A Student's Guide to 50 European Novels has been edited by Abraham H. Lass and Brooks Wright. A well-known teacher, school administrator, and writer, Mr. Lass is principal of Abraham Lincoln High School in Brooklyn, New York. He is the author of **How To Prepare for College, The College Student's Handbook, The Way to Write,** and he also writes a syndicated newspaper column, "College and You." Brooks Wright is an associate professor of English at the City College of New York. He is the author of **Interpreter of Buddhism: Sir Edwin Arnold** and numerous professional articles.

The plot summaries, critical essays, and character analyses collected in this volume and its companion works, **A Student's Guide To 50 American Novels** and **A Student's Guide to 50 British Novels,** are designed to enrich the reader's understanding and appreciation of the great and famous books that are a vital part of our literary heritage. A special section on "How To Read a Novel" provides the reader with the basic skills and insights that will give his reading new and more meaningful dimensions.

A Student's Guide to
50 European Novels

edited by Abraham H. Lass
Principal, Abraham Lincoln High School, Brooklyn, New York

and Brooks Wright
Associate Professor of English, The City College, New York City

WSP
ñ WASHINGTON SQUARE PRESS, INC. • NEW YORK

A STUDENT'S GUIDE TO 50 EUROPEAN NOVELS

A *Washington Square Press* edition

1st printing......................October, 1967

L

Published by
Washington Square Press, Inc., 630 Fifth Avenue, New York, N.Y.

WASHINGTON SQUARE PRESS editions are distributed in the
U.S. by Simon & Schuster, Inc., 630 Fifth Avenue, New
York, N.Y. 10020 and in Canada by Simon & Schuster
of Canada, Ltd., Richmond Hill, Ontario, Canada.

To Betty and Janet
and
Betty

Preface

"Of making many books there is no end," goes the complaint in *Ecclesiastes;* and the modern reader is tempted to add, "and much study of books-about-books is a weariness of the flesh."

What purposes, then, are to be served by this book?

We hope to reach two kinds of readers. First, the reader who is not yet the reader he wishes to be—who knows there is much in store for him, who has not tasted more than a portion of the feast, and who is grateful for a bill of fare. To him we offer an overview so that he may fall to with a whetted appetite. He will *know about* these novels (characters, plots, themes, styles) before he goes on to *know* them. Second, the reader who has sampled many of these novels and needs little more than a review of what he has already enjoyed or a reference guide as an ever-ready help for study.

For each novel we present:

1) an annotated list of the main characters,
2) a full, clear, comprehensible summary of the significant incidents and themes,
3) a digest of present-day critical opinion of the novel, placing it in its proper context in the development of the novel and indicating how contemporary readers and critics evaluate it,
4) a biographical sketch of the author.

While no selection of titles could please everyone, we believe that the novels chosen for this book will challenge the intelligent person to make his own rich and varied reading program. Here are the masterpieces and the milestones, the "classics and commercials," the great books and the near-great. Here are the seed books, the novels from which have sprung new novels and new ideas. All of them are still widely read and discussed. They are part of every reader's heritage.

If these novels have one thing in common despite differences in age and manners, it is that they have all (in Wordsworth's phrase) "kept watch o'er man's mortality"; they have something everlasting to report to us about ourselves, and they report it in the syllables of art.

To read or to reread these novels—and this book will have achieved its purpose if it sends you back to the originals—is to take part in a magnificent adventure of the spirit: to understand what made D. H. Lawrence say, with an artist's pardonable license, "Being a novelist, I consider myself superior to the saint, the scientist, the philosopher, and the poet. The novel is the one bright book of life."

Contents

How To Read a Novel

Why do we pick up a novel? For the moment, the world we know is too much for us—or it is not enough. We seek surcease, or discovery. And so we turn a page and step into another man's world.

In one novel we may find what Graham Greene calls "an entertainment," a tale unfolded for our enjoyment; we shall not even mind a few tears in the telling of it. In another novel, perhaps we find a few of the answers. What we have only half-suspected of human experience is blindingly clear in the author's searchlight; a facet of man has been illuminated.

Often a novel offers us both adventure and insight. From the moment that Don Quixote fares forth across the Campo de Montiel until he returns with his squire to their village, we share the terrifying and never-before-imagined excitements of the windmills, the battle with certain skins of red wine, the great adventure of the Cave of Montesinos, the disenchanting of the peerless Dulcinea del Toboso. Yet it is a means to exploring ourselves, for the Knight of the Mournful Countenance is no mere *picaro*. When we are home again, we are richer for understanding illusion and reality, life in its sublimest and simplest terms.

"Every novel worthy of the name is like another planet, whether large or small, which has its own laws just as it has its own flora and fauna," said François Mauriac, author of *Thérèse Desqueyroux*.

Whatever the novel, it is well to look sharp in the writer's planet. Each novel is the individual vision of an artist, his direct impression of reality. To share his discoveries we must look at the view he sees from his personal porthole. If every prospect immediately displeases and every man seems vile, we may be allowing our prejudices to come between us and the writer's sights. The great Lope de Vega scoffed, "There is none so foolish as to praise *Don Quixote*"; the critic Sainte-Beuve thought *Madame Bovary* "too crude" for most women to read, and indeed as soon as that novel appeared in the *Revue de Paris* both the *Revue* and Flaubert were prosecuted for outraging public morals and religion. (As recently as 1966, the Ladies' Auxiliary of River City, Iowa, complained that the town library had books by Chaucer, Balzac, Flaubert, and Rabelais.) Zola's novels about the Rougon-Macquart families "shocked France to the core," and Proust's *Swann's Way* was rejected by several editors, including André Gide. Before we complain to the novelist that we find his planet uninhabitable, we should permit him to show us its "manners, climates, councils, governments."

The Novelist's View of Reality

Very well, says the reader to the novelist with humility, show me a slice of life.

Novelist A may choose to cut his slice horizontally; Novelist B, vertically. It calls for close attention.

A, following a straight chronological line, begins at the beginning of his hero's story, goes on through the middle until he comes to the end, and then stops. Pierre Prentice is born, goes to the lycée, meets Lucie at a fête, weeps his pints, is off to the wars, and (after a suitable number of complications linked by character and motive) marries or dies.

B, on the other hand, is going to ignore chronology and cut Pierre down the middle for our examination; like Macbeth, he'll "unseam" him from the nave to the chaps. He will disclose his memories, agonies, ecstasies, reveries—with no respect for time. There will be a flashback to the Duchesse de Cénard's salon, when Lucie first met that emotional brigand Gaston Mondieu and Pierre had the strange encounter with Colette. If Novelist B is quite modern, he will not end his novel at all, but will leave his hero (who is not a hero at all) in the middle of a moment of consciousness which can be traced backward or forward in time, as the reader wishes.

The meaning of the real, the nature of reality, has been a point of dispute among novelists, as it has been between philosophers and physicists, for more than half a century. One of the most illuminating quarrels was between Virginia Woolf

and a group of novelists—Bennett, Wells, Galsworthy—
whose materialism seemed to her the negation of life. In
Mr. Bennett and Mrs. Brown, she pointed out how they had
crowded out reality with the furniture of their novels; they
had laid so much dull stress on environment, social setting,
the fabric instead of the substance, that the essence of being
had escaped them.

In a famous statement in her essay "Modern Fiction" in
The Common Reader, Mrs. Woolf put the case for all the
novelists of sensibility, the "stream of consciousness" stylists,
who were to follow. "Life is not a series of gig-lamps sym-
metrically arranged," said Mrs. Woolf (demolishing Novelist
A); life is *"a luminous halo, a semi-transparent envelope"*
which surrounds man from the beginning of consciousness to
the end.

Mrs. Woolf's own luminous style, a subtle handling of the
undercurrents of consciousness, is an almost lyrical flow. In
her work, in Joyce's, in Proust's, the range of implicit experience seems limitless. One of Mrs. Woolf's characters, Mrs.
Ramsay, in *To the Lighthouse,* speaks of the "wedge-shaped
core of darkness" in the depth of being herself, when life sinks
down for a moment and there is no need to act. Of course
this is a very different kind of reality from that in many novels,
or for that matter in many people's experience. Meeting it in
prose fiction today, the reader does well to approach it as he
approaches the reality of a poem: with a response to its
rhythms, its imagery, its timeless flow of memories and
impressions.

Character in the Novel

Mr. Bennett and Mrs. Woolf, Zola and Proust were agreed
on one point at least: the essential concern of the novelist is
with "character in itself"; only if the characters are real has
the novel any chance of surviving.

The reason for this, perhaps, is that the characters above
all in a novel, in E. M. Forster's word, can *solace* us. We who
can hardly understand ourselves, much less one another, meet
in the novelist's world "a more comprehensible and thus a
more manageable human race" and we have the immensely

comforting illusion of understanding, at last, the secret, invisible truth of people.

When the reader puts together all the clues to character that the novelist has included in his book, when he perceives the truth of Levin or Raskolnikov or Julien Sorel, even though none of these may know it of himself, he is almost like the Creator in all-knowing wisdom.

Yet, according to Elizabeth Bowen ("Notes on Writing a Novel"), characters are not *created* by the novelist, but *found;* they preexist in his consciousness and reveal themselves as he is writing, as might "fellow-travellers seated opposite one, in a dimly lit railway carriage."

What the novelist is inviting the reader to do, then, is to *recognize* the people of the novel as they play their roles in the story.

We use the word *play* advisedly; the people of the novelist's world are very busy every moment. They are making choices of alternative behavior; they are speaking or not speaking in a certain way; when they are not around, they are being discussed by other characters.

To recognize Emma Bovary, the reader of Flaubert might well imagine that he is watching her in a drama literally played upon a stage. He may ask himself the same questions about the people in a novel that he subconsciously asks about the figures in greasepaint who move before the footlights:

What is the effect on these people of the *setting* they are in?
What do I know of the *antecedent action?*
What signs of *motive* do I perceive?
Where is the evidence of *conflict,* within and without?
How does this person see himself? How does he wish others to see him? How is he seen by others?
How does he give himself away—in gesture, inflection, choice of words?
Where is the *climax* of this person's conflict? Is it inevitable?

And so on. It is a game only a little different from the one the reader enjoys every day. Listening to his neighbor protest, "I am the last person in the world to gossip," he knows her for a talebearer; trying to solve the riddle of the face opposite him in the subway (eyes full of pain, slack mouth, shaving cut on chin), he wonders what it all means. In novels, however, the characters are explicable; the writer has willed it so. If the reader is perceptive enough, he can pluck out the heart of each man's mystery.

Sometimes the clues are tiny. Every reader understands the significant event, the major decision. But it is also a revealing incident, says Henry James, when a woman stands up with her hand resting on a table and looks at you in a certain way. A chance word or sigh, Forster reminds us, is just as much evidence as a speech or a murder.

The playwright, of course, has always understood this, and that is why we urge the reader of novels to behave as if he were watching a play.

Chekhov, in whose dramas there is no melodrama, only the reverberation of the thousand small shocks that make life palpable, said in one of his letters that the things that happen onstage should be as complex and yet as simple as they are in daily reality. "For instance, people are having a meal at a table, just having a meal, but at the same time their happiness is being created, or their lives are being smashed up."

How many meals are eaten in novels! And every one of them is "evidence." In *The Red and the Black*, Madame de Rênal has to take her place at lunch after Julien Sorel has just walked coldly away from her. Monsieur de Rênal and Madame Derville speak of nothing except Julien's imminent departure. And so Madame de Rênal complains of a migraine and goes off to bed, to weep in freedom, "suffering the cruel torments of the passion into which chance had led her." In *War and Peace*, the Rostov family is at dinner. The count has received a letter from their Nikolushka—he has been wounded—how are they to prepare the countess for the news? Anna Mihalovna chatters of rumors about the war, of how long since there has been a letter from dear Nikolai. Natasha, reading expressions, guesses what has happened, wriggles about in her chair, is rebuked by her governess, blurts out the news to Sonya—how vividly we see the young girl! In *Swann's Way*, when Swann goes to dine at the Verdurins' (where he first knows Odette), he meets a whole class of people, self-assertive, bourgeois, underbred; Proust spins a web of social values at the dinner table. In *The Magic Mountain*, Hans Castrop is in the dining room of the sanatorium when the exotic young Russian girl whom he loves, Clavdia Chauchat, enters. She slams the door to attract his attention, and Hans jumps. Somehow, Mann suggests, Clavdia's entering the dining room that way, and Hans's reaction to her bad manners, are clues to their characters.

Once fully perceived, living characters in novels are life stretchers for us all. We love, suffer, hate, comprehend vicariously. They satisfy our hunger to share the news about the human condition. Real people have a way of keeping themselves to themselves; characters in novels often open their hearts. We are in torment with Jean-Christophe; we learn that struggle is life itself; we come to the fruition of genius with him.

Sharing is a two-way journey. What is the reader's part? Empathy, imaginative sympathy, understanding of human values. As the characters grow larger in our imagination and sympathy, they take on meanings larger than themselves, possibly larger than life. In Kafka's *The Trial*, the commonplace young bureaucrat, Joseph K, charged with a nameless crime by unidentified accusers, who tries to disentangle reality from the nightmare engulfing him, becomes a symbol of modern man, who has ceased to understand human destiny.

At the very least, the reader of novels will have, as Thoreau did at Walden, a great deal of company in his house, especially in the morning, when nobody calls.

The Novelist at Work

"Why should a story not be told in the most irregular fashion that an author's idiosyncrasy may prompt," asked George Eliot ("Leaves from a Notebook"), "provided that he gives us what we can enjoy?"

"Every novelist ought to invent his own technique," said François Mauriac *(Writers at Work, The Paris Review Interviews)*. ". . . The great novelist doesn't depend on anyone but himself. Proust resembled none of his predecessors and he did not have, he could not have, any successors. The great novelist breaks his mould; he alone can use it. Balzac created the 'Balzacian' novel; its style was suitable only for Balzac."

No two novelists are alike; there are as many kinds of novel today—there have always been as many kinds of novel

—as there are readers to discover them. Without too much
literary analysis, it is possible to satisfy one's curiosity about
the way in which a novelist has set about making us enjoy his
book.

Here is a brief list of checkpoints. Each novelist will have
approached a checkpoint in his own way.

Description of the Characters

The storyteller is no painter, but he must leave images in
the reader's mind.

In *Madame Bovary*, Flaubert sketches Emma Bovary and
her husband with rapid brilliance:

> Charles jogged back and forth across the countryside
> under snow and rain. He ate omelettes at farmhouse
> tables, thrust his arm into damp beds, had his face
> spattered with jets of warm blood at bleedings; he
> listened to death rattles, examined the contents of basins,
> handled a lot of soiled underclothing. But every night he
> came home to a blazing fire, a well-set table, a comfort-
> able chair, and a dainty, prettily dressed wife smelling so
> sweet that he never quite knew where the scent came
> from, and half wondered whether it wasn't her skin that
> was perfuming her slip.

(The translation is Francis Steegmuller's.)

A long way from Emma, here is Zola's Nana, in her debut
on the stage. Her tuneless young voice (she is eighteen) and
her awkwardness have not pleased the audience.

> Nana, in the meantime, seeing the house laughing,
> began to laugh herself. The gaiety of all redoubled itself.
> She was an amusing creature, all the same, that fine girl!
> Her laughter made a love of a little dimple appear in her
> chin. She stood there waiting, not bored in the least,
> familiar with her audience, falling into step with them at
> once, as though she herself were admitting, with a wink,
> that she had not two farthings' worth of talent, but that
> it did not matter at all, that in fact she had other good
> points. . . . When she came to certain rather lively
> verses, a delicate sense of enjoyment made her tilt her

nose, the rosy nostrils of which rose and fell, while a
bright flush suffused her cheeks. She still swung herself
up and down, for she only knew how to do that. And the
trick was no longer voted ugly; on the contrary, the men
raised their opera-glasses.

It is not hard to see the same vivid model in this passage
as in Manet's painting called "Nana," though we are told he
and Zola were not inspired by each other.

Quite unlike the technique of the impressionist painters
is the descriptive style of certain contemporary novelists
(Alain Robbe-Grillet or Marguerite Duras, for example) who
borrow from *cinéma-vérité;* the narrator's eye reports all it
sees (or so we are told) and the reader selects the significant
details of character.

Point of View

In *The Craft of Fiction*, Percy Lubbock says that the whole
intricate question of method in the novel is governed by the
question of the point of view: "The question of the relation
in which the narrator stands to the story." Mr. Lubbock tells
us that the novelist can describe his characters from the outside, as an impartial or partial observer, or from the inside, as
a presumably omniscient force. He can also take the viewpoint
of one character who does not know the motives of the others.

Henry James felt that the novelist should stick to one point
of view in a story and not shift arbitrarily; Forster, on the
other hand, cites a number of instances where a novelist has
been able to manage more than one shift rather well—genius,
as always, making its own rules. Contemporary writers frequently *must* shift the narrator voice from character to character, to reveal more than one point of view, to show time and
space not as they "actually" are but as different people perceive them. In Gide's *The Counterfeiters*, as Henri Peyre has
pointed out, there is the French novelist's "obsession to see
himself seeing himself." For our part it matters very little how
the novelist manages his camera eye, just so he puts in focus
for us a world that is both plausible and lasting. What he
shows us will depend on his *moral* lens.

Stendhal, writing to Balzac: "I see but one rule, *to be clear*.
If I am not clear, all my world crumbles to nothing."

Plot, Story, Theme

These are words to play with: when they are well handled by the writer, the reader does not have to notice them at all. But if you lift an eyebrow at cavalier treatment of textbook terms, here are some definitions:

The *story* is the answer to "And then what happened?"
The *plot* tells why it happened just that way.
The *theme* explains the writer's need to tell this particular story.

Or in Forster's delightful simplification: "The King died and then the Queen died" is a story. "The King died and then the Queen died of grief" is a plot. (We do not have a theme for this yet.)

Causality is everything. Well, nearly everything. In his introduction to Henry James's *The Princess Casamassima*, Lionel Trilling outlines the story which runs through a number of nineteenth-century novels in different countries: the story of the young man from the provinces, of humble and even mysterious origin, who moves into society. In one way or another, this is the skeleton of *The Red and the Black*, *Great Expectations*, and *The Great Gatsby*. Yet plot, story, theme are nothing without the essence of all, which is the novelist's personal idiom, his statement outside logic or causality, a statement poetic in that it is always its own excuse for being.

And that brings us to the question of style.

Style

In Leo Tolstoi's *Talks with Tolstoi*, we have the following description of a writer's approach to his art:

Sophie Andreevna said: "It was the last time Turgenev stayed at Yasnaya, not long before his death. I asked him: 'Ivan Sergeevich, why don't you write now?' He answered: 'In order to write I had always to be a little in

love. Now I am old I can't fall in love any more, and
that is why I have stopped writing.' "

And Tolstoi himself, speaking in exasperation:

> One ought only to write when one leaves a piece of
> one's flesh in the ink-pot each time one dips one's pen.

Lest you think, "Ah well, the Russians—!" here is another
novelist's statement of what it means to write. Arnold Bennett,
in his *Journals:*

> The novelist should cherish and burnish this faculty
> of seeing crudely, simply, artlessly, ignorantly; of seeing
> like a baby or a lunatic, who lives each moment by itself
> and tarnishes by the present no remembrance of the past.

There we have it: On every page the novelist has left his
signature for us to read. The oldest quotation of all, Buffon's
"The style is the man," is still the most accurate.

And now we come back to the question of how to read a
novel. Why, by sitting down in an armchair, seeing that there
is a good light over our left shoulder, and turning the page.
Here we are in another man's world.

The Sixteenth
Century

Gargantua
and Pantagruel

by

FRANÇOIS RABELAIS (c 1490–1553)

The Characters

NOTE: *These are listed roughly in the order of their first appearance; the citation following each entry gives the book and chapter. For reasons of space, the list is limited to Books I (Gargantua) and II (Pantagruel). All names are given as they appear in the French text. The etymologies are for the most part based on the edition by Abel Lefranc.*

Alcofribas Nasier (anagram of François Rabelais)—Pen name of the author (title page).

Gargantua (the name is legendary and antedates Rabelais)— The jolly, gluttonous giant who is the hero of Book I.

Grandgousier (big throat)—Father of Gargantua. In I he is the ruler of a small territory near Chinon; in II he is the King of Utopia; generally, however, his character is that of a genial country gentleman (I:3).

Gargamelle (throat)—Mother of Gargantua (I:3).

Thubal Holofernes (two Biblical names)—Gargantua's first tutor, an old-fashioned pedant (I:14).

3

Eudemon (happy, fortunate)—A page who becomes Gargantua's companion (I:15).

Don Philippe des Marays (possibly an actual but unidentified person)—A gentleman with whom Grandgousier consults about Gargantua's education (I:15).

Maître Janotus de Bragmardo (perhaps a caricature of an actual scholar)—A logician sent by the Sorbonne to recover the bells of Notre Dame; a rheumy, incoherent pedant (I:18).

Ponocrates (strong worker)—Gargantua's tutor in humanistic studies (I:15).

Gymnaste (athlete)—Gargantua's squire (I:18).

Philotomie (man of honor)—Gargantua's steward (I:18).

Rhizotome (root cutter)—Gargantua's page and gardener (I:23).

Picrochole (sharp bile)—The warlike and arrogant king of Lerné, representing a certain M. de Sainte-Marthe with whom Rabelais' father had a lawsuit (I:25).

Toucquedillon (braggart)—One of Picrochole's knights (I:26).

Frère Jean des Entommeurs (variously translated: by Urquhart as "Friar John of the Funnels"; by Smith as "the Trencherite"; by Putnam as "the Hacker")—The valiant monk of Seuillé who defends the Abbey from Picrochole (I:27).

Ulrich Gallet (presumably Jean Gallet, who represented Rabelais' father in his lawsuit with Sainte-Marthe)—Ambassador of Grandgousier to Picrochole (I:30).

Pantagruel (a legendary name antedating Rabelais; originally a minor devil associated with thirst)—Son of Gargantua and hero of Books II–V, a courteous and liberally educated prince (II:1).

Badebec (for the possible meanings, see Lefranc)—Mother of Pantagruel, who dies in childbirth (II:2).

Epistemon (wise)—Tutor of Pantagruel (II:5).

The Limosin student—A student at the University of Paris who speaks a grotesque Latinate jargon (II:6).

Panurge (able to do anything, hence a rogue)—The unscrupulous and picaresque companion of Pantagruel (II:9).

Baisecul and Humevesne (names corresponding to two familiar English obscenities)—Two litigants whose case is decided by Pantagruel; their speeches are utter nonsense (II:10).

Thaumaste (admirable)—An English scholar (perhaps Sir Thomas More) who debates with Panurge (II:18).

Eusthenes (sturdy)—A companion of Pantagruel (II:23).

Carpalim (swift)—Another companion of Pantagruel (II:23).

Anarche (lawless)—King of the Dipsodes (thirsty ones) defeated by Pantagruel (II:26).

Utopia (nowhere)—The name of Gargantua's kingdom, taken from the book of that name by Sir Thomas More.

The Story

Gargantua is an amiable giant dwelling near Chinon. His father, Grandgousier, described grandiosely as the King of Utopia, is really a country squire with only a few square miles of territory. Except for his vast capacity for food and drink, Gargantua resembles other growing children. His father, dissatisfied with his son's tradition-bound education, sends him to Paris with a tutor named Ponocrates who exposes him to the new humanistic learning of the day. He has a number of adventures in that city, such as stealing the bells of Notre Dame to hang on his mare's bridle. While he is there, war breaks out between his father and a neighboring monarch named Picrochole, who may represent a certain landowner with whom Rabelais' father had a lawsuit. The *casus belli* is merely the theft of some cakes by the subjects of Picrochole, but the war is prosecuted with heroic bloodthirstiness. Summoned home, Gargantua routs the enemy with the help of a rollicking monk, a kind of French Friar Tuck, Jean des Entommeurs. In gratitude, Gargantua builds for Brother Jean a fine abbey organized on principles diametrically opposed to medieval monasticism: the inmates, both men and women, may marry, and they pass their time not at prayer but in gentlemanly sports and humanistic studies. The motto of the abbey is, "Do what you will."

The second book is a somewhat feebler repetition of the first. Pantagruel is the son of Gargantua from whom he inherits his good nature and gross appetite. Like his father, he goes to Paris where he distinguishes himself in legal and philosophical debate. Here also he makes a friend of Panurge, the anti-hero of the story, a rogue whose relation to Pantagruel suggests that between Falstaff and Prince Hal.

News now comes that the Dipsodes (or thirsty ones) have invaded Utopia. Pantagruel returns and defeats the enemy by emptying his bladder and drowning them all.

In Book III, Panurge, who remembers that by law newly married men are exempt from military service for one year, proposes to marry, and asks for advice. The friends debate the problem back and forth, discuss the character and status of women generally, and consult a number of learned authorities including a theologian, a lawyer, an astrologer, a doctor, a philosopher, and a jester. The responses are uniformly discouraging, but Panurge, undaunted, wants one more opinion; he proposes to consult the Oracle of the Holy Bottle. The third book closes with a description and eulogy of an herb called the Pantagruelion, with which the travelers provision themselves. The plant is actually hemp, the reason for the name being that Pantagruel is a thirsty giant, and hemp (in the form of a hangman's noose) causes a constriction of the throat.

The journey to find the oracle occupies the fourth and fifth books. (Scholars have seen in these the influence of narratives of exploration, especially of the expeditions in search of the Northwest Passage.) The travelers touch at many strange lands which allegorically represent the various institutions which Rabelais was satirizing: the clergy, the law courts, the exchequer, the schools of philosophy, and the like. A few of the episodes are simply travelers' yarns with no ulterior meaning; one story, of a land so cold that men's words freeze solid and thaw out in the spring, is repeated in the tales of Baron Munchausen.

The conclusion of the fifth book is clearly allegorical, the Holy Bottle, according to most commentators, being not merely wine, but Truth itself, after which all seekers thirst. Before reaching their goal, the travelers pass through Lantern Land, inhabited by honest, studious folk. To light their way, they select the lantern of one Pierre Amy. Rabelais at this point is paying a gracious tribute to an old friend of that name, a Franciscan friar who first taught him Greek. Finally, they reach the oracle itself, presided over by a priestess called Bacbuc. She gives each one a glass of clear water in which each tastes his favorite beverage, just as the Truth is one,

though men understand it differently. The message of the
oracle should also be understood symbolically; it is the one
word, DRINK. Some scholars have speculated that Rabelais
intended to carry the story further, at least bringing Pantagruel back to his own country, but as it stands the book
closes with this noble and appropriate climax.

Critical Opinion

Let us face it: Rabelais is more admired than read. Many
people start to read him, attracted as a rule by his reputation
for bawdiness; they usually conclude that the bawdry is certainly there, but that it is hardly worth the erudition and the
persistence needed to dig it out. In many ways Rabelais'
great work presents the same problems as Joyce's *Ulysses*:
they are both extremely long-winded, are packed with learned
allusions in a dozen languages, refer to people and episodes
which would have been long since forgotten had the author
not happened to remember them, rely heavily on puns and
verbal stunts, and teem with enormous lists and catalogs.
Their tone is burlesque and parodic, their language alter-
nates between pedantry and slang, and both are generally
believed to have a symbolic meaning over and above the
literal story. To master Rabelais in detail is the work of a life-
time; the casual reader need not be ashamed to skip and skim.
One should begin by reading *Gargantua* in its entirety, then
select from the other four books according to one's taste. Those
who are interested in Rabelais' views on the learning and institutions of his day should read about the learned gentlemen
whom Panurge consults in Book III, Trippa, Bridoye,
Rondibilis, and the rest, and then turn to the satirical and
allegorical passages of Book V: the Isle of the Papimanes, the
land of the Furry Cats, and the oracle of the Holy Bottle.
Readers who simply want a pleasant, well-told story will find
scores throughout the book.

Rabelais' reputation for obscenity was largely a discovery of
nineteenth-century readers, especially Victorian Englishmen;
his contemporaries seem not to have noticed it. Many other
writers of the period are almost as free-spoken. The authorities
tried to suppress Rabelais' writings on grounds of heresy
rather than immorality. On the whole, it is gluttony, rather

than lechery, which dominates the book, and the gamier passages are scatological, rather than pornographic. Sex is represented as a healthy animal pleasure, of the same order as eating and drinking. There is no suggestion of perversion or neurosis, nor does Rabelais sentimentalize sex or make a religion of it, as does D. H. Lawrence. Moreover, his hero Pantagruel is not a monster of drunkenness or vice; he is a courteous, intelligent, cultivated, and upright prince. All the evidence indicates that Rabelais was the same sort of person: a humane and genial man, who loved life in all its aspects, and who applied his great gifts of learning and intelligence to an examination of the major problems of his day. His treatment of these issues is sometimes bawdy, sometimes erudite, but always acute and level-headed.

Rabelais lived in an exciting age when the revival of classical studies was transforming almost every aspect of European culture. The new learning demanded a new approach to education; the curriculum would have to be far broader and include more secular learning than before. Rabelais pokes fun at the old system in the person of Thubal Holofernes, the sophist who took five years to teach Gargantua his alphabet both forward and backward. The new system is represented by the humanist Ponocrates. Chapters 23 and 24 of *Gargantua* describe the course of studies which Ponocrates considered appropriate for a liberally educated man. An impossibly strenuous curriculum, it is admirable in its breadth and combination of theoretical and practical subjects. Besides the usual studies in language and literature it provides for training in music, painting and sculpture, botany, medicine and gardening, fencing, swimming, and games. Rabelais did not wish to train specialists or ivory-tower scholars; he was interested in the education of the whole man.

Because of Rabelais' anticlericalism and his interest in science, it is sometimes argued that he was a freethinker, perhaps a materialist. There is no real evidence for this, and the occasional expressions of Christian piety in his writings seem too sincere to be seriously questioned. However, in Rabelais' time many sincere churchmen were driven to criticize the Church. Not all of them were Protestants; some, like Erasmus, remained in the Catholic fold. Rabelais was one of these. He was outspoken in his attack on many Catholic institutions, especially the monastic system, which he believed from personal experience to be stultifying and illiberal, but he was no heretic and he was not interested in becoming a martyr. His language is sometimes so reckless as to suggest a Protestant polemic, yet he was certainly no Calvinist. One need only compare Calvin's Geneva with Rabelais' Abbey of Thelème, over the door of which was written "Fais ce que voudras"—do what you wish. Only a man who believed that human nature is basically sound could have chosen that motto.

Rabelais' opinion of lawyers finds its expression in the incoherent speeches of Baisecul and Humevesne, in the bumbling old Judge Bridoye, who decides cases by throwing dice, and in Grippeminaud, the cat who devours everything that falls into his clutches. His opinion of military conquerors is evident in his treatment of Picrochole, the petty king who dreams of being an Alexander. By contrast, Grandgousier is a model ruler: peaceable, conciliatory, and willing to fight only as a last resort.

The tone of these volumes is generally mock-heroic and burlesque, so that if one is to enjoy them to the full one should have some idea of the writers whom Rabelais parodies. The great Picrocholine War pokes fun at the old romances of chivalry and the popular chapbooks about giants and heroes; the delicious point of the story lies in the fact that the war is set in the area immediately around Chinon, so that tiny hamlets are described as if they were cities and half-acre fields as great provinces. The other tradition of heroic poetry from which Rabelais draws is of course the epic tradition of Homer and Vergil: the list of Gargantua's allies (I:42) is based on the catalogue of ships in the *Iliad;* Epistemon's descent to Hades derives from the *Odyssey;* and there is a good parody of a Homeric simile in 1:44. The pretentious language of scholarship is another obvious object of ridicule. In Book III there are passages written in the jargons of the law, medicine and theology. In each instance inflated language is used to make the speaker ridiculous.

Rabelais' language is something about which only a Frenchman should presume to speak with authority, but even in translation one can feel its exuberance. The words pour out in torrents: archaism and neologism, courtly speech and peasant dialect, learned words and slang, scraps of Greek, Latin, Hebrew, English, Dutch, German, Danish, Basque

and languages of Rabelais' own invention. Nothing could be
more unlike the polished neoclassicism of later French prose;
the words pile up in lists and catalogs that swell into whole
chapters by themselves. This unpruned extravagance is an
expression of the same vitality that runs through every part
of the book: Gargamelle's meal of tripe, Pantagruel's diet as a
baby, Picrochole's dreams of conquest, Panurge's practical
jokes. Everything Rabelais thought of, whether words or
images, swelled to gigantic size. His love of language was an
expression of his abounding love of life.

The Author

Rabelais' writings are so overwhelming in their impact that
they often prevent us from seeing Rabelais the man as clearly
as we should. Consequently all sorts of legends have grown
up about him: that his father was an innkeeper, that he was a
drunkard and a sensualist, and that he died uttering
blasphemies. Scholars have been obliged to devote much
effort to disentangling the facts from the fable. We still do not
know when Rabelais was born, but the date was sometime between 1483 and 1495, and the place probably La Devinière,
near Chinon in the Loire Valley. His father, a lawyer and a
man of some consequence among the wealthier bourgeoisie
of the town, appears in the writings as Grandgousier. It is sur-
mised that Rabelais was the youngest child, and that he was
dedicated to a monastic life at an early age, perhaps as young
as seven or nine; but he was never happy as a monk, as his
writings clearly show. After moving from one religious house
to another, he became a secular priest and studied medicine
at the University of Montpellier. Medical students today may
well envy his record: he matriculated in 1530, was lecturing
on Hippocrates in 1531, and by 1532 was appointed staff
physician at the hospital in Lyons.

Lyons was then a center of publishing and had an active
intellectual life in which Rabelais took part. Here, too, he
began the books which made him famous. Exactly how he
started writing is not certain, but we know that in 1532 there
appeared a popular chapbook entitled *The Great and Priceless
Chronicle of the Great and Enormous Giant Gargantua*—not

by Rabelais, though he may have edited it. This book suggested to him the possibility of writing a sequel, tracing the adventures of Pantagruel, son of Gargantua. When the story proved popular, he decided to provide a better prologue to it by writing his own account of Gargantua. This was the book of that title, which was therefore the second to be written though it stands first in the series. The third and fourth books continue the adventures of Pantagruel, and are called simply *The Third Book (Le Tiers Livre)* and *The Fourth Book (Le Quart Livre)*. The *Fifth Book (Le Quint Livre)* appeared posthumously and its authenticity has been seriously questioned. The usual theory is that it is a first draft of chapters written by Rabelais but left in an unfinished state and prepared for publication by another hand.

Rabelais wrote during the early years of the Reformation when even the suspicion of heresy could get a man in trouble. The danger was real: his friend, the publisher Étienne Dolet, was later burned on a charge of heresy. Rabelais was neither a Protestant nor a freethinker, and no heretic in any doctrinal sense, but he was an irreverent critic of the ecclesiastical system. He had already experienced some inconvenience as a young man when his superiors in the Franciscan order, suspicious, no doubt, of anyone better educated than themselves, tried to prevent him from studying Greek. Now he found himself under attack from the theologians of the Sorbonne, at that time the custodians of orthodoxy in France. Accordingly he put himself under the protection of Cardinal Jean du Bellay, serving him as a private doctor and trusted adviser, and traveling with him as far as Rome. From 1546 to 1547 he was in Metz, then outside of France and out of reach of the Sorbonne. In 1550 he was presented with the living of the parish of Meudon, a few miles outside of Paris, where he served for three years and then resigned, perhaps under pressure from the authorities who had condemned *The Fourth Book*. He died in 1553 and is said to have been buried in Paris, but his grave has been lost.

Rabelais was a man so varied that everyone can find what he wants in him. Some see him as a rollicking winebibber, others as a sober reformer who clothed his moral teachings in bawdiness to win a wider audience. Neither view can be maintained without serious qualification. Whatever else he may have been, Rabelais was a perfect mirror of his age; every aspect of the life and thought of his times is illustrated in his writings. His love of learning and his zest for life are wonderfully characteristic of the early Renaissance.

The Seventeenth Century

Don Quixote

by

MIGUEL DE CERVANTES SAAVEDRA
(1547–1616)

The Characters

BOOK I

Don Quixote (assumed name of Alonso Quijano, this last
name being variously spelled)—The hero, an elderly gentleman of emaciated appearance, obsessed with the belief
that he is the last of the knights-errant.

Sancho Panza (*panza*—belly or paunch)—Don Quixote's
squire, a peasant whose practical view of life is at the
opposite pole from his master's romantic idealism; his character is a mixture of simplicity and shrewdness.

Dulcinea del Toboso (name given by Don Quixote to Aldonza
Lorenzo)—A strapping country girl whom Don Quixote
in his imagination endows with all the graces of a highborn lady.

Juana Panza (in Book II called Teresa)—Sancho's wife, as
simple and earthy as her husband.

Pero Pérez—Curate of Don Quixote's village, who attempts
to restore him to his sanity.

Master Nicholas—The village barber.

15

Maritornes—A serving girl at the inn.

Ginés de Passamonte—A galley slave freed by Don Quixote; in Book II he appears as a strolling puppeteer.

Fernando—A young nobleman not to be trusted with women.

Cardenio—A young gentleman in love with Luscinda.

Luscinda—In love with Cardenio, but betrothed by her parents to Fernando.

Dorotea (known to Don Quixote as the Princess Micomicona) —A girl betrayed by Fernando.

Anselmo, Lotario, and Camila—Characters in Cardenio's "Story of the Man Who Was Too Curious for His Own Good."

Captain Ruy Pérez—A Spanish soldier recently escaped from captivity in Algiers.

Zoraida—A Moorish girl, in love with Ruy Pérez, who has left Algiers with him and desires to be baptized a Christian.

Juan Pérez de Viedma—Brother of the Captain, now a judge.

Clara—Daughter of Juan.

Luis—A young gentleman in love with Clara.

Roxinante—Don Quixote's lean, rickety horse.

Cid Hamete Benengeli—An imaginary Arab historian cited by Cervantes as the source of his information.

Book II

Sansón Carrasco—A bachelor of the University of Salamanca, about twenty-four, fond of practical jokes.

Don Diego de Miranda—A wealthy country gentleman, courteous and affable.

Don Lorenzo—Son of Don Diego, a college student with ambitions to become a poet.

Camacho—A rich peasant.

Quiteria—A girl betrothed to Camacho.

Basilio—A poor peasant in love with Quiteria.

The Duke and Duchess—Hosts to the Don, who play on him a rather heartless series of practical jokes.

Doña Rodriguez de Grijalba—Duenna to the Duchess.

The Distressed Duenna—The assumed name of one of the Duke's servants, who takes part in an elaborate hoax of the Don.

Altisidora—A girl who pretends to be in love with Don Quixote.

Doctor Pedro Recio Tirteafuera—Sancho's doctor during his governorship of Barataria.

Ricote—A Morisco exile, disguised as a German pilgrim.

Roque Guinart—A Catalonian bandit.

Don Antonio Moreno—A wealthy gentleman of Barcelona.

Anna Felix—Daughter of Ricote, disguised as an Arab captain.

The Story

BOOK I

In a small village in the territory of La Mancha in sixteenth-century Spain there lives a gentleman named Alonso Quijano whose chief delight is to read old chivalric romances about knights-errant who travel about rescuing damsels, fighting giants, and slaying dragons. As a result of steeping himself in this literature, he becomes convinced that the ancient institution of chivalry can and should be restored. Accordingly, he resolves to become a knight-errant. He finds an old suit of armor, a rusty sword, and a barber's basin to serve as a helmet, and mounting a broken-down old horse called Roxinante, he sets out to seek adventures. Moreover, since all knights-errant in the stories are represented as being in love, he picks a simple, coarse country girl whom he has scarcely seen and who knows nothing of him, gives her the high-sounding name of Dulcinea del Toboso, and endows her in his imagination with all the virtues of a beautiful and highborn lady. For himself he picks the name of Don Quixote. Now it only remains for him to be duly knighted—something he cannot do for himself.

Don Quixote's travels bring him to a small inn which in his imagination appears to be a great castle. He asks the lord—that is, the innkeeper—to dub him knight with all the appropriate ceremonies. The innkeeper, taking his guest for a harmless lunatic, plays out the role, much to the amusement of the rest of the company. Returning to his village, the new-made knight engages a peasant named Sancho Panza to act as his squire, assuring him that when the two have made their fortunes by knight-errantry, Sancho is to be rewarded by the grant of an island of which he will be governor.

The adventures that befall the two are generally farcical and turn out badly. The Don's imagination, however, is able to convert the most ridiculous situation into high romance. There are too many episodes to be summarized here. Some, however, are so famous that they are known to everyone and have even passed into proverbial speech. Thus the expression "to tilt at windmills" is an allusion to an adventure in which Don Quixote comes upon a row of windmills, mistakes them for giants with whirling arms, attacks them with his lance, and is thrown from his horse. Another time he takes a herd of sheep for a great army, attacks it, and is soundly drubbed by the shepherds. Once at night he and Sancho come upon a building which they take for a castle and from which there emanate frightening sounds. They wait until daybreak to attack the "fortress," only to find that what they have heard is the machinery of a mill. On another occasion, while staying at an inn, the Don attacks a row of wineskins and imagines that the wine which spurts out is blood. When confronted with the evidence of his mistakes, Don Quixote has a convenient and unanswerable explanation: the giants only *seem* to be windmills or wineskins; actually their form has been changed by malicious enchanters for the purpose of deceiving their gallant enemy.

The adventures of Don Quixote and Sancho are entwined with several subplots that are more conventional. The principal one involves two pairs of young lovers, and describes the obstacles that must be overcome to bring them all safely to the altar. Another subplot deals with a Spanish prisoner of war who escaped from the hands of the Moors in Algiers, bringing with him a lovely Moorish girl. These adventures are further extended by stories which the characters tell to amuse each other, so that there are digressions within digressions.

Meanwhile the family and friends of the Don become anxious for his safety. The village barber and curate seek him out, and pretend that the welfare of his lady Dulcinea requires him to return home. They persuade him to enter a cage and carry him off ignominiously in an ox-cart. The knight is now confused and weak; his housekeeper and niece welcome him home with relief and try to nurse him back to health.

BOOK II

Don Quixote is restored to health but not to sanity. After a time, he and Sancho set out on their travels again. They begin by going to Toboso to behold the lovely Lady Dulcinea, whom neither knows by sight. Sancho supposes that by now his master is mad enough to believe anything, and tells the Don that the first peasant girl they meet is Dulcinea. Don Quixote, however, can still recognize a peasant when he sees one, and tells Sancho that if this wench is his lady, then wicked enchanters must have cast a spell over her and changed her form. In the chapters that follow, Sancho pays dearly for this deception.

After many adventures, Don Quixote comes to the castle of the Duke and Duchess who have heard of his extraordinary deeds and who set about to play a series of practical jokes on their guest. The jest is simply to take the Don at his own estimate, to entertain him as if he were Sir Lancelot or Sir Roland, to ask his help in succoring maidens in distress, and, in short, to stage a play which for the Duke is comic, though for the Don it is deadly serious. The gentlemen and servants of the Duke's household are instructed to take part in the hoax. The climax is an elaborate pageant featuring beautiful nymphs and fearsome enchanters, in the course of which Don Quixote is told that Dulcinea can be freed from her enchantment if Sancho will voluntarily receive three thousand three hundred lashes across his buttocks. Don Quixote is ready to apply the lashes at once, but Sancho wins the concession that he may administer the punishment himself at his own good time.

The Duke also fulfills Don Quixote's promise to Sancho by giving him an island to govern. The "island," called Barataria, is only a small village on the Duke's estate, the inhabitants of which are instructed to obey their new "governor." Sancho, though he is simple and illiterate, is not stupid; he discharges his duties conscientiously and wisely. He is, however, tormented by his official physician who allows him to eat none of the food he likes most. When a mock attack is staged on the town, Sancho is badly pummeled. Finally, after twelve days of rule, Sancho resigns, declaring as proof of his honesty that he is leaving his post as penniless as he came.

Don Quixote is finally brought to his senses by a young
man of his village named Sansón Carrasco. Disguising himself as a knight, Sansón challenges the Don to combat, on
condition that the defeated party shall obey the commands
of the victor. Sansón wins the duel and imposes the penalty
that the Don shall go home and not take up arms for a year.
Don Quixote is dismayed, but keeps his word; he even suggests that if he can no longer play knight, he will play shepherd
and live the idyllic life described in pastoral poetry. This
project is cut short, however, by the Don's illness. He takes
to his bed and, to the surprise of all around him, becomes
suddenly quite sane. Sancho urges his master to get better so
that they may be shepherds together and continue the quest
of Lady Dulcinea, but the Don—now Señor Alonso Quijano
again—rebukes him, renounces all his fantasies, makes his
will, and in a sober Christian fashion breathes his last.

Critical Opinion

Whatever else *Don Quixote* may be, it is unquestionably a
satirical parody on the romances of chivalry. Since these books
are almost wholly unread today, except by scholars and specialists, and even King Arthur no longer stirs the imagination
of most boys, the modern reader of Cervantes may feel that
his author is beating a dead dog. In the sixteenth century,
however, such works were still popular. The most successful
of them all, Ariosto's *Orlando Furioso*, appeared in 1532.
Knighthood was no longer in flower, of course, and yet it was
still possible—or had recently been so—to find men whose
characters had been molded by the old ideal. Bayard, known
as "le chevalier sans peur et sans reproche," died as late as
1524, while Cervantes' patron, Don John of Austria, may be
regarded as the last of the crusaders. Cervantes has sometimes been described as the man whose mockery administered
the *coup de grâce* to the ideals of the Middle Ages. But to
understand him in this way is to oversimplify his point of
view. Though *Don Quixote* pokes fun at the romantic tradition of knighthood, there was more than a touch of the knight-
errant in Cervantes' own character. He realized that the chivalric romances were utterly unreal, but he had a strong linger-
ing affection for them.

We must bear this ambivalence in mind in trying to understand Cervantes' complex attitude toward his hero. In some chapters the Don is merely ridiculous. Thus, when he makes himself sick from a medicine of his own preparation, we feel little sympathy for him: he is being a silly old man and it serves him right if he throws up. These chapters for the most part come early in the story. As the novel progresses we discover that the Don, for all his madness, has innate human worth and dignity. He gains stature especially in Part II where he is unfailingly self-respecting and self-possessed, courteous, grave, and honorable. By contrast, the sensible people about him, like the Duke and Duchess, strike us as cruel and ignoble. By the time the Don arrives at the Duke's court, our sympathies are wholly on his side. We have learned to love the old knight, not in spite of, but because of, his delusions. This book, then, though it is comedy, is not low comedy or farce; it is a wise and very human-hearted comedy in which mockery is tempered by compassion, and the humor is very close to pathos.

Considered from the most serious point of view, *Don Quixote* may be read as a philosophical exploration into the nature of reality and illusion. The question confronts us in every chapter. To begin with, there is the problem (easily overlooked) of the imaginary Arab historian, Cid Hamete Benengeli, whom Cervantes cites as his source for the story, though he warns us that Benengeli may not be reliable; he may have jealously minimized the true glory of his hero. Then there are the apocryphal stories about the Don written by Avellaneda. These, Cervantes tells us, must be rejected as fictions. In short, by warning us against the fictions of others, Cervantes almost persuades us that his fictions are truth, though even this truth, we are told, may not be wholly reliable.

The problem of reality and illusion is even more insistently put in the crucial question: just how mad is Don Quixote? Admittedly there are times when, by any psychiatric standards, he is delusional and disoriented. At other times, he is reasonable enough on all matters that do not touch on his one obsession. Mark Van Doren suggests that perhaps he is acting a role, and that he knows exactly what he is doing, just as the child who plays Superman is not deceived by his own game. Moreover, this acting is not in vain, for it creates the very thing that it imitates. Suppose that a man, in pretending to be a poet, managed to write excellent poetry; he would no longer be pretending. This is Don Quixote's attitude toward knighthood. Admittedly, he tells us, chivalry has become rare in these degenerate days, but if only men will think, feel, and act like knights, they will be knights in fact. Thus it becomes hard to say what is fantasy and what is reality; reality is the fiction men live by.

It is remarkable how the Don's reality manages to impose itself on everyone else. Consider, for example, Don Quixote's proposal to make Sancho the governor of an island as reward for his faithful service. Sancho is understandably skeptical, but he is too tactful to reject an offer made in such good faith. Then—incredibly—the dream materializes. The Duke, acting out what he conceives to be an elaborate practical joke, orders his retainers, including a village of several thousand people, to behave as if Don Quixote's crazy dream had actually come true. The result is that the Don gets what he wants, and everyone else is made to act like a fool. Sancho, for his part, takes his job seriously and governs his "island" so well that his laws are remembered long after he leaves office. The joke is on the Duke. The final irony comes in the last chapter. The Don, now on his deathbed, renounces all his dreams, like a child who puts away his toys at bedtime. Perhaps he has realized all along that they are only toys. But now Sancho pleads with him to keep up the game: if he will only recover, the two can go on looking for the fair Dulcinea. The tables are now completely turned, and we no longer know who is the wise man and who the fool.

Indeed, one of the striking features of this story is the way in which the characters of knight and squire gradually grow together until they become virtually one man. At first, the two men are poles apart. Sancho is convinced that his master is mad, and constantly argues or expostulates with him. Sometimes they even quarrel. After months of shared experience, however, their personalities blend, until each takes on some of the speech habits of the other. Sancho learns the high-flown jargon of chivalry and the Don begins to talk in homely proverbs. Their partnership is almost like the relation of body and soul, and their arguments together suggest the *débat du corps et coeur* which was a familiar form of dialogue in late medieval literature. Alternately, we may think of the two as representing the tension between reason and imagination, or pragmatism and idealism, which exists in every one of us.

Here, then, lies the secret of *Don Quixote*'s popularity and its claim to immortality. It is not just a satire of a decaying institution. Its theme is permanent and universal. The knight in shining armor who travels about the world performing valiant deeds is a permanent and archetypal figure of the human imagination. Sometimes he is called Hercules or Perseus, Amadis or Roland, Davy Crockett or Superman or Batman. Beside these heroic figures the human imagination creates the anti-hero, whose practical and earthbound personality is the necessary foil and complement to that of his companion: Prince Hal has his Falstaff; Sherlock Holmes has Doctor Watson. Each is necessary to the other, and each is a part of our own inner life.

The Author

The details of Cervantes' life have been obscured by time and legend, but the main outlines are clear enough. He was born at Alcalá de Henares in 1547, the son of a not very successful apothecary. His education was unsystematic, since the vagaries of his father's practice took him to various cities. It was an exciting time in Spanish history. The hereditary enemy, the Moors, had been expelled from the peninsula only a short time before, but continued as formidable opponents throughout the Mediterranean. Spain was part of a Hapsburg empire that included Austria, the Low Countries, Naples, Sicily, Sardinia, Burgundy and parts of Germany. It was also the focus of a great overseas empire from which vast wealth poured in, stimulating a brilliant flowering of the arts and letters. It was the beginning of Spain's Age of Gold.

In his early twenties, Cervantes went to Italy in the suite of Cardinal Acquaviva, the Papal legate to Spain. He was not yet a man of letters, although a handful of his poems on the deaths of Don Carlos and Queen Isabella had attracted favorable notice. Casting around for some road to advancement, he enlisted in the Spanish army in 1570 as a private soldier, and saw action the following year in the famous naval battle of Lepanto. This engagement marked the beginning of the end of Turkish power in the Mediterranean; in it an alliance of Christian nations led by Don John of Austria defeated a formidable Turkish fleet and released thousands of European galley slaves. It was a brilliant and dramatic victory. Cervantes, though sick with a fever, fought well and was wounded three times.

Cervantes took part in a less successful action in 1573–1574 in Tunis where an attempt was made to relieve the Spanish garrison at La Goletta (there is a circumstantial account of this venture in *Don Quixote*). Then in 1575 he set out for Spain, bearing a letter from Don John recommending him for a commission. On the way home, his ship was captured by Barbary pirates. Cervantes was taken to Algiers and held for ransom. His letters from Don John proved his undoing, for his captors, taking him for a person of importance, set the ransom very high. The next five years Cervantes spent in brave but fruitless efforts at escape. Several times he was captured, severely punished, and almost executed.

In 1580 Cervantes was ransomed for five hundred ducats and returned to Spain. For a short time he saw service in Portugal, but from 1582 on he devoted himself largely to literature. Prolific though he was, his reputation rests on one book. His many plays added nothing to his reputation, his poetry proved mainly that he was no poet, and his pastoral novel *La Galatea* is now unread. His private affairs at this time are obscure. It is clear that he had an illegitimate daughter, though her mother remains a shadowy figure. In 1584 he married Catalina Salazar y Palacios, a girl eighteen years younger than himself, who brought him little dowry. The two were uncongenial, and for most of their marriage they lived apart.

Cervantes had long hoped to find a government post. In 1587 he was given the job of requisitioning supplies for the projected invasion of England. The work was difficult and thankless. On one occasion, in obedience to instructions, he took some supplies belonging to a cathedral chapter and was temporarily excommunicated. In 1590 he tried to find a place in the colonial administration in America, without avail. He seems to have been a conscientious but disorderly administrator. By 1597 his accounts were in such disarray that he was dismissed from public service and jailed for a time in Seville. Little is known of his life in the years immediately following, except that he lived in extreme poverty and that he must have been at work on *Don Quixote*.

The book on which his immortality rests was published in 1605 (Part I), and, despite the envious or spiteful comments of Lope de Vega and other literary men, was an immense and immediate success. The knight and his squire rapidly became proverbial and gave rise to a new adjective: quixotic. The book was several times reprinted and translated during the author's lifetime, although Cervantes never became rich from it. Indeed, he might never have gotten around to finishing the story as planned had not a certain Alonzo Fernández de Avellaneda (possibly a pseudonym) published his own continuation in 1614. Under this spur, Cervantes finished and published Part II the following year; the concluding chapters contain a number of attacks on his literary enemy.

Cervantes' later writings are uneven, but one book at least, the *Exemplary Tales (Novelas exemplares)*, is worthy of the author of *Don Quixote*. His last work was *Persiles y Sigismunda*, a diffuse and fantastic story which he finished on his deathbed. He died in 1616 in Madrid. The exact location of his grave is unknown.

The Eighteenth
Century

Candide

by

VOLTAIRE (FRANÇOIS MARIE AROUET)
(1694–1778)

The Characters

NOTE: *Of the dozens of characters in* Candide, *only the following play any continuing role in the story. The rest appear incidentally for a page or two, to illustrate some great misfortune or conspicuous piece of folly.*

Candide—The hero, a likable and ingenuous youth whose name expresses his innocence.
Cunégonde—The daughter of the Baron of Thunder-ten-Tronckh, loved by Candide.
Pangloss—Candide's tutor, a philosopher who believes that he lives in the best of all possible worlds. The name means "all tongue," an allusion either to his learning or to his wordiness.
Cacambo—Candide's servant, part Spanish and part Indian; shrewd, resourceful, and devoted to his master.
Martin—A poor scholar whom Candide befriends. His pessimistic view of life is the counterpoise to Pangloss's optimism.

The Story

In Westphalia in the eighteenth century there live a minor but self-important nobleman, the Baron of Thunder-ten-Tronckh, his fat wife, the Baroness, and his daughter, the beautiful Cunégonde. Attached to their household are a tutor, Dr. Pangloss, and an amiable, openhearted youth named Candide, the Baron's illegitimate nephew. Pangloss is a philosophical optimist who believes that everything is as it must be, and that everything necessarily happens for the best. Candide accepts this doctrine without question. Then one day he is caught by the baron kissing Cunégonde, and is expelled from the castle. As he sets out on his wanderings, he begins his initiation into real life, and gradually learns how much suffering, vice, and stupidity there is in the world.

Almost at once, Candide is pressed into the service of the Bulgarian army, which is at war with another power, the Abares. After an especially bloody engagement, he deserts in horror and makes his way to Holland. Here he meets a miserable beggar who proves to be his old tutor, Pangloss. From him Candide learns that Westphalia has been devastated by war and Cunégonde killed with all her family. They proceed together to Portugal, and, after nearly being drowned at sea, land just in time to see the city of Lisbon destroyed by the great earthquake of 1755. The Holy Inquisition, believing that the earthquake is a judgment on the city for the sin of harboring heretics, has Pangloss hanged and Candide flogged.

Candide is nursed back to health by a mysterious woman who—to his great joy—turns out to be his lost Cunégonde. She has not died after all; she admits that she has been raped and disemboweled, but, as she explains, neither of these accidents is necessarily fatal. For the present, she is joint mistress of two men, a Jewish banker and the Grand Inquisitor himself. Candide manages to kill both men and steal enough money so that he can escape with Cunégonde in a ship to Buenos Aires. There other misfortunes befall them. Cunégonde attracts the eye of the Spanish governor, and Candide is obliged to flee to Paraguay, then governed by the Jesuits as a military theocracy. The commandant (who is both a colonel

and a priest) receives Candide hospitably and reveals himself
to be Cunégonde's brother. When the commandant learns that
Candide still loves his sister, he forces Candide to flee for his
life.

In the company of a servant, a half-breed named Cacambo,
Candide next visits the mythical kingdom of Eldorado, where
gold and gems are as common as sand and pebbles. More
remarkable still, all men are wise and virtuous. Since everyone is just, there are no lawyers, and since everyone is devout, there are no priests. The arts and sciences are supported by the state, and all men, even the humblest, enjoy a
luxurious standard of living. Although these people treat
their visitors hospitably, Candide still longs to find Cunégonde.
At length he is allowed to leave, taking with him enough
jewels to make him fantastically wealthy by the standards of
the outside world.

The two make their way to Surinam, where Cacambo is sent
to Buenos Aires to bribe the governor into giving up Cunégonde, and Candide takes a ship to Europe. He also strikes
up a friendship with a man of letters named Martin whose
pessimistic view of life is a wholesale refutation of Pangloss's
optimism. The trip is spent in one long argument over good
and evil, vice and virtue, fate and free will. Finally the
two reach Paris, where Candide is enabled to form his opinions of Paris society, the theater, books and critics, gambling
and theology. Other adventures take them to Venice, where
Candide continues to learn from a nobleman, Signor Poco-
curante, who is bored with everything, and from six kings,
who have all lost their thrones in one way or another. By
now Candide is fully convinced that there is nobody (outside of Eldorado) so rich or so powerful as to escape the unhappiness that is man's common lot.

Putting Christendom behind them, Candide and Martin
push on to Constantinople where, by a series of happy coincidences, they are reunited with Cacambo, Cunégonde,
Pangloss (who was not thoroughly hanged in Lisbon) and
even with Cunégonde's brother, as quarrelsome as ever.
Cunégonde is by now wrinkled and ill-tempered, but Candide embraces her politely and marries her out of a sense of
duty. Most of the jewels from Eldorado are gone, but with
what remain Candide buys a modest farm just outside the

city and settles down to raising fruit which Cacambo sells in the markets.

Now at last Candide achieves a certain measure of philosophic calm. He no longer enjoys great wealth or the joys of romantic love. But by dint of honest, wholesome work, he and his household enjoy modest security and peace. Cunégonde even becomes a good cook. Pangloss, the same argumentative, pedantic philosopher as always, tries to prove that things really are for the best in this best of all possible worlds, but Candide is cured of philosophizing, and abstract arguments no longer interest him. His only reply is, "Let us cultivate our own garden."

Critical Opinion

Candide is a brilliant improvisation, and should not be judged as if it were a carefully planned novel. Obviously Voltaire never took his plot seriously, or expected his readers to. The episodes are strung together with so little continuity that most of them could be shuffled about without affecting the story, and what continuity there is depends on a series of preposterous coincidences. Clearly Voltaire was not writing an adventure story, but parodying one. The characterization is equally sketchy: the characters are not portraits but caricatures, intended to voice an opinion or illustrate a vice. Indeed, the plot demands these two-dimensional characters, for if they could be accepted as real people, their misfortunes would be terrible, not comic, and we should be offended by the flippant tone of the book.

This bantering tone, which strikes the reader from the very first page, is established mainly by the careful manipulation of ironic effects. Voltaire delights in juxtaposing incongruous ideas or images; for instance, when Cunégonde describes the *auto-da-fé* at Lisbon, she says, "I had an excellent seat; and refreshments were served to the ladies between the Mass and the execution." The effect, of course, is to suggest that even the execution is not so shocking as the frivolity of the spectators. A similar device is to ridicule the technical terms of philosophy by using them in unexpected or even bawdy contexts, as when the lovemaking of Dr. Pangloss is described as a lesson in experimental physics. Some of the

best lines are epigrams or outrageous paradoxes, like Cunégonde's remark that a lady of honor may be raped; it only
strengthens her virtue. But the chief and recurring device is
the ironic insistence, at each fresh turn of misfortune, that
Candide lives "in the best of all possible worlds." Throughout,
Voltaire restricts himself to a very elementary vocabulary and
to grammatical constructions as simple as Candide himself,
but the simplicity is the work of great sophistication.

Still, for all its banter, *Candide* is serious enough. The
satire is expressed in the play of words, but it is based upon
the play of ideas. The chief butt of its ridicule is the optimistic philosophy associated with the German philosopher Gottfried Wilhelm Leibnitz (1646–1716) and with the English
poet, Alexander Pope (1688–1744). Both these men addressed
themselves to the ancient problem of evil: in a world that is
presumably made by an all-wise, all-loving and all-powerful
God, how can we explain the existence of sin, suffering, and
death? Leibnitz's analysis distinguishes three kinds of evil:
metaphysical evil (finitude and imperfection), physical evil
(chiefly pain), and moral evil (or vice). He then attempts to
explain and justify each kind by showing that it is inevitable,
or that it actually serves some greater good. Thus men feel
the pain of fire so that they will not let themselves be burned,
and undergo death so that the world will not be overpopu-
lated. The burden of the argument is that evil is a necessary
part of the divine plan which in its totality is good. In other
words, we experience the one combination of good and evil
which permits the greatest good to emerge, and so the world
is, if not perfect, at least the best possible. Pope carried the
argument still further, or at least stated it more recklessly, in
his poem, *An Essay on Man*:

> All Nature is but Art unknown to thee;
> All Chance, Direction which thou canst not see;
> All Discord, Harmony not understood;
> All partial Evil, universal Good:
> And spite of Pride, in erring Reason's spite,
> One truth is clear: *whatever is, is right.*

This kind of optimism *Candide* attempted to refute chiefly
by arguing that human instinct revolts against it; there is too
much suffering in the world to be explained away so glibly.

Voltaire does not argue with Leibnitz; he simply exposes his
hero to so much pain that phrases like "the best of all possible worlds" become a mockery. As Candide exclaims, "If this
is the best, what are the others like?"

Voltaire could at least contend that he had not fabricated
evidence to support his view; many of the events in *Candide*
actually happened. Thus the war between the Bulgarians and
Abares is actually the Seven Years' War; the six dethroned
kings in Venice are historic figures; the English admiral who
is executed to encourage the rest is the unfortunate John Byng;
and so forth. However, the prize exhibit in Voltaire's collection of horrors is the earthquake which in 1755 destroyed
most of Lisbon and buried thirty thousand people under the
rubble. Here was a calamity so overwhelming that it could
not be explained as contributing to some greater good. As
Voltaire observed, "Had Pope been in Lisbon, would he
have dared to say, 'All is well'?"

There are many things besides optimism which Voltaire
attacks. Chief of these is war. Nowhere in *Candide* does he
write with more cold anger than in the description of the
Abarian village "which the Bulgarians had burned in accord-
ance with international law." After war, he attacks religious
intolerance and cruelty, especially in the chapters dealing
with the Inquisition. Pride of rank is made ridiculous in the
Baron of Thunder-ten-Tronckh; pedantry in the person of
Pangloss. In addition, Voltaire takes occasional shots at people with whom he had quarreled personally: Dutch publishers, French critics, and the whole German nation.

The kingdom of Eldorado would seem an exception to this
catalog of misery and folly, since all men there are wise and
virtuous, but the reader is not expected to suppose that such
a place could ever exist. Its function in the book is to under-
score the evils of the actual world by presenting an ideal society for comparison. There are several aspects of Eldorado
that are especially Voltairean: we note the respect that is
paid to science and technology, and the fact that there are
no lawyers (Voltaire had been trained as one). More important, the people are all deists, that is, they believe in a god
who is known not by revelation or miracles, but by reason
and conscience, and who is worshiped without church or
priesthood.

Voltaire does not allow his hero to stay in Eldorado. Candide returns to the real world and finds a partial cure for at least some of life's evils: to work hard and avoid theories. This world may not be the best possible, but it can be improved. This is what Candide means when he tells Pangloss to cultivate his garden.

Candide is a delight to read. Its clear and graceful style makes it a classic model of French prose. Readers of all countries take pleasure in the urbane wit, the light tone, and— behind all the joking—the intensity of moral conviction. Voltaire has the merit of seeing with great clarity certain truths so obvious that many people in every age overlook them: that war and bigotry are evil, that greed and stupidity are rampant in the world, that society can and should be improved. If Voltaire were alive today, he would undoubtedly say that nothing in the past two hundred years since *Candide* was written has made the book any less true or timely.

The Author

Poet, playwright, novelist, critic, historian, philosopher and social reformer: Voltaire was all of these, and in none was he great; yet in all he did he displayed such brilliance, verve, versatility and polish that he stands out as the most universal genius of his age. His real name was François Marie Arouet; Voltaire was a pseudonym the origin of which has been variously explained. He was born in 1694 in Paris of bourgeois stock, his father being a notary. He got his education from the best teachers of the day, the Jesuits; their piety did not stick, but their literary training did. When Voltaire left school at seventeen, his father determined to make a lawyer of him, but young Arouet balked, and found more pleasure in the company of literary freethinkers. Soon he won a reputation as a wit, as a young man with radical ideas, and as a writer of satirical verses. In fact, he was so successful that he was credited with writing some anonymous poems that were not his at all, and one of these, a satire on the social abuses of the time, earned him eleven months in the Bastille. Though the conditions of detention were so mild as to be more an insult than an injury, Voltaire acquired a hatred of the arbitrary exercise of authority which remained his chief passion all his life.

On his release, he produced a play, *Oedipe,* an attack on pagan superstition which actually was directed against the religion of his own time. He also issued the first version of his epic poem on Henry IV, later known as the *Henriade.* These won him, while still in his twenties, the favor of the king and the rank of the leading author in France. Then Voltaire was again struck down by the insolent exercise of privilege: after a personal quarrel with a young nobleman, the Chevalier de Rohan, he was publicly thrashed by the Chevalier's servants and again thrown into the Bastille. Though he was smarting for revenge, Voltaire decided it was more prudent to live under free institutions, and in 1726 he left for England, where he stayed three years.

It has been said that "Voltaire left France a poet; he returned to it a sage." Certainly England broadened his experience. Here he learned a new language, studied a new literature, and could say what he wished without fearing arrest. He made friends with the chief writers of the day, including Swift and Pope, whose talents were in many ways akin to his own. He studied the works of Newton, who saw the world as an orderly and rational structure ruled by physical laws, and of the deists like Shaftesbury, who taught that man can be virtuous and worship God without the help of scriptures or churches. In particular, he fell under the influence of the rationalist and empiricist philosopher John Locke.

In 1729 Voltaire returned to France and resumed his brilliant career. By now, thanks to royalties and prudent investments, he was on his way to becoming rich. The years from 1734 to 1749 he spent comfortably as the accepted lover and permanent fixture in the home of the Marquise du Châtelet, a clever woman of literary and scientific tastes, who shared his enthusiasm for Newton and Locke. All this time he continued to write plays, stories, poems, histories, philosophy, and a popularization of Newtonian physics. In 1746 he was elected to the French Academy. For a time the king was his best patron. Then Voltaire tactlessly wrote a poem in praise of the royal mistress, Mme. Pompadour, which pleased neither the queen nor the king. Fortunately Frederick the Great had for some time urged him to visit Prussia, and Voltaire found it prudent to accept the invitation.

At first Voltaire was received in Potsdam with every mark of favor: a pension, a coach, and a court title. The king fancied himself a patron of the arts, and saw in Voltaire a brilliant addition to his literary circle. Voltaire, however, was as irrepressible in Prussia as he had been in France, and quarreled with everyone, including Frederick. By 1753 he was on his travels again. He even considered emigrating to Pennsylvania, but the fear of seasickness kept him back, and he chose Geneva instead. Here the Puritanism of the city distressed him; he could not even produce the amateur theatricals which he loved. Finally in 1760 he settled at Ferney, an estate across the frontier in France, but so close to the Swiss border that he could easily escape to either country from the bigotry of the other.

The last years at Ferney were as busy as any in Voltaire's life. He was now extremely rich, and used his capital to develop the industries of the village. He was internationally famous, and all Europe came to see him. With those who did not come he kept up a tireless correspondence, sometimes writing thirty letters a day. The plays, histories, tales and essays never stopped. And what was most of all to his credit, he became a kind of international public defender for persons suffering from intolerance or religious persecution.

Voltaire died quite literally of an excess of public adulation. In 1778 he was persuaded to revisit Paris, where a play of his was to be produced. He entered the city like a conquering hero, received visitors by the hundreds, and was crowned with laurel while the crowds roared and women swooned with excitement. The strain was too great for a man of eighty-six, and in May he died. He thus escaped by a few years witnessing the French Revolution, the excesses of which would probably have appalled him, but for which he had to some extent prepared the way.

Voltaire illustrates most of the virtues and some of the vices of the century. As a writer he is always witty, clear, urbane, and intelligent. As a thinker he is lucid rather than profound. His talent lay in popularizing the ideas of others. He was not really a philosopher, but the greatest philosophical journalist of all time. His temper is rational and skeptical, giving little scope for the feelings. Orthodox Christians, at least in France, have always regarded him as a monster of irreligion. Actually he was a deist who did not hate religion, only superstition and bigotry. His tragedies and epics are no longer read, but his lighter pieces, especially the philosophical tales like *Candide,* are so witty, so polished, so thoughtful, so civilized, that they are still the delight not of France alone but of the whole world.

The Nineteenth
Century

The Red and the Black

by

STENDHAL (MARIE-HENRI BEYLE)
(1783–1842)

The Characters

Julien Sorel—The hero, a young man of peasant origins, intelligent, proud, ambitious, ready to use others to serve his ends.

Père Sorel—Julien's father, a carpenter, shrewd, harsh, and grasping.

M. de Rênal—The Mayor of Verrières, a self-important manufacturer who wishes to rank with the nobility.

Mme. de Rênal—The Mayor's wife, a woman of aristocratic connections, simple, natural and unworldly. Her deepest love is for her children.

Valenod—Rênal's principal rival in Verrières, a vulgar and unscrupulous parvenu.

Curé Chélan—An elderly priest, recently ousted from his living; a genuinely good man who is concerned for Julien's professional and spiritual welfare.

Mme. Derville—Cousin and companion of Mme. de Rênal.

Elisa—A servant in the Rênal household who falls in love with Julien.

Fouqué—A friend of Julien who has a lumber business, an honest, loyal and unpretentious young man.

41

Abbé Pirard—Director of the seminary at Besançon, an austere and devout Jansenist.

Marquis de la Mole—Julien's employer in Paris, a former émigré noble now restored to a position of wealth and influence who treats Julien with great courtesy and consideration.

The Bishop of Agde—A youthful prelate involved in right-wing conspiracy.

Mathilde de la Mole—Daughter of the Marquis, a proud, intelligent, high-spirited and sarcastically witty girl of nineteen or twenty, drawn to Julien because he is more forceful and ambitious than the men in her own circle.

Norbert de la Mole—Mathilde's brother, a rather ordinary and uncomplicated young man.

The Chevalier de Beauvoisis—An elegant young gentleman with whom Julien fights a duel.

Conte Altamira—An Italian count who has taken part in a liberal conspiracy and has fled his country under sentence of death.

Mme. de Fervaques—A pious widow to whom Julien declares his love in the hope of making Mathilde jealous.

Prince Korasoff—A Russian who fancies himself a man of the world and gives Julien instructions in the art of seduction.

Marquis de Croisenois—Mathilde's fiancé, amiable, witty and well bred, but otherwise a nonentity.

M. de Frilair—A priest at Besançon, the political and professional enemy of Pirard.

The Story

France in the 1820's was in the grip of political and religious reaction. Charles X ruled by divine right. In the army and in the government the nobility were back in the saddle, having learned nothing during their twenty years of exile. The church also was reestablished, and its prelates wielded great political influence.

Julien Sorel, a boy of eighteen living in Verrières, a small town in the Franche-Comté, is intelligent and ambitious. Although his father is only a peasant, Julien has received a fair education and is eager to occupy a position in life equal to his abilities. A few years before he could have entered the

Napoleonic army, where even a common soldier could rise, like Bernadotte, to become a king. Now that the country is at peace and ruled by the Bourbons, the only road to power for a poor boy is to enter the church. Accordingly, Julien studies Latin and theology with a view to entering a seminary; in the words of the title of the book, he chooses the clerical black rather than the military red.

Julien's reputation as a scholar wins him a post as tutor to the children of M. de Rênal, the Mayor of Verrières. Julien is smarting with a sense of social inferiority and is determined not to be treated as an inferior. In a short while, he is deeply involved in an affair with his employer's wife. His motives are neither love nor sensuality so much as a wish to test his nerve, to prove to himself that he can get what he wants, and to strike a blow at his employer. The affair proceeds so recklessly that the secret leaks out, and M. de Rênal receives an anonymous letter denouncing the lovers. By extremely adroit maneuvering, they turn suspicion from themselves, but Julien is obliged to leave Verrières and enter the seminary at Besançon.

Seminary life is no refuge from the world, however; it is Julien's initiation into a particularly vicious and cutthroat brand of politics. He tries to excel in his studies only to discover that his fellow students do not respect intelligence and resent those who have it. Because of his independent spirit, he is nicknamed Martin Luther and subjected to all kinds of petty indignities. His ability does earn him the respect of the director, Abbé Pirard, an austere and dedicated man. A power struggle, however, is under way between Pirard, a Jansenist, and a pro-Jesuit faction led by the Vice Principal. Julien is caught up in the intrigue. He conducts himself as prudently as he can, winning some points of advantage and losing others. At length Pirard, worn out and discouraged, resigns his post and leaves for Paris, taking Julien with him.

Julien now becomes private secretary to a wealthy and influential nobleman, the Marquis de la Mole, and a member of his household. In addition to performing his work admirably, Julien acquires some urban polish and sophistication, learns to dress well, frequents the theaters and opera, and even fights a duel. His employer shows his trust by using him as an emissary in a secret and dangerous political mission. Julien's triumph, however, is an affair with the daughter of the house, Mathilde de la Mole, a girl of about nineteen.

Mathilde is a high-spirited girl who admires men of spirit and who finds most of the men in her own circle insipid and uninteresting, not excepting her official fiancé, M. de Croisenois. Her ideal of manhood is an ancestor, Boniface de la Mole, the lover of Marguerite of Navarre executed in 1574 for his part in a conspiracy. After Boniface was beheaded, the queen took his severed head and buried it with her own hands. Mathilde is fascinated by this sentence of death, which she declares is the one distinction that cannot be bought. She sees in Julien some of the qualities which she admires in her ancestor, and is drawn to him despite his plebeian origins. The lovemaking of the two young people is almost a kind of warfare in which Julien is constantly on his guard against being tricked or betrayed or made a fool of. For him the conquest of Mathilde is a social triumph and a test of will. At one point they break off, and Julien pays court to a fashionable widow in the hope of making Mathilde jealous. At length it develops that Mathilde is pregnant; she now accepts him without reservation and announces to her father that she plans to marry his secretary.

De la Mole is furious, for he had dreamed of giving his daughter to a duke, but he consents to the marriage, and, to make Julien a little more acceptable as a son-in-law, provides him with a private income, an army commission, and a minor title. Before the ceremony can take place, however, the marquis makes inquiries about Julien in Verrières. He receives a damaging letter from Mme. de Rênal, denouncing Julien as a social climber and a schemer who insinuates himself into wealthy families and plays on the affections of the women for his own advantage. This letter, which is far from representing Mme. de Rênal's true feelings, has been dictated by her confessor. It precipitates a tragedy.

The marquis is furious and refuses to allow the marriage under any conditions. Julien is beside himself with vexation; he rushes off to Verrières, buys two pistols, and avenges himself on Mme. de Rênal by shooting her while she is kneeling in church. The wound is not fatal, but Julien is arrested and tried for attempted murder. His arrest brings him some peace of mind. He cooperates with his prosecutors and invites death during the trial by refusing to defend himself. Since efforts have been made to influence the jury (the local clergy take the lead in this piece of corruption) there is a good chance that Julien may be acquitted. Unfortunately, one of the jurymen is a former rival for the affections of Mme. de Rênal who nurses his old grudge. The jury finds Julien guilty and he is beheaded. Mme. de Rênal dies soon afterward, not of her wounds but of a broken heart, while Mathilde buries her lover's severed head as Marguerite of Navarre had done for her unlucky ancestor. In death, at least, Julien has enabled her to act out her most precious fantasy.

Critical Opinion

In February of 1828, an execution took place in Grenoble which was to provide Stendhal with the plot of his best-known novel. The criminal was Antoine Berthet, the son of a Dauphinois blacksmith, an intelligent but unstable young man who had served as a tutor in the family of M. Michoud de la Tour, a friend of Stendhal. Either he corrupted Mme. Michoud or she him. At any rate, their affair resulted in Berthet's being dismissed and placed in a Catholic seminary. When his superiors decided that he was not fit for the priesthood, he returned to his mistress, only to find that a second young man was now serving in the double capacity of tutor and lover. After a short stay in a second seminary, Berthet obtained another post as tutor in the family of Comte de Cordon; a romance with the daughter of the family led to a second dismissal. Now made desperate by so many checks, and enraged with Mme. Michoud, he shot her during mass in the village church, but succeeded only in wounding her. For this assault he was sent to the guillotine.

The story of Julien Sorel follows this one so closely that no one could mistake the parallel; in fact, the family of Mme. Michoud de la Tour never forgave Stendhal for the novel. There were others in Grenoble who might have recognized themselves in certain of the subordinate characters: Mme. Derville, Abbé Chélan, Father Pirard, Valenod and Fouqué. In a broader sense, all of France sat for its portrait in *The Red and the Black (Le Rouge et le Noir)*, for Stendhal was careful to show how his characters played their part in the social and political movements of the day. We see the aristocracy trying to live as they had done before the Revolution and plotting to recover absolute political power. We see the bourgeoisie growing rich from business and manufacturing and trying to dignify themselves with titles of nobility. We see the Bonapartists still cherishing dreams of imperial glory, and the church, now restored to political power, exercising it without scruple. The novel is a sociological study, admittedly unfriendly and partisan, of France under the last Bourbon king.

In this society, Sorel typifies those men who had risen to power a generation earlier, during the turmoil of the Revolution and the Empire: men of the people, with nothing to lose and everything to gain, ambitious, unscrupulous, and energetic, men like Danton, Robespierre, or Napoleon himself. Born out of his time, Sorel becomes a secret worshiper of Bonaparte; he keeps a portrait of the emperor in his mattress, and the *Memorial of Saint Helena* is his favorite reading. The Napoleonic myth has molded his character, or, if you will, corrupted it. Sorel never acts as most people do, from simple emotion, or easy self-indulgence; his every act is a conscious exercise of will, a trial of strength which he sets for himself. He even makes love grimly and joylessly in order to satisfy himself that his will is stronger than that of the women whom he seduces.

Sorel is obsessively class-conscious; he can never forget that he is a peasant living among aristocrats, and he is always on the watch for snubs and insults, most of them quite imaginary. Thus, when he first meets Mme. de Rênal, he imagines she is insulting him, whereas she, in fact, sees in him only an attractive boy who will be kind to her children. He fights a duel with de Beauvoisis because of a rude glance from one of that gentleman's lackeys. When he enters Mathilde's bedroom, he comes armed to the teeth for fear of an attack by Norbert or de Croisenois, neither of whom even suspects what is afoot. And when he finally takes possession of Mathilde, it is with the grim satisfaction that he has done so instead of the marquis. There is much self-pity and self-deception in all this; Julien's torment springs largely from the fact that he cannot see either himself or others as they are, and turns even love into an act of class warfare.

In her own way, Mathilde is equally the prisoner of her fantasies. She dreams of the energetic days of the wars of religion, and really loves not Sorel but her own ancestor, Boniface de la Mole, who was loved by a queen and who died on the scaffold. Sorel's death enables her to act out her fantasy to the very end, burying her lover's head with her own hands, as Marguerite of Navarre had done. Thus the book ends with a melodramatic gesture which might have been appropriate in the sixteenth century, but which is utterly out of place in the nineteenth, except perhaps as an ironic commentary on the times.

For most critics, the chief problem in the book is Sorel's attack on Mme. de Rênal, an action for which we are quite unprepared. Indeed, everyone involved seems to be acting out of character. Granted that Mme. de Rênal, under great pressure from her spiritual director, might have written a letter so damaging to the man she loved, can we assume that so worldly a man as the count would have taken at face value such a letter, coming as it did from a cast-off mistress? Presumably, he believed the letter because he wanted to believe it; it gave him a weapon to use against the man who had betrayed his confidence. Even so, Sorel's position was still a strong one; Mathilde was pregnant and wished to marry him; sooner or later the count would have to bow before these realities. Why then did the strong-willed Mathilde lose her head and summon Sorel to Paris, instead of simply arguing with her father till she won her point? Finally, how can we explain Sorel's action? An ordinary man might, in the height of passion, try to strike at the person who had so cruelly ruined his prospects, but Sorel was not an ordinary man. Never in his life had he done anything which was not calculated to advance his interests. In the long trip to Verrières (before the days of railroads) he would have had time for reflection. Are we to suppose, as some critics have suggested, that he was actually out of his mind?

All these questions and others like them have been examined by F. W. J. Hemmings (*Stendhal: A Study of His Novels,* 1964), who suggests that Sorel acts as he does in order to vindicate his integrity. All his life he has been made to feel inferior to the aristocracy, and now a noble has accused him of ignoble behavior. The charge is plausible enough, too plausible to be simply argued away. Only by some decisive act can he clear himself of the imputation of baseness. He must do the one thing he would not do if he were really a calculating schemer: he must throw away every advantage which he is on the point of gaining, his wife, wealth, career and title of nobility. Sorel goes to the guillotine deliberately, and even with a certain serenity of mind; he is his own master at last.

The Charterhouse
of Parma

by

STENDHAL (MARIE-HENRI BEYLE)

The Characters

Lieutenant Robert—An officer in Napoleon's Italian army, presumably Fabrizio's real father.

Marchese del Dongo—A Milanese noble attached to the Austrian cause; a fat, stingy, pasty-faced reactionary.

Marchesa del Dongo—His young wife.

Angelina Valserra (Gina), Contessa Pietranera, later Duchessa Sanseverina—Sister of the Marchese; beautiful, brilliant, passionate, resolute, and unscrupulous.

Ascanio del Dongo—Eldest son of the Marchese, as reactionary and as treacherous as his father.

Fabrizio Valserra, Marchesino del Dongo—The hero, an impetuous, handsome, harum-scarum youth.

Priore Blanès—A kindly old priest whose hobby is astrology.

Limercati—A rich young man, for a time Gina's lover.

Margot—A vivandière who befriends Fabrizio at Waterloo.

General Fabio Conti—A Parmesan general, member of the Liberal party, pompous and vindictive.

Clélia Conti—His daughter, charming, gentle and loving.

Conte Mosca della Rovere—Prime Minister of Parma, about fifty, a shrewd, experienced, and worldly politician.

Ranuccio-Ernesto IV—Prince of Parma, an absolute monarch, not wholly stupid, but demoralized and made cruel by fear of assassination.

Duca Sanseverina-Taxis—An elderly aristocrat, personally inoffensive, but eager for an honorific appointment that will dignify his not very ancient title.

Rassi—The Fiscal General (Chief Justice) of Parma, a detested reactionary.

Ferrante Palla—A physician, poet and revolutionary.

Clara-Paolina—Consort of the Prince, a shy woman, unhappy because her husband has a mistress and does not speak to her.

Landriani—Archbishop of Parma, a shy, honest old man, risen from the populace, easily intimidated by men of rank.

Marchesa Balbi—Mistress of the Prince, conspicuous mainly for her stinginess.

Marchesa Raversi—Leader of the Liberal opposition, a determined virago.

Marietta Valserra—A pretty young actress.

Giletti—Marietta's lover, thin, ugly and vindictive.

"La Mammaccia"—A grasping and dishonest old woman who acts as Marietta's mother.

Lodovico—Fabrizio's loyal manservant; in his spare time he writes sonnets.

Conte Zurla—Minister of the Interior.

Fausta—A celebrated singer.

Conte M—A jealous, conceited young man, in love with Fausta.

Don Cesare—Brother of General Conti and chaplain at the Fortress of Parma.

Princess Isotta—An elderly Princess of the ruling house, and a confirmed old maid.

Marchese Crescenzi—A rich man betrothed to Clélia, but otherwise a nonentity.

Ranuccio-Ernesto V—The heir apparent of Parma, a painfully shy boy, interested only in mineralogy.

General Fontana—Aide-de-camp of the Prince.

Gonzo—A hanger-on of the Marchese Crescenzi.

Annetta Marini—A merchant's daughter, in love with Fabrizio.

Sandrino—Fabrizio's son by Clélia.

The Story

The Charterhouse of Parma (La Chartreuse de Parme) is laid in northern Italy, beginning in the last years of the Napoleonic era and continuing into the period of reaction that followed. The hero, Fabrizio, is ostensibly the second son of a conservative old nobleman, the Marchese del Dongo, though there are strong hints that the boy is actually the son of an officer in Napoleon's army. His childhood is made unhappy by his unsympathetic father and his arrogant elder brother, Ascanio; his warmest affection is for his aunt Gina, Contessa Pietranera, an extremely clever and beautiful woman, now a widow. As he grows up to be extremely handsome and charming, her tenderness for him ripens into a love which has strongly incestuous overtones, although they never become completely overt or explicit. Fabrizio's transition from boyhood to manhood is marked by a quixotic adventure. When Napoleon returns from Elba, Fabrizio, full of enthusiasm for the imperial cause, hurries off to France to join the army and manages to reach Waterloo. The experience is so confusing that he hardly knows what has happened to him. With the final collapse of the Napoleonic cause, Fabrizio returns to Italy to find the country firmly in the grip of a reactionary Austrian government. His brother has denounced him to the police, and his future, either as a soldier or a statesman, is compromised.

His aunt Gina is now the mistress of a certain Conte Mosca, Prime Minister of the independent Principality of Parma which he governs with all the astuteness of a Metternich. To establish her in Parma, Mosca marries Gina to an elderly and wealthy duke who is happy to be rewarded for his cuckoldry with a coveted decoration. In Parma, Gina proves to be the prettiest, cleverest, and most influential woman at court, so that even the Prince, Ranuccio-Ernesto IV, casts a hungry eye at her. Gina and the Conte make plans for Fabrizio: the only career open to him is the Church. As a nobleman, he will not be expected to be either pious, learned or chaste; his family connections and Mosca's influence will eventually make him archbishop of Parma. Accordingly he is sent to study theology for four years in Naples. He returns a Monsignor though not yet an ordained priest.

Fabrizio is now such a presentable young man that the Conte suffers pangs of jealousy. Fabrizio, however, feels only affectionate gratitude for his aunt—no more—and he has no wish to hurt his friend Mosca. Accordingly, he takes as his mistress a young actress named Marietta. The affair, begun so lightly, ends in a tragic brawl with a rival, a commonplace actor named Giletti. After killing Giletti in self-defense, Fabrizio again has to run from the police. Ordinarily he could expect a rapid acquittal for the homicide, except that political considerations have given the episode an exaggerated importance. The Liberal faction at Parma seizes on it to embarrass their enemy, Mosca. The prince, smarting from his rejection by Gina, is delighted to strike back at her through her beloved nephew. Fabrizio is sentenced in absentia to twenty years' imprisonment. Unless he is judicially cleared, his clerical career is over.

Gina threatens the prince that she will leave Parma if Fabrizio is not freed. Ranuccio-Ernesto, torn between his desire to have Gina and his desire to humiliate her, responds treacherously. He pardons Fabrizio, omitting certain phrases that would render the pardon irrevocable. Then once the boy is in the grasp of the police, he has him incarcerated in the Fortress of Parma. Fabrizio, however, is not deeply dejected. The governor of the fortress, General Conti, has a pretty young daughter named Clélia, whose window faces the prison. Fabrizio is able to communicate with her and, for the first time in his life, falls seriously in love.

While Fabrizio is languishing happily in confinement, Gina is scheming to set him free. The daring escape plan involves several high officials whom Mosca bribes. Fabrizio, once free, thinks of nobody but Clélia, and has no eyes for his aunt. Gina now realizes that neither she nor Fabrizio nor Mosca will be safe so long as the prince lives. Her next scheme is to have Ranuccio-Ernesto assassinated. Among her many admirers, a slightly insane poet named Palla, a fanatical republican, yields to Gina's kisses and her money, and consents to poison the prince. After fulfilling his bargain he goes beyond his instructions and raises a republican revolution in Parma, which Mosca easily suppresses.

Gina and Mosca are now riding the crest of their wave.

The new prince, a shy boy interested only in mineralogy, yields to Gina's insistence that Fabrizio must be exonerated. For this, she requires not a pardon, but a new trial, and a trial means that Fabrizio must surrender himself. Mosca proposes that Fabrizio be lodged in the city jail, which he, as minister of police, controls; but the love-sick Fabrizio surrenders instead at the fortress, where he can see Clélia again. This prison is controlled by Mosca's chief enemy, Rassi, the Fiscal General. Soon it appears that Rassi intends to have his prisoner poisoned before the trial can take place. For the second time, Gina must plot to free him. She goes to the prince, who is too ingenuous to believe that any citizen, especially an innocent one, can be exposed to poisoning in a prison of his. However, after only a short reign, he has learned to like the taste of absolute power, and he finds Gina just as attractive as his father had. He consents to free Fabrizio in exchange for Gina's favors.

Once Fabrizio has been safely acquitted and reinstalled in his ecclesiastical dignities, Gina tries as long as she can to postpone payment of her debt to the prince. The prince will not be put off, but his victory does not last long. Within half an hour after he has left her bed, Gina leaves the country and settles in Naples, where the loyal Mosca eventually joins her. She leaves Fabrizio in Parma, where, as the coadjutor with right of succession to an elderly archbishop, he is the most powerful ecclesiastic in the place. Marriage to Clélia is now, of course, out of the question; she becomes the wife of a wealthy, pompous marchese.

At this point in the novel Stendhal introduces a short, bittersweet concluding movement about the love of Fabrizio and Clélia. After Clélia's marriage, Fabrizio's haggard expression secures him an undeserved reputation for piety, and his anguished manner in the pulpit makes him a fashionable and popular preacher. For some time the lovers avoid each other, but neither her married state nor his clerical vows are a permanent obstacle. Eventually the two yield to their passion. Clélia has, to be sure, made a vow to the Virgin never to see Fabrizio again; she honors the vow by meeting him only in the dark. A child is born, Sandrino, who dies at the age of two. Soon after, Clélia also dies. Fabrizio is devastated; he has grasped for worldly happiness and success and has been thwarted at every turn, most cruelly where his heart was most deeply involved. The only course that remains to him is to retire from the world, so that the diocese shall not be disgraced by an unworthy archbishop. Despite all his sins as a prelate, he is still a good enough Catholic, and sufficiently honest with himself, to realize that there is much on his conscience that must be cleared. Accordingly he withdraws to the Carthusian monastery in Parma, the "Charterhouse" of the title, to spend his last sad days.

Critical Opinion

During Stendhal's years as consul at Civitavecchia, one of his hobbies was to buy or copy old accounts of crimes and scandals that occurred in Rome during the sixteenth and seventeenth centuries, the same sort of material that Browning used as the source of *The Ring and the Book*. In his collection was an account of the life of young Alessandro Farnese, later Pope Paul III and the founder of the Farnese fortunes. According to this account, Alessandro owed his advancement in the Church to the influence of his aunt, mistress of Cardinal Rodrigo Borgia. In his youth he was jailed for abducting a young noblewoman, escaped from prison, but nevertheless managed to become cardinal and Pope. His mistress presented him with a son who became Duke of Parma. This little sketch of seven hundred words was the starting point of *The Charterhouse of Parma*, so that the atmosphere of the novel, with its intrigues and poisonings, incestuous passions and easy amours, suggests the Italy of the sixteenth century rather than the nineteenth. Stendhal chose to modernize the story, possibly because the career of Paul III was so much a matter of history that it could not well be tampered with for artistic reasons. Accordingly he chose the scene he knew best: northern Italy in his own day. Tact obliged him to change the details considerably; he described Parma as it might have been had the Farnesi continued to rule there. Actually that dynasty had become extinct in the eighteenth century, and in Stendhal's day Parma was governed by Napoleon's second wife, Marie Louise of Austria, for her times a relatively liberal and enlightened ruler. The character of Stendhal's despotic prince may have been modeled on that of the neighboring Duke of Modena, Francis IV.

Parma is a small state, and the drama of politics, enacted on this narrow stage, becomes petty. Intrigue rules, rather than diplomacy, and the fate of ministers is settled in bedrooms. The prince is a caricature of an autocrat. Though he is not stupid or cowardly by nature, he obliges his prime minister to look under the bed each night for possible assassins. The conservative leader, Mosca, is an enlightened man compelled to head a despotic government. The leaders of the opposition are far less liberal. The generals are afraid of gunpowder, and worry chiefly about the number of buttons on their soldiers' uniforms. Rassi, the Fiscal General, is a villain out of old-time melodrama, and the maneuverings of these men suggest *opéra bouffe*. Only at two points does a more serious note intrude. Two figures transcend this world of petty court intrigue: Napoleon, who for a few years swept away the old dynasties and gave Italy a modern government; and Ferrante Palla, the revolutionary, who represents the new Italy being born—the country that Silvio Pellico and Mazzini were already dreaming of.

The vitality of this story is derived less from its politics than from a trio of brilliant characters: the glittering Duchessa Sanseverina, the worldly-wise Mosca, and the handsome scapegrace, Fabrizio. All three are thoroughly amoral, yet we cannot help but like them for their charm, their resourcefulness, their insouciant gaiety in the face of danger. Mosca is the wisest, and his words sound like the maxims of de La Rochefoucauld. Gina is the most vital. But Fabrizio is perhaps the finest of all, since he is the only one who undergoes any maturation or refinement of character. That he is capable of high idealism is shown by his behavior as a boy at Waterloo. Later he falls into a life of pleasure seeking and religious hypocrisy. Yet, by the end of the story, if he has not achieved real holiness, he has at least risen to the level of honorable self-abnegation. Though apparently an anti-hero, he contains within him, unknown to himself, the stuff of which heroes are made.

One of the defects of the story is that the last years of Fabrizio's career and the change of heart that led him to take refuge in the monastery are rather hastily treated. The story of an archbishop in love would make a novel in itself, and his state of mind after Clélia's death needs to be analyzed to seem convincing. The fault is not Stendhal's, but the publisher's. The original novel had to be curtailed and Stendhal died before he could rewrite it as projected. As it is, one feels that the plot is ample enough for three novels at least.

The Charterhouse of Parma is one of those books whose greatness is universally recognized though readers are often hard put to say just where it lies. Moralistic critics are bewildered by its amorality and lack of high seriousness. Formalistic critics are troubled by its sprawling organization. Despite these flaws, it continues to live through its abundant vitality.

The Author

Stendhal's real name was Marie-Henri Beyle, though at times he tried to distinguish himself with a spurious nobility by signing himself Henri de Beyle, the sort of thing Julien Sorel would have done. Actually, Beyle was of solid bourgeois stock, his father being a lawyer in Grenoble. He was born in 1783. His mother died when he was seven, leaving him to be raised by his father, a stern, dry, cautious man, and by his Aunt Séraphie, both of whom he detested. His early education was in the hands of clergymen, and was largely responsible for his later anticlericalism. In fact, his whole character was formed in reaction against his father and preceptors: he was turbulent, skeptical, egotistical, sensual, and undisciplined.

Beyle's love for literature was fostered by his maternal grandfather, a doctor with cultivated and literate tastes. At the age of thirteen he was sent to the École Centrale in Grenoble, where he distinguished himself in mathematics, and seemed destined to proceed to the École Polytechnique at Paris and become an engineer. He arrived at the capital in 1799, the day after the *coup d'état* which made Napoleon master of France. Forgetting his prudent plans to be an engineer, Beyle threw himself into the imperialist venture on which the country was now launched. A distant relative named Daru, who was in favor with Napoleon and who later became secretary of state, found him a clerical post in the War Office. This proved too tame, and the following year young Henri, only seventeen, received a commission as second lieutenant and was sent to join the French army in Italy.

Though Beyle knew nothing of Italy when he went there, it was to become his second country and the scene of one of his major novels. He was delighted with the Italian opera, with the music of Cimarosa and the painting of Correggio; he was attracted by the Italian temperament, which seemed more passionate and forceful, less civilized (in the bourgeois, nineteenth-century sense of the word) than the French. Italy, especially Rome and Milan, became so much a part of him that he once proposed to inscribe on his tomb the words, "Enrico Beyle, Milanese." Above all, he fell in love with Italian women; his private life from this time on is largely a record of his love affairs.

The years that followed were full of activity. In 1806, he reentered the government service and was given an administrative post in Brunswick, then occupied by the French. Here he learned a little German, moved in good society, and was treated with a respect flattering to his self-esteem, but found himself generally bored. Later he traveled much in Germany and Austria, was sent on a government mission to Vienna, and followed the emperor's army to Russia. Here he saw the battles of Smolensk and Borodino, watched Moscow burn, and found the conflagration esthetically satisfying. Then with equal self-possession, he retreated with the army back into western Europe. Napoleon's empire was now collapsing, and when Paris fell Beyle left France, realizing that his career in government was finished.

Now that the Bourbons ruled France, Beyle turned to literature, and hereafter we shall refer to him as Stendhal, the name which he made famous. His writings during the twenties were very miscellaneous: lives of celebrated composers, a history of Italian painting, a treatise on love, a guidebook to Rome, and various magazine articles published in London and Paris. He lived rather precariously in Italy, France, and England. The change of government in 1830, which placed a bourgeois monarch, Louis Philippe, on the throne, opened up to Stendhal the possibility of reentering public service. That same year he was appointed consul in Trieste, where his reputation for radicalism made him unwelcome to the Austrian authorities. Next, he was transferred to Civitavecchia in the Papal States; the salary was lower, but his beloved Rome was close at hand. He remained in this post for the rest of his life, although his health obliged him to be absent for long periods of time.

The Red and the Black was written during the last year of the reign of Charles X. By the time it appeared in 1831 it was already out of date, at least as an attack on the Bourbons. During the following decade Stendhal wrote two auto-biographical works, *Memoirs of an Egotist (Souvenirs d'Egotisme* 1832) and *Life of Henri Brulard (Vie de Henri Brulard* 1835–1836), together with an unfinished novel, *Lucien Leuwen* (1834–1835). Not wishing to be turned out of a second consulate, he left these unpublished in his life-time. In 1839 he published his second masterpiece, *The Charterhouse of Parma,* a story of adventure and intrigue set in Italy. After a long illness, Stendhal died in Paris in 1842 of a stroke.

Stendhal's reputation was slow to mature. He claimed he wrote "for the happy few" and predicted that he would not be appreciated until 1880. In this he was right. Perhaps the trouble lay in the fact that he did not fit any of the literary stereotypes of the day. His love for heroic egotists like Napoleon set him apart from the men of the eighteenth century, and yet he did not exactly resemble the romantics either. He lacked the grandiose posturing of Hugo or the sentimentality of Lamartine. Only when these men no longer dominated the literary horizon was it possible to see where Stendhal's greatness lay: in his psychological realism.

Les Misérables

by

VICTOR HUGO (1802–1885)

The Characters

Jean Valjean—The hero; at first a simple, hardworking peasant; later rendered bitter and disillusioned by his life as a convict; finally a worthy and inoffensive man, redeemed by the example of the saintly Bishop Myriel and by his love for his foster daughter, Cosette. Alias Père Madeleine, Ultimus Fauchelevent, Urbain Fabre, #24,601, and #9,430.

Charles François Bienvenu Myriel, Bishop of D-(Monsieur Bienvenu)—A saintly old man, remarkable for charity and good works.

Mlle. Baptistine—His sister, a spinster.

Mme. Magloire—His housekeeper.

G——A former member of the revolutionary National Convention, with a noble passion for social justice.

Petit Gervais—A Savoyard organ-grinder about twelve years old.

Felix Tholomyès—A Parisian student sowing his wild oats.

Fantine—Mistress of Tholomyès. By disposition modest and reserved, she is forced by circumstances to become a prostitute.

Friends of Tholomyès and Their Mistresses:
  Listolier—Dahlia
  Fameuil—Zephine
  Blacheville—Favourite
Thénardier—Sergeant, innkeeper, con man and criminal; a grasping and unscrupulous man. Alias Jondrette, Fabantou.
Mme. Thénardier—His wife, equally unscrupulous.
Euphrasie (Cosette)—Daughter of Fantine, foster daughter of Valjean, a gentle, affectionate girl.
Eponine—Daughter of Thénardier, a wretched but good-looking girl, in love with Marius.
Azelma—Second daughter of Thénardier.
Javert—Police officer, a man of incorruptible tenacity.
Fauchelevent—An old man, formerly a notary, in the end a gardener in the Convent of the Petit Picpus.
Bamatabois—A provincial dandy who insults Fantine.
Sister Simplice—A Sister of Charity, of saintly character and incorruptibly truthful.
Scaufflaire—Keeper of a livery stable at M— sur M—.
Champmathieu—A peasant suspected of being Valjean.
Colonel Baron Georges Pontmercy—A gallant officer at Waterloo, later an inoffensive old man interested in cultivating flowers.
Mother Innocent—Prioress of Petit Picpus.
Marius Pontmercy—Son of the Colonel, a generous-spirited young man devoted to the memory of his father.
Gavroche—A gamin, the son of Thénardier.
M. Gillenormand—A bourgeois of the old regime, a cranky, domineering old man.
Mlle. Gillenormand—His daughter, a prudish spinster.
M. Mabeuf—An old friend of Pontmercy, a botanist and a bibliophile.
Abbé Mabeuf—His brother.
Mère Plutarch—His housekeeper.
Théodule Gillenormand—Grandnephew of Gillenormand, a handsome young officer.
Students and conspirators in the uprising of *1832*:
  Enjolras—A twenty-two-year-old militant revolutionary, young, handsome and serious.
  Combeferre—The philosopher of the group.
  Prouvaire—The son of a rich man, a naturally shy and gentle youth, sentimental and romantic.

Feuilly—A fan maker, self-educated.

Courfeyrac—A playful and high-spirited boy, the son of a noble.

Bahorel—Bold, generous, quarrelsome, talkative, prodigal.

Lesgle (Laigle) de Meaux (Bossuet)—Cheerful but unlucky.

Joly—A medical student and a hypochondriac.

Grantaire—A physically ugly skeptic.

Mère Bougon—Landlady of the Maison Gorbeau.

Bandits of the Patron-Minette—

Gueulemer—A great, hulking brute.

Babet—Thin, shrewd, formerly a tooth puller.

Claquesous—A mysterious, dark man, a ventriloquist. Alias Le Cabuc.

Montparnasse—Young, good-looking, and rather a dandy.

Other criminals associated with Thénardier:

Bigrenaille.

Brujon.

"Deux Milliards."

Magnon—A servant of Gillenormand, by whom he has two sons.

Toussaint—Servant to Valjean.

Mère Hucheloup—Innkeeper in the Rue de la Chanvrerie.

Boulatruelle—A road laborer of Montfermeil.

The Story

The plot of *Les Misérables* is vast and intricate, but its central thread follows the adventures of a peasant named Jean Valjean during the first third of the nineteenth century. Valjean is a convict, condemned to the galleys for stealing a loaf of bread to keep his family from starving. Because of several attempts to escape, his term is extended to nineteen years. In 1815 he is released, a bitter and desperate man, and finds his way to the town of D—— in southern France. Because he is a galley slave, no one will give him shelter until the bishop of the town, a saintly man, offers him lodging and courteous treatment. Valjean rewards this hospitality by stealing the bishop's silver during the night. Soon after, the police pick him up with the loot and bring him back. The bishop, to Valjean's astonishment, assures the police that the silver is a gift, and even reproaches his guest for not having taken the candlesticks as well. This generosity, the first that Valjean has known in years, touches and reforms him. Thereafter, he resolves to be worthy of the bishop's trust and to live as virtuous a life as possible.

Several years later, we meet Valjean in a town in northern France where he has established himself under an assumed name as a manufacturer of cheap jewelry. Thanks to a few simple improvements in the process of manufacture, he becomes wealthy, gains the trust of the townspeople, and even is appointed mayor (a position which an ex-convict might not legally hold). The police inspector of the town, Javert, is a grimly persistent sleuth who comes to suspect his superior's true identity. He is on the point of denouncing him when word reaches him that a man supposed to be Valjean has been arrested on another charge and is about to be sent back to the galleys. In embarrassment, he confesses to the mayor what his suspicions have been, and offers to resign, but the offer is not accepted. Valjean now knows that he is permanently safe from exposure, but the news forces him to a hard choice, since he realizes that an innocent man will suffer in his name. In a heroic gesture of renunciation, he goes into the courtroom, reveals his identity and voluntarily returns to the galleys.

After several years, Valjean escapes and returns to the north, where he has hidden a large sum of money, the fruit of his years as a capitalist. This sum is enough to keep him in comfort and allow him to indulge in quiet philanthropy. His first act is to seek out a small girl named Cosette. She is the daughter of Fantine, one of his former employees, who became a prostitute in order to support her daughter. Fantine is now dead, and Cosette is being raised by foster parents who exploit and abuse her. Valjean adopts the girl as his daughter and gives her all his love and care. Together they go to Paris, where Valjean finds a post as a gardener in a convent and Cosette becomes a charity pupil. In this retreat, Valjean shakes off Javert, who is still looking for him, and spends several years in safety.

As Cosette grows up, she attracts the interest of Marius Pontmercy, a young student in Paris. Marius has been raised by his grandfather, a bourgeois of the old school, but he worships the memory of his father, an army officer made a

baron by the gift of Napoleon. At twenty, Marius is supporting himself in penury and associating with radical friends. He
and Cosette meet in the Luxembourg Gardens and carry on
a secret correspondence despite Valjean's attempts to keep
Cosette and himself hidden.

The story comes to a climax amid the stirrings of civil unrest. In 1832, an unsuccessful revolt of the socialists against
the monarchy breaks out in Paris. In this, Marius and his
friends take part, and Valjean, whose concern for social
justice is greater than his fear of discovery, also joins. In the
midst of the street fighting, he meets his old enemy Javert,
whose life he now holds in his hands. Although a single
bullet would free him forever from fear of arrest, Valjean lets
Javert go. This magnanimity shakes Javert's moral universe,
which has been based on strict legalism. For the first time, he
realizes a convict may be a better man than a law-abiding
citizen. His whole life as a police officer has been lived on
false premises. Rather than arrest Valjean, he puts his affairs
in order and commits suicide.

Meanwhile, in the street fighting around the barricades,
the rebels are surrounded and outnumbered. Marius is badly
wounded. Valjean lifts him on his back and carries him down
into the sewers, which provide a secure if unpleasant passage
away from the area of fighting. Marius is brought home to
his grandfather, unconscious and almost dead. When he
comes to, he does not know who has saved his life.

Valjean now decides not to stand in the way of Cosette's
happiness. He realizes that she loves Marius and should
marry him. After settling a large fortune on her, he withdraws
to a secluded life, fearing that the presence of a former
galley slave might be an embarrassment to her, now that she
is a baroness. Marius at first accepts this arrangement, but
when he learns that Valjean is the man who saved his life,
he and Cosette hurry to their benefactor's bedside in time for
one last glad, tearful reunion before the old man dies. On his
deathbed, Valjean gives Cosette the candlesticks with which
the saintly Bishop Myriel had won his soul so many years
before.

Critical Opinion

Les Misérables, begun as early as 1840 under the title of *Les Misères,* occupied Hugo intermittently during the next decade, was resumed in 1860 in Guernsey, and was finished the following year. It is one of those books which inevitably tempt one to use the word epic, both for its size and its scope. In sheer bulk it is impressive: five volumes each of novel length. Its scope is more impressive still: it is about everything. At its core, of course, is the history of Jean Valjean, with the pendant love story of Marius and Cosette. Much of this is based on actual fact. Bishop Myriel was actually Bishop Miollis of Digne, in southern France, and Valjean is based in part on a certain Pierre Maurin, a released galley slave whom the bishop befriended. M—— sur M——, where Valjean became a capitalist, is actually Montreuil-sur-mer. Marius is Hugo himself as a young man, and Colonel Pontmercy is in part General Hugo. The uprising of 1832 was, of course, recent history.

Les Misérables is a novel with a thesis: it is an attack on injustice. Hugo is exposing a barbaric system of law and punishment which sent men to the galleys for trivial offenses, was centered on punishing rather than reforming the criminal, made no allowance for extenuating circumstances, and provided for no parole. Beyond these obvious abuses, Hugo points an accusing finger at the society which created and tolerated them. His concern with social issues is, however, rather general, suggesting a sympathetic observer somewhat removed from the scenes he describes. We do not detect here the realism of Zola's *Germinal,* which gives the very smell, taste and feel of poverty, nor do we find any interest in the workings of the economic system.

Hugo is more at home in discussing politics. His estimates of the Empire, of the Bourbon restoration, and of the July monarchy are thoughtful and (if one can tolerate a certain amount of bombast) worth reading. The study of Louis Philippe, for instance, is a masterpiece of characterization. Marius undergoes a development of his political opinions very like Hugo's own: first he is royalist, then Bonapartist, and finally republican. It is curious that although Hugo served in several legislatures, he shows no knowledge of practical politics. He does, however, have a feeling for the mystique of political movement, and the enthusiasms that made men fanatical supporters of the Empire or sent them to die on the barricades.

Most of all, *Les Misérables* is a moral and religious study of sanctity, perhaps the most difficult of all themes for a novelist. Bishop Myriel is clearly a saint of sorts, and his moral influence on Valjean is decisive in changing him from a criminal to a good man. Valjean is not quite a saint himself, but he is a model of charity and self-sacrificing love, who in his turn is able to influence and redeem others. The moral lesson comes straight from the Gospels: even desperately evil men can be redeemed by acts of love and forgiveness. Myriel accepts Valjean, even though he is a convict, and forgives him the theft of his silver. Valjean does not shrink from contact with Fantine, even though she is a prostitute. Javert sees the moral foundations of his life crumble under him when Valjean spares his life. And if Hugo seems guilty at times of idealistic sentimentality, let us remember that Valjean's original, the convict Maurin, was charitably received by Bishop Miollis and did in fact end as an honest man.

In addition to these social, political, and moral themes, Hugo has thrown in a vast amount of miscellaneous information and commentary with no organic bearing on the story. Thus we have what amount to independent essays on the history of slang, life in convents, the sewers of Paris and the battle of Waterloo. Some of these are striking in their own right. Thus the account of the sewers is a combination of realism and symbolism that anticipates Zola. The account of Waterloo is a masterpiece of elaborate exposition. Finally we should note Hugo's affectionate vignettes of the old quarters of Paris. Even as he wrote, these districts were being demolished to make way for new, wide boulevards, and Hugo's descriptions are therefore full of antiquarian nostalgia for streets and buildings that were rapidly vanishing. Few authors have had such a keen sense of the city as a living organism with its processes of life, metabolism and death.

Without doubt *Les Misérables* is a masterpiece, but it is not flawless. Even if one accepts its sprawling, rambling construction, it has other faults. The plot depends too much on melodrama and coincidence for modern taste; the style is often flashy, relying excessively on glib antitheses; the tone is often pretentious and bombastic, suggesting a humorless writer who could never tell when his sublimities were overdrawn. Despite these defects, Valjean and his bishop have achieved literary immortality, and no one who has read *Les Misérables* can ever forget them.

The Hunchback of Notre Dame

by

VICTOR HUGO

The Characters

Quasimodo—A deaf hunchback, the bell ringer of Notre Dame. He is a strong, ugly man, savage toward those who ridicule him, and shut off from humanity generally, except for his master, Claude Frollo.

Archdeacon Claude Frollo—An austere and learned priest, who practices alchemy. A life of celibacy and study has warped his personality and made him morbidly passionate.

Pierre Gringoire—A minor poet and playwright. Apart from a certain natural vanity about his writing, he is a good-humored and accommodating person of bohemian habits.

La Esmeralda—A young gypsy dancer, cheerful and pretty.

Phoebus de Chateaupers—A handsome young captain beloved by Esmeralda. He is self-centered and fickle with women, a swaggerer and a swearer.

Jean (Jehan) Frollo du Moulin—Claude's brother, a wastrel and a scapegrace.

Pâquette-la-Chantefleurie (Sister Gudule)—A recluse in mourning for her child who has been abducted by gypsies.

Fleur-de-Lys de Gondelaurier—Fiancée of Phoebus.

Dame Aloïse de Gondelaurier—Her mother, a respectable widow.

Jacques Charmolue—Proctor of the ecclesiastical court, in charge of the interrogation of Esmeralda.

Leaders of the Beggars of Paris:

Clopin Trouillefou: "*King of Tunis.*"

Mathias Hungyadi Spicali: "*Duke of Egypt and Bohemia.*"

Guillaume Rousseau: "*Emperor of Galilee.*"

Oudarde, Gervaise, and Mahiette—Three widows.

Louis XI—The king, a crafty old man, stingy and cruel.

Guillaume Rym—A citizen of Ghent and an agent of the king, a crafty intriguer.

Jacques Coppenole—A hosier from Ghent, delegate to the French court, a plebeian and a democrat.

The Story

The scene is Paris in January, 1482. The city is agog over a delegation of Flemish citizens who have arrived for the marriage of the dauphin to Margaret of Burgundy. The annual Feast of Fools is in progress, a kind of licensed saturnalia at which all sorts of gaiety and disorder are allowed. Among the throngs in the streets is a gypsy girl, Esmeralda, who earns her living by singing, dancing, and performing tricks with a little trained goat. Esmeralda is not a gypsy by birth, however; sixteen years before, the gypsies stole her from her cradle, leaving in her place an ugly, deformed little boy. The unhappy mother believed that her child had been eaten; in her grief she shut herself up in an anchorite's cell in the Place de Grève, near the cathedral, and now lives there as a recluse dependent on public charity. Esmeralda, of course, knows nothing of all this. Her only link with her past is an embroidered baby's slipper which she carries with her in a bag about her neck. Someday, she hopes, it will lead her to her mother.

Esmeralda is young, beautiful, and chaste. She has the misfortune to attract the lustful attentions of Archdeacon Claude Frollo, one of the clergy of the Cathedral of Notre Dame. Frollo has hitherto lived a life of austerity and scholarship, and his long self-denial has made him all the more vulnerable; the signs of repressed passion are visible on his tight, nervous lips, stern face, and smoldering eyes. In secret he studies alchemy and is reputed to be a sorcerer.

Frollo's chief act of humanity has been to adopt and raise from childhood a boy who, sixteen years before, was exposed outside the cathedral in the hope that some charitable person would have pity on the foundling. This is Quasimodo, now a man of twenty, an unspeakably ugly and deformed hunchback; he is obviously the same child whom the gypsies left in exchange for Esmeralda. Frollo's kindness is rewarded by doglike devotion; his master is the one person whom Quasimodo loves, since all other men tease or torment him or shrink from him in disgust. Quasimodo lives in the cathedral where he is the bell ringer. The booming of the great bells has made him deaf, but he loves them and the church which is his only home.

As part of the festivities, the city of Paris presents a morality play in honor of the royal wedding. The author is a penniless scholar named Gringoire who is also attracted, though less intensely than Frollo, to the pretty gypsy dancer. After the performance, Gringoire, who has not been paid for his efforts, is wandering footloose through the dark streets of Paris and comes upon Esmeralda being attacked by two men. He is not very effective in her defense, but fortunately a captain of the guard rides up at that moment and rescues her. One man escapes, and so the authorities never learn that he is Frollo, the sinister priest. The other assailant is Quasimodo who is arrested and put in the pillory. As he stands there, his back bloody from whipping and exposed to the jeers of the crowd, he begs for water, and Esmeralda finds enough charity in her heart to hold a cup to his lips. The half-human hunchback is touched to the point of tears by this unexpected act.

Gringoire, meanwhile, has no place to sleep. He stumbles on in the dark and blunders into the heart of the thieves' quarter, where no honest man would knowingly venture alone and unarmed. The thieves capture him, and, finding he has no money, are on the point of killing him, when it occurs to somebody that their prisoner could just as well be offered in marriage to one of the gypsy women. Esmeralda steps up, recognizing in him the man who had tried to help her earlier, and agrees to marry him in gypsy fashion for a term of four years in order to save his life. This agreement is an act of pure humanity; the marriage is not consummated, for Esmeralda is in love with Captain Phoebus de Chateaupers, the handsome officer who rescued her from Frollo. Gringoire, meanwhile, joins the gypsies and, since no other livelihood is open to him, becomes a street acrobat.

Archdeacon Frollo, though foiled once, has not abandoned his prey. To get at her, he uses Captain Phoebus, who, though he is engaged to a respectable woman, has arranged a rendezvous with Esmeralda. She in her innocence expects to become his wife, and waits for him in a garret in a squalid quarter of the city. Frollo follows Phoebus there, spies on them, and then, overcome by jealousy, bursts in, stabs Phoebus, he supposes fatally, and escapes for the second time.

Esmeralda is arrested and charged with the attempted murder of Phoebus. Actually her crime is simply that she is a gypsy and therefore suspected of witchcraft. Even her goat is so clever that the judges believe it to be a witch's familiar. Under torture Esmeralda confesses to everything demanded of her, and is sentenced to be executed. Phoebus is not dead, only badly wounded, but he does nothing to save her, wishing to keep his hands clear of the unsavory affair. Frollo, too, knows that Esmeralda is innocent, and contrives to visit her cell, offering her freedom in exchange for her love. She, however, shrinks from him in horror. Frollo resolves that if he cannot have her, no one shall. He prefers to see her die, to rid himself of his torment.

On the day of the execution, Esmeralda is led, according to custom, to the porch of Notre Dame where the clergy, Frollo among them, are to pray for her repentance. As she kneels there, Quasimodo suddenly and dramatically drops by a rope from the gallery above and carries Esmeralda off into the church. She is now safe, for the cathedral is a sanctuary where even the worst criminals are free from arrest. Quasimodo bears her, unconscious, to a room in the tower, brings her food and clothing, and waits on her devotedly, for he has not forgotten her kindness when he was in the pillory, and adores her as devotedly as his master, though far more reverently.

Esmeralda is, of course, a prisoner still, for she will be arrested as soon as she leaves the cathedral. Gringoire now proposes, with some prompting by Frollo, to raise an insurrection of all the thieves in Paris and free Esmeralda. That night a mob of gypsies and vagrants silently swarms through the city and assembles in front of the locked doors of Notre Dame. Quasimodo, watching from his tower, does not realize that these are Esmeralda's rescuers; he only knows that the church is under attack and his beloved gypsy in danger. He conducts a heroic one-man defense of the cathedral, hurling beams and stones, overturning scaling ladders, and pouring molten lead on the attackers. Eventually the king's men, led by Chateaupers, ride up and disperse the mob.

Meanwhile, as the battle rages in front of the cathedral, Frollo and Gringoire slip in and, unknown to Quasimodo, spirit Esmeralda away. In the confused chase that follows, they find their way to the Place de Grève, the very spot where Esmeralda was to have been hanged. Again Frollo offers her a choice between himself and the scaffold, and again she refuses him. Nearby is the cell of the recluse, Sister Gudule, who for years has nursed a fanatic hatred of all gypsies. Dragging Esmeralda to the cell, Frollo thrusts her hand in at the window, shouting, "Sister Gudule! Here is an Egyptian! Avenge yourself on her!" The old hag grasps Esmeralda like a trap, not knowing that it is her own daughter, and holds her prisoner. But Esmeralda still has the little shoe in a bag about her neck. In the struggle the old woman recognizes the very shoe she had embroidered for her lost child. Now she is as eager to save Esmeralda as before she was to denounce her, but it is too late. The officers arrive and hang the girl on the spot.

The execution is witnessed from the tower of Notre Dame by Frollo and Quasimodo. As Esmeralda drops into the noose, Frollo breaks out in a fiendish, insane laugh. Quasimodo cannot hear it, but he sees; with a sudden angry lunge he pushes his master over the edge of the balustrade. Frollo falls; he catches with his hands at a gutter, hangs there a minute as the pipe bends beneath his weight, and then plunges to the pavement below. In the excitement that follows, Quasimodo disappears. Making his way to the common pit at Montfaucon, where the bodies of executed persons are thrown, he dies clasping Esmeralda's body in his arms.

Critical Opinion

The Hunchback of Notre Dame (*Notre Dame de Paris*), though it was written by Victor Hugo, is a monument to the genius of Sir Walter Scott. It is perhaps the chief example in

French of the historical romance which, in Hugo's day, was enjoying its first vogue, thanks to the enormous success of the Waverley novels which burst on a delighted public between 1815 and 1830. The characteristics of this genre are a vigorous plot and strong action, much picturesque description, local color, and historical detail offering or professing to offer a vivid reconstruction of life in centuries past. Another and related influence that affected Hugo was the Gothic novel, which was popular in the late eighteenth and early nineteenth centuries, and which ran strongly to sensational plots, gloomy castles, and fragile damsels swooning in the arms of sinister, passionate men. Archdeacon Frollo, with his white face and burning eyes, his thwarted lust, and his reputation for sorcery, is derived from Ambrosio in M. G. "Monk" Lewis's *The Monk*.

Such a novel requires that the characters be striking rather than subtle; we recognize them immediately as sinister, virtuous, or grotesque as the case may be. Such elements of complexity or of surprise as they may display derive from Hugo's favorite device of ironic antithesis, the combination of incongruous traits in one person. Thus Esmeralda, who grows up amid crime and violence, is innocent and virginal; the austere archdeacon is seething with repressed sexuality; the ugly Quasimodo is full of love and devotion, while Chateaupers is the opposite: fair on the outside and treacherous within. More convincing, perhaps, though no less dramatic, are the crowd scenes in which large masses of ordinary people, assembled for a play, an execution or a riot, give us a vigorous impression of actual life.

The "character" which dominates the book from start to finish, however, is the great cathedral of Notre Dame which has a distinct personality, and which, in its vast, intricate, solemn structure, is clearly intended as a symbol of the spirit of the Middle Ages. Hugo lavishes pages of description on the old church with its high vault, its gargoyles (of which Quasimodo almost seems to be one), and the great bells which are its clamorous voice. Other pages of equally loving description are devoted to medieval Paris, in an imaginative reconstruction based on careful historical research. These passages are a testimony to the shift in popular taste in the early nineteenth century which led to a renewed appreciation of the great Gothic monuments of medieval France.

The Hunchback of Notre Dame is not long, but it is rather

loosely constructed. Hugo's desire to present not just a story but a panoramic view of an age is undoubtedly responsible for its many digressions. Thus the account of the visit of the Flemish envoys, the character of Louis XI and the debate between the autocratic king and the democratic Coppenole, symbolically set in the Bastille, are quite irrelevant to the fate of Frollo and Esmeralda, interesting though the material may be in its own right.

Had Hugo lived a century later, he would probably have chosen to present his story as a movie script rather than a novel. The vivid scene of the night attack on the cathedral, in which Quasimodo throws down the scaling ladders and pours boiling oil on the attackers, and the death of Frollo, who hangs precariously to a sagging gutter before plunging two hundred feet to his death, are perfectly cinematographic; in fact, almost identical scenes have appeared in literally thousands of films. As for the role of Quasimodo, it would seem to have been written expressly for Lon Chaney, who played the part in the 1923 silent movie classic.

The Hunchback of Notre Dame is a good example of a novel once popular and still famous, now on its way to becoming a period piece. As such, it is best read either by a completely naive or quite sophisticated reader. Hugo is one of those literary giants whom the twentieth century finds it a relief to be able to ignore. And yet the reader who can approach the book on its own terms, as the reader of 1831 would have done, will find in it all the virtues of the historical romance: excitement, verve, picturesque scenes, and, if not life itself, at least a highly diverting substitute for it. One biographer of Hugo, André Maurois, while conceding the artificiality of the characters, still pleads in their behalf:

> These characters have achieved a life of their own in the minds of readers in all countries and all races. They have about them the primitive grandeur of epic myths, and that inner truth bred of their author's private phantoms.

The Author

Victor Hugo was the son of a Napoleonic general. His family was bourgeois, with peasant antecedents not far in the background. Hugo's own account of his life, suggesting a more distinguished ancestry, is one of his less successful works of fiction. His childhood was chaotic. His parents were not on good terms, and generally lived apart, while the children passed back and forth between them. Most of Hugo's early years were spent abroad wherever his father was stationed. For a time the general was in Madrid, where he appeared to have brilliant prospects. He was the governor of three provinces and was given a title as a Spanish count, while his sons were enrolled in a school for scions of the Spanish aristocracy. The students, however, rejected the Hugo boys as parvenus and as French, so that their stay there was not happy. One biographer suggests that from these experiences there springs Hugo's ambivalent feeling toward the aristocracy: his longing for prestige and titles, coupled with liberal-democratic principles.

When Napoleon fell, the fortunes of the Hugo family fell with him. Back in Paris, Victor's education continued in an unsystematic way which may account for some of his intellectual superficiality in later life. His mind was nourished mainly on his private reading; he soon developed into an extremely precocious boy, and began to write regularly in his teens. His mother's death when he was nineteen left him penniless: for a year he maintained himself writing doggedly on the edge of starvation.

At twenty he published his first poems, the impeccably royalist sentiments of which won him a pension from Louis XVIII. On these prospects he married a childhood friend, Adèle Foucher; the wedding was marred by the behavior of his brother Eugène, who also loved Adèle, and who went insane the next morning. Hugo also began to attract the attention of his literary idol, Chateaubriand, who called him an "enfant sublime." Soon he took his place among the rising authors of the day: de Vigny, Nodier, Gautier and Lamartine. At first he was a royalist in politics and a traditionalist in style (the two went necessarily together), but romanticism was in the air. In 1827, he wrote a play, *Cromwell,* which broke decisively with the conventions of neoclassicism, and with it a preface which was a manifesto of the romantic movement. This was followed by *Hernani* (1830), the production of which marked a decisive victory for the new manner. The performances were interrupted by demonstrations which came close to riots. Hugo's venture on the stage won him fame, wealth, and also a mistress, an actress named Juliette Drouet, to whom he addressed most of his love poems, and to whom he remained faithful for more than thirty years. He did not, on the other hand, allow Adèle a like freedom with her lover, the critic Sainte-Beuve.

In the years that followed, poems, plays, and novels poured from Hugo's pen in a steady stream. *The Hunchback of Notre Dame* appeared in 1831, dashed off in six months in a last-minute fulfillment of a publisher's contract. Fame and honor came freely; in 1841 Hugo was elected to the French Academy, and in 1845, after shifting his allegiance from the Bourbons to the house of Orleans, he became a peer of the realm.

In politics Hugo had a talent for exactly reflecting the opinions of the majority of Frenchmen. After the revolution of 1848 he discovered that he was a republican, and ran for the presidency. When Louis Napoleon became president in December of that year, Hugo at first supported him, but later turned against him, perhaps in chagrin at not receiving a cabinet position. After the *coup d'état* of 1851, in which Napoleon proclaimed himself emperor, Hugo left the country and settled in the Channel Islands, on British soil but French-speaking territory. Here he stayed for nearly twenty years, a self-conscious and dramatic exile, refusing offers of amnesty and writing shrill vituperation against Napoleon III. Here too he completed *Les Misérables* (1862).

The establishment of the Third Republic made possible his return, to the adulation of the entire country. Once again he sat in the legislature, though without any influence as a practical politician. His literary output continued as voluminous as ever, though its quality in the last years added little to his stature. He died in 1885 and was buried in the Pantheon.

In lands where French is not spoken, Hugo is known chiefly as a novelist; in France he is known as a poet. The variety and skill of his metrics, the subtlety of his vowel harmonies, and the departure from the conventions of neoclassicism made him the most influential French poet of his generation. He displays with heightened emphasis many of the vices and virtues of his English contemporary, Tennyson: the vast productivity, the technical virtuosity coupled with a mediocre intellect, and a sure sense for saying impressively what his middle-class readers already obscurely felt. Hugo's vanity amounted almost to a messianic complex and led him repeatedly into pompous, tasteless, humorless bombast. A colossus standing astride the nineteenth century, he had to be overthrown if French literature was to breathe freely in the twentieth.

Eugénie Grandet

by

HONORÉ DE BALZAC (1799—1850)

The Characters

Grandet—A cooper and winegrower of Saumur, shrewd, stubborn, and miserly.

Mme. Grandet—His timid, submissive wife.

Eugénie Grandet—Their daughter, innocent, pious, and self-sacrificing.

Charles Grandet—Grandet's nephew, at first an affected and dandified young man, later a cynical opportunist.

Nanon—The servant of the Grandets, a big, sturdy, faithful, hardworking peasant girl.

Townspeople of Saumur—Cruchot, the notary; Judge Cruchot de Bonfons, his nephew; de Grassins, the banker; Adolphe de Grassins, his son; Abbé Cruchot, a priest; Madame de Grassins.

The Story

During the Bourbon restoration, the richest man in Saumur is old Grandet: cooper, vintner, and former mayor. He is too shrewd and closemouthed to reveal the exact size of his fortune, but the townspeople estimate it at several million francs. Consequently his only child, Eugénie, is the most desirable heiress in the province. Her chief suitors are Judge Cruchot, son of Grandet's lawyer, and Adolphe de Grassins, son of his banker. Eugénie, completely innocent and submissive, has no preference, so Grandet shrewdly plays the candidates off against each other.

Grandet has a brother who years before went to Paris where he built up a sizable business as a wine merchant. This brother's son, Charles Grandet, is also mentioned as a possible match for Eugénie. One day, while Cruchot and de Grassins are playing court to their heiress, Charles appears unexpectedly for a visit of some weeks. An elegant Parisian, his luxurious tastes and fashionable wardrobe dazzle everyone; Eugénie is bewitched and falls in love with her cousin. Charles is the bearer of a letter from his father to old Grandet, the contents of which he is unaware. From it Grandet discovers that his brother has failed in business and killed himself in shame; he commends Charles to Grandet's care, begging him to give the boy a new start in life, preferably by sending him to the Indies with enough capital to start in business. When Charles learns what has happened, he is prostrate with grief. Grandet is annoyed at the responsibility that has been thrust on him, while Eugénie and her mother are full of sympathy. In the emotion of the moment, Charles and Eugénie declare their love and promise that when the fates reunite them they will marry.

Eugénie has a plan to help her fiancé. Over the years her father has given her a collection of gold coins for her dowry. Many of them are collectors' items, and their value is about six thousand francs. She persuades Charles to accept these as a loan, but knowing what her father will think, she keeps the transaction a secret. Meanwhile Grandet has his own plans for his nephew. He consents to pay Charles's fare to the nearest seaport, buys from him a sizable collection of family jewelry at less than full value, and persuades Charles to assign to him all interest in his father's estate, debts and all. With Charles out of the way, Grandet liquidates his brother's assets, reinvesting a good portion for himself. With what is left he makes a partial payment to the creditors, postponing payment of the balance. In time most of the creditors are willing to compromise, and Grandet buys back their notes for a fraction of their original value.

While Grandet is congratulating himself over this coup, he learns that Eugénie has disposed of her coins. He grieves not only over the financial loss, but also because he prizes the coins for their rarity and is dumbfounded by Eugénie's unexpected display of independence. In his heart he has always regarded the coins as his own. Eugénie is confined to her room on bread and water. She submits to her punishment with stubborn defiance while the servant Nanon secretly brings her delicacies at night. Mme. Grandet, who has never opposed her husband before, now stands by Eugénie, but, torn by the quarrel, she enters a fatal decline. Grandet realizes that his wife is dying and that Eugénie is in a position to insist on a division of the estate; in short, it behooves him to treat her decently. Once Mme. Grandet is dead, he persuades Eugénie to make over her estate to him, which she does with proud indifference.

Grandet finally dies, still so obsessed by his love of gold that when the priest enters bearing the viaticum Grandet reaches not for the consecrated host, but for the gold pyx. Eugénie, now worth nineteen million francs, is still unmarried. Cruchot and de Grassins renew their attentions, but she is still waiting for Charles, who has not written her in seven years. When Charles returns, he has changed greatly. He has made a fortune as a slave trader, growing cynical and unscrupulous in the process. He is now negotiating a socially brilliant marriage with the ugly daughter of a count. Eventually he writes Eugénie a cold letter of rejection, returning her loan.

Charles's marriage is threatened, however, for the count is reluctant to give his daughter to the son of a man who has defaulted on his debts. Eugénie has it in her power to break Charles since her uncle's estate is now in her control. If she simply does nothing—as is her full legal right—her former lover cannot marry. Instead, with contemptuous generosity, she settles her uncle's debts in full and with interest. Charles is astonished to learn how wealthy a woman he has passed up, but it is too late now, for Eugénie has finally given her hand to de Grassins. It is a marriage of convenience, undertaken with the understanding that it will not be consummated. In time, de Grassins dies, leaving Eugénie a widow who has never known married love or motherhood. She devotes herself to a retired, pious life, shutting herself up in her father's grim old house, and living—apart from her generous charities—with utmost personal frugality. The author hints on the last page that she may remarry, but the reader may be allowed to doubt it.

Père Goriot

by

HONORÉ DE BALZAC

The Characters

Père Goriot—A retired manufacturer whose life is wholly centered in his selfish and ungrateful daughters.

Countess Anastasie de Restaud—Goriot's elder daughter, a beautiful but self-centered woman.

Count de Restaud—Anastasie's husband, embarrassed by his unfashionable father-in-law and heartless to his wife.

Baroness de Nucingen (Delphine)—Goriot's second daughter, eager to be accepted by the nobility.

Baron de Nucingen—Delphine's husband, an unscrupulous financier.

Eugène de Rastignac—A young man of an impoverished but noble family, who comes to Paris to advance himself; he is ambitious, impulsive, and well intentioned, but corruptible.

Viscountess de Beauséant—A cousin of Eugène, brilliant and talented.

Mme. Vauquer—The proprietress of a cheap boardinghouse, stingy and small-minded.

Victorine Taillefer—An innocent, gentle and affectionate young girl living in the Maison Vauquer.

Mme. Couture—A relative and guardian of Victorine.

Vautrin—An escaped convict, determined, intelligent, resourceful, and cynical about human nature and society.

Poiret—A retired clerk.

Mlle. Michonneau—A desiccated old maid.

Horace Bianchon—A generous and kindly medical student, later a famous doctor.

Count Maxime de Trailles—Lover of the Countess de Restaud, a dandy and a compulsive gambler.

Marquis d'Adjuda-Pinto—Lover of the Viscountess de Beauséant.

Sylvie and Christophe—Servants at the Maison Vauquer.

The Story

In the year 1819, there comes to Mme. Vauquer's boarding-house, a respectable but shabby establishment in a seedy section of Paris, a young law student, Eugène de Rastignac. Well born but poor, he hopes to redeem his family fortunes in Paris by rising professionally or socially. He carries letters of introduction to a cousin, the Viscountess de Beauséant, whose sponsorship wins him entrée into the most exalted circles of Parisian society. Intoxicated by this life, he forgets his studies and plunges into expensive self-indulgence in which his mother and sisters support him by selling their jewelry.

One of the boarders at the Maison Vauquer is a retired manufacturer of vermicelli named Goriot. Originally quite rich and respected by the tenants accordingly, he is now living in the cheapest apartment and his clothes are thread-bare. Gradually the story of his misfortunes comes out. His two beautiful girls have married well; one is a countess and the other a baroness, but they are vain and self-indulgent, and their husbands, although they like having a rich father-in-law, are embarrassed to have him under their roofs. Goriot, who has always spoiled his children, now consumes his life savings to gratify their whims, paying not only their debts but those of their lovers. Once the money is gone, however, he is no longer allowed to visit them, and must content himself with occasional glimpses in public.

Eugène meets Goriot's eldest daughter, the Countess de Restaud, and without knowing the relationship, becomes infatuated with her. At first she welcomes him to her home, but when she discovers that he is a friend of her father she drops him. At the suggestion of his cousin the viscountess, Eugène woos the second sister, the Baroness de Nucingen, a social climber who yearns to be received by Viscountess de

Beauséant. She accepts Eugène as her lover to secure this invitation. At the same time, she appeals to Eugène's sentiments by making a conspicuous if inexpensive display of affection for her father. Goriot responds by setting Eugène up in a comfortable bachelor's apartment where the lovers may meet and he may visit them both.

There is another scheme afoot by which Eugène may make his fortune. In the Maison Vauquer lives Victorine Taillefer, the daughter of a wealthy man who suspects her legitimacy and will not acknowledge her as his own. Meanwhile she lives in poverty, nursing her expectations. Another boarder, the intelligent, unscrupulous, and rather sinister Vautrin, points out to Eugène that if Victorine's brother should die, her father, rather than see the family become extinct, would acknowledge his daughter. In that case, her husband would succeed to the fortune. Vautrin proposes that Eugène make love to Victorine while he, Vautrin, sees that the brother dies unexpectedly and in such a way that no one can trace the crime. In return, he asks merely that Eugène hand over to him one fifth of the profits.

Eugène is properly shocked at this proposal, especially since he finds it more amusing to be the lover of Delphine than the husband of Victorine. Vautrin, however, confident that he can corrupt his young friend, works on him with cynical persistence. Eugène yields to the extent of flirting tentatively with Victorine and allowing her to fall in love with him. Then the plot comes to a head. Victorine's brother is killed in a duel, but Eugène declares in horror that he cannot marry the girl. At this moment, Vautrin is arrested. Two boarders, discovering that he is an escaped convict, denounce him to the police.

Meanwhile, old Goriot is dying. His last days are made wretched by the demands of his daughters. Anastasie has sold her husband's family jewels to pay her lover's gambling debts, and Goriot must pledge his annuity to meet the obligation. Besides, there is a matter of a thousand francs for a lamé evening dress. Delphine has nothing on her mind but the invitation, which Eugène has secured for her, to the Viscountess's ball. She insists that he take her there while her father is literally on his deathbed. Goriot dies tended only by Eugène and a kindhearted medical student, Bianchon. He is buried at their expense, and neither daughter attends his funeral.

Eugène is revolted by his initiation into Parisian society, which proves more heartless and corrupt than he had ever dreamed. He resolves now to act without scruple in dealing with such people. He despises society although he still wishes to conquer it. His first step is to dine with Delphine de Nucingen.

Critical Opinion

Balzac has been called one of the most *necessary* authors of his century. This ambiguous adjective indicates his key position as a writer in touch with the chief currents of romanticism and realism, and it pays tribute to his industry as the chronicler of French society in his generation, an achievement so vast that no man can profess to know anything about the age of Louis Philippe who has not studied the work of Balzac. At the same time, *"necessary"* suggests that most critics praise Balzac with some qualification, directed sometimes at the style, sometimes at the plot. But whatever the exact terms of these reservations, everyone agrees that Balzac is the sort of writer whom no one can ignore.

First, consider the scope of his novels, which are known collectively as *The Human Comedy (La Comédie Humaine)*. They total ninety-six books, most of them set in France during the four reigns of Napoleon, Louis XVIII, Charles X and Louis Philippe. The characters are drawn from all classes, from the aristocracy to the underworld. In all, there are about two thousand of them, and their careers can be traced from one novel to another. Not all the books were completed; we have the titles of fifty more works which were sketched out or merely projected. The novels are grouped together under broad headings: Scenes of Private Life, of Provincial Life, of Parisian Life, of Military Life, of Country Life, Philosophic Studies, and Analytic Studies. Balzac's classification suggests the work of the great taxonomists of natural history, like Linnaeus. He conceived humanity as a group of related species, the provincial being different from the Parisian as the peasant is from the shopkeeper, all of which he proposed to describe and catalogue.

Of this rich and varied society, Paris is the nerve center. Most of the novels are set there, but even in those set in the provinces, Parisian standards make themselves felt, just as Charles Grandet, in his unhappy visit to Saumur, brings with him the glitter and corruption of the capital. The social leaders are the old aristocracy, now back in their places and trying to make up for the hardships of the Revolution. Their days are numbered, however, for new men have arrived. Former peasants like Grandet are now in the powerful middle class while dubious businessmen like Nucingen push their way into the nobility. Money rules everything. Men are calculating and ruthless, and their wives, who by and large set the tone of society, are no less so. Innocence and integrity survive only in obscure backwaters, in Eugénie Grandet, Nanon, or the sisters of de Rastignac. But Balzac is not sentimental about country life; provincials may be less sophisticated but they are just as ruthless as Parisians, as the domestic struggle between Grandet and his daughter demonstrates.

Balzac's judgment on society is harsh. He finds it dominated by intrigue, whether in love, business, politics or society. These several types of intrigue merge: a man may court a woman because he needs her dowry as capital, or use the favor of his mistress to advance himself politically. It is silly to charge *The Human Comedy* with immorality, as some of Balzac's contemporaries did; the ethical judgments which it makes are clear and firm. One does suspect, however, that Balzac writes with far more zest about vice than about virtue. We are more likely to remember a powerful figure like Vautrin than the insipid Victorine.

Many of Balzac's characters can almost be reduced to a formula which defines their position in society or accounts for their actions. They are in the grip of a single overriding passion: Goriot loves his daughters, Grandet loves gold, and Delphine wants social recognition. Others are simply social types: Nucingen the banker, Nanon the faithful servant, Mme. Vauquer the penny-pinching landlady, Poiret the petty clerk. Most of these are static characters, predictable and almost automatons. Those who are not static are likely to deteriorate, like Rastignac, who comes to Paris full of good intentions but is corrupted. Occasionally a character is neither predictable nor convincing: a sophisticated worldling like Charles Grandet would hardly become a devoted lover overnight, or so easily change his role from gentleman to slave trader to gentleman again. The most remarkable character is the convict Vautrin, a brilliant, baleful figure who seems a creation of pure imagination. Actually he was modeled on the famous detective Vidocq.

Balzac is famous for his realism of scene and setting, an excellent example of which is his description of the Maison Vauquer, with its air of shabby, respectable poverty. Every spot on the curtains and every flyspeck on the picture frames is enumerated. Yet the total effect of such a description is more than realism. One feels that Balzac is describing not so much a boardinghouse as a state of mind, and that the seedy drawing room is a projection of the personalities of Mme. Vauquer and her lodgers. Similarly, Paris is not just a city, but a spiritual condition: brilliant, corrupt, built on broken hopes and ruined lives, the city of Baudelaire's poetry. Balzac is certainly a realist, and yet most readers sense that his novels are a little more than real. What brings these social documents to life is the author's powerful poetic imagination.

The Author

There is a noble French family named de Balzac, but Honoré is not one of them. Birth records show that the family were originally peasants named Balssa, and that the particle *de,* indicating nobility, is pure imposture. The author's father was a provincial lawyer in Tours, where Balzac was born in 1799. After education in the local schools, he studied law in Paris and was then apprenticed to a notary in whose office he spent three years. His experience of the law gave him a firsthand knowledge of business, and insight into the more selfish motives of human action. When, however, Balzac senior proposed to set his son up in practice, Honoré rebelled. In his twenties he busily turned out novels and short stories by the dozen, in not one of which did any critic see signs of promise. His next venture, which was even less successful, was a flyer in publishing. Later he ran a type foundry. After three years, the business went bankrupt, leaving Balzac with debts which his mother eventually paid.

In 1829 Balzac went back to writing novels, both to pay off his debts, which were chronic, and to win fame, which he

craved. He set himself a killing pace. Each evening he retired about six o'clock, slept till midnight, awoke, dressed
himself in a white monastic robe which was his working uni-
form, and then wrote at frantic pace, often until the next afternoon, sustaining himself with great draughts of coffee. As the
stories accumulated he conceived the grand plan of linking
them so as to form a loosely connected social history of his
time, to be called, in imitation of Dante, *The Human Comedy*.
The scheme was never finished according to Balzac's grandiose
plan, but, even so, it extended to nearly a hundred titles.
These won him the fame he wanted, and might have made
him rich but for his incurably spendthrift habits.

Three mistresses, all of them members of the aristocracy,
played important roles in Balzac's life (although he did not
deny himself other temporary and more plebeian amours). In
such matters Balzac was as much a climber as de Rastignac
or Charles Grandet. The first was Mme. de Berny, a woman
of the *ancien régime*, old enough to be Balzac's mother; one of
her sons was just his age. The relationship was rather
maternal, and continued on a Platonic basis long after it had
ceased to be physical. The second affair was with the Marquise
de Castries, a literary lion hunter who was more interested in
Balzac as a celebrity than as a man. Balzac avenged himself
on her by using her as the model for several unflattering portraits of titled ladies. The most romantic of all his attachments was to a Polish countess named Hanska who began by
writing him anonymous letters which were signed "the
stranger." Since the letters hinted that their writer was beautiful, unhappily married, and extremely rich, Balzac was interested at once. A rendezvous was arranged in Switzerland
and the relationship placed on a regular basis. The count
raised no objections, and after a few years obligingly died.

Meanwhile, Balzac was busy with other projects, although
one wonders how he found time for them all. He dabbled in
politics and ran without success for the Chamber of Deputies.
He got into several lawsuits, brought on by his lighthearted
way of honoring his literary obligations. He also conceived the
idea of reopening some Roman silver mines in Sardinia to
recover metal from the slag heaps. But Balzac talked too
freely about this scheme, and another speculator got on the
scene first. To the end of his days, Balzac never gave up his
dream of making a fortune in business.

Balzac's views on religion were complex. Nominally a Catholic, he was from childhood much influenced by his mother, who had a large library of works on Rosicrucianism, Swedenborgianism, and Illuminism. One would not suspect from reading *Eugénie Grandet* that the author harbored such views, but his novel *Seraphita* contains a systematic exposition of them. In politics, he began as a Bonapartist, but was converted, perhaps by the influence of Mme. de Berny, to the cause of the Bourbons. However, despite his theoretical approval of a despotic government, he usually regarded himself as beyond the more onerous restrictions of the law; in 1835 he went to jail rather than do military service with the National Guard.

Balzac's death was brought on in part by overwork, in part by the rigors of traveling to Russia in winter to visit Mme. Hanska. Though they were engaged, the marriage was long delayed since it was necessary to obtain the permission of the Czar. It finally took place in 1850, and the couple returned to Paris, where Balzac had built his bride a house and filled it with *objets d'art*. The romance that had sustained the two for so long evaporated soon after marriage, when it developed that the countess's fortune was not so large as he had supposed, nor his debts so small as he had represented them. He died a few months later of bronchitis and heart disease. In his last hours, he expressed a wish that Dr. Bianchon be summoned. Bianchon was one of his own fictional creations, a medical student in *Père Goriot* whose aid he had invoked for more than one of his characters. So compelling was the imaginary world which he had conjured into being, that in the end it became for him completely real.

Mlle. de Maupin

by

THÉOPHILE GAUTIER (1811–1872)

The Characters

Mlle. de Maupin (disguised as the Chevalier Théodore de Sérannes)—A girl of about twenty, a Lesbian disguised as a young gentleman.

D'Albert—A young poet, introspective and restless in temperament; he professes to be looking for an ideal mistress, but actually appears to be a latent or potential homosexual.

Rosette—A vivacious young widow of twenty-four, mistress of D'Albert but in love with Théodore.

Ninon (disguised as Isnabel)—A girl of fourteen or fifteen, traveling with Théodore as a page.

Alcibiades—Brother of Rosette.

The Marchioness—Rosette's aunt, an aristocrat with the bearing and manners of the old regime.

Graciosa—Correspondent of Mlle. de Maupin.

Silvio—Correspondent of D'Albert.

The Story

A young poet named D'Albert is in search of a mistress, an ideal woman with whom he can enjoy an ideal love. Unfortunately, his standards are impossibly high, and his experience in seducing women of quality (for he will accept no others) is limited. At length, with the help of an acquaintance, he strikes up a liaison with Rosette, a pretty young widow of twenty-four, as approachable as one could wish, who gives every evidence of being in love with him. The relationship seems satisfactory in every way, and yet D'Albert is still unsatisfied. Rosette, lovely though she is, is still not perfection, and at times D'Albert wonders whether, despite appearances, she truly loves him. Though Rosette is not the woman he is seeking, D'Albert remains with her, partly so as not to wound her feelings, and partly out of habit. In this mood of impatience, he meets a young gentleman named Théodore de Sérannes, one of the many guests at Rosette's country estate. All he knows of Théodore is that he is an old friend of Rosette, and he suspects that his mistress intends to use this young man to make him jealous. Théodore is extraordinarily beautiful in an ambiguous, feminine way; in fact he perfectly conforms to the ideal of loveliness which D'Albert has been seeking so long in vain. Instead of being jealous, D'Albert is drawn to this stranger, and is appalled to realize that he is in love with a man.

But is he? The truth is that, unknown both to D'Albert and Rosette, Théodore is a girl, Mlle. de Maupin. Impatient and fretful with her sheltered life as a woman, and in independent circumstances, answerable to no one, she resolves to see how men live, once they are away from the proprieties of the drawing room. Training herself to ride like a man and to fence, she then dresses herself as a traveling student and sallies out to seek adventures. Despite her obviously effeminate appearance, she learns to drink and swagger enough to be accepted by men as one of them. Invited by a friend to Rosette's country estate, she is embarrassed to find that her hostess has fallen in love with her, and that the other members of the family are doing all they can to promote the match. "Théodore" is perplexed, but feels that the disguise must be kept up. One night she is surprised in Rosette's bedroom by Alcibiades, Rosette's brother, who demands that she either marry his sister or fight a duel. "Théodore" has no choice but to fight; rather surprisingly, she wins, wounds Alcibiades lightly, and beats a quick retreat.

Continuing on her travels, "Théodore" picks up a small girl

of fourteen or so, who falls in love with her and disguises herself as a page in order to join her. Some time later—we do not learn exactly how or why—she returns as a guest with her page to Rosette's estate. She finds Rosette killing time with her new lover, D'Albert, whom she does not love, and whom she is quite willing to drop if only "Théodore" will have her.

At this point the two threads of the story—the adventures of D'Albert and of Mlle. de Maupin—converge. D'Albert is distressed by his perverse love, and at the same time half hopes, half suspects that "Théodore" is not what he seems. His suspicions grow when the guests decide to put on a performance of *As You Like It*. D'Albert plays Orlando and "Théodore" is Rosalind. Seeing "Théodore" in a woman's costume, D'Albert is satisfied that his beloved is a girl after all, and that the situation in the play parallels reality. After the performance he writes a passionate letter, addressed both to Théodore and Rosalind, declaring his love for her under either name. There is a long wait, during which D'Albert is racked with anxiety. Then one night, Mlle. de Maupin comes to his room dressed as Rosalind and gives herself to him. When D'Albert has taught her all he knows about the art of lovemaking, he falls asleep exhausted. Toward morning Mlle. de Maupin steals from his bed into Rosette's and stays there until noon. The next day she rises early and leaves, taking her page with her. A week later a letter arrives for D'Albert explaining that their love cannot continue. Her last request is that he care for Rosette. "Love each other well in memory of me, whom both of you have loved, and breathe my name sometimes in a kiss."

Critical Opinion

When a male homosexual falls in love with a Lesbian, what happens? One would think that the literary form best suited to such a situation would be the limerick, but Gautier chose to write a novel. Or rather, he did not write a novel; he recorded an erotic daydream; for neither the characterization nor the plot nor the style is appropriate to the novel, at least as it is traditionally understood.

By any ordinary definition, a novel demands more careful

organization than we find here, and a more consistent handling of the narrative point of view. The story begins as a letter written by D'Albert to his friend Silvio, a letter so long as to strain the patience of any correspondent. Silvio, however, is not a character who figures in the story; he exists only so that D'Albert may confide in him. Next the tale shifts to a conventional third-person narrative which quickly gives way to a dialogue printed as a play. The epistolary convention is resumed as Mlle. de Maupin begins a series of equally improbable letters to her confidante, Graciosa. Finally, the third-person narrative appears again, although this time the author intrudes and speaks at length in the first person.

Nor is the characterization in the novel any more satisfying. Théodore and Rosette are not people at all; they are erotic fantasies existing only as phases of D'Albert's imagination: Rosette as the perfectly compliant mistress he thinks he wants, and Théodore as the pretty boy whom he wants in fact. Any reader will want to raise practical questions about the plot: Why was the marchioness eager to marry her niece to a complete stranger, knowing nothing about his family, his income, or his prospects? After Mlle. de Maupin had wounded Alcibiades in a duel, how could she return to the same house a few months later as a guest? When she abducted little Ninon as her page, did not the child's parents try to trace them? And while she is devastating the hearts of her two lovers, why do we hear nothing further about Ninon —what is she up to? And finally, what is the time and place of the story? There is a reference to the Argand lamp, invented in 1785; otherwise the story could just as well have been laid in the sixteenth or early seventeenth century, that is, during the French Renaissance which Gautier loved so well.

All these criticisms are perhaps irrelevant, for *Mlle. de Maupin* was not meant to be a traditional novel. Instead it is a typical piece of romantic art, careless of the traditional rules and the distinctions between the genres, thoroughly subjective, and constantly turning into reverie or internal monologue. Reason and reality were not regarded as the instructors of romantic art, but its enemies. About halfway through the book, D'Albert writes to his friend Silvio a description of an ideal theatrical performance as he imagines it, a description that is almost a manifesto of the principles of Gautier's art. It runs in part as follows:

But there is a theatre which I love, a fantastic, extravagant, impossible theatre, in which the worthy public would pitilessly hiss from the first scene, for want of understanding a single word. . . .

The characters are of no time or country; they come and go without our knowing why or how; they neither eat nor drink, they dwell nowhere and have no occupation; they possess neither lands, incomes, nor houses; only sometimes they carry under their arm a little box full of diamonds as big as pigeons' eggs; as they walk they do not shake a single drop of rain from the heads of the flowers nor raise a single grain of the dust on the roads. . . .

The dialogue is most universal: the lion contributes a vigorously uttered oh! oh!—the wall speaks through its chinks, and provided that he has a witticism, rebus, or pun to interpose, any one is free to interrupt the most interesting scene: the ass's head of Bottom is as welcome as the golden head of Ariel; the author's mind may be discerned beneath every form, and all these contradictions are like so many facets which reflect its different aspects while imparting to it the colours of the prism.

Obviously Gautier was writing under the influence of an undigested diet of Shakespeare; he was bewitched by the opalescent magic of *A Midsummer Night's Dream,* but understood nothing of Shakespeare's dramatic power.

An interest in Lesbianism is itself characteristic of a certain current of romantic taste. One encounters it in Coleridge ("Christabel"), Baudelaire ("Lesbos," "Femmes damnées"), and Swinburne ("Anactoria," *Lesbia Brandon*), to mention only the more famous writers.[*] The exploration of sexual perversion was part of the romantic program of extending the boundaries of human experience into strange and unexplored areas. Some writers evoked the past (Scott), others traveled in imagination to new continents (Chateaubriand), invoked the Devil (Goethe's *Faust*), took drugs (De Quincey) and cultivated their hallucinations (Nerval, Rimbaud). Still others, like Verlaine and Baudelaire, explored the byways of sex, writing of them with a shudder of mingled fascination and revulsion, a superheated self-consciousness that is utterly un-

---

[*] For a fuller treatment of the subject, see Mario Praz, *The Romantic Agony.*

like the easy sensuality of pagan antiquity. Comparable themes are found, of course, in post-romantic novels of the nineteenth and twentieth centuries, but by then the temper had changed. With Zola, and the naturalists after him, Lesbianism is treated as something ugly and squalid (see, for example, *Nana*). In the Freudian era it is treated clinically, as a symptom of an emotional disorder. But no one today would adopt the rapturous, sentimental tone of Gautier; that would seem merely unsophisticated. Or for a contrast of another sort, compare *Mlle. de Maupin* with Shakespeare, especially *Twelfth Night*, *As You Like It*, and *The Merchant of Venice*. In all of these, women disguise themselves as boys; in fact, the situation is one of the clichés of Renaissance comedy. There, however, the mood is graceful, idyllic, and artificial; by comparison, Gautier seems prurient. His prurience lies not so much in the choice of his theme, as in the way he flirts with it, sidles up to it, and then veers away.

The style of *Mlle. de Maupin* is not really appropriate to a novel; it smacks more of the essay. D'Albert's description of his ideal theater will give us a clue to what Gautier was trying to do:

> . . . his (the lover's) principal business is to drop clusters of pearls and bunches of roses from his lips, and to scatter poetic gems like a true spendthrift; often he effaces himself entirely, and lets the author court his mistress in his stead.

The modern reader may find that some of Gautier's poetic gems are rhinestones; they give the impression of a clever and articulate undergraduate, blessed with more ingenuity than taste, trying very hard to be literary.

One may well ask why this novel remains in print today, and presumably still finds readers. Some undoubtedly pick it up because of the notoriety which it brought its author a century and a third ago. These readers hope that because it was shocking once it will be still. Others will read it sympathetically because of the author's real achievement in other fields; after all, he was the author of *Enamels and Cameos* (*Émaux et Camées*), which is no small distinction. Still others will find it an interesting period piece, an example of romantic taste, which one may read with the detached but affectionate interest which one gives to the not-too-recent past.

The Author

Théophile Gautier was a fertile and versatile writer, author of scores of works of fiction, poetry, drama, travel, and miscellaneous journalism, now remembered as one of the most flamboyant young men of the romantic generation, and as one of the originators of the doctrine of "art for art's sake." He was born at Tarbes in the far south of France, but grew up in Paris and was educated at the Collège Charlemagne. His first love was painting, and, if literature had not claimed him, he would be remembered as one of the same generation as Corot, Gerard, and Petrus Borel. In literature, he remains something of a painter still, as the repeated references to color in *Mlle. de Maupin* testify. While he was still a boy, his fancy was caught by the poets of the sixteenth and early seventeenth centuries, a school then largely ignored in favor of the classical writers of the age of Racine. An essay on Renaissance literature, written when he was only eighteen, came to the attention of the critic Sainte-Beuve, who in turn introduced him to the principal authors of the day, notably Hugo and his circle.

When Hugo's play *Hernani* appeared in 1830, Gautier was a leader of the claque that applauded that revolutionary work. His cherry-colored waistcoat and his mane of flowing hair were symbols of the youthful extravagance of a circle which included Musset, de Vigny, de Nerval, Dumas, and Delacroix. Their motto was *"morte aux péruques,"* or "death to the wigs," that is, to the old-fashioned classicists whose taste they ridiculed. In many ways, they resembled the bohemians and beatniks of our own day.

The experience of *Hernani* led Gautier to give up painting for writing. To earn a living, he became a journalist specializing in artistic and dramatic criticism. A series of travel books describing experiences in Spain, Italy, Algiers, Turkey and Russia must also be included among his journalistic works. *Mlle. de Maupin* appeared in 1835, when Gautier was twenty-four. It was in some ways his most unusual book and earned him a quite undeserved reputation for depravity. His greatest work, however, was *Enamels and Cameos,* published in 1856 and revised in 1872. This was a slim collection of poems, written for the most part on the slenderest of subjects, but polished with a meticulous care that suggests the carving of a gem. Their appeal is almost wholly to the eye, offering little either to the mind or heart. The last poem, entitled "L'Art," is a famous and much-quoted manifesto of Gautier's artistic principles: that the finest work is that done in the most difficult medium, and that the artist must avoid anything easy, vague, or imprecise.

These poems became the models for the disciples of the doctrine of "art for art's sake," a formula which originally meant simply that art has no aim other than beauty and perfection of form. At times, in the writing of lesser authors, this dictum was invoked merely as a device to secure the author immunity from criticism of any kind, especially moral criticism; but as a serious literary program it had an important influence, leading in poetry to the marmoreal objectivity of the Parnassians, and in fiction to the dispassionate realism of Flaubert. In England, Pater and Wilde were especially influenced by Gautier.

Gautier was personally quite uninterested in politics, and so, unlike Hugo and others of that generation, he had no difficulty in accepting the Second Empire of Napoleon III. He died in 1872, after surviving the defeat of France and the civil strife which followed. These last years were painful to him: "I live by habit," he wrote, "but I no longer care to live." However, to the extent that academic historians of literature can confer immortality, Gautier is still alive.

Dead Souls

by

NIKOLAI GOGOL
(NIKOLAI VASSILIEVICH GOGOL-JANOVSKY)
(1809–1852)

The Characters*

Pavel Ivanovich Chichikov—The protagonist, an opportunistic
  adventurer with an affable manner which inspires confidence in everyone.

Manilov—A landowner with whom Chichikov does business,
  an amiable, ineffective and undistinguished person.

Mother Korobochka—Another landowner, an old hag, foolish
  in most matters but narrowly shrewd in anything pertain-
  ing to the management of her estate.

Nozdryev—A third landowner, boastful, swaggering, hard-
  drinking and exuberant, a cardsharp and a pathological liar.

Sobakevich—A fourth landowner, a sturdy, roughhewn, coarse,
  bearlike man.

Plewshkin—A fifth landowner, miserly to the point of mono-
  mania.

Selifan and Petrushka—Chichikov's servants, stolid, stupid,
  and unwashed.

---

* See Note on Russian Names, p. 173.

Others—The governor, the governor's daughter, the chief of police, the postmaster, the district judge, two unnamed ladies.

The Story

Pavel Ivanovich Chichikov is a man who lives by his wits. He poses as a "collegiate counselor." Actually, he has been in the government customs service, from which he has been expelled for collusion with smugglers. His main asset is a pleasant, insinuating manner which wins the confidence of people with money and influence. This gift serves him in an ingenious get-rich-quick scheme. At this time Russian law decreed that landowners should pay taxes according to the number of "souls," that is, serfs, on their estates. This figure, computed at each census, remained fixed until the next, on the assumption that births would roughly compensate for deaths.

Chichikov travels about the country offering to buy title to "dead souls," serfs who have died since the last census. The landowners are glad to oblige since if they can present the tax authorities with a legal bill of sale for their property, their assessment will be correspondingly reduced. Chichikov's plan is to take his title deeds—which of course look legitimate enough—and mortgage his nonexistent property for real money.

In the first chapter, Chichikov arrives at a small provincial town and surveys it thoroughly: its economic state, the names of the principal landowners, the character of the officials, and the number of serfs. The local gentry take him for a person of consequence and find him charming. They invite him to parties and entertain him at their country estates, while their wives and daughters flirt with him. In the meantime, he busily buys title to as many dead souls as he can, invariably pledging the owner to secrecy about the real nature of the transaction. When the purchase is registered at the district court, word gets around that Chichikov is fabulously rich. He himself lets it be known that he has an estate in the Ukraine where he plans to settle his serfs.

Chichikov's scheme collapses through the indiscretion of the people with whom he does business. One of them suspects that she has been swindled, and inquires about the going rate for dead serfs. Another gets drunk at the governor's ball and blurts out the truth, though he is such an inveterate liar that nobody knows whether to believe him. The word gets around that Chichikov has been trying to win the hand of the governor's daughter. Others suggest that he is a spy, or even that he is Napoleon Bonaparte in disguise. Chichikov has to leave town in mad haste, and the last we see of him he is dashing across the countryside in his carriage to meet his next adventure.

Critical Opinion

Dead Souls is only a fragment of a novel. Gogol planned to complete it in three parts, of which the present book is the first. A few fragments survive to show what the whole was intended to be. In the succeeding episodes, Chichikov was to have more adventures, in the course of which he would meet a number of truly virtuous people: an honorable merchant, a just governor, an ideal landowner, and a perfect woman. These were to exert a reforming influence on him, so that the novel was to be the history of his regeneration, and—on an allegorical level—a parable of Russia herself, what she was and what she might become.

The critics have found these unfinished fragments artificial and unconvincing. Chichikov is such an engaging rogue that we do not want him reformed, and the virtuous characters lack the vitality of those in the book as it now stands, a robust, comic vitality which may remind American readers of certain passages in *Huckleberry Finn*.

Probably, then, the unfinished state of the novel is no great loss to art. However, its incompleteness does explain one anomaly of structure: the unexpected last chapter. Here, after Chichikov has failed in his scheme and left town, the author goes back in time and gives us the facts of his hero's early life of which we have so far known nothing: his family, his schooling and his government career. In a conventionally constructed novel these facts would have been introduced early, perhaps in the second chapter. But if one judges the story in the perspective of Gogol's grand unrealized plan, this flashback is appropriately placed.

In its present form, the book is complete in itself. It is a devastating satire on Russian society in the early nineteenth century. *Dead Souls* is a rogues' gallery of unforgettable scoundrels, brilliantly portrayed: the suspicious Mother Korobochka, Manilov the nonentity, Nozdryev the liar, the bearlike Sobakevich, miserly Plewshkin, and a whole swarm of extortionate officials, gossipy women, and drunken serfs. The novel's attack on officialdom especially angered the government. One of the passages to be censored was the episode of Captain Kopeikin, an officer who has been maimed in the Napoleonic Wars, and drags himself around government offices hoping for a pension or indemnity. He proves such a nuisance that he is put in jail, and eventually becomes a robber. The Czarist government was not prepared to admit that such things could happen.

The reader is readily persuaded to accept this picture of Russia because Gogol is so obviously faithful in depicting the physical minutiae of daily life. He devotes long passages to such matters as the architecture of a village street, the layout of a manor house, the contents of a storeroom, the legends on shop signs, and the condition of the pavements. Consequently the book has a richness of visual detail, some of it homely and some of it grotesque, that is missing in a writer like Tolstoi. Because of this fidelity to appearances, some critics have treated Gogol as nothing more than a simple realist. Actually the details are carefully chosen to stress the moral theme of the book: the vulgarity and spiritual emptiness of Russian life. Even so simple a detail as two women kissing each other is made to carry a weight of social commentary:

> As soon as the "lady delightful in every respect" was informed of the arrival of the "pleasant lady" she hurried out to meet her. The ladies clutched each other's hands, kissed, exclaimed like two young girls meeting not too long after graduation from boarding school before their mamas have had time to make it clear to them that their papas aren't equals in wealth and standing.

In all this display of false values, Chichikov is the chief exhibit. He may be cleverer and better washed than the rest, but inwardly he is as empty—an opportunist without roots or values who never suspects that his soul is as dead as those he trades in.

In the midst of this unrelieved picture of tawdriness and knavery, the reader is startled to meet occasional lyrical passages in which Gogol steps out of his story to apostrophize Russia—her language, her landscape, her vastness, her haunting appeal. The suspicion arises that Gogol is simply trying to throw the government censors off the trail. Actually the suspicion is an unworthy one. Gogol was intensely patriotic —chauvinistic if you will. But there is nothing inconsistent in an author's castigating the land he loves, precisely because he loves it so. On the last page of the novel, as Chichikov drives off pell-mell in his carriage, Gogol compares his country to a troika hurtling across the world:

> And where do you fly to, Russia? Answer me! . . . She doesn't answer. The carriage bells break into an enchanted tinkling, the air is torn to shreds and turns into wind; everything on earth flashes past, and, casting worried, sidelong glances, other nations and countries step out of her way.

The Author

Gogol's life was short and troubled. He was born in 1809 of a family of petty gentry in the Ukraine. An ancestor had served under the kings of Poland, but this foreign strain was an embarrassment to him. Fairly early in life he abbreviated his Polish-sounding name of Gogol-Janovsky to plain Gogol. His father died while Nikolai was in his teens; his mother, who pampered and adored him, outlived him.

After graduating from the gymnasium at Nyezhin at nineteen, he set out for Saint Petersburg. He considered becoming an actor and for a time worked as a government clerk. His first important books were on Ukrainian themes: sketches of rural life and folklore which won him a wide audience, *The Evenings on a Farm Near Dikanka* (1831–1832). He also planned a history of the Ukraine in the Middle Ages. The book was never written, but on the strength of it he held for a time a lectureship in history at the University of Saint Petersburg. He proved incompetent both as a scholar and a teacher, cut most of his classes, and resigned after sixteen months. Later he supported himself by teaching at a girls' school and by private tutoring, but he was never especially learned or even widely read; in fact he has been called the least educated of the great Russian writers of his time.

Gogol's love of Ukrainian history finally found its proper expression in *Taras Bulba*, a swashbuckling romance in the manner of Sir Walter Scott, set among the Cossacks. His taste for grotesque folklore appears in an eerie tale, *Viy* (1835), about a man who is destroyed by demons. *The Overcoat* (1842) is an important landmark in the development of the Russian short story, a pathetic story of a petty civil servant whose one dream is to possess a fine coat.

Government corruption is the theme of *The Revisor (The Government Inspector, or The Inspector General*, 1836), a play about an engaging impostor who wanders into a town that is nervously awaiting a visit from a government inspector. The local officials, who have a good deal on their consciences, take him for the inspector in disguise. Much to his surprise, he is flattered and feted until he is found out. The play ends with the unexpected and devastating arrival of the real inspector. In many ways the theme anticipates *Dead Souls*. The play would certainly have been banned except for a miracle: the Tsar himself read it in manuscript and ordered that it be performed. The play was a great success, but it did not make Gogol personally popular. In the same year, he left Russia, and for the rest of his life, except for short visits, he remained abroad. *Dead Souls*, with its unforgettable pictures of Russian life, was written in Rome.

By all accounts, Gogol was deeply neurotic and subject to spells of deep depression, morbid self-doubts, and paroxysms of obsessive piety. So far as one can judge after more than a century, his problems were basically sexual. He simply had no interest in women. He did, it is true, propose marriage to one girl, but the relationship was to be completely spiritual. His ambivalence toward women appears in the characters he creates. Either they are hags like Mother Korobochka or they are untouchable goddesses who resemble, as one Russian critic points out, the pictures on boxes of chocolate. Being unable either to accept or to change himself, Gogol took refuge in religious exercises, agonized prayer, and self-flagellation. His comic vision of life, which had kept him in wholesome contact with reality during his early and middle years, faded, and he later began to see himself in grandiose terms as a moral teacher and a prophet.

Gogol wrote a sequel to *The Government Inspector*, interpreting that hilarious comedy as an allegory about the conscience. He continued *Dead Souls* in order to show the reformation of Chichikov, and he published a series of letters to his friends which glorified everything in Russian life, including serfdom and autocracy, that was traditional, Slavic, and opposed to the humanist culture of Europe (*Selected Passages from Correspondence with My Friends*, 1847). His friends were not appreciative, and one, the critic Byelinsky, wrote an angry reply that became almost a manifesto for those intellectuals who were oriented toward European liberalism.

With this new rejection, Gogol's confidence in himself was shattered. The ruin was completed by Count Alexander Tolstoy (not to be confused with the famous Leo) who introduced him to the man who became Gogol's spiritual director in his last years: Father Matvey (Matthew) Konstantinovsky. Both Tolstoy and the priest were fanatically orthodox and antiliberal, and to them Gogol submitted himself in masochistic self-abnegation. Father Matthew was opposed to all art and literature, and reduced his disciple to a state of quivering terror with his threats of hellfire. Finally, one night in February, 1852, Gogol made the ultimate sacrifice: he destroyed the manuscript on which he had been working for ten years, the unfinished portion of *Dead Souls*. His boy servant Semyon, realizing what his master was about, fell on his knees and begged him to stop. Gogol grimly went ahead, and when the manuscript was in ashes, he crossed himself, kissed Semyon, and lay down to weep. From then on he had no further wish to live. He sank into deep depression and weakness, refused food, and fought off his doctors. Nine days later he died. His last words were, "Give me the ladder!" but what he meant nobody knew.

The Count of
Monte Cristo

by

ALEXANDRE DUMAS père (1802–1870)

The Characters

Edmond Dantès—A sailor from Marseilles, betrothed to Mer-
cédès. Originally open and trusting, after his imprison-
ment he becomes obsessed with a desire for vengeance. As
Count of Monte Cristo he is ostentatiously rich and power-
ful, generous to his friends, elaborately vindictive to his
enemies, at all times mysterious.
Names assumed by Dantès:
  Abbé Busoni.
  Lord Wilmore.
  Sinbad the Sailor.
Louis Dantès—Father of Edmond.
M. Morrel—A Marseilles merchant, owner of the *Pharaon*.
Julie Morrel—His daughter.
Maximilian Morrel—His son, later in love with Valentine de
  Villefort.
Haydée—Daughter of Ali Pasha of Janina, sold into slavery
  by Mondego and redeemed by Monte Cristo.
Fernand Mondego—A Catalan fisherman, later a soldier and

military adventurer in Albania, ultimately a lieutenant general with the title of Comte de Morcerf.

Mercédès—His cousin, betrothed to Edmond, later married to Fernand.

Vicomte Albert de Morcerf—Son of Fernand, betrothed to but not in love with Eugénie Danglars.

Danglars—Supercargo on Dantès' ship, later Baron Danglars, a banker.

Baroness Danglars—His wife, formerly in love with de Villefort.

Eugénie Danglars—His daughter, an independent girl who wishes to be an actress.

Louise d'Armilly—Companion and music teacher to Eugénie.

M. Noirtier—A bold and resolute Bonapartist conspirator.

Gérard de Villefort—His son, the *procureur du roi* (public prosecutor), a generally conscientious official, but unscrupulous where his ambition is concerned.

Marquis and Marquise de Saint-Méran—Members of the old aristocracy, parents-in-law of de Villefort.

Renée de Saint-Méran—Their daughter, first wife of de Villefort.

Valentine de Villefort—Daughter of Renée, in love with Maximilian Morrel.

Héloïse—Second wife of de Villefort.

Edouard—Son of de Villefort by Héloïse.

General Flavien de Quesnel—A royalist general, killed in a duel by Noirtier.

Baron Franz d'Epinay—His son, betrothed to Valentine.

Gaspard Caderousse—Neighbor of Louis Dantès, a tailor and later an innkeeper.

Madeleine Caderousse (called La Carconte)—His wife.

Abbé Faria—A prisoner in the Château d'If, a learned man who befriends and instructs Dantès.

Luigi Vampa—A Roman bandit.

Peppino—A shepherd, later one of Vampa's band.

Major Bartolomeo Cavalcanti—An Italian adventurer.

Benedetto—Illegitimate son of de Villefort and the Baroness Danglars, posing as Andrea Cavalcanti, son of the major.

Servants of the Count of Monte Cristo:
  Bertuccio.
  Ali.
  Baptistin.

Friends of Albert de Morcerf:
  Beauchamp.
  Debray.
  Château-Renaud.
D'Avrigny—De Villefort's physician.

The Story

It is not possible, within the compass of this book, to summarize all 118 chapters of *The Count of Monte Cristo (Le Compte de Monte Cristo)*. In what follows, therefore, the main strands of the narrative are presented separately, rather than interwoven in chronological order.

The story begins in 1815, with Louis XVIII ruling in Paris and Napoleon in Elba. The hero, Edmond Dantès, is a sailor from Marseilles, the first mate of the three-master *Pharaon*. During a passage from Naples to Marseilles, the captain of the *Pharaon* dies suddenly, leaving Dantès in command, a post which the owner of the ship, M. Morrel, proposes to make permanent. Furthermore, Dantès is on the point of marrying a beautiful Catalan girl named Mercédès. Thus it appears that he is about to achieve his two chief ambitions in life although he is only nineteen. Dantès, however, has enemies. One is Danglars, the supercargo of the *Pharaon*, who wishes to be captain; the other is Fernand Mondego, Mercédès' cousin, who wishes to marry her. These two men, with the help of a drunken neighbor named Caderousse, plot to put Edmond out of the way.

They are helped by the turbulent political situation. Just before the captain of the *Pharaon* died, he had asked his mate to deliver a sealed package to Napoleon at Elba. Dantès delivers the package, receiving in return a letter addressed to a M. Noirtier in Paris. Dantès has no political convictions and no knowledge of the contents of this correspondence; he cannot know that he has been made a messenger in a conspiracy to restore the emperor. Unfortunately Danglars is aware of what is afoot. He writes a letter to the local authorities denouncing Dantès as a Bonapartist and allows Fernand to deliver it. Dantès is arrested only a few hours before his marriage.

The official to whom Dantès has been denounced is M. de

Villefort, the public prosecutor, and son of the same Noirtier to whom Dantès is carrying the emperor's letter. As a servant of the Bourbon regime, de Villefort is in a tight spot, for his father is a notorious Bonapartist. As he reads the letter which Dantès carries, he realizes that if it should ever become public, his career will be ruined. Accordingly, he burns the evidence and sends Dantès to the Château d'If, a prison on an island in the harbor of Marseilles reserved for dangerous political offenders.

During the Napoleonic restoration of the One Hundred Days, Morrel tries to obtain the release of Dantès on the strength of his services to the emperor, which he somewhat exaggerates. However, before anything can be done, the regime falls and the Bourbons are restored. Dantès, now branded as a desperate Bonapartist, remains in the Château d'If for fourteen years, brooding bitterly over the injustice that has been done him. Another prisoner there is the Abbé Faria, an Italian priest whom the authorities consider insane because he tries to bribe his way out of prison by offering them a fortune in buried treasure, of which only he knows the location. Dantès communicates secretly with the abbé and befriends him. Faria is extremely intelligent and teaches his fellow prisoner many things, including several languages. The treasure, he assures Dantès, really exists, and if the two can escape together they will share it. Unluckily, before they can do so, the abbé dies. Dantès now sees only one route of escape. He drags the abbé's body to his own bed and puts himself into the sack in which Faria has been laid out for burial. When the sack is thrown into the sea, Dantès cuts himself loose and swims to freedom.

The abbé's treasure—a hoard dating back to the early sixteenth century—is on an uninhabited islet in the Tuscan archipelago called Monte Cristo. Dantès makes his way there and finds that his friend's story is true. He is now rich beyond all calculation and powerful enough to do whatever he wishes. He vows to avenge himself on the four men who had him jailed: Fernand Mondego, Danglars, Caderousse, and de Villefort. This vengeance must be a masterpiece of poetic justice. Dantès will not strike the blow himself; each villain must be trapped by his own vices—greed, treachery, or ambition. Finally, each must be made to recognize what he has done and who the avenger is. For so devious a plot, Dantès needs a disguise and he needs time.

Accordingly, some years later, in 1838, there appears in Italy a mysterious stranger, fantastically rich, styling himself the Count of Monte Cristo. His manner of life is oriental in its opulence. He is accompanied by a Greek girl whom he has purchased as a slave in Constantinople, and his personal servant is a Nubian mute. His agents are everywhere and he knows everything. When necessary, he travels disguised as a priest or an Englishman. Rumor has it that he is Maltese, has discovered a silver mine in Greece, is in league with pirates and bandits, and has seraglios on three continents. His manner is masterful and distinguished. Wherever he goes he creates a sensation which is accompanied—at least among the ladies—by a shudder of fascination and fear.

The Count's first debt is to Morrel, his old employer and benefactor. He arrives at Marseilles in time to help Morrel out of grave difficulties, for the firm has lost all its ships at sea and can no longer meet its claims. The Count poses as the agent of an English banking house, buys up Morrel's debts, saves Morrel from suicide, and gives him a new ship.

Caderousse is the least guilty of the Count's old enemies, since he was only a passive accomplice in the plot. Knowing the man's greed, the Count disguises himself and, on suitable pretext, gives him a valuable diamond. Caderousse and his wife are not satisfied with this windfall. Wishing to enjoy their wealth twice over, they sell the stone to a jeweler and then kill him to recover it. For this crime Caderousse is sent to the galleys. Later he escapes, but meets his death when he tries to blackmail a former accomplice, Benedetto, the illegitimate son of de Villefort.

Fernand Mondego is the chief enemy, since he has profited from Dantès' imprisonment by marrying Mercédès. In the intervening years, he has served in the French army and then become a military adventurer in the Balkans. After rising to power in the service of the Albanian, Ali Pasha, he has betrayed his master to the Sultan, returned to France a rich man, and become a lieutenant general styling himself the Comte de Morcerf. Morcerf's son, an honorable young man who knows nothing of his father's true character, is reluctantly engaged to Eugénie, the daughter of Danglars. Monte Cristo hints to Danglars that there is a skeleton in the Morcerf family closet. Danglars investigates and the engagement is broken off. Soon hints appear in the papers about the betrayal of Ali Pasha, and the House of Peers launches an investigation. The principal witness is Haydée, Monte Cristo's companion, who, it develops, is the daughter of Ali Pasha himself and remembers Morcerf distinctly. Morcerf's wife and son leave him, renouncing his name and fortune, and Morcerf commits suicide.

De Villefort, the man who sentenced Dantès, has now risen to be crown prosecutor (*procureur du roi*), although he has serious crimes on his conscience. Years before he had a child by the wife of Danglars, apparently born dead. De Villefort buried the baby secretly in the garden, but by an improbable series of events it was recovered, revived, and raised by a smuggler named Bertuccio. This child is Benedetto, whom we have already met as an accomplice of Caderousse. He rapidly displays criminal tendencies, robs his foster parents, and is sent to the galleys.

While these complicated events are unfolding, de Villefort also begets, by his first wife, a legitimate daughter named Valentine and, by his second, an unpleasant little son named Edouard. Héloïse, the second wife, lives only for her son, and wishes to destroy all the heirs who stand in the way of his inheriting the fortune accruing from her husband's first marriage. Normally this inheritance would descend to Valentine unless, of course, some accident should occur. At this point, the Count of Monte Cristo befriends the family, wins the confidence of Héloïse, and, under pretext of giving her a medicine for her asthma, supplies her with a bottle of poison.

In the following months a series of mysterious deaths strike de Villefort's family: first the parents of his first wife, then his father's manservant, who accidentally takes a drink meant for his master, then Valentine, who does not die but falls critically ill. De Villefort realizes that his wife must be the assassin and that it is his official duty to arrest her. He confronts her with the evidence and offers her the chance to commit suicide. Without staying to see if she accepts the offer, he hurries off to court to seek a death sentence for Benedetto, charged with the murder of Caderousse. Benedetto, who now knows his parentage, claims the crown prosecutor as his father and denounces him in court for having virtually committed infanticide. Crushed, de Villefort returns home to find that Héloïse and Edouard have killed themselves, and that Dantès is standing by to gloat. In a few minutes the crown prosecutor goes insane.

Danglars escapes more lightly. In the years since 1815, he too has risen, has become a banker, received the title of Baron, and married an aristocratic wife. Monte Cristo is able to wound him in his two most vulnerable spots: his social ambition and his greed. Danglars' daughter is reluctantly engaged to Albert de Morcerf, but when the Ali Pasha scandal leaks out, Danglars looks for a more acceptable son-in-law. Monte Cristo offers Benedetto, the escaped convict. Suitably groomed and furnished with a princely income and spurious genealogy, Benedetto is presentable enough to impose on Danglars. The marriage contract is on the point of being signed when the police come to arrest Benedetto for the murder of Caderousse.

Danglars is publicly humiliated, but he must suffer more. Monte Cristo has letters of credit on Danglars' bank for five million livres. He cashes them at a time when Danglars' credit is overextended. Danglars is ruined and flees to Rome where he is immediately taken prisoner by bandits acting on orders from the Count. They carry him to a cave and proceed to starve him until he is happy to pay five thousand louis d'or for a single chicken. This treatment lasts for some weeks until Danglars' remaining wealth has all been extorted from him. At length Monte Cristo releases him, but meanwhile his hair has turned white.

Monte Cristo does not extend his vengeance to the children of his enemies. (The death of Edouard is an accident which he did not foresee.) He befriends Albert de Morcerf, and forbears to punish Mercédès. As for Valentine, he saves her from death by poison, spirits her away from her father's house, and enables her to marry the man she really loves, Maximilian Morrel, the son of his old benefactor. The old debts of love and hate are now paid, and Monte Cristo remorsefully wonders if he has not been presumptuous in playing the role of God's avenging angel. However, he still has Haydée, and the prospect of happiness beckons. Saying farewell to Valentine and Maximilian, he leaves as mysteriously as he came.

Critical Opinion

The Count of Monte Cristo was written in collaboration with Auguste Macquet and A. P. Fiorentino. The title was suggested by memories of the island of Monte Cristo, which Dumas had seen from a boat in 1842, though he never actually set foot on it. The theme of the mysterious stranger came from a short story by Peuchet in *La Police Devoilé*. Originally the story was intended to begin in Italy (note that Chapter XXXI reads like an opening chapter), and the prior history of the Count was to be told in retrospect. At Macquet's suggestion, the first thirty chapters dealing with the imprisonment of Dantès were added later. Accordingly, the story now falls into three divisions: Marseilles, Rome, and Paris. The novel was published in 1844 in twelve volumes, and eight years later it was dramatized, yielding four plays.

The Count of Monte Cristo is one of those books which never stimulate the reader to thought, and yet do not allow him to stop before the last page. Its appeal today is largely to children, mainly perhaps to boys in early adolescence. It was not, however, intended as a child's book. Perhaps readers in the 1840's were less jaded or less sophisticated, for, while it was appearing in serial form, everyone in Paris read it and hailed one another in the streets to learn if Dantès had escaped yet from the Château d'If. Gautier, Balzac, Stevenson, and Andrew Lang all testified to its magic. This popularity demands some explanation, for the book, while it is clearly a masterpiece of its kind, is not the sort of masterpiece that most critics bother to examine.

It is easy to find flaws in *The Count of Monte Cristo*. The plot—enormous, intricate, and full of elaborately contrived coincidences—cannot possibly be taken seriously, except by that willing suspension of disbelief which, according to Coleridge, is necessary for poetic faith. This overcrowding of incident arises from the fact that the novel first came out in serial form, and a story that is "to be continued in our next issue" must hold its readers by giving them at least one exciting episode per chapter. As for the enormous length and occasional prolixity, this is explained by the fact that Dumas was paid by the line. (To take advantage of this arrangement he once invented a character who spoke only in mono-syllables; when the publishers refused to pay for less than a half-line, the character was killed off.)

Nor can we say much more for Dumas' characters. His villainous villains, heroic heroes, and maidenly maidens are without complexity or depth. Today they would belong in a grade B movie or a children's television program. The one memorable creation is Monte Cristo himself, not because he is any more real than the rest, but because he is so utterly and wonderfully unreal. In terms of literary genealogy, he is descended from the heroes of Byron. He has the tall figure, black hair, and pale complexion of the Byronic hero, also the same masterful will, the mystery which obscures his origins, the worldly poise which covers the scars of a past love. There is a long line of such characters in the novels of the nineteenth century, a later example being Captain Nemo of Jules Verne's *Nautilus*.

It would be naïve, however, to object to *The Count of Monte Cristo* on these grounds; the art of melodrama is not the art of Henry James, and it must obey its own laws. The secret of melodrama is wish fulfillment: the hero must act out the reader's fantasies for him. Obviously Dantès in some ways resembles Dumas himself: his generosity, his extravagance, his love of dramatic gestures. In his island cave, he lives the sort of life that Dumas dreamed of and very nearly achieved. The terrible vengeance which he wreaks on those who have hurt him undoubtedly represents the compensatory daydream of a poor boy whose grandfather was a marquis and whose grandmother was a slave. Even today Monte Cristo stirs the imagination of everyone who has ever dreamed of being rich and powerful and glamorous. Dantès is a figure of purest myth, so compelling that the guides in the Château d'If will now show you the cell where he was imprisoned.

The Author

On his birth certificate, dated 1802, the full name of Dumas is given as Alexandre Dumas Davy de la Pelleterie. Davy de la Pelleterie was the name of his grandfather, a French marquis who settled as a planter in Santo Domingo. Dumas was the name of his grandmother, a Negro slave. His father, a tall

and handsome mulatto, enrolled in the army as a private
just before the Revolution, and, thanks to Napoleon's policy
of opening promotions to all able men, became a major general by the age of thirty. After a falling-out with Napoleon,
he retired to a country village near Paris, married a local girl,
and died at forty-four. His only child, Alexandre, inherited
from his mother his blue eyes and light skin, from his father
a robust body and tightly curled hair.

Dumas' education was rudimentary. At sixteen he was
little more than a raw country bumpkin. He was, however,
restless, the capital with its excitement beckoned, and with
the help of an old comrade-in-arms of his father's, he secured
a job in Paris as secretary to the Duc d'Orléans. Once established in the city, he became stagestruck, haunted the theaters, and—although he had had no previous literary training
or ambition—tried his hand at writing plays of his own. If
Dumas knew nothing else, he did know what was dramatically effective, and his plays were popular. Much of their success came from the fact that they broke with the stilted tradition of neoclassic tragedy; instead of classic themes treated
with strict decorum of style they used sensational plots,
Gothic settings, brooding Byronic heroes, and other melodramatic devices. The most famous was *La Tour de Nesle*
(1832), an historic drama crowded with gloomy dungeons,
secret panels, and corpses.

Encouraged by his success, Dumas took a mistress, a dressmaker named Catherine Lebay, who was the mother of another Alexandre Dumas, later famous in his own right as the
author of *Camille (La Dame aux Camélias;* operatic version,
La Traviata). Catherine was followed by a long series of
women, usually actresses, the last and most famous of whom
was Adah Menken, an American bareback rider from New
Orleans, who also enjoyed the friendship of other men of
letters, including Gautier, Swinburne, and Dickens. He was
briefly married to one of his mistresses, a fat actress named
Ida Ferrier, but the relation, which had lasted amiably for
some years, did not survive the strains of matrimony.

Today Dumas is remembered chiefly as a novelist. His
career in fiction began in the 1840's when he struck up a
friendship with a teacher named Macquet, who came to him
for help in revising a play. The two conceived a plan for an
historical novel based on an old book, published in 1700,

entitled *Mémoires de Monsieur d'Artagnan.* This became *The Three Musketeers (Les Trois Mousquetaires).* Scholars have long argued over how much was written by Dumas and how much by Macquet; it would seem that Macquet did most of the historical research and wrote a rough draft of the story, which Dumas then completely rewrote. In this way Dumas and his collaborators were able to turn out an incredible number of books, two or three at a time, and six or ten volumes long. Dumas was often accused of running a novel factory and enriching himself by the labors of ill-paid hacks. The ethics of the situation are ambiguous, but it is clear that Macquet and the rest considered themselves well paid for their work, and Dumas, always generous, was happy to acknowledge their help. Moreover, none of his associates ever produced anything memorable alone; the magic was all Dumas'.

The Count of Monte Cristo appeared at virtually the same time as *The Three Musketeers,* and was just as popular. Others almost as well known were *Twenty Years After (Vingt Ans Après,* 1845), *Queen Margot (La Reine Margot,* 1845), *La Dame de Monsoreau* (1846), *Forty-five Guardsmen (Les Quarante-Cinq,* 1847–1848), *Le Vicomte de Bragelonne* (1848–1850), *The Queen's Necklace (Le Collier de la Reine,* 1849–1850), *Black Tulip (La Tulipe Noire,* 1850), and *Olympe de Clèves* (1852). Most were swashbuckling romances set in the sixteenth, seventeenth and eighteenth centuries, some were contemporary, and others were detective stories. Probably no one has read them all; the complete works of Dumas, published between 1860 and 1880, run to 277 volumes. Many became plays, and in 1847 Dumas opened his own theater to produce them.

These novels made Dumas rich, but no fortune was too big for him to squander. He built himself a great villa outside Paris and named it "Monte Cristo"; the descriptions make it sound like a sultan's palace in a De Mille spectacular. Here Dumas, as vain and delighted as a child, presided over a motley crowd of friends, actresses, curiosity seekers, and parasites. Then came the revolution of 1848, which was bad for the theatrical world, especially for Dumas' theater. His own extravagance pushed him further toward ruin. When there was no wine for the servants he broke open a case of champagne. Finally the villa had to be sold, and, in 1851,

Dumas took refuge in Brussels, out of reach of his creditors. Two years of hard work and prudent management enabled him to return to Paris more or less solvent. He now began a third career, this time as a journalist. In 1853 he founded a daily paper for which he wrote most of the articles. But the taste of Parisian readers was now changing, and Dumas began increasingly to look like a has-been.

His energies did not fail him, and in 1860 he set off to Italy to help Garibaldi capture Naples from the Bourbons. It is said that the famous red shirts of Garibaldi's soldiery were his suggestion. For a time he acted as supervisor of archeological investigations at Pompeii, then, tiring of the job, returned to Paris. The last decade of his life was of a piece with the rest, only diminuendo. His vitalities began to flag at last, and his son, now a respectable author of moral plays, tried to put a brake on his father's excesses. By 1870, Dumas was destitute and an invalid, a crumbling mountain of a man, tended by his children in Alexandre's villa near Dieppe. As he lay dying, the Prussian troops were entering the town, but nobody had the heart to tell him. According to his biographer, André Maurois, a kindly smile lingered on his lips to the very end.

Madame Bovary

by

GUSTAVE FLAUBERT (1821–1880)

The Characters

Charles Bovary—Medical officer in a small Normandy town, the devoted husband of Emma Bovary. He is an honest mediocrity, well intentioned, placid, and unambitious.

Héloïse Dubuc—The first Mme. Bovary, an ugly middle-aged widow who becomes a nagging, jealous wife.

Emma Bovary—The protagonist, second wife of Charles Bovary. Although she is a peasant's daughter, she has impossibly romantic aspirations which make her perpetually dissatisfied with her lot.

Berthe Bovary—The only child of Charles and Emma.

Charles Denis Bartholomé Bovary—The father of Charles Bovary, a retired army officer, who fails at everything he tries, and sinks into dissipation.

Mme. Bovary Senior—Charles's mother, protective and managing, jealous of her daughter-in-law.

Rouault—Emma's father, a well-to-do peasant, a simple, hearty, robust man, fond of his comforts and of his family.

Marquis d'Andervilliers—A local politician and member of an old and aristocratic family, who invites the Bovarys to dinner and gives Emma her one taste of fine living.

Léon Dupuis—A lawyer's clerk who becomes Emma's lover.

Of no great strength or depth of character, he appeals to her because he reflects her mood and adopts her sentiments.

Rodolphe Boulanger—A country gentleman, another lover of Emma's. Self-centered and sensual, to him the liaison is just another diversion.

Homais—The local pharmacist. An anticlericalist in the tradition of Voltaire, he sees himself as embodying the forces of enlightenment and progress; actually he is shallow, pompous, argumentative and self-seeking.

Bournisien—The parish priest, a hardworking, unimaginative man.

Dr. Larivière—A distinguished physician from Houfleur.

Lheureux—An unscrupulous shopkeeper who lures Emma to financial ruin.

Guilloumin—A lawyer.

Hippolyte—A stableboy.

The Story

The place is Normandy, the time, the second quarter of the nineteenth century. Charles Bovary, the son of a retired army officer, a sturdy, plodding, unimaginative country boy of fifteen, comes to Rouen to attend school. Though he has no great ability, his mother pushes him hard, and he finally manages to qualify as an officer of health, an inferior grade of doctor. His mother locates a practice in the small country town of Tostes, and even finds him a wife, a widow much older than he, supposedly wealthy, who proves to be jealous and domineering.

Charles finds pleasure and escape in the company of one of his patients, the prosperous farmer Rouault, and of his pretty daughter, Emma, who has enjoyed a convent-school education and has pretensions to taste and genteel manners. Charles's wife is jealous, but her unexpected death from a hemorrhage removes her from the picture, leaving Charles free, after a decent wait, to marry Emma. For him the marriage is a love match, and in his placid, undemonstrative way he is completely happy.

Emma, on the other hand, is a romanticist whose taste has been formed on the sentimental novels and poetry of the day. She hopes to find in marriage an intense emotional fulfillment such as she has read of in books. But after the honeymoon she is bored, and cannot believe that her quiet routine with a stolid, unambitious man represents the happiness she has dreamed of. Her restlessness is increased by an invitation to a dinner and ball given by the Marquis d'Andervilliers. This brief glimpse of a wealthy, luxurious life makes her all the more dissatisfied with Tostes. She begins to read fashion magazines, dreams of moving to Paris, and tries to introduce a few touches of elegance into her bourgeois household. Finally her frustration and ennui take the form of symptoms of illness, and Charles, for the sake of her health (she is now pregnant), moves to the small market town of Yonville l'Abbaye.

Yonville is a sleepy, nondescript place where nothing happens. The Bovarys are made welcome by Monsieur Homais, the pharmacist, who wishes to impress the new doctor and win his support, and by Homais' boarder, a law clerk named Léon Dupuis, who tries to impress Emma by sharing her romantic fantasies. Bovary settles down to his usual routine, while Emma indulges in dreams of love for Léon—a love which is not consummated or even declared. At length Léon, who is impatient with provincial life, leaves to seek his fortune in Paris.

Emma, now at loose ends emotionally, attracts the attention of Rodolphe Boulanger, a fashionable bachelor and gentleman farmer who has settled nearby. She becomes his mistress. The affair is only a gallant diversion for him, but for her it promises to be the great passion she longs for. As she grows more reckless, she becomes more extravagant, and without her husband's knowledge, goes heavily into debt to a village merchant, Monsieur Lheureux.

Meanwhile, Charles is persuaded by Homais to attempt a corrective operation on Hippolyte, the stableboy at the local inn, who has a club foot. Emma, who sees a chance to make her husband a professional success at last, joins the persuasion. Though Charles lacks the necessary skill, he operates. Gangrene develops and a surgeon has to be summoned to amputate the leg. While the patient's shrieks ring through the village, Charles stays in his house, heartbroken and humiliated. Emma, turning against him in contempt, decides to elope with Rodolphe. Rodolphe, however, is bored with her and afraid of forming any permanent ties. He sends her a letter

breaking off the affair. Emma falls into convulsions and is ill
for months. She recovers slowly, and for a time develops an
intense interest in religion, which she indulges with the same
sentimental ardor which she formerly gave to adultery.
Finally she is well enough so that her husband takes her to
Rouen to see the opera. There they meet Léon, who has returned from Paris a much more worldly and sophisticated
man than before.

Emma now starts an affair with Léon, and, on the pretext
of taking music lessons, is able to meet him once a week in
Rouen. To finance these trips, she borrows further from
Lheureux and persuades Charles to give her power of attorney to handle his accounts. This she uses to intercept
payments from his patients and even to sell property without
his knowledge. At length the affair with Léon runs its
course, as he finds it a risk to his advancement, and she discovers that adultery can be as banal as marriage. One day,
after a quarrel with Léon, she returns home to find a court
judgment against her for 320 pounds, to be executed within
twenty-four hours.

By now half insane with desperation, Emma visits one
moneylender after another, tries to persuade Léon to commit embezzlement, and pleads with Rodolphe, who coldly
turns her away. A lawyer to whom she goes for help takes
advantage of her desperation and makes advances to her. At
length she dashes into Homais' shop, forces the assistant to
give her the key to the drug closet, swallows a handful of
arsenic, and goes home to die. As her agony increases,
Charles becomes paralyzed with panic, Homais is incompetent, and a distinguished doctor summoned from Honfleur
arrives too late to help.

After the funeral, Charles, prostrate with grief, tries to set
his household affairs in order. Gradually he learns of his
wife's extravagance and dishonesty. At last he unearths
letters from Rodolphe and Léon and realizes that Emma has
not loved him. Soon after, he dies, completely crushed, and
his daughter, Berthe, is sent to be raised first by her grandmother who dies the same year, then by a poor aunt, who
puts her to work in a factory. Homais, on the other hand,
prospers, and after much manipulation and self-advertise-
ment achieves his highest ambition: he is awarded the medal
of the Legion of Honor.

Critical Opinion

Madame Bovary does for the romantic movement what *Don Quixote* does for the age of chivalry. Flaubert's aim was to examine the principles and emotions of romanticism which he had once considered valid, and to show how they bring about the ruin of an empty-headed woman who takes them seriously. In so doing he was exorcizing part of himself. His picture of a splenetic, frustrated, illusion-ridden personality is so complete that it has added a new word to the French language: *Bovarisme*.

Flaubert claimed to pass no judgment on his characters. He saw himself simply as a clear-sighted and dispassionate observer of human folly. Actually, he had strong opinions about his characters, and he does not really leave us in any doubt as to what they are. He obviously had no love for Emma, although his attitude toward her is complicated by his realization that there was a good deal of her in his own personality. His keenest ridicule is reserved for Homais, the druggist, who is everything Flaubert detests in the French middle class: self-seeking, vulgar, pretentious and stupid. On the other hand, the old peasant Rouault is sympathetically treated, and the dull-witted Charles Bovary wins our pity, even our respect, mainly because he never pretends to be more than he is.

Flaubert's chief weapon is irony and bathos, the most extended example being the scene at the agricultural exhibition, where the love dialogue between Emma and Rodolphe is interwoven with the speech of the chairman awarding prizes for pigs and manure. Elsewhere, Emma's vague, yeasty longings are summed up in one short anticlimactic sentence: "She wanted to die, and she wanted to live in Paris." Even minor incidents are turned to an ironic purpose, as when the boy Justin, weeping on Emma's grave, is mistaken by the sexton for someone stealing potatoes.

As a conscientious realist, Flaubert took care to ground every detail of his story in fact. There really was a Norman country doctor who died of despair over his wife's infidelity; the village of Yonville is actually Ry, not far from Honfleur; a number of minor characters have been identified as real people, and as for Homais, the most devastating caricature in the book, it is said that every druggist in Normandy took offence at him.

Generally Flaubert's realism expends itself on prosy, commonplace objects; but there are times, like the death scene of Emma, when he produces gruesome or disgusting details which anticipate the naturalism of Zola. (It is said that Flaubert threw himself so intensely into writing this scene that he could taste arsenic in his mouth and became actually ill.) Other details become symbols, as when Emma finds the faded bridal bouquet of the first Madame Bovary, pricks her finger on the wire, and wonders what would happen if she were to die also.

Flaubert's famous style set a standard of excellence which has yet to be surpassed. His obsessive search for the *mot juste*, or the exactly right word, is something which French readers can best appreciate. Even in translation, however, the careful architecture of the book is obvious, and some of the rhythm of the paragraphs and sentences is also in evidence. The reader should note, for example, the effect of the short, understated sentences which close many of the chapters. They seem unemphatic, yet they sting like whips.

Madame Bovary, in short, is the classic novel of the realist movement, whether one reads it for its psychological insight, for its solid use of realistic detail, for its masterful handling of irony, or for the authoritative control of its style. Some critics have argued, and with reason, that it is the most perfect novel of its century.

The Author

The life of Gustave Flaubert has few dramatic episodes. His one passion was his art, and that he practiced with utter singleness of purpose. He was born in Rouen in 1821 of middle-class parents. His father was a distinguished doctor who served as the model for Dr. Larivière in *Madame Bovary*. Gustave spent his childhood on the grounds of the hospital where his family lived. The death scene of Emma Bovary was written by one who as a child had peered through the windows of the dissecting room to watch autopsies.

At eighteen, Flaubert was sent to Paris to study law, a

subject which he found incomprehensible and gave up with relief. In 1844 he settled with his parents on a family estate near Rouen called Croisset. Here he spent the rest of his days in rigid routine and almost monastic seclusion, writing and rewriting with a painstaking thoroughness that is now legendary. To achieve the proper rhythm of a sentence cost him agonies, and he would spend days in the revision of a single page. Chronic illness, either neurotic or neurological, deepened his isolation, which was interrupted by rare trips to Paris, by visits from literary friends, and by two trips outside of Europe. In 1849–1851, he traveled with a friend to Egypt, Syria, Turkey and Greece. In 1858, he visited the site of Carthage to collect local color for his work.

Flaubert never married. In his youth, he felt a Platonic love for a certain Mme. Schlesinger, who appears as Mme. Arnoux of *Sentimental Education (L'Education Sentimentale)*. Later he took as mistress a third-rate poetess named Louise Colet. The relationship, however, interfered with his writing, and was therefore conducted largely by mail. The arrangement was not satisfactory to Louise, who threw herself at him so violently that she once had to be forcibly ejected by the guards from a railway waiting room where she had followed him. Finally, during the writing of *Madame Bovary*, Flaubert dismissed her abruptly.

Madame Bovary appeared amid difficulties. It was first published in serial form by the *Revue de Paris,* a magazine suspected by the censors of radical views, and one which the government was eager to suppress. The theme of the novel— adultery—offered a handy pretext for prosecution, and the publishers, eager to avert any trouble, tried to excise certain passages. When Flaubert refused to accept the revisions, the government brought proceedings against him and the magazine for offending public morality and religion. The trial (which resulted in an acquittal) was a *cause célèbre*. The novel became famous overnight.

Flaubert's later years were painful. The Franco-Prussian War disrupted his life when Croisset was occupied for some months by German soldiers, his friends were dying off or were alienated, his family suffered financial reverses, and his health was getting worse. He continued to work despite illness and melancholy, and died suddenly of apoplexy in 1880.

By temperament Flaubert was a romanticist who forced

himself to be a realist. He shared with the writers of the romantic generation a melancholy temperament, a taste for irony, a dislike of the bourgeoisie and a love of exotic places, like Egypt and Carthage. On the other hand, his native romanticism was disciplined by studied objectivity, by the care with which he excluded his own personality from his writing, and by the meticulous realism with which he recorded the minutiae of ordinary life. This tension between romanticism and realism appears in the alternation of themes of his novels. His first major published work was *Madame Bovary* (1857), which is deliberately antiromantic. It was followed by *Salammbô* (1863), a picture of ancient Carthage with its bloody, barbaric magnificence. In 1873, came *Sentimental Education*, which is set in modern Paris and is largely based on recollections of Flaubert's own student days. This was followed by *The Temptation of Saint Anthony* (*La Tentation de Saint Antoine*, 1874), which presents the torments and ecstasies of the early Christian ascetic. *Three Tales* (*Trois Contes*) appeared in 1877, and expresses both moods: it contains the story of Herodias, which satisfied Flaubert's love for ornate orientalism, and on the other hand, it includes "A Simple Heart" ("Un Coeur Simple"), the story of a simple Norman servant woman, whose life is so narrow that her frustrated emotions find their chief outlet in devotion to a stuffed parrot. This little story is a model of disciplined style and structure. Despite its dryly objective manner, it suggests a compassion for its protagonist which is rare in Flaubert's earlier work. Flaubert also wrote a comedy, *The Candidate* (*Le Candidat*, 1874), which was a failure, and an unfinished novel, published posthumously, *Bouvard et Pecuchet* (1881), which was to be a comprehensive satire on human society. *Madame Bovary*, however, is his masterpiece, and remains perhaps the most distinguished example of the realistic novel.

Oblomov

by

IVAN ALEXANDROVICH GONCHAROV
(1812–1891)

The Characters *

Ilya Ilyich Oblomov—A gentleman living on income from his lands; honest and sweet-tempered, but irresponsible and pathologically lazy.

Zahar Trofimich—Oblomov's lazy, dirty, quarrelsome but faithful manservant.

Volkov—A friend of Oblomov, preoccupied with social activities.

Sudbinsky—A friend, a career administrator in the government.

Penkin—A literary friend.

Ivan Gerasimich Alexeyev—Another friend, a complete nonentity.

Mihey Andreyich Tarantyev—An impudent, ill-natured parasite, professedly a friend of Oblomov.

Andrey Ivanich Stolz—Oblomov's closest friend, businesslike, efficient and enterprising.

Anissya—Oblomov's cook, married to Zahar.

Olga Sergeyevna Ilyinsky—A young girl loved by Oblomov.

° See Note on Russian Names, p. 173.

Intelligent, spirited, she wants to arouse Oblomov from his lethargy.

Marya Mihailovna—Olga's aunt, sedate and unemotional.

Baron von Langwagen—An old friend of Marya Milhailovna, a courteous man of the world.

Sonichka—A friend of Olga.

Agafya Matveyevna Pshenitsyn—A widow, Oblomov's landlady.

Ivan Matveyich—Agafya's brother, a petty government clerk, shrewd and unscrupulous.

Vanya—Agafya's son.

Masha—Agafya's daughter.

Andrey—Son of Agafya and Oblomov.

Irina Panteleyevna—Wife of Ivan Matveyich.

The Story

One of the evils of a serf-holding society, apart from injustice, is the demoralizing effect on the serf-holder who grows accustomed to living on the labors of others and never learns to do any useful work of his own. Ilya Ilyich Oblomov is such a man. A bachelor of about thirty, he lives in a Saint Petersburg apartment on the income from a medium-sized estate of about three hundred serfs. His household consists of a cook, and a valet named Zahar, an old family retainer who is dirty, negligent, quarrelsome and dishonest, but who nevertheless follows his master with blind feudal loyalty. Ilya Ilyich has left his native village of Oblomovka initially to make a career in some government office in the capital. Not liking a life of responsible routine, he has left his job and spends his time vegetating. He lies in bed till afternoon, is prostrated by the simplest decisions, neglects his correspondence, and pays no attention to his estate, which is mismanaged by a succession of dishonest or incompetent agents.

Since Oblomov is pleasant, inoffensive, and undemanding, he has friends who visit him (he is far too lazy to visit them). They are interested in improving his career, his health, his social life or his mind, but the only one who can arouse him to anything like action is an old childhood comrade, Andrey Ivanich Stolz. Stolz is half German, and from his father he has inherited an industrious, methodical, unromantic, aggressive approach to life. He is now a young businessman on the way up, obviously destined to achieve wealth and influence.

Through Stolz, Oblomov meets a young woman, Olga Sergeyevna, who stirs his torpid heart to an unexpected flurry of love. Olga recognizes in Oblomov a sweet-tempered and affectionate nature, but her chief interest is to use her ascendancy over him to remodel his personality, to arouse him to responsible and creative activity, and to turn him into a man like Stolz. Oblomov wavers erratically between industry and foot-dragging. He loves Olga and wants to be worthy of her, but at the same time he fears that she cannot really love him, or else loves him for the sake of something that he is not and cannot be. The love affair, therefore, pursues a rather jerky course, in which ardent declarations of passion alternate with hesitancy and tears. The crucial test of Oblomov's determination is to ask her aunt for Olga's hand in marriage and to declare publicly that he is engaged to her. This moment is indefinitely postponed while Oblomov draws up plans for a new house and awaits news from his bailiff about his financial situation. Finally Olga, recognizing that her sluggish fiancé will never do anything, breaks the engagement. To hide her chagrin, she goes traveling through Europe, and eventually marries Stolz.

Oblomov, meanwhile, settles deeper than ever into a morass of indolence. He has managed to uproot himself sufficiently to move (under threat of eviction) to a suburban apartment owned by a young widow, Agafya Matveyevna Pshenitsyn. Mentally, she is even more torpid than Oblomov, but she is a busy housekeeper, a good mother, and a bountiful cook. Oblomov surrenders to her comfortable ministrations as if he were falling asleep in his mother's arms. Agafya's unscrupulous brother takes advantage of the situation to make Oblomov sign IOU's for money he has never borrowed, and otherwise to milk him dry. Oblomov is rescued by the providential appearance of Stolz, who not only straightens out his debts but even takes over the management of Oblomovka and turns it into a paying property. Eventually Oblomov marries Agafya and has a child by her, whom he names Andrey after his friend; but he never bestirs himself to go back to Oblomovka or even to visit Olga and Stolz. In the course of time, he dies peacefully in his sleep of an apoplectic stroke brought on by his sedentary life. Stolz adopts young Andrey, who will thus be saved, we presume, from the insidious influence of Oblomovism.

Critical Opinion

Certain figures in literature (Gargantua, Don Quixote, Mr. Pickwick) are such complete expressions of their type of personality that they are prototypes of that character, which is thereafter known by their name. Oblomov is one of these. When Goncharov's novel appeared, the public was becoming accustomed to the new school of realism in Russian literature and to sociological commentary like that in *Fathers and Sons*. At first *Oblomov* was universally interpreted as a study of the deterioration of character in a serf-holding society, the product of generations of inherited privilege. Oblomovka, the native village of Ilya Ilyich, is a drowsy backwater untouched by European influence, and, for all its bucolic charm, it represents the kind of life that the progressive forces of the time wished to sweep away. Of this semi-medieval life the manservant Zahar is a product and a symbol. On a lower level, he is another Oblomov. Stolz belongs to the new generation that was expected to transform the country. Significantly he is only half Russian, his father being a German, a people that for Goncharov would seem to epitomize everything that is practical, disciplined, scientific, anti-romantic and progressive. Stolz's slightly insensitive, pushing, middle-class ways disturb the aristocratic torpor of his friend Ilya. The issue between the old life and the new, between Oblomov and Stolz, must be resolved, we know, in favor of the new, yet the author allows us a certain ambivalence of feeling toward both. Thus we laugh at the people of Oblomovka, yet not without secret envy for their old-fashioned, dreamy, impractical way of life. Similarly we respect Stolz, and yet not without some distaste for his doctrinaire, busybody nature. The tension between the two is characteristic of all societies in transition.

While modern critics do not slight the sociological side of *Oblomov*, they are especially aware of its importance as a psychological study. Oblomov's lethargy is not just the vice of a single class or even of a whole nation. There is a streak of Oblomovism in us all. It represents the wish to return to the peaceful, vegetative life of the womb. Oblomov's warm, dark bedroom, where he lies dozing swaddled in an old dressing gown, is an approximation of the intrauterine existence. His childhood, during which he was coddled and spoiled, did nothing to cut the umbilical cord. Olga is the one force strong enough to rouse him, but when she is on the point of success, his whole being rises in protest. The procrastination, which finally destroys his engagement to Olga, is a not-quite-conscious defense mechanism. In a sense, Oblomov is not defeated by life. He triumphs over it, for not all the coaxing of Olga nor the gadfly persistence of Stolz can make him do what he does not wish to do. He conquers them by sheer inertia.

For this reason, *Oblomov* is a comedy, not a tragedy. By classical definition, tragedy is an action in which a noble or potentially great figure is destroyed by some flaw in his own makeup: the ambition of Macbeth, for instance, or the noble gullibility of Othello. But Oblomov is not really destroyed, unless a peaceful death in his sleep can be called destruction. He defies duty and common sense and gets away with it. He belongs with Gargantua and Falstaff and the other heroic gluttons of literature. Certainly, for all his pathological laziness, he is not contemptible. Since he has never lived in the world, he retains an unspoiled innocence that all his friends find compelling. Olga especially comments on his "dovelike gentleness." He believes in loyalty and purity and the dignity of man. There is not a grain of cynicism in him, and when he criticizes the life of his upper-class friends as superficial, restless and selfish, he displays a firmer understanding of moral values than they do.

Since the whole point of the story is that nothing ever happens, the plot is simple and uncomplicated, and the subordinate material, like Olga's marriage to Stolz, remains peripheral. The pace is slow. The structure is carefully planned with architectural skill and studied opposition of themes—Russia and Europe, aristocrat and bourgeois, country and city, Agafya and Olga, Zahar and Stolz. Certain images are repeated like symbols: the spray of lilac that Olga carries, or the Oriental dressing gown that enfolds Oblomov in his moments of contemplative withdrawal. Perhaps the most notable passage is Oblomov's dream of his childhood in Chapter 9, Part I. This is an idyllic picture of an innocent and unsophisticated life in a rural district where money is hardly ever used and even the days are reckoned by the feasts of the church rather than by the civil calendar. But this happy Arcady is located in the past and can be reentered only in a dream. Perhaps that is all it ever was.

The Author

Ivan Alexandrovich Goncharov wrote slowly and sparingly, and, so far as readers outside of Russia are concerned, he is remembered for a single book. He was born in 1812 in a provincial town in the Volga region. His father, a wealthy merchant, sent him at ten to study at a Moscow gymnasium and later at the University. Most of the intellectual leaders of his generation were students at about the same time, but Goncharov did not belong to their circle. His aim was to become a career bureaucrat, and he spent much of his life working for the Ministry of Finance. He did his writing in his spare time, without the pressure from publishers that so harassed Dostoevski. His first novel, *A Common Story*, was a tale of a naïve provincial idealist who comes to the capital, loses his illusions, and turns into a cynical opportunist. In some ways, the theme suggests *Oblomov* though with a different ending.

The only even remotely venturesome episode in Goncharov's life was a trip to Japan as secretary to a trade mission. He traveled by sea, in the days before the opening of the Suez Canal, and returned overland across Siberia before the railroad had been built. So strenuous a trip was certainly not in character for so sedentary a man. According to one story, he volunteered for the assignment without thinking, and, finding himself taken at his word, could not back out. His journal of the voyage was published as *The Frigate Pallas* (1857). *Oblomov* appeared in the same year, and was immediately recognized as a work of major importance, at least in Russia. English readers had to wait sixty years for a translation.* About the same time, Goncharov left his post in the Ministry of Finance and took a position as literary censor for the Ministry of Education, a dull and distasteful

---

* *Oblomov* has been translated three times into English; the first version (1915) is seriously inadequate. More recent translations are by N. A. Duddington (1929) and D. Magarshack (1960).

job, and certainly inappropriate for one who was himself a novelist, but one which he discharged in a less illiberal spirit than most censors would have done.

Goncharov's third novel, *The Precipice* (1869), was the fruit of many years' work. About provincial life on the Volga, it is memorable for a picture of an old-fashioned household firmly ruled by a benevolent old matriarch. Goncharov was convinced that Turgenev had plagiarized from this book, but his suspicion seems to have been a symptom of the paranoia which afflicted him in his old age. He never married. His last years were spent in a long and lonely retirement which turned him into a sort of Oblomov himself, although far more irascible and suspicious than his gentle and placid hero.

Fathers and Sons

by

IVAN SERGEYEVICH TURGENEV (1818–1883)

The Characters *

Nikolai Petrovich Kirsanov—A middle-aged country gentleman, kindly and gentle, deeply fond of his son.

Pavel (Paul) Petrovich Kirsanov—Nikolai's brother. In his
youth he has had an unhappy love affair which has left him
a moody, solitary bachelor. A thorough aristocrat, his manner is aloof, his dress and grooming immaculate, his speech
at times caustic.

Arkady Nikolayevich Kirsanov—The elder son of Nikolai,
just out of the University. Basically he is a simple, affectionate person, but much under the influence of his brilliant
and bitter friend Bazarov.

Fedosya Nikolayevna Savishna (Fenichka)—Nikolai's mistress, a gentle, shy, pretty peasant girl.

Mitya—Nikolai's illegitimate son, a healthy baby a few months
old.

Yvgeny (Eugene) Vasilich Bazarov—A brilliant young medical student, a friend of Arkady. A nihilist, he mocks at
everything, especially stupidity, sentimentality, and self-
deception.

* See Note on Russian Names, p. 173.

Vassily Ivanich Bazarov—Yvgeny's father, a retired army doctor, a simple man living placidly in the country.

Arina Vlassyevna Bazarov—Yvgeny's mother, an old-fashioned gentlewoman, unintellectual and superstitious, but kind and motherly.

Matvey (Matthew) Ilich Kolyazin—A government official, a relative of the Kirsanovs. He is genial and self-important, not an original or clever man, but an able politician and administrator.

Viktor Sitnikov—A young man, a hanger-on and imitator of Bazarov.

Avdotya (Eudoxia) Nikitishna Kukshin—A well-to-do woman separated from her husband. She thinks of herself as an emancipated woman, reads European books, and studies chemistry.

Anna Sergeyevna Odintsov—A wealthy widow, loved by Bazarov. She has an open and unconventional mind, but no strong convictions or emotional attachments.

Katerina Sergeyevna Loktiv (Katya)—Younger sister of Mme. Odintsov, quieter and more conventional.

Princess K.—An elderly relation living with Mme. Odintsov, extremely ill-natured.

Father Alexei—The Bazarov's parish priest.

Piotr—Nikolai's dandified manservant.

The Story

The Kirsanovs are a family of Russian country gentry, rather more attractive than some of their class. Nikolai Petrovich is a well-intentioned man with views which were advanced in their time. His more old-fashioned neighbors still think of him as a radical. He has emancipated his serfs and now is struggling with the problems of collecting rent from his estate. A widower, he has taken the peasant girl Fenichka as his mistress, and refrains from marrying her only out of deference to the class prejudices of his brother, Pavel. Pavel is a retired army officer, now living with Nikolai. A burned-out love affair has left him without ambition or purpose. Arkady, Nikolai's son, is a cheerful, good-natured young man in his early twenties.

In May, 1859, Arkady, who has just graduated from the

university, returns to his father's estate, bringing with him his friend Bazarov, a brilliant young medical student under whose spell he has fallen. Bazarov is a nihilist; he reverences nothing and mocks at everything. He is impatient of any kind of sentiment, professes to have no illusions, ridicules all Russian social classes, and scoffs openly at everything old-fashioned. This unsettling guest stays for a long visit, affecting his hosts in various ways. Nikolai is bewildered, Pavel is affronted, and Arkady worships him; only Fenichka and the baby feel at ease with him.

During their stay, the two young men make trips to the nearby provincial capital where they meet a wealthy young widow, Anna Sergeyevna Odintsov, and her sister, Katya. Anna, who has a quick and unconventional mind, finds the young men diverting and invites them to visit. During their stay, Bazarov falls in love with Anna despite all his nihilist principles, but, though something of a flirt, Anna is the sort of woman who does not fall in love. She is alarmed at the violence of the passion she has aroused, and pulls back from the relationship. Arkady, who follows his friend in everything, at first imagines that he too is in love with Anna, but actually he is more drawn to Katya, whose tastes are closer to his own.

Arkady and Bazarov next visit Bazarov's parents, who live quietly in the country. The father is a retired army doctor and his wife a simple, old-fashioned woman. Both adore their son. During this visit, Arkady finds that the gap between his friend and himself is widening. He is not really a nihilist at heart, and he resents Bazarov's gibes at his Uncle Pavel. The two young men nearly come to blows, but decide instead to go back to the Kirsanov estate. There Bazarov consoles himself for the loss of Anna by flirting with Fenichka, Nikolai's mistress. Though nothing happens beyond a kiss more or less stolen by force, the scene is observed by Pavel, who challenges Bazarov to a duel. Bazarov is unhurt and Pavel only scratched. The two are more or less reconciled and invent a story to explain their disagreement.

During his convalescence, Pavel finds that the duel has stirred up powerful memories of the woman whose love he lost in his youth. He begs Nikolai not to risk losing a woman who truly loves him, and urges him to marry Fenichka. In the meantime, Arkady's love for Katya has matured. He proposes marriage and is promptly accepted. This step marks the final break with Bazarov and his nihilism. One feels that as Arkady grows older he will become much the same sort of man as his father: a conscientious landlord, an affectionate husband, and a good citizen, a man of enlightened views, but no revolutionary.

As for Bazarov, he says his farewells to Arkady and Anna and returns in a sulk to his native village where he settles down as his father's medical assistant. He is, however, bored and restless. One day, to occupy his mind, he undertakes an autopsy of a patient who has died of typhus. The dissecting knife slips and cuts his hand. A few days later he dies of the disease himself, bitterly but bravely. The story ends happily, however, for the Kirsanovs have a double wedding, and even Anna finds herself a husband whom she does not love, though someday she may. Pavel retires to Germany where he continues his empty life alone. The peaceful grass waves over the grave of the bitter and tormented Bazarov.

Critical Opinion

The plot of *Fathers and Sons* is simple and rather loosely put together. In fact, Turgenev's novels typically consist of memorable vignettes and character sketches, rather than carefully articulated plots. The story does involve two love affairs, a duel and a death, material which another author might have turned into something romantic or melodramatic, but here these exciting events are understated. The real theme is in the title: a confrontation between two generations, largely a matter of temperament and ideas, finding expression simply in talk.

The conflict is a familiar one. The older generation of the fathers is either frankly Tory, like Pavel, or timidly liberal, like Nikolai. The sons deride their elders as stick-in-the-muds and take pleasure in shocking them. Nikolai admits that there is nothing new in the situation; in his youth he too had reminded his parents that they belonged to a different generation. Now his own son is the rebel. The conflict ends predictably, however, for we feel sure that Arkady, once he has settled down with his rather conventional wife, will be the same sort of person in the context of his own times that his father was in his.

The great question mark is Bazarov. We cannot predict how he will turn out, and, since he dies young, we never know. Without doubt, he is Turgenev's most famous character. Most of Turgenev's men are neurotic cripples like Pavel, or gentle nonentities like Nikolai. But Bazarov is different, leaving his mark on everyone he meets, whether they hate him, like Pavel, worship him, like Arkady, or fight clear of him, like Anna. Although people always characterize him in terms of his opinions, it is really as a personality that he makes his mark. He is courageous in the face of death and severe in his judgments, especially with fools. In manner he is deliberately blunt and sarcastic. When at length he falls in love, it is not with the easy emotion of Arkady's wooing, but with a violent passion that makes his body tremble. Except for servants and children, everyone is in awe of him. When he dies, we know that Arkady and Katya, in their placid existence together, will always remember this strangely disturbing force that once touched their lives.

Bazarov is the first nihilist, or, to be more exact, the word was first made familiar by Turgenev's use of it in this book. Actually, the word appears as far back as 1836 to designate a philosophical skeptic who denies that anything exists. Turgenev uses nihilist to mean one who recognizes no established principles and takes no authorities for granted, however respected they may be. And so Bazarov scoffs at religion, at poetry (especially the romantic poet, Pushkin), at patriotism, at politicians (including liberal parliamentarians), at nature (which the romantic generation worshiped) and even at love, where it is a matter of sentiment and not of biology. There is, however, one general principle which he does recognize, and to which even his nihilism is secondary: "Our actions are governed by utility," he says. "In these days negation is the most useful thing of all—and so we deny." In other words, nihilism is simply the strategy which his utilitarianism demands in the present historical context. Alternatively, we might label him a nominalist (there is no such thing as science in general, he argues, only particular useful arts) or as a positivist (he believes that one chemist is worth thirty poets). Needless to say, positivism and utilitarianism are quite familiar to English-speaking readers, with the difference that the

English representatives of the school are usually academic people who lack Bazarov's flair for insult. Real Bazarovs are rare, but his imitators, like Arkady and Sitnikov, are a dime a dozen wherever undergraduates congregate. Presumably, they will continue to exist so long as their elders are pompous and intellectually lazy.

It is commonplace to remark that Turgenev's women are often more impressive than his men. There are several notable women in this novel, divided about evenly between the liberal intelligentsia and the authentic Russians, untouched by western ideas. Mme. Kukshin illustrates the intellectual woman at her most grotesque. She dabbles in chemistry, in architecture, and in American literature, preferring Emerson to George Sand. She is superficial, affected, nervous, unsatisfied. Mme. Odintsov, more original and intelligent, recognizes Bazarov's qualities better than anyone else, and is the only person in the book sufficiently unprejudiced and forthright to be a match for him. And yet, at the center of her personality, lies some neurotic scar which makes her incapable of serious attachments. Although she sometimes achieves serenity, she is never really happy.

At the other extreme is Bazarov's mother, "a genuine Russian gentlewoman of the old school; she might have lived some two centuries back, in the old days of Muscovy." Arina Vlassyevna believes in omens and spirits. At most she writes one or two letters a year, but she is kind to the servants, is charitable to beggars, and loves her son. A good woman, obviously, and Turgenev regrets that such people have become rare. Then there is the shy, delicate and lovely Fenichka, who is as authentically Russian as Arina. Her mute, self-effacing love is born of the Russian peasant's capacity for endless suffering.

These characters suggest the tension in Turgenev between the western and the Slavic ideals. Bazarov is a new kind of Russian, neither serf nor noble, but an independent spirit who promises to lift Russia out of her oriental lethargy. Fenichka is the opposite ideal, intuitive rather than intellectual, strong in her simplicity and in her closeness to the life of the people. Those critics who believe that there is in the Slavic soul a peculiar profundity lacking in the western European will find in Fenichka a heroine after their heart. When Turgenev created Bazarov, he wrote as a Westernizer; when he created Fenichka, he wrote as a Slavophile.

The Author

Ivan Sergeyevich Turgenev is, among the Russian authors of his generation, the most European in his orientation, the first to be admired in the West. He came from a family of well-to-do country gentry. His mother was an autocrat of the old school who treated her serfs with utter indifference to their humanity. Mme. Turgenev had had a miserable childhood and marriage, and in her bitterness she became a tyrant to everyone, including her own children. Ivan's education was a blessed escape, first to Moscow, then Saint Petersburg, and finally Berlin. He returned to Russia in 1841 at the age of twenty-three, held a civil service post for a time, and then turned to a literary career, despite his mother's disapproval. For some years until she died, he lived a somewhat bohemian life. Thereafter he was comfortably wealthy.

Turgenev never married. As a young man he, the man who was to be famous as the enemy of slavery, bought a serf girl from his cousin and installed her on the family estate as his mistress. He wearied of her after a year or so, but not before he had become the father of an illegitimate daughter whom he conscientiously educated and supported till her marriage. His greatest love, however, was for a singer, Pauline Garcia, later Mme. Viardot. Their relationship was quite Platonic (Turgenev could always satisfy his physical needs elsewhere). Mme. Viardot merely tolerated him and her husband found him no threat. Turgenev, nevertheless, remained infatuated with her, following her all over Europe. It was her attraction, quite as much as any native intellectual bent, that made him a cosmopolite. From 1856 till 1883 he lived in the West, and went home only for short visits.

Turgenev's first major book, written in the forties and published in 1852, was *Annals of a Sportsman,* a collection of sketches of country life. Despite the innocent title, the true theme was the relation of serf and master. Turgenev did not sentimentalize the peasants, but he treated them as human beings; that was revolutionary enough. Since emancipation of the serfs was imminent, the book had a strong topical interest. It was received as an important piece of social protest, and its influence has been compared to that of *Uncle Tom's*

Cabin. In fact, it is supposed to have influenced the Tsarevich, later Alexander II, in his determination to abolish serfdom. In the same year, Turgenev was imprisoned for a short time for his laudatory obituary of Nikolai Gogol, author of *Dead Souls;* his standing as an enemy of tyranny was thus confirmed by his own sacrifice.

Turgenev's next books again dealt with social themes. *Rudin* is a picture of a revolutionary, supposedly modeled on Michael Bakunin, whom Turgenev had known in Berlin. *A Nest of Gentlefolk* is set among the aristocracy; its chief character, Lavretsky, one of Turgenev's unheroic heroes, is an ineffectual man torn between the woman he has married and the woman he loves. Turgenev's greatest novel was *Fathers and Sons* whose hero, Bazarov, was modeled after a Russian doctor whom Turgenev had met in Germany in 1860. Nobody liked Bazarov. The conservatives found him subversive, and the radicals complained that they had been caricatured. One wonders just how Turgenev felt about his own hero. Intellectually, he is at one with Bazarov, but his instinctive sympathies were with the older generation.

The reception of *Fathers and Sons* reinforced Turgenev's determination to stay in Europe. Consequently, his later novels were attacked as retrospective and out of touch with current realities. In Europe, however, he was well received, especially among the realists: Flaubert, Edmond de Goncourt, Alphonse Daudet, and Émile Zola. The five used to dine together regularly and called their meals the "dinners of the hissed authors." On the other hand, Turgenev's relation with Dostoevski was impossibly bitter, while with Tolstoi he fought a duel.

Turgenev's last years were empty of major external adventure or incident. In 1867 there appeared *Smoke,* a study of a weak man in the grip of a fascinating woman. Ten years later came *Virgin Soil,* a picture of another ineffectual hero who aspires to be a popular leader, but who breaks himself against the inertia of the Russian peasant. This, too, was badly received in Russia. Turgenev continued to live mainly in France, with occasional trips home, a kindly old man with gout. Towards the end, critical hostility began to wane. When he died, he was hailed as one of Russia's very great writers. Turgenev lacks the epic sweep of Tolstoi or the passion of

Dostoevski. His novels are for the most part low-keyed portraits of a dying class. Nevertheless, many critics regard him as the greatest craftsman of the three.

Germinie Lacerteux

by

EDMOND LOUIS ANTOINE HUOT DE
GONCOURT (1822–1896)
JULES ALFRED HUOT DE GONCOURT
(1830–1870)

The Characters

Germinie Lacerteux—Servant to Mlle. de Varandeuil, a plain,
simple girl, devoted to her mistress. Her naturally affectionate nature leads her into a series of love affairs which
result in debt, drunkenness, degradation, and finally death.

Mlle. Sempronie de Varandeuil—An elderly spinster of a noble
family ruined by the Revolution. She is rough in manner
but kindly at heart, fond in her gruff way of her many
great-nephews and nieces, and deeply attached to Germinie.

Mère Jupillon—Proprietor of a dairy store and a friend of
Germinie, outwardly sentimental, inwardly selfish and
calculating.

Jupillon—Schoolboy son of Mère Jupillon, later Germinie's
lover. He is vulgar and self-centered and takes shameless
advantage of her.

Adèle—A servant living in the same building as Germinie.

Médéric Gautruche—A sign painter and for a time Germinie's
lover, lively and entertaining, but a spendthrift and a
drunkard.

The Story

Germinie Lacerteux is a peasant girl who comes to Paris
at the age of fourteen to earn her living. After various jobs,
in the course of which she is neglected, ill-treated, and on one
occasion assaulted, she finds refuge as maid-of-all-work to
Mlle. de Varandeuil, an elderly aristocrat living on a small income. Her mistress, despite her gruff manner, is kind to her,
and Germinie is devoted in return.

Germinie has a normal woman's capacity for love, but is
too plain to attract men. For a time she develops a sentimental
attachment for her confessor, until he realizes what is happening and puts her in the care of an older priest. Thereafter she
loses all interest in religion. She is fond of her niece, and
allows her sister and brother-in-law to take advantage of her
affection by extracting money from her. In particular, she is
fond of a schoolboy named Jupillon whose mother keeps a
dairy store. As Jupillon grows up, Germinie falls frantically in
love with him, making herself ridiculous by following him
to dance halls and taverns, though he is at least ten years
younger than she.

Jupillon, embarrassed, publicly humiliates her. She buys his
love by setting him up in business with money saved from her
earnings. He shows his gratitude by giving her an illegitimate
child, but will not marry her or support the baby. Finally
Mère Jupillon forces the two to separate, much to the relief of
the boy, who has taken up with a younger, prettier girl. When
the baby dies, Germinie loses her last hope for a normal, happy
life.

Thereafter her degradation proceeds rapidly. She allows
Jupillon to take two thousand francs from her, though she
knows that he does not love her and that she will be in debt
for the rest of her life. On another occasion, she steals money
for him from Mlle. de Varandeuil. A second pregnancy results
in a nearly fatal miscarriage. Though her mistress suspects
nothing, the neighbors subject her to daily insults which
destroy what is left of her self-respect. For a time she con-
templates suicide, then turns to heavy drinking. After Jupillon
leaves her, she takes another lover, a sign painter named
Gautruche who is more of an alcoholic than she. The relation-

ship has more in it of masochism than of love. She is not ashamed to spend half the night outside Gautruche's door waiting for him to come home. She finally breaks off when Gautruche proposes marriage, for this would involve leaving Mademoiselle, the only person ever to be kind to her.

Germinie is only forty-one when she dies, but she looks at least fifty. Prematurely worn out by her debauchery, she succumbs to pleurisy and an ulcerated lung. Mlle. de Varandeuil is grief-stricken when she realizes that she has outlived every person whom she has ever loved, even Germinie. But her sorrow turns to disillusionment after the funeral as one by one the tradesmen of the neighborhood come to collect Germinie's unpaid debts. Soon the whole truth is out. At first Mlle. de Varandeuil is furious. Then her anger gives way to pity for Germinie's suffering. She goes to Montmartre, the cemetery where Germinie has been buried in a common pit, and finds that there is not even a cross over the grave, only markers to indicate the burials for each day of the month. "What must be left of Germinie must be about there . . . to pray over her, one must pray at random between two dates."

Critical Opinion

When critics protested against the sordid and depressing theme of *Germinie Lacerteux*, the authors had an unanswerable defense: every word of it is true. The Goncourt brothers actually had a servant, Rose Malingre, who had watched over them from childhood with the gruff tenderness of an old watchdog and who had tyrannized over them with the assurance of a trusted servant who is too much of a friend ever to be dismissed. In 1862 she fell ill and was taken to the country for a change of scene; instead of improving she began to develop unmistakable signs of tuberculosis. When she was brought back to Paris, the doctors gave her only a few weeks to live, and her whole mind and character were crumbling as fast as her body. Jules took her to the hospital in a cab, and then broke down in tears. A few days later she was buried in a common grave at Montmartre. After the funeral, Jules's mistress, a midwife named Maria, told the brothers facts which her professional ethics had till then obliged her to keep secret: that Rose had had two children, one of whom had lived for six months, that she had taken the son of a dairy woman as a lover and set him up in rooms at her own expense, that she had run into debt and stolen from her masters, and that she had contracted pleurisy from watching in the rain outside her lover's apartment to see what other women he brought there. The brothers were naturally shocked, but at the same time delighted. Here was material for a book. And so the whole pitiable story was set down, except that for themselves as Rose's employers they substituted a cousin, Cornélie le Bas de Courmont, and Rose's lover, actually a boxer, became a glove-maker. Maria's professional experience provided them with information about childbirth and puerperal fever. For the final scene, Jules did a watercolor of Rose's grave which they kept by them as they wrote.

This reportorial technique undoubtedly accounts for the organization of the story, in which clinical details accumulate as a series of short vignettes, in chapters of one or two pages each, and are never organized into extended scenes. The conversations rarely go beyond a few exchanges: scraps of dialogue overheard, trailing away or interrupted by rows of dots. The only passages of extended narration are the two flashbacks at the very start of the book, one telling of Germinie's early life and the other her mistress's. Structurally they are the least satisfactory part of the book, being rather contrived and awkwardly introduced.

In his self-centered way, Edmond later imagined that he and his brother had invented naturalism. Actually, it is fairer to see these two on a line of development that runs from Flaubert to Zola. We can assess their contribution by comparing them with the other two. *Germinie Lacerteux* irresistibly invites comparison with Flaubert's novella, "A Simple Heart" ("Un Coeur Simple"). This, too, tells the story of an old and trusted servant, Félicité, who lives in a small Norman town. Here we have the same mute loyalty to a gruff mistress, the same themes of religious devotion and of love conferred on a succession of insensitive or unworthy objects, the same accumulation of minute detail, ending in a clinical description of the last illness. Flaubert, however, uses more of the traditional craft of the novelist and pays more attention to organization and conventional plotting. Details, for instance, are introduced early in the story which prepare the way for events that happen much later, and the transitions from one episode to another are meticulously managed. *Germinie Lacerteux* advances by a nervous succession of scenes which usually begin and end abruptly. The chief difference, however, lies in the author's attitude toward the principal character. Félicité is a household drudge who never does anything that gets her talked about: she is not promiscuous, does not drink, and never steals. Flaubert was able to find her interesting despite or even because of her dullness, whereas the Goncourt brothers never saw Rose as a subject worthy of their art so long as they supposed she was a woman like Félicité; she did not become interesting until she could be seen as a pathological specimen. Both authors adopt a detached, objective manner, but beneath it one senses Flaubert's sympathy and compassion; one finds none in the Goncourts. The one episode which vibrates with real feeling is the scene in which Mlle. de Varandeuil leaves Germinie at the hospital and then breaks down in tears in the cab. As we have noted, the tears were Jules's own, the emotion authentic.

The novels of Zola, such as *L'Assommoir* or *Germinal,* are characterized by the same interest in factual detail, the same preoccupation with poverty and degradation, the same sense of fatality. We note without regret the absence of Zola's pretentious theories about heredity and the organic causes of vice. We miss Zola's powerfully poetic imagination, which could endow a mine shaft or a waterwheel or a public market with independent life and personality. The Goncourts, like Zola, are careful to establish the social milieu of their characters, but draw no conclusions about the facts they describe. Unlike him, they have no interest in social reform. Zola's propagandism is undoubtedly an artistic blemish, but at least it suggests that the author cared for something besides himself. In avoiding social preachments, the Goncourts practiced a more austere art, but the impression they leave is simply one of fastidious distaste for petty shopkeepers, workmen, and poor people generally.

At times we feel that Germinie submits so abjectly to her fate that she never becomes a well-defined human being. The most sharply outlined figure in the book is actually her employer, Mlle. de Varandeuil, a woman whose character has been shaped by misfortune quite as much as Germinie's. Used as a character in another story, she could have been either tragic or comic. Germinie, on the other hand, is merely pathetic. As we watch her sink ever deeper into the mire, we feel sorry for her and for Mademoiselle, but that is all. There is no illumination, no catharsis, only an oppressive sense of doom. We feel it was too bad that it all happened, but then, it couldn't have been helped.

The Authors

The story of the Goncourt brothers is almost solely the story of their books and opinions; it is singularly lacking in dramatic action. Edmond and Jules were born in 1822 and 1830, respectively, the sons of a retired army officer from Lorraine. Though not aristocrats in their own right, they had aristocratic connections and they clung with passionate insistence to the prefix *de* in their name, the sign of nobility. They grew up in Paris, were educated there, and remained confirmed Parisians all their lives. At one point, Edmond studied law, but without enthusiasm. In 1848, the death of their mother left them with a modest income, large enough to give them leisure to indulge their interests and spend their time writing.

Successful literary collaboration is not easy. Between brothers it is almost unheard of. The Goncourts are, with the brothers Grimm, the most notable instance. They lived together, shared the same tastes, pursued the same hobbies, worked on the same books, kept one diary, and developed a shared personality, so that they might almost be regarded as one author in two bodies. They are treated as such in all the literary histories. It is hard to know exactly what each brother contributed, but one may guess by comparing their joint work with the books which Edmond wrote alone. Apparently Edmond was the scholar and organizer, while Jules, younger and livelier, was the imaginative stylist. Jules thought of himself as more "Latin" in temper, and of Edmond as more Teutonic.

The Goncourts claimed for themselves three major achievements: to have rediscovered the eighteenth century and made it fashionable in the world of taste, to have done the same for Japanese art, and to have been the founders of naturalism. All three claims must be viewed with some qualification, but they do indicate where the Goncourts' interests lay. Their fondness for the eighteenth century, beginning with their collections of old books, prints, and bibelots, bore fruit in a series of books on the period: *Art of the Eighteenth Century (L'Art du dix-huitième Siècle*, 1859-1875), *History of French Society During the Revolution (Historie de la Société française pendant la Révolution*, 1854), *Intimate Portraits of the Eighteenth Century (Portraits intimes du dix-huitième Siècle*, 1857–1858), *The Woman of the Eighteenth Century (La Femme au dix-huitième Siècle*, 1862), and others. These go beyond the usual histories of the time in the fullness with which they re-construct the life of the period, even restaurant menus being used for documentation.

The Goncourts' interest in Japan went back to the 1850's, when oriental art was imperfectly known and collecting diffi-cult. Their contribution was necessarily one of appreciation rather than scholarship. They were enthusiastic collectors themselves, and, toward the end of his life, Edmond wrote studies of Utamaro (1891) and Hokusai (1896).

The Goncourts' naturalistic writing would seem at first glance to harmonize badly with their fastidious aestheticism in other matters. It was, however, a natural outgrowth of their interest in the minutiae of experience, their reportorial love of detail accurately presented. For them, the supreme value in a novel was its fidelity to actual life, and if that truth offended the sensibilities of the middle-class reader, so much the better. Their principal novels in this vein were *Charles Demailly* (1860), a picture of a writer persecuted by his colleagues and deceived by his wife; *Soeur Philomène* (1861), a story about nursing; *Renée Mauperin* (1864), based on the life of a child-hood playmate; *Germinie Lacerteux* (1864); *Nanette Salomon* (1867), a picture of artistic and bohemian life, with an anti-Semitic bias; and *Madame Gervaisais* (1869), a portrait of their aunt. Several of these were made into plays, with indif-ferent success.

As sometimes happens with bachelors, the Goncourts' lives became increasingly self-centered and detached from other people. Love in the ordinary sense of the word never touched them, since it would have threatened their relationship, under-mined their egotism, and interfered with their writing. When necessary they took mistresses, sometimes the same one, but they never allowed themselves to become too deeply involved. Toward other writers they adopted a tone of systematic denigration, and filled their journals with waspish comments about their contemporaries. Sainte-Beuve in their eyes was cowardly, Gautier boorish, Flaubert pigheaded, Taine fatuous, Renan insufficiently patriotic, and Baudelaire a bourgeois who spent his life trying to acquire the elegant distinction of being thought mad. As for Shakespeare, he lacked imagination. The ordinary business of daily living was a torment to them. Their pages are full of petulant complaints about crying babies, noisy church bells, and a neighbor who inconsiderately died—this last being described as one of their many "pinpricks." This morbid sensitivity they ascribed to their constant and nervous preoccupation with their art. It was the cross which as geniuses they were obliged to bear.

In 1870, Jules died. For some months, his mind had been deteriorating. First he developed a morbid intolerance of noise, then lapses of memory, finally incoherence and delirium. Edmond ascribed his brother's death to his relentless effort to cultivate a carefully wrought style and impeccable literary form, and to his sensitivity—so necessary to a writer—which made him vulnerable to the most trifling irritations. Jules's own entry in the journal tells us what was really wrong. It was syphilis.

Edmond continued to live for another quarter century, and wrote four novels by himself: *La Fille Élisa* (1875), a study of prostitution; *The Zemganno Brothers (Les Frères Zemganno,* 1879), the story of two acrobats whose brotherly affection recalls the Goncourts' own; *La Faustin* (1882), on the life of the actress Rachel; and *Chérie* (1884), based on a personal and confidential story told him by a young girl of his acquaintance. He left his entire fortune to establish an academy of ten authors and to endow a prize bearing his name. Today it is a highly coveted honor for French authors. The journal, the first volumes of which appeared during Edmond's life, was finally published in full in 1959 and provides an invaluable eyewitness account of the French literary scene during the later nineteenth century.

Crime and Punishment

by

FYODOR MIKHAILOVICH DOSTOEVSKI
(1821–1881)

The Characters *

Rodion Romanovich Raskolnikov (Rodya)—The hero, an
ex-student without means, who dreams of proving that he
is superior to the ordinary run of humanity, a generous
person, but moody and morbidly excitable.

Pulcheria Alexandrovna Raskolnikov—Rodion's mother, a
widow living on a small pension.

Avdotya Romanovna Raskolnikov (Dounia)—Rodion's sister,
an intelligent and spirited girl, engaged to Luzhin.

Piotr Petrovich Luzhin—Dounia's fiancé, a pompous, self-
centered, self-made man.

Arkady Ivanovich Svidrigaïlov—Formerly Dounia's employer,
an unprincipled sensualist and probably a murderer, coldly
purposeful, strong-willed, without hypocrisy or illusions.

Marfa Petrovna Svidrigaïlov—His deceased wife.

Dmitri Prokofich Razumihin—A friend of Rodion, a generous
and impulsive young man.

Semyon Zaharovich Marmeladov—An unemployed government clerk, a drunkard and a masochist.

---

* See Note on Russian Names, p. 173.

Katerina Ivanovna Marmeladov—His wife, an irritable consumptive, tormented by memories of the social position she has lost.

Sofya Semyonovna Marmeladov (Sonia)—His daughter, a saintly, long-suffering girl who turns to prostitution to support her family.

Polenka, Lida and Kolya—Children of Katerina Ivanovna.

Alonya Ivanovna—A grasping old pawnbroker.

Lizaveta Ivanovna—Her pious, simpleminded half-sister.

Porfiry Petrovich—A police investigator with a flair for psychology.

Zametov—A head clerk in the police department.

Nikodim Fomich—District superintendent of police, nicknamed "the explosive lieutenant."

Lebetzniakov—A friend of Luzhin, an emptyheaded liberal.

Amalia Ivanovna Lippewechsel—The quarrelsome German landlady of the Marmeladovs.

Kapernaumov—Sonia's landlord, a tailor with a cleft palate.

Praskovya Pavlovna—Rodion's landlady.

Nastasya—A servant of Praskovya Pavlovna.

Ilya Petrovich—Assistant clerk at the police station.

Zossimov—A young doctor, Razumihin's friend.

Natalya Yegorovna—Daughter of Praskovya Pavlovna, now deceased, Rodion's former fiancée.

Koch and Pestryakov—The men who discover the murder of Alyona Ivanovna.

Nikolai—A painter who confesses to Rodion's crime.

The Story

Rodion Romanovich Raskolnikov, a poor young law student in Saint Petersburg in the 1860's, has stopped attending classes. His mind is in a ferment with new and unconventional ideas filtering into Russia from the West. He believes that men are divided into two classes: the ordinary herd, for whose guidance moral laws have been devised, and the exceptional men, like Caesar or Napoleon, who make their own laws. To find out if he is one of the exceptional few, he proposes to kill someone, preferably a worthless or hateful person whose death would harm nobody. He chooses as his victim an old pawnbroker named Alonya Ivanovna. Since she is reputedly rich, the crime will have the double advantage of relieving Rodion's poverty. After much tortured debate with himself, he goes to the woman's apartment and brutally murders her with an axe. At this moment Alonya's half-sister, an inoffensive woman who lives with her, unexpectedly returns to the room. Rodion is obliged to kill her, too. Losing his head completely, and forgetting to look for any money, he grabs a few trinkets that customers have left in pawn, and manages, more by luck than anything else, to escape unnoticed.

Rodion's crime affects the lives of others, since he has friends and family. First, there is his mother, a gentle and affectionate woman who sends him money when she can. His sister, Dounia, has been serving as governess for the children of a man named Svidrigaïlov. When her employer made improper advances to her, she left him and is now engaged to a self-important bourgeois named Luzhin. Rodion, realizing that Dounia is making a mercenary marriage in order to help him financially and professionally, opposes the match. A third woman in his life is Sonia, the daughter of an unemployed clerk named Marmeladov, whom Rodion has casually met and befriended. The family are desperately poor because of Marmeladov's improvidence and drunkenness. Sonia has turned to prostitution to support them. When Marmeladov is accidentally killed, Rodion gives the family money and tries to help them. Last but not least, Rodion has a good friend in a fellow student named Razumihin.

By the time Rodion has hidden his loot and concealed the other evidence, he is almost out of his mind with emotional strain. The pressure grows even greater when he is summoned to the police station to answer a complaint about a bad debt. He swoons in the presence of the officers and is carried to his room, where Razumihin tends him through several days of fever and delirium. Rodion's nervousness nearly betrays him as he listens to his friends discuss the murder by his bedside. Under a strong compulsion to confess, he all but admits the crime to a police clerk, and he attracts attention to himself by visiting the scene of the murder and behaving in an agitated fashion. He also returns to the police to claim a watch which he had pawned with the old woman. While there, he is interviewed by the police inspector at work on the case, Porfiry Petrovich, who approaches the problem psychologically and whose shrewd insights direct his suspicions toward Rodion.

Meanwhile, Rodion's mother and sister have arrived in the capital in preparation for Dounia's wedding to Luzhin. Rodion promptly quarrels with his prospective brother-in-law, and Luzhin, in return, acts with such pompous arrogance that Dounia dismisses him. Dounia's former admirer, Svidrigaïlov, also appears in town. His wife has died under suspicious circumstances and he wishes to take up with Dounia. He is prepared to offer her ten thousand rubles, but Rodion and his sister see grave danger in any connection with so unscrupulous a man. Fortunately, Dounia and Razumihin are by now falling in love, and their relation ripens into a normal youthful romance.

Rodion is now obliged to go to the police again to pick up his pawned watch, for if he fails to do so he clearly invites suspicion. Porfiry Petrovich, acting on a report of Rodion's behavior when he visited the pawnbroker's apartment after the crime, interrogates him again, playing cat and mouse with him and driving him to the edge of distraction. The interview is unexpectedly broken up when the house painter Nikolai, who had been in the apartment house at the time of the murder, suddenly appears and confesses to the crime. Rodion has had an unexpected reprieve, but the urge to confess is now so strong that he goes to Sonia and tells her the whole story.

Despite her occupation, Sonia is a deeply religious woman. Instead of shrinking from Rodion, she pities him, at the same time urging him to confess his crime and assume the burden of expiatory suffering. Soon after, Porfiry Petrovich approaches Rodion with the same suggestion. The painter Nikolai is innocent, Porfiry explains, but he is a religious fanatic who believes that the sins of the world can be wiped out by voluntary vicarious suffering. He has made a false confession so that he may suffer after the model of Christ's atonement. But the evidence still points to Rodion. Rodion is shaken still further to learn that Svidrigaïlov has also discovered his secret. He occupies the apartment next to Sonia and was listening during the confession.

Svidrigaïlov intends to use this information, not to hurt Rodion, but to blackmail Dounia into accepting him as a lover. If she will consent, he tells her, he will help Rodion escape the country. In a tense scene, Dounia defends herself with a revolver; the bullet only grazes Svidrigaïlov and she cannot bring herself to fire another. Svidrigaïlov realizes that he will never win her consent. Taking the revolver from her, he leaves the room and shoots himself.

At length, driven more by moral and psychological pressures than by external threats, Rodion goes to the police station and confesses his crime. He is sentenced to Siberia, where Sonia accompanies him to wait for his release. Although Rodion is not yet truly penitent for the murder, we are given to understand that with Sonia's influence he will eventually achieve genuine contrition and religious conversion.

Critical Opinion

Rodion Raskolnikov has been called the Russian Faust. Both men are poor students, but proud and ambitious. Both are tempted by pride of intellect to commit sins. Both fail to find the happiness they seek, and both are redeemed by the love of a devout woman. In each instance, the goal of the hero's ambition is undefined, even in his own mind. Rodion's motives are extremely confused. At first Dostoevski seems to have envisioned the problem in these terms: If a man can, by the murder of a worthless human being, achieve a great and undeniable good, is the crime justified? The problem is stated in these terms in Chapter 6, Part I, and Rodion justifies the act to himself by arguing that the money he will steal from Alonya Ivanovna will save his sister from a hateful and mercenary marriage. Since, however, he does not become a penny richer despite his crime, it would seem that money was not his real motive. Later another theory is introduced. We learn that Rodion has written a magazine article arguing that for certain exceptional men ordinary morality does not obtain. They live by their own laws. Rodion defends this thesis in conversation with Porfiry Petrovich, yet it is already clear, even to himself, that he is not one of the exceptional men of whom he dreams. There is nothing especially Napoleonic about killing two defenseless women. Furthermore, if he really had been a superman, he would have acted without debating the matter with himself, and he would certainly not have felt an urge to confess afterward. In the end, Rodion is reduced to claiming that he killed Alonya Ivanovna only to prove that he had the right to do so. In short, he gives the impression of being driven by forces of which he is incompletely aware. One senses that in killing the pawnbroker he is trying to kill something within himself, the weak and submissive side of his personality of which he is ashamed.

The battle in Raskolnikov's soul is symbolized by three figures. The first is Porfiry Petrovich, who stands for the law. No vulgar policeman or sleuth out of a detective story, he is rather fond of his victim and honestly concerned for him. Still, a crime has been committed, and it is Porfiry's business to see that justice is done. The second figure is Svidrigaïlov, who is the resolute amoralist that Raskolnikov would like to be. Although a sensualist and probably a murderer, he is not wholly evil; he is intellectually honest and capable of occasional acts of benevolence. His virtues, however, are not at war with his vices, as are Raskolnikov's. Both are an expression of one undivided and inflexible will. Finally there is Sonia who represents the divine grace that transcends morality. These three contend for Raskolnikov's soul like the good and bad angels in a medieval morality play. In the end Sonia appears to be winning, though not yet completely.

Raskolnikov's situation may also be analyzed as a battle between reason and feeling, if we bear in mind that Dostoevski believed rationalism was evil and more harmful to human love than hate itself. At the start of the novel, Raskolnikov is an intellectual in the grasp of an obsessive idea. At the end, his eventual reformation is understood to depend on his being able to forget ideas, so that life will replace theory. All the evil or contemptible people in the book are rationalists in one way or another: the sinister Svidrigaïlov, the practical Luzhin, and the silly Lebetzniakov, while the admirable figures are chiefly moved by feeling: Pulcheria, Dounia, Razumihin and Sonia.

The reader will be struck by Dostoevski's insistence on suffering as the only way to salvation. To the unreligious man, this emphasis may seem morbid. Dostoevski was led to this belief partly by his experience as a convict, but also by the piety of the Russian Orthodox Church, which has always laid great stress on suffering and humiliation, not as a way for a criminal to pay a debt to society, but as a way for a Christian to imitate Christ.

The theological name for this voluntary abasement is kenosis (literally, "emptying"), and it is most strikingly illustrated

in the novel by the painter Nikolai, who makes a false confession simply so that he may suffer. Significantly, Nikolai is
an Old Believer, the member of a sect, the Raskolniki, with
the same name as Rodion's. Sonia's own kenosis is prostitution, which in her is not a sin, but an illustration of Paul's
statement in the Epistle to the Philippians that everyone who
humbles himself will be exalted. Even so grotesque a figure
as Marmeladov, who is undoubtedly a masochist, also experiences his kenosis, and when he exclaims that he wishes
to be crucified, he too identifies himself with Christ. He is
thus closer to salvation, with all his sins, than his proud,
quarrelsome wife, despite her efforts to maintain her good
name. The reader must try to understand these characters,
not from the perspective of Protestant individualism, in which
each man stands naked and alone before his God, but from
the standpoint of Orthodox piety, which conceives of the
church as a mystical community of salvation in which each
man must bear the sins of all.

If the reader cannot accept Dostoevski's theology, he must
nevertheless respect his psychology. At a time when most academic psychologists were trying to understand the mind in
purely physical terms, Dostoevski understood it as the seat of
emotional forces and unconscious conflicts. His characters are
often abnormal, even grotesque, but they are convincing.

Crime and Punishment is so impressive a book that it
seems petty to point out its occasional weaknesses. The most
serious flaw is its excessive dependence upon chance; for instance, that Svidrigaïlov should live next to Sonia and Luzhin
in the same building as Marmeladov seems highly improbable. Some scenes are sheer melodrama, such as the episode
in which Luzhin accuses Sonia of stealing, or the interview
between Dounia and Svidrigaïlov. Svidrigaïlov himself is a
mystery and his suicide is never properly explained. It cannot be simply a matter of frustrated sensuality, for he can
always find women. Presumably it is meant to demonstrate the
bankruptcy of his self-willed amorality, but the point is not
made clear. And finally the epilogue, with its loose ends and
the fresh questions which it raises at the last moment, vio-
lates the unity of structure which has been maintained up to
that point. But the reader can disregard these blemishes.
Crime and Punishment is indisputably a masterpiece.

The Brothers Karamazov

by

FYODOR MIKHAILOVICH DOSTOEVSKI

The Characters *

Fyodor Pavlovich Karamazov—A provincial landowner, a coarse sensualist and a buffoon.

Adelaida Ivanovna Miüsov—First wife of Fyodor Pavlovich, an heiress.

Sofya Ivanovna—Second wife of Fyodor Pavlovich, a helpless and innocent girl who dies insane.

Dmitri Fyodorovich Karamazov (Mitya)—Son of Fyodor Pavlovich by Adelaida Ivanovna, a passionate, unstable man.

Ivan Fyodorovich Karamazov—Elder son of Sofya Ivanovna, a restless intellectual.

Alexey Fyodorovich Karamazov (Alyosha)—Younger son of Sofya Ivanovna, a kindly, gentle and devout boy of twenty.

Grigory Vassilyevich—A loyal old servant of the Karamazov family.

Marfa Ignatyevna—Grigory's wife.

Lizaveta Smerdyastchaya—A half-witted girl.

Pavel Fyodorovich Smerdyakov—Illegitimate son of Lizaveta, possibly the son of Fyodor Pavlovich and now his valet. He is a shallow, insolent person, also an epileptic.

Yefim Petrovich Polenov—A benefactor of the Karamazov children, who pays for their education.

° See Note on Russian Names, p. 173.

Piotr Alexandrovich Miüsov—A cousin of Adelaida Ivanovna.

Piotr Fomich Kalganov—An idle young man, related to Miüsov.

Maximov—An elderly landowner.

Father Zossima—Elder of the local monastery, famous for his spiritual counsel.

Father Païssy—A monk, Alyosha's spiritual director after the death of Father Zossima.

Father Ferapont—A crazy, fanatical ascetic.

Mihail Ospovich Rakitin—A theological student, a malicious opportunist.

Mme. Hohlakov—A scatterbrained, middle-aged widow.

Lise Hohlakov—Mme. Hohlakov's crippled daughter, a mischievous, neurotic and willful girl.

Katerina Ivanovna—Dmitri's fiancée, a proud, handsome, theatrical, possessive woman.

Agafya Ivanovna—Her sister.

Kuzma Kuzmich Samsonov—A clever, grasping old merchant.

Agrafena Alexandrovna Svyetlov (Grushenka)—Mistress of the merchant Samsonov, loved by Dmitri.

Fenya—Grushenka's servant.

Nikolai Ilyich Snegiryov—A discharged officer, burdened by an invalid family.

Arina Petrovna—Snegiryov's insane wife.

Ilyusha—Snegiryov's young son, a passionate, defiant boy, devoted to his father and bullied by his schoolmates.

Nina and Varvara—Daughters of Snegiryov.

Nikolai Ivanovich Krassotkin (Kolya)—A good-natured, daredevil schoolboy of thirteen.

Anna Fyodorovna Krassotkin—His doting mother.

Smurov—A schoolboy.

Marya Kondratyevna—A neighbor of Karamazov.

Gorstkin (Lyagavy)—A peasant trader of Volovya.

Pyotr Ilyich Perhotin—A young official.

Trifon Borissovich—Innkeeper at Mokroe.

Mussyalovich—Grushenka's Polish lover, a venal swindler.

Vrublevsky—Companion of Mussyalovich.

Mihail Makarovich Makarov—Captain of police, an old-fashioned officer.

Mavriky Mavrikyevich Schmertsov—Inspector of police.

Nikolai Parvenovich Nelyudov—Investigating lawyer.

Ippolit Kirillovich—Deputy prosecutor, an able and ambitious man, consumptive.
Fetyukovich—Dmitri's lawyer from Moscow.
Dr. Herzenstube—A conscientious, mediocre physician.
Dr. Varvinsky—District medical officer.

The Story

Fyodor Pavlovich Karamazov is a landowner in a small provincial Russian town shortly after the liberation of the serfs. Though nominally a gentleman, and fairly well off, Karamazov lives on the fringes of respectable society which he scandalizes by his disorderly life, his flagrant sensuality, and his idiotic buffoonery. He is twice a widower. His first wife deserted him, leaving a son, Dmitri, now twenty-seven; and his second wife died of abuse, after bearing two children, Ivan, now twenty-four, and Alexey, or Alyosha, who is twenty. All the children were neglected and raised by servants and relatives. In addition, Karamazov is thought to have seduced or raped the village half-wit and to have had by her a fourth son, Pavel, surnamed Smerdyakov or "Stinky." Smerdyakov is now his father's valet and cook. These four young men are utterly different. Dmitri is an ex-army officer with a taste for dissolute living which he inherits from his father. He is as careless of money as his father is grasping, and constantly in debt. In exchange for paying Dmitri's bills, Karamazov has forced his son to renounce all further claims on the estate. The second son, Ivan, an intellectual living in Moscow, has cut loose from his roots in Orthodox Christianity without finding any other spiritual home. Alyosha, on the other hand, is religious. A gentle, affectionate, healthy, good-looking boy, he has become a novice at the local monastery. Smerdyakov, though he is a capable servant, is resentful of his position. He is ambitious and sly, fawning and insolent by turns, and an epileptic.

In the monastery Alyosha comes under the influence of his spiritual director, Father Zossima, a monk famous for his sanctity. Since ill will is running high between Dmitri and his father, the elder Karamazov suggests that the entire family consult Zossima to seek a reconciliation. Alyosha fears some joke but arranges the interview. His worst fears are realized.

Karamazov behaves like a clown, quarrels with his sons, is impertinent to the monks, and embarrasses everyone. Fortunately, the monk is not offended, only deeply concerned for the welfare of his guests. He gives some brief but searching advice to Karamazov and Ivan. To Dmitri he says nothing but only makes a low bow in recognition, as he later explains, of the terrible suffering which he foresees that Dmitri must undergo. Alyosha he commands to leave the monastery and enter the world, where humanity and more especially his brothers will need him.

Dmitri at this time is involved in a complicated love affair. A while before, as a young officer, he was attracted to Katerina Ivanovna, the handsome and proud daughter of a colonel. Her father, he discovers, has embezzled regimental funds and is threatened with disgrace if the money is not returned. Dmitri proposes to make good the debt in exchange for Katerina's favors, an insulting offer which he makes only to humiliate a woman who has hitherto ignored him. Katya, out of loyalty to her father, agrees to make the sacrifice, but Dmitri, whose more honorable side is now aroused to generosity, makes her an outright gift of the necessary money, four thousand rubles. Katerina, who loves dramatic situations in which she can suffer conspicuously, now feels obligated to Dmitri and is convinced she loves him. The two become precariously engaged.

Dmitri, however, is unstable and sensual. He has scarcely become engaged when he becomes infatuated with Grushenka, a young girl kept by an old merchant, Samsonov. When Katerina entrusts Dmitri with three thousand rubles to be sent by post to her sister in Moscow, Dmitri steals the money and squanders most of it in three days with Grushenka. He is now almost penniless. He cannot leave Katerina, to whom he is bound by his debt, nor can he marry Grushenka, who is not likely to marry a pauper. To make matters worse, old Karamazov is also interested in Grushenka, and is trying to bribe her away from Samsonov with the very money which Dmitri regards as his rightful share of the estate. Meanwhile, Katerina and Ivan are seriously attracted to each other. Dmitri is pleased by this development which will free him from his engagement, but Katerina is grimly resolved to sacrifice her life to Dmitri's rehabilitation, and will not encourage another lover.

Smerdyakov, who has been biding his time, now comes to Ivan with a shocking proposal made, however, so obliquely that Ivan can if he chooses fail to understand its tenor. Dmitri, Smerdyakov explains, is in a state of mind in which he could easily kill his father. Old Karamazov fears this, and barricades himself in the house at night. He will open the door only if he hears a secret knock, known only to Smerdyakov, which is to announce the arrival of Grushenka. But Smerdyakov has betrayed the signal to Dmitri, who can thus enter when he chooses. If necessary, Smerdyakov can feign an epileptic fit, so that no one will suspect his complicity, and Ivan can leave the coast clear by going out of town. Furthermore, if Karamazov lives to marry Grushenka, the children will inherit nothing, whereas if he dies soon he dies intestate. The sons will be his heirs . . . and so forth. Ivan rushes from the room in a frenzy of horror and revulsion and, washing his hands of the whole business, leaves for Moscow. He has, however, thus opened the way for the very tragedy which Smerdyakov has outlined, so that the latter can hardly be blamed for drawing his own conclusions. Obviously, if Karamazov dies, Ivan will get a third of the estate, while, if Dmitri is sent to Siberia, Ivan will get half and be free to marry Katerina as well.

Dmitri's soul is now a whirlpool of anger, guilt, and frustrated desire. Above all else, he must restore Katerina's money so that he may leave her and marry Grushenka before his father gets her. He tries frantically to borrow the money, but to no avail. Going to Grushenka's house, he finds her not at home and suspects that she has already stolen away to his father. Grabbing a small brass pestle from the kitchen, he dashes off to his father's house and steals into the garden. Here he is surprised by an old servant, Grigory. They grapple and Dmitri strikes down the old man with a blow of the pestle. Covered with blood, he makes his way back to Grushenka's house only to find that she has gone off with another man—a Pole who had seduced her five years before and deserted her. Now he has returned and she is ready to come at his call.

Dmitri catches up with Grushenka at a nearby village. The Polish lover proves to be only a petty card sharp who can be bought off. Dmitri gives him money to leave. He and Grushenka then begin a wild bout of festivity, calling in dancers and musicians and treating all the peasants lavishly. This fact is later used against Dmitri who, only a few hours before, was generally supposed to be penniless. Nor does Dostoevski tell us at this point where Dmitri has gotten the money. While the feasting is at its height, the police break in to arrest Dmitri. His father has been killed and three thousand rubles have been stolen.

After interrogation, during which he makes a poor impression because of his wild language, Dmitri is put on trial. The prosecution is able to make a convincing case, since Grigory's testimony puts him at the scene of the crime, and since Dmitri's sudden and lavish expenditure of money can be accounted for only by the theft. Dmitri explains that although he had taken three thousand rubles from Katerina, he had not spent it all. He had kept back half, hoping he would someday have courage to make full restitution, and it was this money that the witnesses had seen in his possession after the crime. He is obstinate in insisting that he did not kill his father.

While the trial is in progress, Ivan has several interviews with Smerdyakov. The valet, in a tone of insolent familiarity, admits that he is the murderer, and that he acted on what he assumed to be Ivan's tacit instructions. Though Ivan did not strike the blow, he is an accessory to the crime, and stands to benefit by it. For his part, Smerdyakov plans to use the money he has stolen, plus what he can get from Ivan by blackmail, to go to Moscow and open a restaurant. Ivan, in horror, declares that he will tell the truth in court and denounce Smerdyakov. He then returns to his rooms in a state approaching delirium. The following day he gives his testimony, but nobody believes him. In his speech he seems obviously close to insanity. Smerdyakov cannot be subpoenaed, for he has hanged himself.

The denouement comes with the concluding speeches of prosecution and defense, followed by a verdict of guilty and a sentence to Siberia. There is a final scene of reconciliation with Katerina and parting with Grushenka. Ivan and Katerina propose to arrange an escape, and have collected a large sum of bribe money for the purpose, but Dmitri refuses. Though he is wrongly convicted, he is a sinner nonetheless and will accept his sentence as a necessary atonement for his other misdeeds.

In addition to the main story, there are several subordinate plot lines, all relating to Alyosha. One involves a crippled girl named Lise to whom Alyosha is for a time engaged. Another, so extensive as to be almost a novel within a novel, gives the history of Father Zossima and the circumstances which led to his becoming a monk. Still another relates to a cashiered army officer named Snegiryov whom Dmitri insults and whom Alyosha in his kindness attempts to help. Snegiryov has a son named Ilyusha (Ilya), whom Alyosha befriends. Ilyusha's death, surrounded by his weeping family and a band of loyal schoolmates, gives Alyosha an opportunity to declare his faith in the resurrection of the body, and thus to close the novel on an affirmative note.

Critical Opinion

The Brothers Karamazov is the product of the religious fervor of Dostoevski's last years. It is a long book, full of digressions, as if the author, sensing that his days were numbered, had sought to cram into it everything that still remained for him to say. He has chosen as his theme a family which, in its several members, represents the different aspects of Russian life. Fyodor Pavlovich, the repulsive father, is the least admirable: a violent, sensual man, but impressive for his very vitality. Alyosha is Holy Russia of Orthodox Christianity, a serenely devout youth whose modest, loving, happy personality is a blessing to everyone about him. Ivan is that aspect of Russia that touches Europe, a restless, deracinated skeptic. What then of Dmitri? According to Kirillovich, the prosecutor, Dmitri is Russia herself in all its contradictions. He shares his father's violence and sensuality, though without his meanness. He gets drunk and quotes Schiller in his cups. He has moments when he yearns for holiness, though fitfully and ineffectually. He is mercurial and immature, contemptible and noble in one moment, often base yet always able to see how base he is. From the point of view of the practical, temperate, bourgeois European, he is turbulent, unpredictable, and altogether exhausting.

Nevertheless, one can argue that Dmitri is the real hero of the story, or, at least, that he constantly threatens to depose Alyosha from that role. Alyosha is the hero in a didactic sense, that is, he is the model held up to our admiration (an admiration which few readers will begrudge), and yet he is always on the sideline of the main action. Even his engagement to Lise Hohlakov is a passive affair. He allows her to take the initiative, and, when that neurotic and spoiled little lady decides to break off the engagement, he remains unperturbed. Dmitri is the hero in a dramatic sense. He takes a major part in the action, and we are genuinely in doubt as to what his fate will be, as we never are with his brother. We might compare him to the hero of a medieval morality play like *Everyman*. Alyosha is in a state of grace. Ivan is damned or in danger of damnation, while Dmitri's soul is a battleground for good and evil angels. The good angels have not yet swept the field, but the battle appears to be turning in their favor.

Paradoxically, Dmitri's very sinfulness will be the means of his salvation, for his realization of how vile he is leads him to a repentance not possible to more self-righteous people. He knows very well that he has robbed Katya, struck Grigory, and longed for his father's death, so that his punishment, though technically a miscarriage of justice, is no more than he deserves. Gradually and with much rebellion of spirit, he will accept his suffering and see it, not as hell but as purgatory. This is a process which D. H. Lawrence flippantly described as "sinning your way to Jesus." A more appropriate comment would be the words of Jesus himself: except a seed fall in the ground and die, it shall not bring forth fruit.

If Dmitri is the hero, who is the villain? The obvious answer is Smerdyakov, the fawning, sexless, epileptic flunky with no emotions except jealousy and ambition, a man so base that it never occurs to him that other people have moral scruples. He is the one who actually strikes the death blow, and yet he is so far below the sphere of moral conflict, as Alyosha is above it, that he does not make a very impressive villain. Morally or psychologically speaking, the villain is Ivan. He has desired the murder, even if he did not commit it, and he has unconsciously or half-consciously instigated it. It was he who speculated that if God does not exist, then anything is permissible, and it is partly his fault that Smerdyakov took him at his word. Smerdyakov is an extrapolation of one side of Ivan's personality, embodied in a much cruder man. He stands in much the same relation to Ivan as Svidrigaïlov to Rashkolnikov in *Crime and Punishment*, and like Svidrigaïlov he unexpectedly commits suicide. His motives are not fully explained. Presumably he acts not out of fear of punishment—for it turns out that no one believes Ivan's story anyway—but because he realizes that he has made a blunder, and that Ivan is not the superman he took him for. Before he dies, however, he forces Ivan to see his guilt so clearly that Ivan is driven into hell: he goes insane.

Psychoanalytically oriented critics have made much of the fact that Dostoevski afflicted Smerdyakov with his own disease, epilepsy. It is surely no coincidence that Dostoevski's own father was murdered, not by his sons, to be sure, but by his serfs, in rebellion against their master's brutality. Dostoevski was properly shocked by his father's death. Yet might it not have come in answer to a wish so hidden that even he was not aware of it? In creating Smerdyakov, Dostoevski drew a murderer who was at once a servant and a son, and then, in making him an epileptic, placed his own signature upon him. In Freudian theory the desire to kill the father springs from a sexual rivalry for the mother. This part of the Oedipal drama Dostoevski has assigned to Dmitri. Both he and his father are rivals for Grushenka, and, when Dmitri stands outside his father's bedroom window, he believes she is inside. At that moment he does not strike Karamazov, but he does strike, and believes he has killed, old Grigory, the father substitute who cared for him as a child.

This analysis has so far paid no attention to Father Zossima. The spiritual biography that occupies most of Book IV is dramatically a digression whose very style separates it from the rest of the book. Nevertheless, even if Zossima is a bit remote from the violent tragedy of the Karamazovs, his presence is needed to maintain the balance of the book. He is Alyosha's good angel, as Smerdyakov is Ivan's evil angel, and he insures that the moral spectrum extends both up and down, as close to heaven as it does to hell. Without Alyosha and Zossima the atmosphere of the story would be intolerably suffocating, and the reader might lose his moral bearings. The subplot dealing with Ilyusha and his friends is even harder to integrate with the main action, and at times it is sentimental in a way that puts modern readers on their guard. Its function would seem to be that it shows Alyosha *in action*. Zossima has sent him into the world there to find his proper sphere of usefulness. On leaving the monastery, he finds the quarrel

between Dmitri and his father too far advanced for him to
deflect its course. He can only provide moral solace. With the
schoolboys, who are still young and plastic, it is another matter, and Alyosha, who is hardly more than a boy himself,
finds his proper work among them.

In addition to the main figures, the book is packed with
a large number of subordinate characters who are fully and
carefully delineated: the histrionically suffering Katya, the
fanatical Father Ferapont, and the thirteen-year-old daredevil,
Kolya. Mme. Hohlakov, though more two-dimensional than
the others, is still a richly comic figure. Subordinate to these
is a swarm of other figures who appear for only a paragraph
or two: servants, policemen, beggars, Poles, an unnamed general's widow, an innkeeper, and a number of officials, all of
whom, for the brief time that they are in the spotlight, are
fully and convincingly real.

One of the most famous passages of the novel is the Parable
of the Grand Inquisitor, Ivan's fantasy about Christ who returns to earth, only to get into trouble with the ecclesiastical
authorities. This interlude is a tour de force which can and
probably should be read in isolation. It expresses, of course,
Dostoevski's detestation, as a Russian Orthodox believer, of
the Roman Catholic Church. Its main theme is that men fear
moral responsibility, and that Christ's teaching laid on them
a burden of freedom which they are reluctant to bear. The
Church has relieved them of this burden, and so is forced to
condemn even the Founder of Christianity as subversive. In
a larger sense, Dostoevski is attacking all benevolent despot-
isms, especially Socialism, which seek to make men happy
by limiting their freedom.

As a Christian, Dostoevski takes man's moral responsibility
seriously indeed, and by the same token he shuns any facile
optimism about human nature. He rejects all social philoso-
phies which explain moral evil as the consequence of unfavorable environment, and which propose to cure man's
sinfulness by manipulating that environment. The kingdom
of heaven will not come by social engineering, but by love
and forgiveness. The theme of *The Brothers Karamazov* is
not crime followed by reformation, but death followed by
resurrection.

The Author

Unlike Tolstoi, Dostoevski came from the middle class, and the characters of his novels are not peasants and nobles, but students, businessmen, and government employees. The setting is not the steppes, but the capital and its crowded tenements. Dostoevski's father was an army surgeon, a harsh disciplinarian who was killed by his own tenants. His mother came from a Moscow merchant's family, an affectionate though not very forceful person, rather like Pulcheria Raskolnikov. At the age of seventeen Dostoevski was sent to a military academy, which he detested; at twenty-three he resigned his commission in order to write.

Dostoevski's early novels, beginning with *Poor Folk* (1845), show a strong sympathy with the downtrodden and an interest in abnormal psychology. This was a time of social unrest and liberal agitation, and it was therefore natural for the young author to find his way into radical circles. Under the influence of a liberal-minded official, Petrashevsky, he joined a group of advanced thinkers who met to discuss such topics as the abolition of serfdom, the problem of censorship, and Fourierist socialism. There is a satirical picture of these radicals in *Crime and Punishment* in the character of Lebetzniakov. In the reaction that followed the revolutions of 1848, the Petrashevsky circle was rounded up, and in 1849 Dostoevski was sentenced to death for seditious conspiracy. Some of Raskolnikov's feelings during cross-examination undoubtedly derive from this experience. The sentence was commuted to eight years' exile in Siberia, but, with deliberate cruelty, the prisoners were led to the execution ground and actually blindfolded before being told of their good fortune.

Dostoevski's experiences in exile profoundly changed his outlook on life. He learned to accept his punishment as a just expiation, not of the crime with which he was legally charged, but of his sins in general and those of mankind at large, a view which we find expressed in the novels. His sympathy with the exiled, the humiliated, and the dispossessed deepened. He also became seriously epileptic, although he had shown signs of the disease before the exile. His attacks were accompanied by a deep sense of harmony and elation, a symptom now well recognized by neurologists and one which helps to locate with precision the area of the brain involved in the seizure. To Dostoevski it suggested a mystical affinity between illness and spiritual insight.

After his release, he was allowed to enlist in the army and in 1855 his commission was restored. In 1859, he returned to the capital. During his stay in Siberia, he met and married Marie Isaeva, the consumptive widow of a drunken government clerk. Though he loved her, the marriage was not a happy one. Some of her traits appear in the figure of Katerina Ivanovna Marmeladov. Marie died a few years after his return. By then, his affections had already turned to a certain Polina Suslova, a proud, passionate, defiant woman who obsessed him for the short time that she was his mistress. He also became a compulsive gambler, and spent much of his time at the gaming tables of Europe, where he generally lost. Dostoevski had other troubles, too. His stepson proved worthless, his brother was an alcoholic whose family had to be supported, a magazine *(Vremya)* which he started was suppressed by the government, and a second one *(Epokha)* failed.

Crime and Punishment was written at high speed under pressure from Dostoevski's publishers. It went through several preliminary versions, being planned as a diary, a court deposition, and a reminiscence, before assuming its present form. In the years that Dostoevski had been in exile, the intellectual climate had changed. In place of the romantic European liberalism of his (and Raskolnikov's) youth, the mood was now patriotic, Slavophile, and Orthodox. In 1871 he returned to Orthodox Christianity, less out of reasoned belief than for emotional and psychological motives. His last years were relatively happy and successful. In 1867, he left Polina Suslova and married his secretary, Anna Grigorievna Snitkina, who loved him, respected his genius, and did not protest against his compulsive gambling. The period of his greatest works followed: *The Gambler* (1867), *The Idiot* (1868-1869), *The Possessed* (1871), and *The Brothers Karamazov* (1880). He was also active as a journalist and editor. When he died in 1881 he was already a great national figure, and since then he has had a profound influence on European literature.

Anna Karenina

by

LEV (LEO) NIKOLAEVICH TOLSTOI
(1828–1910)

The Characters *

Agafia Mikhailovna—Levin's housekeeper.
Annushka—Anna Karenina's maid.
Chirikov—A friend of Levin.
Golenishchev—A friend of Vronsky, residing in Italy.
Mihail Stanislavich Grinevich—A Gentleman of the Bedchamber, and a friend of Oblonsky.
Hannah—The daughter of Vronsky's English horse trainer, a protegée of Anna.
Kapitonych—Karenin's doorman, loyal to Anna.

THE KARENINS

Alexei Alexandrovich—Anna's husband, a government official; honorable but stiff and self-righteous.
Anna Arkadievna—Karenin's wife and sister of Prince Oblonsky, a beautiful and intelligent woman. After she becomes Vronsky's mistress, the strain of her ambiguous position makes her increasingly angry, suspicious, and self-pitying.
Anny—Anna's daughter by Vronsky.
Seryozha—Anna's son by Alexei.

---

* See Note on Russian Names, p. 173.

Kornei—Karenin's manservant.

Korsunsky—Noted as a social leader, dancer, and master of ceremonies.

Kritsky—A friend and political associate of Nikolai Levin.

Kuzma—Levin's servant.

THE LEVINS

Sergei Ivanovich Koznyshev—Half brother to Konstantin and Nikolai, a well-known scholar and author, an emotionally inhibited, middle-aged bachelor.

Konstantin Dmitrievich Levin (Kostya)—A member of an old family of Moscow nobility, he prefers to live on his estate and derives his chief satisfaction from farming. He is a serious and thoughtful person, much preoccupied with religious issues and agricultural problems.

Nikolai Dmitrievich Levin—Konstantin's brother, originally austerely religious, who has taken up a dissolute bohemian life, and is interested in radical social reform.

Kitty Levin—Levin's wife, née Princess Ekaterina Alexandrovna Shcherbatsky; an uncomplicated, affectionate girl.

Dmitri (Mitya)—The son of Kitty and Levin.

Natalie Lvov—Née Princess Natalia Alexandrovna Shcherbatsky.

Countess Lydia Ivanovna—A friend of Karenin, a meddlesome woman much given to religious enthusiasms.

Makhotin—An officer.

Maria Andreyevna (Masha)—Nikolai's mistress.

Matriona Filimovna—Nurse to the Oblonsky children.

Matvei—Oblonsky's valet.

Princess Miakhy—An eccentric, noted for her blunt speech.

Mikhailov—A Russian painter in Italy who paints a portrait of Anna.

Filipp Ivanovich Nikitin—A veteran; a friend of Oblonsky.

Countess Nordston—A member of the Shcherbatskys' social set. She and Levin dislike each other.

THE OBLONSKYS

Prince Stepan Arkadievich Oblonsky (Stiva)—Anna's brother, a genial, good-looking, easygoing, sensual man.

Dolly Oblonsky—Née Princess Daria Alexandrovna Shcherbatsky (Dolinka, Dollenka, Dashenka)—Stepan's wife, uneasily resentful of his infidelities.

Grisha—Oblonsky's son.

Masha—Oblonsky's daughter.

Vasya—Oblonsky's daughter.

Tanya—Oblonsky's daughter.

Varvara Oblonsky—Oblonsky's aunt.

Petrov—A painter in Germany, infatuated with Kitty.

Anna Pavlovna Petrov—His wife.

THE SHCHERBATSKYS

Prince Alexander Dmitrievich Shcherbatsky—Kitty's father, a kind and courteous old man.

Princess Shcherbatsky—Kitty's mother, ambitious for her daughter to marry Count Vronsky.

Natalia Alexandrovna—Natalie Lvov.

Daria Alexandrovna—Dolly Oblonsky.

Ekaterina Alexandrovna—Kitty Levin.

Nikolai Shcherbatsky—Kitty's cousin.

Sitnikov—Tutor to Seryozha Karenin.

Mikhail Vasiliyevich Sliudin—Karenin's office manager; a quietly efficient man.

Mme. Stahl—A Russian woman living at German spas. She has a reputation for exceptional piety, but is actually a self-indulgent invalid who torments Varenka with her demands.

Varvara Andreyevna Stahl (Varenka)—Friend of Kitty, foster-child of Mme. Stahl, a pious, self-effacing girl.

Stremov—A political opponent of Karenin.

Tushkevich—Lover of Betsy Tverskoy.

Princess Betsy Tverskoy—A friend of Anna, malicious and meddlesome.

THE VRONSKYS

Court Alexei Kirillovich Vronsky—A wealthy landowner and army officer, lover of Anna Karenina, a man of personal charm and some ability, but of no fundamental seriousness of character.

Alexander Kirillovich Vronsky—Brother of Alexei.

Countess Vronsky—Alexei's mother.

Veslovsky—A guest of Levin who tries to flirt with Kitty.
Yashvin—A friend of Vronsky, a compulsive gambler.
Nikolai Ivanovich Sviazhsky—A friend of Levin, a landowner
  interested in local politics.

The Story

Anna Karenina is set in Russia during the 1870's, in Moscow, in Saint Petersburg, and on the country estates of the nobility. The plot focuses on two love affairs: the happy marriage of Konstantin Levin and Kitty Shcherbatsky, and the tragic liaison of Count Vronsky and Anna Karenina. Although the major characters are related and move in the same circles, the two stories are largely independent, except as each is a commentary on the other.

Levin is a country landowner, a noble, but basically a simple and good-hearted man who relishes his life as a farmer and derives his strength from contact with the soil. He is in love with Princess Ekaterina (Kitty) Shcherbatsky, one of the three daughters of a kindly, old-fashioned Moscow nobleman. Kitty is also receiving the attentions, if not the serious courtship, of a handsome and wealthy young man, Count Vronsky. Though she does not really know which man she prefers, her mother persuades her that Vronsky is the better match. When Levin finally plucks up courage to propose to her, she refuses him, and he returns to the country to nurse his wounds there.

Vronsky, however, is not really interested in marriage, and is only flirting. Instead of proposing to Kitty, as he is expected to do, he falls in love with Anna Karenina, the sister of Kitty's brother-in-law. Kitty is brokenhearted, both at being rejected by the man she had chosen, and at having rejected the man who had chosen her. For a time, her health suffers. Then her family send her for a vacation to a German spa where she makes other friends and recovers from her love for Vronsky.

Levin, meanwhile, throws himself into the congenial routine of farm life and into developing his theories of agricultural management. After a suitable wait, he renews his courtship and proposes to Kitty again in a curious scene in which he spells out the initial letters of the words of his declaration of love. Kitty shows her intuitive understanding by replying in the same manner. They are married and are deeply happy. Occasional friction crops up, and brief, unjustified moments of jealousy, but the marriage is basically sound. Kitty proves her strength and emotional stability during the painful last illness of Levin's brother Nikolai, whom she tends with tender and sympathetic competence. Then the birth of a son, Dmitri, brings her happiness and fulfillment as a mother.

The last chapters of the book are given over largely to the development of Levin's religious convictions. Although he is a moral man, and sensitive to religious issues, he is a skeptic. Indeed, even to be married by the rites of the Church and to take the sacrament raises problems of conscience for him. After his marriage, he goes through a period of painful seeking from which he emerges a believer in God, if not exactly an orthodox Christian. He recognizes that his new faith will not solve all his problems, but he feels that his life at last has purpose and meaning.

Anna Karenina's love develops very differently from Kitty's. She is the wife of Alexei Alexandrovich Karenin, a distinguished government official. Though their relations are respectful and correct, there is no love between them, and his distant, ironic manner repels her. At the opening of the book, Anna impresses us as a handsome, vital and charming woman, a loving mother, adored by her nephew and nieces, and able to intervene in a quarrel between her brother and his wife and bring about a reconciliation. When Vronsky shows signs of falling in love with her, she tries to draw back and hurriedly leaves Moscow for Saint Petersburg.

Vronsky, however, is seriously in love for the first time in his life. He pursues Anna on the same train and makes his intentions clear. The affair develops so rapidly that gossip spreads. Karenin (who is more concerned for his reputation than for his wife's affections) tries to warn her to be discreet. She refuses even to discuss the matter and goes recklessly ahead with her affair. In a short time she is pregnant. She informs Vronsky of the fact shortly before he is about to ride in a dangerous steeplechase. He is so unsettled by the news that he falls and is nearly killed. Anna's alarm for her lover betrays her feeling publicly and unmistakably. On the way home she defiantly confesses to her husband that she is Vronsky's mistress, and dares Karenin to do with her whatever he wishes.

Alexei is uncertain whether to seek a divorce. His first instinct is to try to maintain appearances and continue to live with Anna, finding what satisfaction he can in his work. He stipulates only that Vronsky is not to enter his house. When Anna and Vronsky disregard this request, Karenin considers a divorce and approaches a lawyer. At this point, word reaches him that Anna has given birth to a child and is dying of puerperal fever. He hurries to her bedside, and a full reconciliation follows. Anna begs Alexei's forgiveness, Alexei pardons both his wife and her lover, and Vronsky, overwhelmed with shame, tries to shoot himself.

What no one could foresee was that both Anna and Vronsky would recover, and that Anna's deathbed reconciliation with her husband could not stand the strain of daily living with him. Finally the two agree to separate. Anna will surrender custody of her son to Alexei, and will have custody of her daughter by Vronsky. Vronsky will resign his army commission and abandon his career, and the two lovers will leave Russia for Europe.

Anna and Vronsky lead a wandering life for a time, visiting one resort after another, but finally her longing to see her son pulls her back to Russia. Without warning, she forces her way into her former home and into the bedroom of the boy who has been told she is dead. Next she tries to see if she cannot find some part of Saint Petersburg society that will accept her. A few old friends keep up the acquaintance, though with some embarrassment, but when she appears at the opera she is publicly snubbed. Finally she and Vronsky retire to his country estate, where he busies himself with building a hospital for his tenants and making other improvements.

Life on Vronsky's estate is luxurious, even extravagant, but the atmosphere is poisoned by a vague and growing malaise. Vronsky realizes that he has sacrificed his career for the woman he loves, and begins to feel resentful. More especially, he is vexed because his illegitimate daughter must bear Karenin's name. He wants Anna to press for a divorce so that he can have an heir. By this time, however, Karenin has fallen under the influence of a pious countess named Lydia Ivanovna, and refuses, ostensibly because of religious scruples, to grant the divorce. Anna is now increasingly fretful, reproachful, jealous and possessive. She fears losing her lover, and with good reason, since Vronsky's mother is pressing him to marry someone else. Anna quarrels repeatedly with Vronsky, growing increasingly hysterical and unreasonable. At night she takes morphine. Finally in a state of acute depression she throws herself under a train and is instantly killed. Vronsky is shattered by the tragic ending of his love. He continues to live an empty and embittered life, and the last we see of him he is courting death by volunteering for service in Serbia in the war against Turkey.

Critical Opinion

Tolstoi's second masterpiece, *Anna Karenina,* differs from *War and Peace* in many ways, but most conspicuously in that it consciously illustrates a moral lesson: the relation between the sexes is destructive when it is possessive and self-centered, but ennobling when it is inspired by unselfish love. Such a theme might seem to be almost too obvious to be treated with any originality, yet Tolstoi has endowed it with life and authenticity.

The two ways of love are represented, of course, by the marriage of Kitty and Levin on the one hand and the adultery of Anna and Vronsky on the other. At the outset it is by no means obvious that Anna will end tragically and Kitty happily. If anything, Anna has the advantage. She is cleverer and more charming, and Kitty seems rather ordinary by contrast. Nor is Anna by any means evil. She intervenes to save her brother's marriage with Dolly (ironically, as it turns out, since Stepan is unable to help her in a like situation), and, when she suspects that Vronsky is too interested in her, she tries, for Kitty's sake, to discourage him. To some extent, perhaps, fate has cheated her in giving her a husband who, for all his virtues, is stiff and unsympathetic. Still, whatever Karenin's shortcomings, they had not proved insupportable to her until she met Vronsky. Anna, in short, is not predestined to her tragic end. She invites it.

Since both Anna and Vronsky make tremendous sacrifices for each other (he abandons his career and she her reputation), it may seem strange to speak of their love as selfish, and yet it is certainly a grasping, possessive relationship. In fact, it is precisely because she has given up so much for his sake that Anna demands so much of Vronsky: his time, his attention, repeated demonstrations of his love. This jealous possessiveness causes the rift between the two. Anna grows panicky when she senses that she is losing Vronsky. She reacts with self-pity that is in a large measure hatred of the person she has become. Because she is so full of hate, the whole world appears hateful. In this mood she takes her life.

Society plays its part in this downfall. Anna, born a princess, must endure snubs at the opera, cannot go to parties with Vronsky, is dropped or slighted by her old friends, and is forced to chafe in retirement from the world. We are not to suppose, however, that because society condemns her, society is in the right. In Anna's circle, a discreet adultery was considered no grave matter. Her friend Betsy and her brother Stepan manage their extramarital affairs without serious consequences. When Vronsky first becomes involved with Anna, his mother welcomes the affair as being just the right experience to give her son a final touch of worldly polish. She does not turn against Anna until she realizes that Alexei is seriously in love and that his career will suffer. In other words, society turns on Anna, not because it is less corrupt than she, but because it is more so. Anna's crime in the eyes of her friends is that she will not play the game according to the rules; she is too frank and reckless. Had she been an amiable and uncomplicated hedonist like her brother, she would have been a less tragic figure, and less heroic. As it is, she is impressive enough to command our respect and pity, even in her final degradation.

By contrast with Anna, Kitty Shcherbatsky is simply a nice girl and little more, while Levin lacks the poise, the glitter and the charm of his rival. He is not especially clever or articulate, and he has many acts of unchastity to reproach himself for. Nevertheless, Kitty and her husband succeed in their marriage because each honestly cares for the other more than for himself. If Levin finally learns the meaning of the love of God, it is because he has first discovered the love of one woman.

Centered on the domestic problems of two couples, *Anna Karenina* has a much narrower scope than *War and Peace* and a much tighter organization. It is less of a sprawling, national epic and more a novel in the conventional sense. Even so, there are many chapters that have no bearing on the central plot. We see Levin out hunting or at political meetings, Stepan at his office, Karenin in his committee rooms, and Nikolai on his deathbed. Few authors are so prodigal as Tolstoi in creating such scenes; there is enough material here for several novels. Nevertheless, these scenes are not redundant. They offer us a detailed picture of Russian society in the seventies, a society that Tolstoi on the whole condemned. Most of his aristocrats are frivolous and irresponsible, like Betsy Tverskoy, or, if they are personally good, like Prince Shcherbatsky, they are also useless. Some, like Sergei Ivanovich, are seriously concerned with social issues, but these men are deracinated, Westernized Russians, whose brittle intellectuality is without depth or feeling. They mean well, but they have lost their touch with their native soil and traditions, and the institutions they favor seem, at least in Levin's eyes, like exotic plants growing in an alien climate.

Levin is Tolstoi's most autobiographical character, far more so than Pierre in *War and Peace*. Into Levin, Tolstoi has projected his own brooding search for religious truth, his pacifism, his distrust of governmental processes, his love of outdoor labor, and his sympathy with the peasantry. The details of Levin's courtship are taken from Tolstoi's own, as is the episode in which he gives Kitty his diary to inspect, with its account of all his premarital unchastity. Levin's spiritual crisis and conversion is also autobiographical, and the last sentence of the book is Tolstoi's profession of faith:

Now my life . . . regardless of anything that may happen to me . . . is not only not purposeless as it used to be, but has the unmistakable purpose of goodness that I have the power to provide to it.

War and Peace

by

LEV (LEO) NIKOLAEVICH TOLSTOI

The Characters

NOTE ON RUSSIAN NAMES: *In Russia the full name normally has three parts: the given or baptismal name, the patronymic, and the family name. Persons are customarily referred to by the first two. Thus Count Rostov is regularly called Count Ilya Andreich. The patronymic is derived from the father's name by the addition of a suffix meaning "son of." It is therefore a useful guide to family relationships. The patronymic may sometimes appear in a syncopated form: e.g., Andreivich or Andreich. In addition, the Russian language is rich in affectionate diminutives which are freely used as nicknames. Thus Nikolai may appear as Nikolenka or Nikolushka. To complicate matters further, Russian names at this period were sometimes Gallicized, so that Pyotr Kirillovich is invariably called Pierre by his friends. Servants are generally called by a single name: Tihon, Lavrushka. There is wide variation in the way Russian names are transliterated into English, and the degree to which translators try to find English equivalents. Thus Bezuhov may be rendered as Bezoukhov, and Andrey as Andrew.*

PUBLIC FIGURES

Alexander Pavlovich (1777–1825)—Czar Alexander I of Russia.

Napoleon Bonaparte (1769–1821)—Emperor Napoleon I of France.

Kaiser Franz I of Austria (Francis) (1768–1835)—Franz II of the Holy Roman Empire.

General Mihail Larionovich Kutuzov (1745–1813)—Prince of Smolensk, Field Marshal of the Russian forces.

Prince Pyotr Bagration (1765–1812)—Russian general, served at Austerlitz and died at Borodino.

Count Mihail Speransky (1772–1839)—Liberal minister of the Czar, in power 1809–1812.

Count Alexei Andreivich Araktcheev (1769–1834)—Russian Minister of War after 1808.

Count Rastoptchin—Governor of Moscow at the time of the French occupation.

THE PRINCIPAL FAMILIES OF THE NOVEL

THE BOLKONSKYS

Prince Nikolai Andreivich Bolkonsky—Formerly commander-in-chief of the army, now in retirement; an autocrat whose crusty manner covers a genuine love for his children. In old age he becomes impossibly irascible.

Andrey Nikolayevich Bolkonsky—Son of the prince, married to Lizaveta Karlovna and later engaged to Natasha Rostov; an honorable, talented man whose misfortunes make him melancholy and disillusioned.

Lizaveta Karlovna Bolkonsky (Liza, "The Little Princess")—Wife of Andrey, who dies in childbirth.

Marya Bolkonsky (Masha, Marie)—Daughter of Prince Nikolai, who lives in seclusion with her father; a homely, devout woman with a talent for self-abnegation, who eventually marries Nikolai Rostov.

Nikolai Andreich Bolkonsky (Nikolinka)—Andrey's son; a slim, sensitive and eager adolescent.

The Bezuhovs and Kuragins

Count Kirill Vladimirovich Bezuhov—Father of Pierre, a roué, a famous dandy in the days of Catherine the Great.

Count Piotr Kirillovich Bezuhov (Pierre)—Legitimized son of the old count, married first to Elena Kuragin, second to Natasha Rostov. Though not brilliant, he is kind and well intentioned, loyal, and full of idealistic plans for reform. In social circles he is considered slightly ridiculous.

Prince Vassily Sergyevich Kuragin—The heir to Count Bezuhov's fortune until Pierre is legitimized; a worldly man with a sure instinct for self-advancement.

Ippolit Kuragin—Elder son of Prince Vassily.

Anatole Kuragin—Second son of Vassily, dissipated and corrupt.

Elena Vassilyevna Kuragin—Daughter of Vassily, and Pierre's first wife; a beautiful woman, but selfish and stupid.

Katerina Semyonovna (Katish)—Cousin of Vassily.

The Rostovs

Count Ilya Andreich Rostov—A wealthy member of Moscow society, genial, kindly, and improvident.

Countess Natalya Rostov (née Shinshin)—His wife.

Nikolai Ilyich Rostov—His son, without special talent or distinction, but likable enough. From a rather unsteady youth he becomes a responsible head of his family. Engaged to Sonya, he marries Marya Bolkonsky.

Vera Rostov—Eldest daughter of Count Rostov, good-looking and clever, but rather unpleasant in manner. Marries Berg.

Natalya Ilyinishna Rostov (Natasha)—Younger daughter of the count, a warmhearted and high-spirited girl. At first changeable in her affections, in the end she settles down as Pierre's wife.

Piotr Ilyich Rostov (Petya)—Younger son of Count Rostov, an impetuous boy who dies in the campaign of 1812.

Sonya Semyonovna—A niece of Count Rostov, brought up in his family. More self-effacing than Natasha, she is in love with Nikolai, but eventually renounces him.

Alphonse Karlich Berg—An officer who marries Vera Rostov; self-seeking and self-satisfied.

Shinshin—Bachelor cousin of Countess Rostov.

OFFICERS AND GENTRY

Marya Dmitryevna Ahrostimov—An elderly, strong-willed widow, friend of the Rostovs.

Osip Alexyevich Bazdyev—A Freemason who introduces Pierre to the order.

Bilibin—A Russian diplomat at the Austrian court, a witty and sophisticated man with a taste for epigram.

Mlle. Amélie Bourienne—A French emigrée, household companion to Prince Bolkonsky and Marya. Her flirting with Anatole Kuragin prevents an engagement between him and Marya.

Vassily Fyodorovich Denisov (Vaska)—A friend of Nikolai Rostov and an officer in his regiment.

Dolohov—An infantry officer demoted to the ranks for wild behavior, a heavy drinker, swaggerer, and duelist.

Princess Anna Mihalovna Drubetskoy—An impoverished noblewoman.

Boris Drubetskoy—Son of Anna Mihalovna. He has been educated with the Rostov children and is in love with Natasha. He marries Julie Karagin.

Ilagin—An old-fashioned, hospitable country gentleman, neighbor of the Rostovs.

Julie Karagin—A wealthy heiress and friend of Marya Bolkonsky.

Ramballe—A French officer who befriends Pierre in his captivity.

Anna Pavlovna Scherer—Maid of honor to the Empress and a prominent Saint Petersburg hostess.

Tushin—An artillery captain who serves honorably at Austerlitz.

Villarsky—A Polish count and Freemason.

FAMILY RETAINERS, SOLDIERS, PEASANTS

Alpatich—Steward of the Bolkonsky estates.

Dunyasha—Marya's maid.

Platon Karataev—A peasant who shares Pierre's captivity and befriends him, a simple, cheerful, saintly man.
Lavrushka—Valet to Denisov and later to Nikolai Rostov.
Dmitry Vassilyevich (Mitenka)—Steward to Count Rostov.
Tihon—Valet to Prince Bolkonsky.

The Story

War and Peace is a vast and sprawling novel about Russia during the Napoleonic Wars, from 1805 to 1813, with an epilogue set in 1820. The historical background of the story is dominated by Napoleon who, in 1805, had declared himself emperor and was now moving to subjugate central Europe. Against him was marshaled an alliance of Russia, Prussia, and Austria, which he defeated in a series of victories at Ulm, Austerlitz, and Jena. For a time, the Czar made peace (Tilsit, 1807), and even dreamed of dividing the world with his former enemy. The peace was only a breathing spell, however, and in 1812 the French moved east again. The Russian army, now fighting on its own ground, withdrew, forcing Napoleon to extend his lines of communication without any decisive action. After a bloody but indecisive battle at Borodino (September 7, 1812), the Russians fell back beyond Moscow, which was occupied by the French. Here Napoleon waited for the Russians to make peace. Instead they burned the city to the ground. Since Moscow was no longer tenable, Napoleon retreated toward Poland through mud and snow, and was harassed by the Russians, who now took the offensive. By December, 1812, the French army had melted away and the Napoleonic empire had received its mortal wound.

Domestic politics in Russia reflected these events. The Czar had come to the throne in 1801, when Russian culture, at least among the aristocracy, was permeated with French influence. Alexander himself was stirred by the ideals of European liberalism, and, for a time, under the ministry of Count Speransky, Russia saw the beginnings of constitutional reforms. After 1812, a nationalist reaction set in, and a revulsion against things French. Speransky was dismissed and the conservatives came into power. By 1825, the tyranny was so oppressive that some of the nobility attempted an abortive revolt (the Decembrist conspiracy), which ended disastrously.

Against this background, Tolstoi tells the story of three young men of high position, together with their friends and families. There are perhaps a hundred characters mentioned by name, from the Czar to the serfs. The action takes in everything from the councils of empire to the small talk of the soldiery. The focus of attention, however, is on three men: Prince Andrey Bolkonsky, Count Pierre Bezuhov, and Count Nikolai Rostov.

ANDREY

Prince Andrey is the son of Prince Nikolai Bolkonsky, a retired army commander who lives in seclusion with his daughter Marya at his estate, Bleak Hills, near Smolensk. Andrey is married and lives in Saint Petersburg, but he chafes at the restrictions of his life and longs to distinguish himself publicly. The campaign of 1805 offers him the opportunity, and he joins the Russian army as an adjutant to General Kutuzov, leaving his wife, who is pregnant, in the care of his father and sister.

Andrey's service begins soon after the Austrian defeat at Ulm. He takes part in small engagements in Austria and Moravia, and attends the staff conference before the battle of Austerlitz. During that engagement, he conducts himself honorably but is wounded and left on the field. His family suppose him dead although the news is kept from his wife. He makes his way back to Russia and reaches Bleak Hills just in time to witness his wife's death in childbirth. The baby survives, is named Nikolai, and is placed in the care of Marya and the old prince.

Andrey now leaves active military duty and spends most of his time on his estates, brooding. This retirement lasts from 1806 to 1809, when he finally emerges from his shell sufficiently to take an interest in public affairs. For a time he joins the liberal circle around Speransky, but is soon disillusioned. Then he finds new life and hope in the company of Natasha, the daughter of Count Ilya Andreich Rostov.

The old prince, Andrey's father, opposes a second marriage, and demands a waiting period of one year. Andrey agrees reluctantly, and, out of consideration for Natasha, refuses to make the engagement public so that she will not feel bound by any promise to him. He then leaves on business, commending to her his friend Pierre Bezuhov, and urging her to rely on him in any difficulty. Pierre's vicious wife takes advantage of Andrey's absence to persuade Natasha that she should instead accept her brother, Anatole Kuragin. Anatole proposes to elope with Natasha, though he has a wife by a former secret marriage. Natasha breaks off her engagement with Andrey only to learn how Anatole has deceived her. Andrey, bitter and disillusioned, refuses to have anything more to do with her.

In 1812, Napoleon's invasion breaks over Russia. Andrey leaves his father, who has by this time sunk into senile irascibility, and joins the army again. After the capture of Smolensk, Marya and her father evacuate the estate at Bleak Hills. The old prince dies of a stroke and Marya is left isolated among a mutinous peasantry. She is rescued by Natasha's brother, Nikolai Rostov. Andrey, meanwhile, takes part in the battle of Borodino, where he is gravely wounded. He is carried to Moscow, then being evacuated, where he is found by Natasha and her family. They are reconciled at last. She nurses him faithfully until his death at Yaroslavl, some distance to the northeast of Moscow. The boy, Nikolinka, is raised by Marya and her husband (she eventually marries Nikolai Rostov). At the end of the book we see him as an eager and sensitive youth, burning to show himself worthy of his father, whose memory he worships.

PIERRE

Andrey's closest friend, Pierre Bezuhov, the illegitimate son of Count Bezuhov, has been raised in Europe by tutors. At the start of the novel he has returned to Russia where his father is dying. He is a fat, awkward young man, socially inept, and an enthusiastic Bonapartist. After his father's death, Pierre's fortune changes suddenly; his father has provided for his legitimization and succession to the title. Prince Vassily Kuragin, the original heir, tries to destroy the will before it can be registered. Failing in this, he cultivates Pierre and manipulates him into a marriage with his own daughter, Elena Vassilyevna Kuragin. The marriage is unhappy. Elena is beautiful and has a brilliant position in society, but she is utterly selfish, sensual, and corrupt. Pierre comes to suspect her of misconduct with Dolohov, a dissolute friend of his brother-in-law, Anatole Kuragin. There is a duel in which Dolohov is wounded. Finally the husband and wife decide to live apart (1806).

Pierre is now emotionally adrift. For a time his native idealism finds expression in the Society of Freemasons, which he joins at the urging of one Osip Alexyevich Bazdyev. This society appears to him as an expression of purified religion and practical philanthropy. Under its influence he tries to introduce social reforms such as the establishment of schools and hospitals on his own estates. He is not very successful, as his own agents cheat him. Eventually he becomes disappointed in the Freemasons, too, when the fashionable members of his lodge show no interest in his programs of moral and social reform. Bazdyev does accomplish one thing, however: he persuades Pierre to become reconciled with his wife, at least publicly (1809).

Prince Andrey is by now (1810) emerging from his seclusion after his wife's death, and Pierre urges him to marry Natasha Rostov. When Natasha tries instead to elope with Anatole Kuragin, Pierre foils his brother-in-law and shows Natasha how she has been duped by a married man. He also tries to reconcile Natasha with Andrey, but in this he fails. At length, realizing that he is falling in love with Natasha himself, he breaks off communication with her.

Two years later, Pierre is set free by the sudden death of his wife from angina. Public events, however, leave him no time for private concerns. The French have invaded Russia. Pierre witnesses the battle of Borodino as a civilian observer, then returns to Moscow. Most of the citizenry are leaving, but Pierre disguises himself and stays on, entertaining vague plans of assassinating the Emperor Napoleon. After various adventures, he is arrested as an incendiary and barely escapes being executed (1812).

While in captivity, Pierre encounters a man who teaches him more about religion and the love of humanity than the pretentious and cerebral doctrines of the Masons had done. This is Platon Karataev, a simple, illiterate soldier, whose cheerful instinctive goodness is a practical lesson in Christian love. Karataev is executed by his captors, but Pierre still feels his influence.

After an exhausting retreat with the French across western

Russia, Pierre is freed by Cossack soldiery. He returns to Moscow, sets his estates in order, and eventually (1813) marries Natasha. This time the marriage is happy and fruitful. The epilogue shows Pierre seven years later (1820). He is at peace, but his old social idealism is still stirring, and there are hints that he will be one of the liberal conspirators who will take part in the ill-fated Decembrist *coup d'état*.

NIKOLAI

The Rostovs are the third family of the novel. They are not vicious like the Kuragins, or talented like the Bolkonskys. They are decent mediocrities, unreflective, affectionate, and fond of life. Count Ilya Rostov, the father, is kindly and genial, but hopelessly improvident. His household includes his four children and a dowryless niece, Sonya, who is being raised as one of his family. From childhood she has been in love with the eldest son, Nikolai.

In 1805 Nikolai, an officer in the Pavlograd regiment, is sent to Austria, where the Russians are seeking to relieve the pressure on their allies. His first engagement frightens him badly, but he manages not to disgrace himself. In the second, at Schöngraben, he is slightly injured and runs from the field. News of his wound reaches his family, who consider him a hero. Nikolai himself begins to boast about his military prowess. At Austerlitz he is fired with patriotic ardor and dreams of doing some great service for the Czar. During the battle he is actually sent to the Czar with a message, but arrives too late for it to be of any use, and is too awed to deliver it.

Nikolai returns home to Moscow and spends the winter of 1806 in a round of good times. When Pierre fights his duel with Dolohov, Nikolai is Dolohov's second. Dolohov repays his friendship by proposing marriage to Sonya, Nikolai's sweetheart. When she refuses him, Dolohov retaliates by ruining Nikolai at cards. The old count agrees to pay the debt of 43,000 rubles, and Nikolai returns to his regiment much chastened. He sees service in Poland after the battle of Eylau (1807) and witnesses the meeting of Alexander and Napoleon at Tilsit. By now he is a seasoned soldier, bluff, good-natured, and no longer a coward.

Meanwhile, the Rostovs' financial position has deteriorated.

The girls are approaching marriageable age and it is important that they marry well. The eldest, Vera, marries a career officer named Berg who insists on a handsome dowry. The countess is obliged to dismiss one of Natasha's suitors as being too poor. For the same reason, she tries to discourage the romance between Nikolai and his cousin Sonya, and to find Nikolai an heiress. But Nikolai is reluctant to make a mercenary marriage. Natasha becomes engaged to the brilliant and wealthy Andrey, but as has already been related, she proves fickle and breaks the engagement. In the meantime, the lavish living goes on as usual: Tolstoi draws a memorable picture of life on the Rostovs' country estate, with hunting parties, visits to the neighbors, and Christmas festivities (1810).

As with the other two families, the invasion of 1812 brings the Rostovs' affairs to a crisis. Nikolai is with his regiment and is decorated for valor. The youngest son, Petya, is also eager to join up. During the retreat from Smolensk, Nikolai meets and aids Marya Bolkonsky under circumstances that have already been related. He is struck by the romantic possibilities of the situation and begins to regret his youthful promise to Sonya.

When Moscow burns, the Rostovs lose their property, but their chief blow is the death of Petya in a minor skirmish with the French. In 1813 the old count dies, realizing with remorse that he has left the family bankrupt. The estates are sold, and the family moves into hired lodgings. Under the circumstances, marriage between Sonya and Nikolai becomes unthinkable, as both are almost penniless. She writes him an affectionate letter releasing him from his promise.

As the story ends, both the remaining children manage eventually to make profitable matches. In 1813, Natasha marries Pierre who has been quietly in love with her for some time, and Nikolai is free at last to choose Marya Bolkonsky. Now that peace has come, Nikolai settles down to the life of a conservative country gentleman. By responsible management of his wife's property he is able to rebuild the family fortunes. The three families are now united by marriage and happy in their settled domesticity.

Critical Opinion

War and Peace is such a stupendous achievement that it could well be classified as an epic rather than a novel. Certainly there is enough material here for three ordinary novels. Tolstoi has given us not one hero but three, and set them against a background of armies and emperors and the surging currents of European history.

We may approach *War and Peace* from many angles. One of the most obvious is to see it as a study of Russian society, especially the nobility. Here is the privileged class, a Westernized élite, speaking French as freely as their native tongue, who live lavishly and bear themselves with the assurance of men whose right to rule is unquestioned. At the other extreme are the serfs whose drudgery supports the social structure. Tolstoi plays down the possibilities for class conflict which the situation suggests. At one point, at Bogutcharovo, there are rumblings of discontent, but generally the relationship of master and servant is natural and unself-conscious, like that between Rostov and Danilo, or Ilagin and his housekeeper. The one class that is conspicuously absent is the bourgeoisie: the merchants, petty officials and minor clergy. Tolstoi, the aristocrat, had warm affection for the Russian masses, but none for social climbers.

The stage of *War and Peace* is more than Russia; it is Europe. Tolstoi is concerned with the meaning of the vast conflict of forces which were then sweeping across the continent. As opposed to the heroic view of history, which sees great events as the work of great men, Tolstoi sees men as the tools of history, not its creators. Generals and politicians do not understand the forces they fancy they control, and even Napoleon in Tolstoi's view is only a posturing adventurer, helpless once the tide of events runs against him. The historic personage in the story for whom Tolstoi shows most sympathy is not the Czar, not Speransky, the brilliant liberal minister, but Kutuzov: an old, sluggish, purblind soldier who will not fight if he can help it, but who has enough instinctive sense of the Russian character to know when the momentum of history is in his favor.

As the title suggests, the alternations of war and peace

establish the major rhythm of the book and affect the lives of every character in it. There are other contrasts and conflicts. We have noticed the polarity of noble and peasant, of the French and Russian languages, of court and country, of the sophisticated and simple. There are also the contrasts of the affectionate Pierre with his vicious in-laws, the Kuragins; of the brilliant, restless, intellectual Bolkonskys with the more impulsive and unreflective Rostovs; of the fashionable new capital with the comfortable old one; of the gaiety of the Rostovs' party with the solemnity of Count Bezuhov's death; the alternation of hope with depression in Andrey; the clash between the scientific German generals and the intuitive Bezuhov; the contradictions within Pierre, who sets out to kill an emperor and instead saves the life of a child. All these create dramatic tension which Tolstoi heightens by using short chapters and rapid changes of scene, suggesting urgent and rapid movement.

The characters who crowd the book are many and varied, and all, even the minor ones, are memorable as distinct individuals. On the whole, the lesser characters are rather static. They are sharply delineated, but they are shown only from the outside, and change very little. On the other hand, Pierre, Andrey, Nikolai and Natasha are fully three-dimensional. We see them from many points of view: as they appear to each other, to strangers, and to themselves. Furthermore, they change as they mature. Natasha develops from a little girl into a giddy adolescent and ends as a staid wife. Nikolai sows his wild oats but turns out to be a responsible country squire. Even Andrey, as he lies dying, achieves the detachment and serenity which he lacked all his life. The central characters all find fulfillment in one way or another. Tolstoi seems to be saying that the secret of happiness does not lie in the clash of empires or the deeds of statesmen, but in the undramatic private lives of ordinary people who know how to love each other and to open themselves to the common impulses of humanity. Of this life, Karataev is the purest example.

If there is any flaw in the novel, it is in the long discourses on the meaning of history which clog the later chapters. Omitted in the second edition, these were later restored. One wishes that Tolstoi had been content to let history explain itself. Also, certain turns of the plot seem a bit contrived, especially the coincidence which brings the wounded Andrey into the care of the Rostovs. These are, however, trivial blemishes. The book as a whole is so grand in scope, so stirring in its action, so penetrating in its characterization, so convincing in its realism, that the reader feels he is in the presence not of fiction but of life itself.

The Author

Leo Nikolaevich Tolstoi was born in 1828 on his family's estate of Yasnaya Polyana, near Tula, south of Moscow. His people were prosperous country gentry, some of whom served as models for the characters in *War and Peace*. Thus Prince Bolkonsky is Tolstoi's maternal grandfather, Prince Volkonsky, while Nikolai and Ilya Rostov are his father and paternal grandfather. Sonya and Marya also have their prototypes, and the relationship between the two families was much as it is in the novel.

Tolstoi's education was entrusted to French tutors and completed at the University of Kazan, where he spent three years but took no degree. After a period of idleness, he enlisted in the army and spent several years in the Caucasus, followed by service in the Crimean War. This experience gave him the familiarity with army life which is so evident in *War and Peace*. Then after two trips to western Europe, he returned to his family estate, became a magistrate, and started a school for his tenants, organized on the Rousseauan principle that the unsophisticated life of the peasant is morally and intellectually sounder than the artificial standards of civilization.

Tolstoi's marriage in 1862 was a difficult one. His bride, Sophie Behrs, was still in her teens. She was sexually unawakened and quite unprepared for the violence of his physical demands. To make matters worse, he showed her a diary recording his sexual experiences before marriage, a piece of exhibitionistic honesty which merely revolted her. Tolstoi's failure to integrate love and sex led him in the end to denounce all physical love, to preach chastity as the ideal state, and to declare that the greatest of all tragedies is the tragedy of the connubial bed. In spite of these convictions, he still managed to sire thirteen children.

Tolstoi's career as a writer began in 1852 with the story *Childhood*. His army experience provided him with the material for a novel entitled *The Cossacks*, set in the Caucasus, and for his sketches of the Crimean War, entitled *Sevastopol*. His masterpieces are clearly *War and Peace* and *Anna Karenina*. The first of these was begun in 1864 and published in installments from 1866 to 1869. A revised edition appeared in 1873; the final and definitive text in 1886 is in the main a reversion to the text of 1869. *Anna Karenina* was written from 1873 to 1877.

In 1878 there came the great crisis of Tolstoi's life: his religious conversion. Tolstoi had been raised in the Orthodox church but had ceased in his teens to be conventionally religious. In early life he seems to have experienced many of the doubts of his own characters, Pierre and Andrey. At fifty, the desire to find a religious justification for his life became overwhelming. He tells the story of his conversion in *A Confession,* a work which has been compared to the *Confessions* of Saint Augustine. The beliefs at which he finally arrived were, in his opinion, Christianity pure and simple, purged of the corruptions and additions introduced by Saint Paul and others, a Christianity no different in essence from the teachings of Buddha, Socrates, Lao Tzu, or other great teachers. Among the "corruptions" which he rejected were the doctrines of original sin, the atonement, the Trinity and the incarnation. The central core of Christianity he found in the ethic of universal love and the absolute renunciation of violence.

In politics, his views were equally extreme. He held that the state is evil per se, and that all of its institutions, including property and the law, are founded on theft or force. The ideal society is a kind of utopian anarchy. The same ascetic urge that compelled him as a sensualist to denounce sex led him as an artist to denounce art, or at least all art that lacked a clear moral purpose, or did not communicate simple, wholesome emotions. On these grounds, he was led to attack even Shakespeare, as well as most of his own writing up to that time.

Henceforth much of his writing was polemical or didactic, including such titles as *What I Believe, What Then Must We Do?, The Kingdom of God Is Within You,* and *What Is Art?* He began to attract disciples and to acquire an international reputation as a moral teacher. Gandhi was one of his correspondents. After 1884, Tolstoyism became an organized sect, and Yasnaya Polyana was its Mecca. Tolstoi adopted a new way of life in keeping with his views. He dressed like a peasant, worked with his hands, and renounced a meat diet. Believing that wealth is evil, he wished to renounce his property and royalties, but at this his wife drew the line. Accordingly he deeded everything to her and continued to live in his household as before, theoretically penniless, but actually quite comfortable.

Tolstoi's last years were embittered by friction between Sophie and his followers, especially a certain Vladimir Chertkoff who had installed himself as a kind of high priest of the Tolstoian cult. In 1910, finding his position at home intolerable, and feeling perhaps that his conversion had not really brought him peace, he secretly left his wife and home and set out, at the age of eighty-two, as a wanderer. He had no particular goal. He simply pressed on until his health broke down and he caught pneumonia in a small country railroad station. Sophie was summoned, but Chertkoff would not let her see her husband till he could no longer recognize her. On November 9 he died, besieged by followers, reporters, and even newsreel cameras.

Twenty Thousand Leagues
under the Sea

by

JULES VERNE (1828–1905)

The Characters

Captain Nemo—Commander of the submarine *Nautilus,* a man of mystery who, having suffered from oppression on land, has taken to the sea in his search for freedom and for vengeance.

Pierre Aronnax—A Frenchman of about forty, an enthusiastic marine biologist.

Conseil—Manservant to Aronnax, a stolid Fleming about thirty years old, loyal, courageous and imperturbable.

Ned Land—A Canadian harpooner, restless and choleric.

Captain Farragut USN—Commander of the USS *Abraham Lincoln.*

The Story

In 1866, the world is aroused by reports that ships at sea have occasionally sighted a strange object, several hundred feet long, moving at great speed, and at times luminous. Several ships have been rammed by it and nearly sunk. No one knows what it is, but most experts suggest that it is an unknown and extraordinary species of whale. Among these experts is Professor Pierre Aronnax, a French biologist, the narrator of the story. In the summer of 1867, Aronnax, who has just completed an expedition to "the disagreeable territory of Nebraska" and is returning to France loaded with specimens, is invited by the United States government to join an expedition for the purpose of tracking down the unknown beast. With only three hours' notice, he ships aboard the USS *Abraham Lincoln* with his faithful manservant, a Fleming named Conseil. Also on board is a Canadian harpooner, Ned Land, with whom Aronnax becomes friendly.

After some months, the monster is sighted near Japan, and the chase begins. The strange object seems to be playing games with the ship, which it can easily outrun and outmaneuver. At length the *Abraham Lincoln* draws close enough for Ned Land to launch a harpoon. The missile bounces harmlessly off, and a great spout of water from the object breaks over the ship, washing Aronnax and several others overboard. In the confusion which follows, Aronnax, Land, and Conseil cannot get back to the *Abraham Lincoln*, which is disabled and cannot come about. Instead they find refuge on the back of the very creature they have been hunting, and realize, from the bolts and armor plate, that their whale is actually an enormous submarine. They kick against the sides to attract attention, and eight men, their faces covered with masks, draw them inside.

The submarine commander is a mysterious Captain Nemo. The name, Latin for "no one," recalls another traveler, Odysseus, who also called himself "no one." Nemo's past life is hinted at but never fully explained. We gather that, because of some great tragedy, he has cut himself off from human society, and, with a crew of like-minded exiles, has made a new home beneath the waves, the only place where he feels free. Clearly a scientific and mechanical genius, he has designed and built a submarine without precedent for that time. Fabulously rich, he is a man of cultivation and taste, who has furnished his submarine with a library, a pipe organ, and an art collection that might have been culled from the Louvre or the Uffizi. Finally, he is a marine biologist who has assembled a collection of specimens that is the envy and delight of Professor Aronnax.

Toward his guests, Nemo is courteous but reserved. He explains that he cannot release them for fear that his secret will be betrayed, but that M. Aronnax is welcome to explore the depths of the ocean with him. The rest of the novel is an account of the marvels encountered on his underwater excursion. Many pages are devoted to a description of the submarine (which is called the *Nautilus)* and to the details of its construction. We learn, for instance, that it is 232 feet long, is powered by electricity, displaces 50,000 cubic feet, and cost £ 67,500, exclusive of equipment and fixtures. When Aronnax has taken in all the statistics that he (and the reader) can digest, he and his host put on diving suits to explore the ocean bed. Equipped with electric lamps and cylinders of compressed air, they collect specimens of coral, visit a marvelous underwater forest of seaweed, fight with sharks, witness an eruption of a submarine volcano, and explore the ruined cities of Atlantis. Off the coast of Ceylon, they visit the pearl fisheries where Nemo shows his guest an enormous pearl the size of a coconut (Aronnax calculates its value at £ 500,000). Later they pass from the Red Sea to the Mediterranean through an underwater tunnel known only to Nemo. On its most dangerous adventure, the *Nautilus* travels under ice to discover the South Pole, and barely escapes being frozen into the heart of an iceberg.

At times, we get hints that Nemo is more than a refugee from the tyrants of the land. He is carrying on an active war of revenge. On one occasion, Aronnax and his friends are shut in their quarters and drugged. When they come to, they learn that some violent incident has occurred in which a member of the crew has been fatally wounded. As the *Nautilus* cruises off the tip of India, Nemo's face darkens as he speaks of the subjugation of that country. Near Cape Matapan, Nemo delivers a shipment of gold bullion to a Greek diver; one speculates that he may be financing a revolution somewhere, possibly the revolt of Crete against Turkey. The climax of these operations comes off the Scilly Islands, where the *Nautilus* is attacked by a naval vessel. Is it French or British, or of some other nationality? It carries no flag, and so we do not know. Nemo rams the ship and sails on.

Swiftly the submarine plunges northward, and Nemo, convulsed by grief, vengeance, and remorse, stays out of sight of his captives. All supervision and control seem relaxed. Ned Land, who has never given up hope of escape, proposes that as soon as the *Nautilus* surfaces, the three companions try to seize the ship's dinghy and make for the nearest land. They have just climbed on deck and shut the hatch behind them when they hear an outcry from inside the submarine. Nemo, whether by accident or design, has sailed his vessel into the heart of the Maelstrom, a great whirlpool off the coast of Norway, so powerful that it can swallow up whole ships. Aronnax falls unconscious from a chance blow and wakes to find that somehow he and his companions have escaped the Maelstrom and are lying safely in a fisherman's hut on the Lofoten Islands. And what has happened to Nemo and the *Nautilus?* Professor Aronnax never discovers.

Critical Opinion

Why Jules Verne? In a book devoted to the acknowledged masterpieces of the European novel, what place is there for a work of science fiction read chiefly by boys of twelve or thereabouts? One answer is that for every reader who gets through Rabelais or Cervantes there are probably thousands who have devoured Jules Verne with effortless delight. This fact in itself is worth pondering. Verne's achievement was to create a new form of imagination in which the old magic of the romantic movement was wedded to the new magic of science and technology. He was a supreme mythmaker, and in one form or another, his myths are still very much alive.

Let us begin by noting Verne's obvious weaknesses. After all, anyone who turns out sixty-five novels is going to produce a good deal of hack work. The plots are generally too loose, and even the voyage of the *Nautilus* is little more than a series of unrelated episodes alternating with lectures on marine biology. The characters are as lifeless as pasteboard and fall into a few standard types: the intellectual (usually a scientist), the man of action, and the comic commentator (generally a servant). In the present novel, these three are represented by Aronnax, Land, and Conceil. An explanation for these stereotypes may be that Verne wrote with one eye on the theater, and many of his stories brought in additional royalties as plays. Passepartout, Phileas Fogg and Hector Servadac are good roles for character actors.

The most memorable character Verne ever created is Captain Nemo. He has a certain romantic vitality, with his austere manner, his gloomy withdrawal from mankind, his love of nature, his hatred of tyrants, his mysterious history, his burden of grief or guilt. These, however, are also stereotypes derived from the Byronic hero of fifty years before. Even Captain Nemo's style of speech, as he stands on the South Pole and apostrophizes the setting sun, sounds like a bad rhapsody by Chateaubriand. Nevertheless, Nemo proved so popular that Verne could not leave him to perish in the Maelstrom, any more than Conan Doyle could leave Sherlock Holmes in the Riechenbach Fall. He reappears to die once more in *The Mysterious Island* (1875), where the mystery of his life is cleared up at last. Nemo is actually Dakkar, an Indian prince who has fought the British in the Mutiny, has lost his wife and children, and has become a fugitive, roaming the oceans and seeking revenge. This history is the key to a good deal that is unexplained in the earlier book, and yet Nemo as an Oriental is not very convincing. There is nothing particularly Indian about him; he is a man without a country.

Much of the appeal of Verne's novels undoubtedly stems from themes that have the power of myths, and stir our imagination on a preconscious level. The cave, the lonely island, the sea voyage, these are all archetypes as old as Homer. Some can be read as dream symbols of the sort that would interest a psychoanalyst. In one chapter, for instance, the *Nautilus* penetrates a dark underwater tunnel and finds itself in a great womblike chamber in the heart of a volcano. Still other themes in these novels remain as the staple diet of the children's television program: the mad scientist, the interplanetary voyage, the relic of a prehistoric civilization. As for scientific gadgets and mechanical marvels, they still delight adult admirers of James Bond.

Science fiction is not new; it goes back at least as far as *Gulliver's Travels.* In the family tree of literature, Jules Verne lies in the direct line of descent that runs from Edgar Allan Poe to H. G. Wells. Some of his plots are obviously lifted from Poe, who also wrote about balloon voyages, arctic exploration, and a descent into the Maelstrom. Verne, however, loved science as Poe did not, and knew much more about it. He always based his novels on careful research; when mathematical calculations were called for, they were so elaborate and so precise that some people suspected that they had been supplied by the English astronomer Sir John Herschel. The long paragraphs of scientific data are introduced, of course, to make a fantastic yarn sound plausible, but they accomplish more than this; they are a kind of prose poetry. Consider, for instance, the descriptions of marine life in *Twenty Thousand Leagues under the Sea (Vingt Mille Lieues sous les Mers)*. One can imagine Verne raiding some textbook on zoology to produce passages like this:

> The greater number (of plants), instead of leaves, shot forth blades of capricious shapes . . . pink, carmine, green, olive, fawn and brown. I saw there . . . pavonari spread like a fan, as if to catch the breeze; scarlet ceramies, whose laminaries extended their edible shoots of fern-shaped nereocysti, which grow to a height of fifteen feet; clusters of acetabuli, whose stems increase in size upwards, and numbers of other marine plants, all devoid of flowers!

Professor Aronnax is a fearful pedant, but at least he is a lyrical one.

As a scientific prophet, Verne was ahead of his age, but not too far ahead. His predictions must have seemed fairly plausible even in his own day, and by now most of them have come true. We no longer marvel at the electrical equipment of the *Nautilus,* air travel is commonplace, and even the voyage around the moon has come to pass. On the other hand, certain important developments in today's world such as the role of computers and automatic controls in modern technology, or the fearful possibilities of atomic fission, are not even hinted at in Verne. Nor did Verne ever explore the implications of evolution and applied genetics; he was a Catholic who never accepted Darwinism. Today we see Verne in historical perspective as a product of his age, a fate that has also overtaken more recent writers like Conan Doyle and H. G. Wells. But if science becomes obsolete, adventure never does, and for the young reader or the young-in-heart adult who is too innocent to know or care if a story is up to date or not, Verne's novels are as readable as they ever were.

The Author

For a man whose writings were so crammed with extraordinary adventures, the life of Jules Verne was placid to the point of dullness. No doubt the two facts are connected. He was born in 1828 in Nantes, the son of a solid and intensely conservative provincial lawyer. Nantes is a seaport, and the one touch of romance in Jules's childhood was the sea, which was to figure in so many of his stories. At eleven he acted out the dream of many small boys: he shipped as a cabin boy aboard a three-master bound for the Indies. Anticlimactically, he was intercepted at the next port of call and brought home in disgrace by his father. Thereafter he continued to travel, but for the most part only in his imagination.

Since it was assumed that at twenty Jules would enter his father's firm, he was sent to Paris to study law. Paris appealed to him, while the law did not. He preferred to write short stories and plays, some of which were actually produced. Despite pressure from his father to return to Nantes, he took a job as secretary to a theatrical producer. It paid only a hundred francs a month, but it meant a chance to stay in Paris and write. In 1855, he married Honorine Morel, a young widow with two daughters. The marriage was thoroughly happy, but it obliged Verne to look for more profitable work. With money advanced by his father he was able to buy his way into a firm of Paris stockbrokers, and for several years spent his time faithfully at the Paris Bourse. In the back of his mind, however, was still his old dream of becoming a writer.

Verne's talents were diverted from bedroom farces to science fiction by a friend, Felix Nadar, a photographer and pioneer aeronaut whose hobby was photographing Paris from balloons and who dreamed of inventing a workable helicopter. In 1860, Nadar started to build a great balloon called the *Géant* which was to lift a gondola large enough to hold several rooms. Fascinated by the project, Verne wrote a history of balloons and aerial navigation. The publisher Hetzel told him that the manuscript showed promise, but that the public did not want to be instructed; it wanted to be amused. Why not rewrite the whole thing as a yarn? Verne thereupon produced *Five Weeks in a Balloon (Cinq Semaines en Ballon)*, a novel about a group of explorers who travel across Africa from Zanzibar to Senegal in a great balloon, experiencing hair-raising adventures. Verne had hit on a foolproof formula for a successful novel: contrive a fantastic plot and make it plausible by ballasting it with facts and figures. The result is science fiction. A century later Verne's formula still works.

The novel was such a success that Hetzel and Verne signed a twenty-year contract that was to be profitable to both. For the rest of his life Verne wrote Hetzel one or two novels a year, so many in fact that after his death they kept pouring out posthumously for six years more. Some skeptics even thought that Jules Verne was not a man but a *nom de plume* used by a whole stable of anonymous authors. In all, there were sixty-five books in the series, the most famous being *Voyage to the Center of the Earth* (*Voyage au Centre de la Terre*, 1864), *From the Earth to the Moon* (*De la Terre à la Lune*, 1865), *Twenty Thousand Leagues under the Sea* (1870), *Around the World in Eighty Days* (*Voyage autour du Monde en Quatre-vingts Jours*, 1873), *The Mysterious Island* (*L'Ile Mystérieuse*, 1875), *Michael Strogoff* (1876), *The Begum's Fortune* (1879), and *The Clipper of the Clouds* (1886). Of these, *Twenty Thousand Leagues* is probably the best known.

Success brought Verne a number of luxuries: a big house, servants for Honorine, and a private yacht for himself, but it did not stop the flow of books. Seeking greater seclusion, he moved his family to the provincial town of Amiens and settled down to a life of ordered regularity and bourgeois comfort. During the Franco-Prussian War (of which he did not approve), he served as a kind of coast guard officer, patrolling the Somme in his yacht with a handful of superannuated veterans armed with rusty rifles. Fortunately, the Germans did not attack by sea. There was one moment of nearly fatal drama when Gaston Verne, the son of his beloved younger brother Paul, went insane and shot Verne in the leg. Thereafter, Verne was lame, and could no longer sail his yacht. In compensation, he ran for city councilman in Amiens and won. He took the job seriously and derived much innocent satisfaction from it, but resisted all suggestions that he go into national politics.

As the years went by, he grew more retired, more wedded to his bourgeois provincial life, and more melancholy as his old friends and family died off one by one. His later books were not so magical as the old ones. After fifty years his imagination was beginning to flag. He did his best to keep up with the latest inventions, introducing automobiles and radios into his last novels, but the reality of science was outrunning his dreams. Younger writers like H. G. Wells were beginning to write science fiction, too. Still Verne continued to write with dogged persistence. In 1905, he died of diabetes. His name remains a household word to this day.

Nana

by

ÉMILE ZOLA (1840–1902)

The Characters

Nana—A fashionable demimondaine—vulgar, improvident, thoughtless and destructive.

Bordenave—The irascible manager of the Théâtre des Variétés.

Bosc—A somewhat alcoholic actor at the Variétés.

Marquis de Chouard—Father of Countess Sabine, an elderly and respected man, but a lecher like the rest.

Daguenet—One of Nana's lovers. He has run through a large fortune and is looking for an heiress to marry.

Fauchery—A journalist, variously the lover of Nana, Rose Mignon, and Countess Muffat, a cynical and worldly opportunist. The name suggests "false sweetheart."

Foucarmont—A young naval officer in Nana's circle.

Fontan—A second-rate actor; he is brutal to Nana, who loves him and keeps him till he deserts her.

Georges Hugon (Zizi)—A delicate boy in his teens, infatuated with Nana, who treats him as a big baby or puppy.

Philippe Hugon—Elder brother of Georges, whom he elbows aside; he commits embezzlement for Nana.

Mme. Hugon—Mother of Georges and Philippe, a respectable woman deeply wounded by her sons' misconduct.

Labordette—One of Nana's male friends.

Hector de la Faloise—Another of Nana's young men, who comes to Paris to acquire a fashionable tone, and allows himself to be ruined as part of the process.

Mme. Lérat—Nana's aunt, a seedy old woman interested mainly in cards.

Count Muffat de Beuville—A distinguished, devout, and austere aristocrat, sexually inhibited until he meets Nana.

Countess Sabine Muffat de Beuville—Wife of the count. Although she is seemingly as strict and pious as her husband, she has an affair with Fauchery.

Estelle—Daughter of the count, a skinny, colorless girl who marries Daguenet.

Rose Mignon—A comic actress at the Variétés, rival to Nana.

Mignon—Her husband, manager and pimp.

Louis—Nana's son, a sickly child of three or four.

Laure Piédefer—The lesbian proprietress of a restaurant frequented by prostitutes.

Prullière—A comic actor at the Variétés.

Steiner—A wealthy businessman engaged in various highly speculative ventures.

Prince of Scots—Zola's portrait of the Prince of Wales (Edward VII).

Satin—A small-time prostitute; a lesbian in love with Nana.

Tricon—A procuress.

Count Xavier de Vandeuvres—The last of an ancient family, who is obsessively squandering the remains of a vast fortune.

Théophile Venot—A retired lawyer and a devout Catholic, who tries to reclaim Muffat.

Zoé—Nana's maid, a prudent and calculating woman who is saving up money to set herself up as a madame.

Prostitutes—Gaga, Simonne Cabiroche, Clarisse Bresnus, Louise Violane, Blanche de Sivry, Léa de Horn, Lucy Stewart, Caroline Héquet, Tatan Néné, Irma d'Anglars.

The Story

Nana is the daughter of Gervaise, the alcoholic laundress of *L'Assommoir*, and therefore belongs to the hapless family of the Macquart. Zola devotes one sentence to establishing the connection and then ignores it. At the start of the novel she is an actress. Admittedly she can neither act nor sing, but her flamboyant sex appeal makes up for everything else. She quickly becomes the most famous of the Parisian demi-mondaines during the luxurious and licentious Second Empire. The details of her story are crowded to the point of confusion, and need not be summarized minutely, but the main outlines are clear: Nana spreads ruin wherever she goes. She corrupts the Muffat family: the count is her slave, the countess seeks consolation with other men, the count's daughter is married off to one of Nana's old lovers, and even the count's aged father-in-law winds up in her bed. She destroys the Hugon family: Georges, a teen-age boy, commits suicide for her sake and his brother Philippe becomes an embezzler, leaving their mother broken with grief. She destroys Vandeuvres, who kills himself in the flaming ruins of his racing stables. Those who do not die are left bankrupt.

Nana in her turn is victimized by those she loves, like Fontan, an actor who beats her, and Satin, a bedraggled lesbian who tries to drive other lovers away. Above all, she is ruined by her own extravagance. China dishes and crystal scent bottles crumble at her touch, she throws a handful of diamonds into a coal fire to see if they will burn, and her servants make their fortunes on what she throws away. Her life is a swift crescendo of waste and destruction ending in ruin and collapse. She disappears from Paris for a time, and is supposed to be traveling in the East—Turkey or Russia. When she finally reappears, she is dying of smallpox, and the men who have once loved her do not even dare to enter her room.

Critical Opinion

When *Nana* was written, the sentimental theme of the courte-san with a pure heart, yearning for true love, was a cliché of romantic plays and novels: Verdi's *La Traviata*, based on *Camille* by Dumas, is a famous and popular example. Zola's novel was intended to explode this myth. His heroine is no Camille. She is vulgar, unfeeling, and barely literate. Her power over men is purely sensual. This sensuality Zola repre-sents as invariably destructive and degrading; there is, in fact, a distinctly moralistic undertone to the novel which most writers today would try to avoid, and which is hard to reconcile with the psychological determinism in which Zola professed to believe. Despite its theme, *Nana* is not smutty. There is, for instance, no explicit description of the sexual act. In the one scene where Nana's nudity is described in detail, she is warming herself in front of a fire, and is unromantically compared to a fat goose roasting on a spit. The most unpleasant scene of all is the one in which Muffat, the court chamberlain, is made to crawl on his knees and fetch a handkerchief like a puppy; it is the degradation of the situation that disturbs us, not the sensuality. (The scene, incidentally, was probably lifted from Otway's *Venice Preserved*, an English play of the seventeenth century.)

Zola was a naturalist in theory but a symbolist in practice, and much of the coarse poetry of his novels depends on the symbolic power of his imagery. One such image compares Nana to a golden fly, glittering like a jewel, which has been born on a dung heap and flies in at palace windows, spreading poison wherever it lights. Another symbol of Nana's life is her great luxurious bed, a masterpiece of jewelers' work, with gold and silver cupids, flesh-colored hangings, and at the foot a nude figure of Nana herself. Count Muffat has paid for it, and his reward is that the first time he sets eyes on it, it is occupied by his father-in-law, the Marquis de Chouard, an old man whose sexual exertions have reduced him to a state of slobbering, senile paralysis. The furniture in the Muffat home is also an index of moral deterioration. At the start of the novel, the drawing room is austerely furnished in the stiff Empire style, whereas at the end, the new furniture, with its sensuous curves, deep cushions and ornate decoration, is a symbol of the change that has come over an entire society.

Zola's handling of crowd scenes is famous. The subtleties of quiet dialogue were too fine for him, but a bold scene with masses of people in vigorous motion was exactly suited to his genius. One such passage describes a day at the races, when a horse named for Nana wins the Grand Prix. Zola builds up his picture with an accumulation of details and scraps of conversation, shifts the scene often enough to create a sense of busy confusion, and skillfully increases the tempo to a climax amid the roars of the crowd shouting the name of the winning horse, while Nana, flushed with triumph, takes the cheers as if they were meant for her. Another memorable scene is Nana's death. She lies, a rotting corpse in a rented room, while a group of whores stand around her commenting like a Greek chorus, and in the streets outside a mob, gripped by war fever, shouts "To Berlin, to Berlin." On closer analysis, this scene seems contrived. There is, for example, no especial appropriateness in having Nana die of smallpox instead of the more obvious syphilis. Zola chose smallpox presumably because it is so disfiguring, and provided a strong contrast with Nana's former beauty. Furthermore, there is no real connection between Nana and the Franco-Prussian War, except that Zola wished Nana to die along with the empire whose rottenness she typified. And yet, as we read the last chapter, the manipulation of events does not strike us. The scene is as powerful as Zola meant it to be.

Since it was necessary for Nana to die in 1870, Zola was obliged to compress the passage of time. Nana's child Louis was born, we are told, when Nana was sixteen, and yet, at the end of the book, he is still described as a baby. For a teenager, Nana leads a full life. Fortunately we lose track of time amid the crowding, hurrying events, and so we are generally able to think of Nana as a woman in her twenties. Such confusion of time would have been impossible in *Germinal,* with its firm plotting, but in *Nana* Zola is depicting the triumph of chaos. At first the old order, represented by the Muffat family, with its honor and faith and ancient traditions, seems to stand firm; then cracks appear in the structure; finally everything crumbles as fortunes, honor, lives, and even the empire itself are swept into the vortex of destruction.

Germinal

by

ÉMILE ZOLA

The Characters

Étienne Lantier—The hero of the novel, an intelligent man who thinks about social problems and wants to better himself. He is rather timid with girls, and reserved and delicate in his love for Catherine. Although usually self-controlled, he is supposed to have a pathological susceptibility to alcohol. He is the illegitimate child of Gervaise Macquart, the mother of Nana.

Souvarine—A nihilist, formerly a Russian noble and medical student, who fled from Russia after an attempt on the life of the Czar. An intelligent, reserved man, he has cut himself off from all ordinary human ties.

Rasseneur—A former miner, now an innkeeper. As a labor leader, he pleads for moderation and opposes the strike.

Pluchart—A secretary for the Workers' International, a busy, self-important man, interested only in his organization.

Hennebeau—Manager of the Montsou mines, a hardworking and conscientious agent whose great grief is his unhappy marriage.

Mme. Hennebeau—His wife, a vicious and sensual woman.

The Grégoire Family—A bourgeois family, living off the income from their mining stock, personally amiable and kindly, though blind to the gravity of the social tensions about them.

Négrel—Engineer at Montsou and nephew of Hennebeau. Although he is not above cuckolding his uncle, he is professionally competent and shows unusual heroism in rescuing the trapped miners.

Deneulin—Cousin of Grégoire, and owner of the Jean-Bart mine. An honest, likable man who enjoys the respect of his men.

Toussaint Maheu—A miner, a short, sturdy man, occasionally given to outbursts of temper, but a good husband and a sober workman.

La Maheude—His wife, an honest, hardworking woman. In the opening chapters her main concern is to keep her family fed. During the strike she is fanatical and militant; at the end she is numbed and resigned.

Zacharie Maheu—The eldest son, twenty-one years old, thin and anemic.

Catherine Maheu—The eldest daughter, about fifteen, a frail, undernourished, gentle girl.

Jeanlin Maheu—The second son, a vicious child with simian features.

Alzire Maheu—The second daughter, a hunchback.

Bonnemort—Maheu's father, an old man broken by work and injuries; at the end he becomes insane.

Levaque—A miner in Maheu's crew.

La Levaque—His wife, a slatternly housekeeper.

Bébert Levaque—Their son, a big, hulking boy who plays with Jeanlin.

Bouteloup—Levaque's lodger and lover of La Levaque.

Philomène Levaque—A thin, consumptive girl, mistress of Zacharie Maheu, by whom she has two children.

Pierron—Another miner and neighbor of the Maheu family.

La Pierronne—His wife, who keeps a small shop and entertains Dansaert, the foreman.

Mère Brulé—Mother of La Pierronne, a fierce old woman with a fanatical hatred of the company.

Lydie Pierron—A ten-year-old girl, playmate of Bébert and of Jeanlin, who intimidates her.

Maigrat—The storekeeper, who will not extend credit to families unless their daughters sleep with him.

Dansaert—The mine foreman, a coward and rather disliked.

Chaval—A collier, Catherine Maheu's lover, a brutal and insolent man.

La Mouquette—A haulage girl, fat, coarse, sensual and good-natured.

The Story

Montsou is a mining village in northeast France, a squalid place occupied by a few mining officials, a handful of shopkeepers, and a mass of workers who live on the verge of starvation. To Montsou comes Étienne Lantier looking for work. He finds a job at Le Voreux, the principal pit of the district. The first dozen chapters of the novel describe the life of the miner as seen through his unfamiliar eyes. After a time, he takes lodgings with a family of miners named Maheu, and is attracted to their daughter Catherine. Since she has an acknowledged lover named Chaval, he makes no advances to her.

There is another class at Montsou, the wealthy bourgeoisie, including the shareholders and managers. Hennebeau, who runs the mine, in turn takes orders from the directors in Paris. Négrel, his nephew, is an engineer. Deneulin, an independent operator, is trying to rehabilitate a rival pit nearby. Grégoire and his family live comfortably on their investments. Many of the upper class are individually charitable and well intentioned, but they cannot understand the problems of the miners, especially when their own interests are threatened.

Étienne is more intelligent and better read than most of his comrades, and he dreams of correcting the conditions under which he works, the poverty, the dangerous and brutalizing labor. His associates in this hope are Rasseneur, who owns the local pub; Pluchart, an organizer for the Workers' International; and Souvarine, a Russian anarchist in exile. Of these three, Étienne leans most toward Pluchart.

Meanwhile the tension between workers and management is increasing. The issue is the form of payment for timbering, that is, building the props which are needed to keep the tunnels from collapsing. Because the workers are paid for each tubful of coal mined, they are reluctant to spend time on the necessary but unprofitable timbering work. The company, afraid of cave-ins, proposes to pay for the timbering and coal separately. The men suspect a concealed pay cut and go on strike.

Étienne becomes the leader, displacing the moderate Rasseneur. As the strike spreads, misery deepens and violence breaks out. The strikers try to close down the rival pit at Jean-Bart, even though there is no dispute there. They attack the buildings, try to burn them, and succeed in cutting the cables that operate the lifts. A number of miners, including Chaval and Catherine, barely escape being trapped. The damage ruins Deneulin, the owner of the Jean-Bart, and obliges him to sell out to the Montsou monopoly. Next the miners sweep through the streets of Montsou shouting for bread. An unpopular shopkeeper named Maigrat is killed and castrated in a paroxysm of anger and violence.

This tumult is not unwelcome to the company, which now has an excuse to ask for military protection. Troops are billeted in the town, and scab labor is introduced. Chaval is put in charge of the strikebreakers, embittering still further his natural rivalry with Étienne. Soon violence breaks out again when the soldiers, who have been stationed around the pit to protect the strikebreakers, are stoned by the strikers. The soldiers return with a volley of fire which kills a number of villagers, including Maheu.

This new violence obliges the government to bring pressure on the company to reach a settlement. The strikebreakers are dismissed, the pits are reopened, and the miners sullenly go back to work. Then, when all appears quiet at last, Souvarine, the anarchist, takes a hand. He has had no part in the strike, which he considers wasted effort. Now he aims a death blow at the mine by sabotaging the casing of the shaft. Water pours in from underground channels, timbers are swept away, tunnels collapse, and the pit falls in. Even the buildings and machinery are swallowed up.

A number of miners are trapped in the disaster, including Étienne, Catherine, and Chaval, who take refuge together at the upper end of a dry tunnel. The inevitable battle between the two men breaks out, Chaval is killed, and Étienne at last is able to possess the woman he loves—somewhat improbably, it must be admitted, considering the danger, the rising water, and the starved condition of both lovers. Eventually rescuers are able to break through into the prison, but by this time Catherine is dead and Étienne's hair has turned white.

When he has regained his strength, Étienne leaves Montsou for Paris, where he intends to work with Pluchart for the International. As he goes, he visualizes his fellow miners under his feet and thinks of them as the seeds of a new order, now germinating, whose growth will one day crack the earth asunder.

Critical Opinion

The name *Germinal* is taken from the French revolutionary calendar. It is a spring month, a time of sowing and germination, and, as the title of the novel, it suggests both the violence of revolt and the slow organic processes of nature. As the last page makes clear, the miners themselves are the seeds, hidden underground but destined to break out and bear their fruit in a new society. Their sufferings and their struggle are the theme of what is probably the greatest of all novels about the labor movement.

Though he enlists our sympathies in behalf of the miners, Zola is careful not to overstate their case. He distributes his heroes and villains on both sides of the issue, and shows that capital and labor are both caught in the grip of economic forces which they cannot control. The owners and management are not evil men or normally heartless except where their interests are threatened. Deneulin is fair, Négrel is courageous, the Grégoires kindly. Even the company is driven by the pressure of declining markets. In short, the true villain of the story is the economic system itself.

Three men propose three distinct ways of dealing with this system. Rasseneur is the moderate, believing in negotiation and compromise. Étienne is the activist, believing in organization and strikes. Souvarine is the anarchist who does not wish to reform anything; he proposes to destroy the whole system so that a better one may take its place.

Germinal is based on careful research. The strike is a composite of several actual strikes that occurred in the sixties, seventies, and early eighties. To gather material, Zola read newspapers, medical reports and documents. He went into mines and snooped around mining villages; he interviewed engineers, labor leaders and workers. Certain characters, like Rasseneur, were drawn from life. To all this material Zola brought a powerful shaping imagination. We see this creative power notably in his similes, which endow even inanimate objects with a life of their own. Thus the mine is represented as a monstrous beast whose very name suggests its voracity, and which lives by gulping down human lives. When the mine collapses and the buildings fall in, the spectacle is like the death agony of a living thing. Or, for masterly control of atmosphere, consider the description of the mine district in the opening chapters, with its chiaroscuro of hellish flame against hellish blackness. In these passages, Zola the naturalist writes like a symbolist.

The controlling hand of the artist is also apparent in the carefully manipulated contrasts, some of them intensely ironic, between the rich and the poor of Montsou. For instance, a description of the Maheus' breakfast, with its grubby poverty, is balanced by one of the leisurely and luxurious meals of the Grégoires. There is heavy satire in the account of Mme. Hennebeau's slumming tour of the village, during which her visitors profess to be enchanted by the happy, wholesome life they find there. And the climax of irony comes when, after a mob of miners has swept through the streets of Montsou shouting for bread, the police come to restore order, and following them a baker's delivery wagon with an order of patty shells.

The hand of the artist is if anything too obvious at some points, especially the melodramatic scene in which Catherine and the two rival men are trapped together, the battle to the death and the lovemaking in the bowels of the earth. Nor is there much to be said for Zola's attempt to explain his hero's character in terms of heredity. Étienne is the son of Gervaise, the alcoholic laundress of *L'Assommoir*, and from her he is supposed to have inherited a nervous system that goes wild after a single drink. Actually he is the most intelligent, steady, and responsible miner of the lot. We are told that he harbors a homicidal streak in his character, but even this crops out only when the author finds it necessary to kill off Chaval. It would have been better for *Germinal* if Zola had never heard of heredity. Still, these blemishes can be passed over. Here is a sweeping, powerful, brutal book, which explores a grave social injustice with indignation and compassion. And yet it is no mere tract or piece of propaganda; it is also a work of art, and one of the dozen greatest novels in French literature.

The Author

Émile Zola, whose novels dominated the French naturalist
movement, was only half French. His father was a civil engineer of mixed Italian and Greek extraction who had settled in
Provence where he was directing the construction of a water
supply for the town of Aix. His mother came of northern
French stock, hardworking, disciplined, and temperamentally
at odds with the ebullient Provençal types among whom she
found herself. His father died when Émile was only six, leaving his mother to struggle against growing poverty with no
other assets than an unsettled lawsuit against the town of Aix.
Much of Zola's work may be understood as a response to the
influence of his strong, possessive mother, her resentment of
the bourgeoisie, who would not accept her, and her hatred of
the local poor, to whose level she feared to fall. If it is true
that the best sociological critics are those whose own social
position is ambiguous, then Zola was destined to be a social
novelist; his work was his revenge on Aix. It may also have
been the result of his mother's influence that Zola chose sexual
themes to express his rejection of the society that had rejected
him. The poor are promiscuous, the middle class hypocritical,
and the aristocracy depraved: this is a formula that runs
through his novels.

For the ten years of his life from seventeen to twenty-seven,
Zola was a bohemian, not conspicuously successful at anything. He studied at Paris and Marseilles, but took no diploma.
He wrote journalism, art criticism, and potboilers. He shared
rooms for a time with a boyhood friend from Aix, the painter
Cézanne. He worked as a clerk for the Paris publisher and
bookseller, Hachette. At times he was so hard up that he was
reduced to catching the sparrows outside his attic window
and roasting them. He also found a mistress, Alexandrine
Meley, a steady, prudent girl with motherly instincts and
middle-class ambitions, a girl of whom even his mother ap-
proved. The relationship gave him the emotional stability his
work demanded, and in 1870 they were married.

Zola's life work was a series of twenty novels, conceived in
imitation of Balzac's *Human Comedy*, and designed to trace
the fortunes of a single family under the Second Empire. This

family is derived from a single ancestor in the town of Plassans in Provence (obviously Aix). The legitimate descendants, named Rougon, are restless, intelligent men who back Louis Napoleon during the coup of 1851 and ride with him into power. One of them, Eugène, becomes a minister in the imperial government, where his native ruthlessness serves him well. An illegitimate branch of the family, the Mouret, are middle-class entrepreneurs. One of them founds a great Parisian department store and makes a fortune on the ruin of his smaller competitors. Another illegitimate branch, the Macquart, are proletarians; from them come a swarm of prostitutes, criminals and alcoholics, including Nana and Étienne, the protagonists of the two novels discussed in this book. Zola's plan enables him to explore every corner of French society and expose its corruption. His novels are a series of attacks on the officially sanctioned ideals of the day: the honor of the army, the piety of the clergy, the sanctity of the home, the industry of the peasant, the glory of the empire.

This projected series was barely launched when the Second Empire suddenly collapsed, a turn of events which obliged Zola to compress his time scale rather awkwardly and to introduce anachronistic situations which belong better to the eighteen-seventies and eighties than to the fifties and sixties. The French defeat at Sedan also provided material for a great war novel, *The Downfall (La Débâcle)*. Apart from the works already mentioned, the greatest of the series are *Earth (La Terre)*, a gloomy and violent study of peasant life, and *L'Assommoir*, a picture of alcoholic degeneration. Although the main characters in these novels are related, each book stands on its own merits and can be read apart from the rest.

Zola, as a former journalist, was well aware that sensationalism has a cash value, and these novels, which were certainly sensational, made him very rich. In time he realized one goal of an ambitious and self-made man: he moved into a luxurious villa in a fashionable district, which he stocked with expensive furnishings in vulgar and ostentatious profusion. Another goal, election to the French Academy, escaped him, although his efforts to that end were so persistent that he was known as the perpetual candidate.

Zola's enemies pictured him as a monster of vice, wallowing in filth. His defenders saw him as an angry moralist denouncing the vices of his age. He himself professed to be a detached and objective scientist exploring the effects of heredity and environment on the human personality. In this he resembles the French historian Taine, who declared that virtue and vice are natural products, like sugar and vitriol. Of course, Zola was no scientist, and had to rely on the prevailing psychology of the day, which was based on purely materialistic assumptions. Thus antisocial behavior was assumed to be caused by actual physical lesions or degeneration of the nervous system, and these, in turn, were supposed to be hereditarily transmitted. So bewitched was Zola by the prestige of science that he imagined his novels were laboratory experiments in which he endowed a human organism with a certain hereditary makeup, placed it in the controlled environment of his story, and recorded its reactions. This preposterous thesis he defended in a work called *The Experimental Novel (Le Roman Expérimental)*. Probably no author has ever displayed less understanding of his own creative processes.

Zola's literary practice became known as Naturalism, and established a tradition somewhat different from the earlier realism of Flaubert. Flaubert was equally concerned with the appearance of things, and the faithful representation of reality, but he had no especial bias in favor of ugliness and vice. Moreover, his realism was a literary program with no metaphysic behind it. Consequently the influence of the two men was different. Flaubert's descendants were fastidious stylists concerned with perfecting their art for its own sake, while Zola's followers were more likely to be heavy-handed social novelists like Frank Norris.

Once the Rougon-Macquart series was complete, Zola's work took a more optimistic turn. He began seriously to hope that society might reform itself. There are hints of this hope in *Germinal*. It becomes explicit in late novels like *Travail*, which pictures a utopian socialist society. One reason for this change in Zola's mood may have been the change in his private life. For years, his relations with Alexandrine had been embittered by their childlessness. In 1888 he fell in love with a pretty young laundress named Jeanne Rozerat, set up a second ménage for her, and to his great joy, sired two children. When Mme. Zola learned of it, there were furious scenes in which she smashed some of her husband's expensive furniture. For Zola, however, the relationship brought him a release from sexual anxiety and a new confidence in himself as a man. From this time on, he was more serene and fulfilled, although his writing began to lose its power and to become almost sentimental.

There is nothing false or sentimental, however, about his justly famous defense of Alfred Dreyfus, the Jewish army captain whose trial and imprisonment on a trumped-up charge of espionage rocked the Third Republic to its foundations. The controversy found all Zola's old enemies massed in one compact target: the army, the church, the government, the anti-Semites, the well-to-do—what would now be called the "establishment." The missile which he directed against this target was the famous letter, addressed to President Fauré and published in *L'Aurore*, entitled "J'accuse." Zola was deliberately courting a prosecution for libel, and he succeeded. The courtroom gave him the arena he wanted. The trial ended in a conviction which was appealed and reversed. A second trial took place, but before the verdict was announced, Zola, rather reluctantly and on the advice of his lawyers, fled to exile in England, where he bravely endured the cooking and the climate until the honor of Captain Dreyfus was at last vindicated.

Zola's death in 1902 was the result of a pointless accident: a charcoal heater, a plugged flue, and asphyxiation. The whole world united to pay him the homage he had so long deserved. Dreyfus attended the funeral, and Anatole France delivered an eloquent oration proclaiming Zola "a moment in the human conscience." As for Alexandrine, she concluded that her husband was a genius so great that he might make his own code of morals. She adopted his children.

The Twentieth
Century

The Crime of
Sylvestre Bonnard

by

ANATOLE FRANCE
(JACQUES ANATOLE FRANÇOIS THIBAULT)
(1844–1924)

The Characters

Sylvestre Bonnard—The narrator, a kindly and mellow old
man whose life has been wholly devoted to scholarship.

Thérèse—Bonnard's housekeeper, crotchety and inclined to
tyrannize over her master, but loyal and conscientious.

M. Coccoz—A book salesman fallen on hard times, a pathetic
nonentity.

Mme. Coccoz, later *Princess Trépof*—A pretty, vital and resourceful woman. It is hinted that she makes herself attractive to men who can be useful to her.

Dmitri Trépof—A Russian prince, second husband of Mme.
Coccoz, who beguiles his boredom by collecting matchboxes.

Victor Maldent (Bad Tooth)—Bonnard's uncle, a fire-eating
veteran of the Napoleonic Wars.

Michael-Angelo Polizzi—A Sicilian wine merchant, painter, archeologist, con man and pimp. The florid rhetoric of his
speech suggests his dishonesty.

Rafael Polizzi—A Parisian antique dealer, son of the above.

Clémentine de Lessay—The sweetheart of Bonnard's youth.

M. de Lessay—Clémentine's father, a gentleman of the old
regime and a fanatical royalist.

Paul de Gabry—A country gentleman and friend of Bonnard, interested mainly in sports and hunting.

Mme. de Gabry—Paul's wife, a gracious and sympathetic hostess.

Jeanne Alexandre Allier—Granddaughter of Clémentine, natural and lovable.

Maître Mouche—Jeanne's guardian, unscrupulous and probably lecherous.

Mlle. Préfère—The vicious and tyrannical headmistress of Jeanne's school.

Gélis—A protégé of Bonnard who marries Jeanne, a promising scholar with the enthusiasm and cocksureness of youth.

Hamilcar—Bonnard's cat, a quiet recluse like his master.

The Story

The Crime of Sylvestre Bonnard (*Le Crime de Sylvestre Bonnard*) is written in the form of a diary, the first entry dated 1861 and the last 1882. The narrative falls into two almost completely unrelated parts: a short prelude, "The Log," and the main story, "Jeanne Alexandre." The diarist, Sylvestre Bonnard, is an old bachelor who lives quietly with his housekeeper and his cat. He is a distinguished scholar who lives only for his work. His one passion is collecting manuscripts and fine editions.

The first section, covering the years 1861–1869, tells how Bonnard came to possess his choicest manuscript. On the day before Christmas, he is visited by a shabby book salesman, Coccoz, who tries pathetically to sell some of his trashy offerings. Bonnard gets rid of the man as quickly as he decently can. Later he learns that the salesman is desperately poor and lives with his wife, who is pregnant, in an unheated attic apartment in the same building. On a generous impulse, Bonnard orders his housekeeper to send the family soup and firewood, including a large yule log for the holiday.

Returning to his reading, Bonnard's attention is caught by a reference in a book catalog to an ancient manuscript of the *Golden Legend* (a medieval collection of saints' lives) translated into French by a monk called Jean Toutmouillé (literally, "all wet"). Bonnard is feverishly eager to track down this prize and add it to his collection, but the present where-abouts of the manuscript is unknown.

Then, in 1869 it turns up in a private collection in Sicily. After correspondence with the owner, a man named Polizzi, Bonnard makes the long trip south to inspect the manuscript, only to find that Polizzi has meanwhile sent it to Paris, where it is being offered for sale only a few blocks from Bonnard's residence. Bonnard is beside himself with disappointment and suspects that he has been tricked.

In Sicily, Bonnard meets a pretty French woman and her husband, Dmitri Trépof, a Russian prince who travels around Europe collecting matchboxes. Knowing that the Trépofs will understand his feelings as a frustrated collector, he tells them the story of the precious manuscript of the *Golden Legend*. Returning at once to Paris, he tries to buy the manuscript at auction, and bids every franc he possesses, but in vain. The treasure has been bought by an unknown collector who will not reveal his name. A second time Bonnard has the chagrin of seeing the *Golden Legend* escape him. Several weeks later, at Christmastime, there is a knock at the door, and a pretty boy of eight enters with a parcel for Bonnard. Inside it is a box shaped like a yule log, and inside that, buried under a mass of violets, is the manuscript, with a card signed by the Princess Trépof. Thérèse the housekeeper recognizes in the princess the same Mme. Coccoz to whom Bonnard had been kind so many years before.

The story resumes five years later. Bonnard has traveled to a country chateau where, as the guest of the owner, Paul de Gabry, he is to catalog the manuscript in the library. In the Gabry household there is an orphan girl, the daughter of a friend of the family. Her name is Jeanne Alexandre Allier, and she proves to be the granddaughter (in the first edition of the novel, the daughter) of Clémentine de Lessay, whom Bonnard had loved in his remote youth, but who had eventually married another man. The encounter stirs tender memories, and Bonnard vows to devote his last years to looking after the grandchild of his former sweetheart.

Jeanne is the ward of a lawyer, Maître Mouche, who has placed her in a boarding school where she is miserable. Bonnard obtains Mouche's grudging permission to visit the school, which is run by a formidable spinster named Mlle. Préfère. When the headmistress discovers that Bonnard is a bachelor and a member of the Institute, her husband-hunting instincts are aroused, and she proposes that Jeanne should visit Bonnard regularly in Paris, with herself as chaperone, of course. In time, she becomes so importunate that Bonnard is driven to tell her bluntly that he is not interested in marriage. In her vexation, Mlle. Préfère accuses him of taking an improper interest in Jeanne and gives orders that he is not to be admitted again to the school.

Bonnard is so outraged that he is ill for a time. When he recovers, he finds that Jeanne is now being seriously maltreated at the school. Mouche has cut off her stipend, and the headmistress has set her to work at menial tasks. Acting with a determination scarcely to be expected in an old bookworm, he goes to the school, bribes an attendant, and abducts Jeanne, taking her for safety to the Gabry home. Gabry points out that Bonnard has committed a serious crime, punishable by imprisonment. Gabry then goes to see Mouche, hoping that he can be intimidated or bought off. To his relief he finds that the lawyer has decamped, after embezzling large sums of money from his wards and clients.

Jeanne becomes the ward of Bonnard and lives in his house, where she introduces an unaccustomed note of youthful cheer and vitality. Bonnard, who has never been a father, now has the joy of being a sort of grandfather. There is a student named Gélis whom Bonnard is helping with his research. The two young people are drawn to each other and before the year is out they are engaged. Gélis does not expect any dowry, but Bonnard, acting *in loco parentis,* insists that Jeanne must have one. To raise the sum, he sells his books, including the precious manuscript of the *Golden Legend,* in the conviction that life and love and children are more important than any books. This sacrifice, however, is only the start of a new life for him. He retires to a country cottage and trains himself to be a botanist. His last piece of scholarship is a little book on the pollenization of flowers.

Critical Opinion

The Crime of Sylvestre Bonnard was Anatole France's first novel, the book that established his reputation. In time it became a recognized school text, and certainly it is a story that can safely be put into the hands of any child. In many ways, it is closer to Dickens than to the modern novel, relying on a melodramatic contrast of good and evil, an obvious manipulation of coincidence and an unashamed appeal to sentiment. The humor is Dickensian too; Mlle. Préfère is modeled on Mrs. Bardell, of *Bardell vs. Pickwick;* Maître Mouche would have been at home in the firm of Dodson and Fogg; Thérèse, the loyal, grumbling, tyrannical servant, is in a long literary tradition.

Still, the reader should not dismiss this novel as sentimental fluff. What makes it memorable is the personality of Bonnard himself: kindly, mellow, human, and gently eccentric. Anyone can create a villain. It is far harder to draw a convincing picture of a good man. Unless the reader believes that good people do not really exist, or that it is illegitimate to allow one's heart to be warmed by them, he will find in Bonnard a heartwarming character whom it is a pleasure to know.

Penguin Island

by

ANATOLE FRANCE
(JACQUES ANATOLE FRANÇOIS THIBAULT)

The Characters

> NOTE: *The names are given here in the form adopted in the standard English translation, where they are occasionally and somewhat inconsistently anglicized.*

Saint Maël—A Breton saint who baptizes the penguins, a pious, unworldly man.
Oberosia—A clever and sensual woman, later venerated as the patron saint of Penguinia.
Kraken—Husband of Oberosia, and founder of the royal

dynasty of Penguinia, "whose arm was strong and whose mind was subtle."

Trinco—A military adventurer representing Napoleon Bonaparte.

Father Agaric—A tireless and fanatical intriguer for the royalist cause. The name means "mushroom."

Father Cornemuse—Father Agaric's reluctant associate. The name means "bagpipe."

Crucho—Pretender to the throne of Penguinia.

Prince Adelstan de Boscenos—A supporter of the royalist cause.

Amiral (Admiral) Chatillon—A political adventurer, representing General Boulanger.

Viscountess Olive—Mistress of Chatillon.

Pyrot—An army officer representing Captain Dreyfus.

General Greatauk—Minister of War, representing General Mercier, Minister of War during the Dreyfus case.

Madame Clarence—The leader of a fashionable salon.

Eveline Clarence—Her daughter, later wife of Cérès.

Hippolyte Cérès—A Socialist minister of Posts and Telegraph.

Paul Visire—Prime Minister of Penguinia.

George Clair—The anarchist who accomplishes the destruction of Penguinian civilization.

The Story

Penguin Island (L'Isle des Pingouins) is a witty and satirical travesty of French history from the early legendary times down to the twentieth century, with a prophetic glimpse into the future. It begins with a mythical Breton saint, Maël, who by a series of marvelous events travels to the arctic zone. There he finds an island inhabited by large numbers of penguins whom, in his shortsightedness, he mistakes for men and baptizes as Catholics. His blunder causes consternation in heaven, where the saints and doctors of the church debate whether the sacrament is valid. Finally the Lord resolves the problem by agreeing to turn the penguins into men. Maël then conceives the idea of transporting the island back to Europe. He ties a thread to a rock, sets sail in his boat, and miraculously tows the island to the shores of Brittany.

The penguins are quick to learn the vices of mankind. When

Maël in his modesty makes clothes for them, the women discover they are more seductive clothed than naked. Dividing the fields among themselves, the penguins originate property, law, and warfare. They organize a legislative assembly whose first act is to impose taxes.

The cleverest of the penguins are a certain Kraken and a girl called Oberosia, the very girl, in fact, for whom Maël first made clothes. They strike up a liaison and together conceive a profitable hoax. Kraken disguises himself as a dragon, with false horns and tail, and, in this guise, raids the flocks and barnyards of the island. The peasants are terrified at first, but after a time they resist. Maël is persuaded that the dragon can be conquered only if a pure virgin will tie a cord about its neck and lead it away. Oberosia offers herself as the candidate, and the "dragon," actually a frame of wicker covered with skins, is led into the capital where Kraken "kills" it. In reward for his imposture, he receives an annual tribute and establishes a royal dynasty, the Draconids, which takes the dragon's head for its crest. Oberosia is canonized after her death and becomes the patron saint of the land.

In the chapters that follow, Penguin history runs recognizably parallel to that of France. The Middle Ages, the Renaissance, the Reformation, the Revolution and the Napoleonic Wars are all presented in the thinnest of disguises. There is even a short account of the United States as a nation that exceeds even Penguinia in materialism. The largest part of the book, however, is devoted to contemporary events, which, for Anatole France, meant the history of the Third Republic down to the time of writing.

The Republic of the Penguins is nominally a democracy, actually controlled by a financial oligarchy which debates its policies, controls public opinion through the press, and wages war to maintain its foreign markets. A large body of opinion is still monarchist, and favors the restoration of the Draconids (the Bourbons). In particular, two clergymen, Fathers Agaric and Cornemuse, are the moving spirits of the monarchist cabal. They need a popular leader and find him in Admiral Chatillon, the author's name for General Georges Boulanger, who during the years 1886–1889 placed himself at the head of the antirepublican movement in France and came close to winning power in a *coup d'état*. Chatillon's career parallels—with burlesque and irreverent details—the meteoric rise and ignominious fall of Boulanger.

The Dreyfus affair (1894–1906) takes up one entire section of eleven chapters. It was, of course, very recent history when the novel was written. Dreyfus was a Jewish captain in the French army who was court-martialed on charges of treasonable correspondence with a German military attaché. The evidence of Dreyfus's innocence came out two years later, but the army, feeling its prestige at stake, did its best to suppress it. France was torn by the ensuing controversy, in which Catholicism, militarism, anti-Semitism, and antirepublicanism supported the generals, and in which many prominent men of letters, including Zola and Anatole France himself, spoke in Dreyfus's defense. In the novel, Dreyfus appears under the name of Pyrot, and Zola is called Columban. The forged evidence against Pyrot is bitterly satirized, but the author's burlesque is hardly more improbable than the actual facts.

The last chapters are devoted to the political adventures and domestic misadventures of a radical politician and cabinet minister named Hippolyte Cérès. Cérès is married to Eveline Clarence. He is a socialist and anticlerical; she is a Catholic and a devotee of Saint Oberosia, a situation which makes for a number of entertaining ironies. She is also carrying on an affair with the prime minister. Cérès is frantic with jealousy but cannot strike at his rival without ruining his own career. Finally counting on the peaceful sentiments of the country, he spreads rumors suggesting that the prime minister is plotting to lead the country into war. In the agitated state of public opinion that ensues, the war actually comes to pass, and "the whole world was drowned in a torrent of blood." Anatole France in 1908 clearly foretold the First World War.

The last section of the story is an epilogue which projects the history of Penguinia into the future. A plutocratic civilization arises, buildings grow taller, the sky is darkened with the smoke of factories, the air is polluted, the food is synthetic, and the technical systems, vulnerable by their very complexity, are subject to periodic breakdown. At length an anarchist named George Clair takes matters into his own hands. Using extremely powerful bombs no bigger than an egg (did Anatole France envision atomic fission?), he blows up one key building after another. Anarchy spreads, and the social structure of Penguinia collapses. Nothing, however, is really successful, not even annihilation. In the course of time, the fields are tilled again, hunters and shepherds wrest a living from the wilderness, villages arise, then castles and towns, then cities, and finally a great and rich nation to reenact the drama of the Penguins.

Critical Opinion

Penguin Island is the *Candide* of the twentieth century. Like the earlier satire, it has no overall structure; it is a succession of episodes, ranging from one to a dozen chapters each, loosely strung together. In a rough way, they form a burlesque of French history, but with emphasis on two periods: the early legends and the late nineteenth century. The intervening period, which is to say almost everything, is touched on very lightly. The characterization is equally sketchy; some of the figures are sharply defined, but with the sharpness of caricatures, not people.

An analysis of *Penguin Island* is principally an enumeration of the people and institutions which it ridicules. First among these is the early Christian church as represented by Maël: devout, simpleminded, and gullible. The saint's deeds are told in a style suggestive of the sacred legends which France had read as a child. The most incredible events are recounted with an innocent simplicity which covers, but does not conceal, the author's opinion of pious credulity. Religion itself fares no better than the church. In the council in heaven which decides the fate of Maël's penguins, the author does not spare God himself, who is made to speak in a pompous and self-satisfied manner before a conclave of disputatious theologians.

In art and letters, France upholds classical standards of taste and learning. He mocks at the monks who defaced ancient manuscripts to get parchment for their breviaries; he mocks at the primitive painters of the Middle Ages and their modern admirers, the Pre-Raphaelites; he even scoffs at Dante's *Divine Comedy*.

On society's laws and institutions, France has Maël and a fellow monk speak as follows:

"Do you see, my son," he exclaimed, "that madman who with his teeth is biting the nose of the adversary he has overthrown, and that other one who is pounding a woman's head with a huge stone?"

"I see them," said Bulloch. "They are creating law; they are founding property; they are establishing the principles of civilization, the basis of society, and foundations of the State."

Property, in other words, is founded on theft, as the French socialist Proudhon had said. All governments, royal or republican, are equally selfish and silly. Trinco, the military adventurer, plunges the country into misery, and the royalist conspirators like Boscenos and Agaric are ridiculous fanatics. The leaders of the republic are no more virtuous than their predecessors. They fail to get rich only because there are more of them to share the loot. Even the socialists, whom France might have been expected to treat tenderly, are tedious and argumentative politicians, ready to betray the masses from whom they derive their support.

In the end, as we have seen, Penguin civilization falls because it is so complex and so decadent that a single terrorist can destroy it. And yet the author's skepticism can find no consolation even in total destruction. This, too, is a failure, and the tragicomic history has to begin all over again.

The style of this book is Voltairean: the same simplicity of grammatical structure, the same assumed artlessness of tone, the carefully contrived anticlimaxes, the naughty epigrams, the rage against human stupidity and greed.

Women are apt to be the dominant sex in the novel; at least they are more practical, more purposeful, and have fewer illusions. The men, for example, sometimes try to be chaste, but the women are not so silly. Thus Saint Oberosia is revered as a virgin, and she knows how to capitalize on her reputation, but she does not let it inconvenience her. The author comments on her amours with wicked gravity:

. . . the maiden Oberosia had disappeared. Her absence had at first caused no uneasiness because on several occasions she had been carried off by violent men who were consumed with love. . . . It was even remarked that she sometimes went to meet her ravishers, for none of us can escape his destiny.

Children, on the other hand, are never ridiculed. There are not many in the story, but those few are innocent.

Penguin Island is very different from *The Crime of Sylvestre Bonnard*. Where that is genial this is brittle, where that is sentimental this is cynical. But different though the two manners are, Anatole France is master of them both.

The Author

The real name of Anatole France was Jacques Anatole François Thibault. Anatole France was a childhood nickname which became so distinctively his own that he almost forgot how to spell his real one. He was born in Paris in 1844, the son of a bookseller of simple origins, but with gentle and bookish tastes which he bequeathed to his son. The early years of his life are recorded in a series of reminiscences in which truth is charmingly mixed with fantasy: *My Friend's Book (Le Livre de Mon Ami), Pierre Nozière, Little Pierre (Le Petit Pierre), The Bloom of Life (La Vie en Fleur)*.

France was educated at the Collège Stanislas in Paris, a secondary school where he acquired his love of the classics and his dislike of the clergy. He never attended a university; his father's literary friends and his own reading were more than sufficient to fill the gap. He began to write in the late 1860's, producing several volumes of minor poetry that show the influence of Leconte de Lisle and the then fashionable Parnassian poets. In 1876, he was appointed to a minor post in the Senate Library. The duties were negligible, and for twelve years he neglected them. In 1877, he married Valérie Guérin, a woman from a more substantial family than his own, and for a few years lived comfortably with her. In time, however, their temperaments clashed. He was indolent and passive; she was domineering and difficult about money, most of which was hers. They were divorced in 1893. France married again late in life, but for most of the intervening time he was the friend and lover of Mme. Arman de Caillavet, herself a minor novelist. She presided over an important literary salon attended by writers ranging from the aged Renan to the young Proust, and including also such political notables as Briand, Poincaré and Clemenceau. Anatole France was her most impressive literary property. She suggested themes for his work, prodded him when he was lazy, and nourished his literary reputation. A woman of great energy and worldly sense, she made him famous, possibly even happy.

The collected works of Anatole France include poetry, fiction, autobiography, criticism, political commentary and miscellaneous writing in great variety and virtually all of high quality. In addition to *Penguin Island* and *The Crime of Sylvestre Bonnard,* four novels have been especially acclaimed. *Thaïs* (1890) is set in ancient Alexandria at the time when paganism was giving way to Christianity. The heroine is a celebrated courtesan who is converted to the new religion and causes the downfall of the pious ascetic who converts her. The theme gives full scope for the author's sense of the incongruous, his love of ancient legend, and his anticlericalism. *At the Sign of the Reine Pédauque (La Rôtisserie de la Reine Pédauque,* 1894) is a story of eighteenth-century Paris as well as an exploration of the curious byways of occultism. *The Red Lily (Le Lys Rouge,* 1894) is a novel of contemporary society and manners, with a theme of love and jealousy, set in Florence. *The Gods Are Athirst (Les Dieux Ont Soif,* 1912) deals with the French Revolution and the Terror.

Until the 1890's, France was purely a litterateur and preoccupied mainly with the past. His involvement in politics begins with the Dreyfus affair, during which he, with other men of letters, spoke out against the conspiracy to keep an innocent man in prison. His novel *Monsieur Bergeret à Paris* (1901) is a picture of French society during that crisis. His contempt for the right wing did not, however, make him enthusiastic for the middle-class Third Republic. During the early nineteen hundreds, he became an enthusiastic Socialist, serving the cause as a speaker and a writer. It may be doubted, however, if any faith, even the Socialist, could have survived France's skepticism. In the later novels, like *The White Stone (Sur la Pierre Blanche,* 1903) and *Penguin Island* (1908), there are prophecies, not of a workers' utopia, but of a cataclysm which destroys all society.

In 1896 France was elected to the French Academy, a triumph which marks the high point of his public reputation; in private he ridiculed the honor as he did everything else, and he attended the meetings very irregularly. By now he was generally regarded as the leading man of letters in the country. About the same time he purchased a home in Paris, the Villa Thaïs, which became a kind of private museum housing his vast collection of books, antiques, and bibelots. These possessions were the material counterparts of the curious ideas and odd bits of information which fill his writings.

When France died in 1924, he was beginning to seem dated to the younger generation of writers. The literary virtues which he especially preached, pity and irony, were perhaps too delicate to support the weight of twentieth-century violence. Of the two, the sense of pity in him waned as the sense of irony became more acute, until little was left except a corrosive skepticism that verged on nihilism. As a thinker, France now seems broad rather than deep. His specialty is the memorable aperçu, or middle-range insight, which goes below the surface of things but does not reach down to any solid foundation on which any structure can be built. Even his extraordinary command of style—or rather of many styles— is not matched by a comparable skill in constructing plots. There is still enough in his books to delight any reader: the rich erudition lightly worn, the nimble and vigorous intellect, the contempt for folly and the hatred of injustice, the malicious wit, the classical elegance of style, and above all, the complex and fascinating personality of the author, who, though he no longer looms as large as he once did, is still the Voltaire of modern French literature.

Gösta Berling's Saga

by

SELMA OTTILIANA LOVISA LAGERLÖF
(1858–1940)

The Characters

THE PENSIONERS AT EKEBY

Gösta Berling—An unfrocked clergyman turned vagabond, a
warmhearted, impulsive man, the leading spirit among the
gentleman pensioners.

Captain Christian Bergh—A well-intentioned fellow, but
rowdy, stupid, and easily fooled.

Colonel Beerenkreuz—A cardplayer, gambler, and singer.

Major Anders Fuchs—A bear hunter, brave and taciturn.

Master Julius—Short, fat and merry, a singer and raconteur.

Kevenhüller—A German count turned inventor.

Cousin Christopher—An officer of Napoleon's army, now in
hiding, restless and courageous.

Uncle Eberhard—A philosopher, author of a vast work denying the existence of God.

Löwenborg—A timid, gentle, unworldly man.

Lilliecrona—A musician.

Rutger von Örneclou—A lady's man and a dandy.

OTHER CHARACTERS

Margareta Samzelius, née Celsing—A strong, masterful woman, the efficient manager of the Ekeby properties, and patroness of the twelve pensioners.

Major Berndt Samzelius—Her husband.

Altringer—A rich man, formerly Margareta's lover, now dead.

Count Henrik Dohna—The principal nobleman of the district, ugly, stupid, and pompous.

Countess Märta Dohna—His mother, frivolous, pleasure-seeking, insensitive.

Ebba Dohna—Younger sister of the count, a devout girl in love with Gösta.

Countess Elizabeth Dohna—A gay young Italian girl, married to the count.

Captain Uggla—A decayed gentleman.

Gustava Uggla—His wife. She is bitter with her daughter-in-law for not being more in love with her son.

Ferdinand Uggla—A gentle young man, betrothed to Anna Stjärnhök.

Anna Stjärnhök—A beautiful heiress, engaged to Ferdinand but in love with Gösta, who accepts marriage to Ferdinand as an act of holy resignation.

Ulrika Dillner—A faithful old servant of the Uggla family. She marries Sintram.

Sintram—Ironmaster of Fors, the local representative of Satan, and the source of most of the serious trouble in the community.

Melchior Sinclair of Björne—A harsh man who gambles away his daughter's hand, shuts her out of his house, and beats his wife.

Mme. Sinclair—His submissive wife.

Marianne Sinclair—His daughter, a proud woman with an introspective turn of mind.

The Broby minister—A miser.

Baron Adrian—An impecunious gallant who woos Marianne Sinclair.

Captain Lennart—A released convict who devotes his life to tending the sick and the poor.

Mlle. Marie—A spinster of about forty who earns her living by knitting.

The Broom-girl—A half-witted peasant girl, in love with Gösta.

The Story

Värmland is a province in southwest Sweden between Lake Vänner and the Norwegian border. Originally a remote and sparsely populated district, it underwent sudden economic development in the later eighteenth century, when it was discovered that the land was rich in iron ore. Small furnaces and forges mushroomed everywhere, men gambled and made fortunes, and an era of hectic prosperity began. The chief ironmasters lived lavishly on their manors, entertaining with baronial hospitality. This spacious life was at its height after the Napoleonic Wars, when former army officers without occupation found their way to Värmland. Here their experience of the world, their skill as raconteurs, and their ability as drinking companions or partners at a ball made them welcome guests. *Gösta Berling's Saga* is about such men and the life in Värmland during its golden age.

Gösta Berling is a country clergyman who has been dismissed from his living for drunkenness. He becomes a wanderer, and is known to the peasants as "the mad priest." At the depths of his degradation, and on the point of committing suicide, he is rescued by Margareta Samzelius, the wife of a mine operator and the most powerful woman in the province. In her kind, rough way, she gives him the hope he needs to go on living and installs him on her estate at Ekeby as one of the twelve gentleman pensioners who reside there on her bounty. These men are all failures in life, but they are full of spirit, with a talent for hunting, gambling, music, practical jokes, and gallantry. At Ekeby they live a carefree life, irresponsible but not vicious, rather like a gang of high-spirited, rowdy adolescents.

Satan, however, is eager to spread dissension at Ekeby and turn the guests against their generous hostess. Some years before, Margareta had been forced by her parents to marry Major Samzelius rather than the man she loved, and, in consequence, she became bitterly estranged from her family. Once, when her mother visited her, Margareta admitted her but treated her as if she were a perfect stranger in the house. In return, her mother cursed her, and predicted that she would become an outcast from Ekeby. Satan now maneuvers events so that the curse can be fulfilled. He persuades the pensioners that Margareta has sold her soul to him, and as part of the bargain, one pensioner must die each year if he is not to claim her; they are all being entertained, he assures them, merely to fatten them up for the kill. He now offers them a bargain: Margareta's soul is to be spared, but she is to be turned out of her property which the pensioners will take over. For their part, they agree to manage the estate like gentlemen, not like merchants. If any of them in the year to come does anything sensible, useful, or unmanly, the souls of all twelve will be forfeit. The contract is signed with blood on black paper, and Satan vanishes.

The plan turns out as agreed. On Christmas Day, one of the pensioners becomes drunk and blurts out the story of Margareta's love affair years before. Her husband—who has heard nothing of all this—turns her out into the snow. She has no choice but to wander through the countryside looking for her aged mother, to make amends, and to beg that the curse be lifted. The husband bitterly leaves the estate, which he cannot legally dispose of, in the hands of the twelve pensioners, thinking thus to cause the greatest damage to the property his wife brought him. He goes to live nearby on his own property. The pensioners rule for one gay year of merriment and wild escapades, during which the property is mismanaged, the mines cease to produce, and the wealth is dissipated. However, despite their compact with the devil, the twelve are not really bad men. They are still gallant, generous, and impulsive, and their behavior has a quixotic extravagance that verges on the heroic.

The bulk of the book is given over to their adventures, ranging from the violent to the sentimental. Each pensioner has at least a chapter devoted to him, but many of the episodes are slight and isolated from the rest. The main thread of the story follows the amorous adventures of Gösta Berling, the youngest, and ringleader of the twelve. One girl, Ebba Dohna, loves him, but is disillusioned to learn that he is an unfrocked minister. Being deeply pious she dismisses him, and then dies of a broken heart. Another, Anna Stjärnhök, is engaged to a young man of the neighborhood, Ferdinand Uggla. When she shows signs of changing her mind, Berling goes to intercede for his friend. Like John Alden, he falls in love with the lady himself, and the two plan to elope. Their sleigh is attacked by wolves, and the couple have to take refuge at the very manor where Ferdinand Uggla is still impatiently awaiting the arrival of his fiancée. Gösta takes this turn of events as a sign from heaven, and renounces Anna, who obediently goes to her betrothed. A third lover is Marianne Sinclair, a proud heiress whom Gösta woos at a ball at Ekeby. Her father is infuriated that she should love a penniless pensioner, and shuts the door of his house to her. In despair, she tries to freeze herself in a snowbank, but is rescued by Berling and his friends. Soon thereafter she contracts smallpox, which destroys her beauty, and makes peace with her father rather than inflict her ruined face on her lover. The fourth and most serious love is Countess Elizabeth Dohna, whose husband at first loves her devoutly. His mother, however, tries to poison his mind with suspicion that his wife has married him only for his title and his money and secretly yearns for Gösta. Count Henrik has the marriage annulled. For a time the Countess wanders about the country until her child, the Count's son, is born. To give her child a legal father, she begs Gösta to marry her. He does so, and even though the boy dies soon afterward, he remains with the woman whom after so many misadventures he has thus strangely chosen.

At last, the year over and the bargain completed, Margareta Samzelius returns to Ekeby. She is freed of her curse, having found her mother and become reconciled with her. The pensioners welcome her back and nurse her during her last illness. True to their promise they have almost ruined the estate, but now they light the forges, repair the buildings, and proceed to make good the damage they have done. Margareta, much chastened, proposes to leave the property to them, but Gösta will have none of it. He is not the sort of man who can support the responsibilities and temptations of great wealth. He proposes to live out his days in a simple cottage with his countess, working as a peasant and on holidays playing his fiddle for the village dancing. In this way, he hopes to become sober and useful, and perhaps, as a fiddler, he can still bring joy to the hearts of men.

Critical Opinion

A countess who flees with her lover across a frozen lake, two lovers in a sleigh pursued by wolves through snow-filled woods, a woman who wanders for a year and a day because of a mother's curse, twelve cavaliers who sign a pact with the Evil One: how could any modern author choose such shamelessly melodramatic subjects, especially in the 1880's, when the realistic school of Flaubert, Zola and the Goncourts was at the height of its influence? Selma Lagerlöf, however, was a novelist born out of her time. She preferred to be herself rather than to write the soberly realistic stories then in vogue. For her themes she went to the folklore of her native province. In some of these stories there lay a kernel of actual truth. An unfrocked clergyman in the district was still remembered as a charming and gifted if penniless man. He had been befriended by a woman who served as the model for Margareta Samzelius. Other tales derive from peasant superstitions: stories of the devil who writes his bargains in blood, of a great ghostly dog who leaves his flaming footprints in the dark, and of an angry witch who sends a curse of magpies on an evil old woman. These are retold as a child remembers stories, without irony or sophistication, and with a naïve wonder at the marvelous, passionate men whose deeds they record. The very name *saga*, referring originally to the tales of old Norse adventurers, evokes the atmosphere of legendary times when heroes were more heroic and villains more villainous than they can possibly be today.

The writing of *Gösta Berling's Saga* must have been for the author an exploration of her own childhood, a journey back to the roots of her emotional life. She always claimed that the story insisted on writing itself. Moreover, the interesting fact that she began the saga as a poem, then tried to turn it into a play, and only at length decided to write a novel, proves that here is an instance of a theme seeking for its appropriate expression, rather than an artist casting about for a theme.

The first chapter Selma Lagerlöf wrote was the description of Christmas Eve at Ekeby. The rest of the book crystallized about this nucleus. Some of the chapters in the second part appear to have been written simply to fill out a plan which took shape only after the story was well under way. The slight and sentimental tales about Löwenborg, Julius, and Eberhard were surely added simply to insure that each of the gentleman pensioners had at least one chapter to himself. The pious conclusion, which has bothered some critics, may not have been clearly envisioned at the start.

The legendary quality of the saga explains not only its organization, but also its characterization and style. The twelve knights of Ekeby are not rounded psychological studies of real people. Gösta himself suggests that they are reincarnations of the twelve Olympians, or the twelve gods of Odin's court, or the twelve paladins of Charlemagne, now diminished in these degenerate times to failures and vagabonds, but still breathing the carefree spirit of the childhood of the world. They are gallant, pleasure-loving, impulsive, and, above all, childish. Their adventures are a kind of glorious play. The same childishness pervades the several love stories. There is much wooing here. Maidens die for love, and others, more fortunate, are abducted through dark forests behind dashing horses, yet everything is strangely innocent and sexless, like a fairy tale. The Danish critic Brandes commented, "One feels throughout that the narrator is an unmarried lady."

One critic, Alrik Gustafson, remarks that the moral world of *Gösta Berling's Saga* is never dark enough to be really tragic, despite the presence of Satan. The moral conflict does not lie between good and evil, but between two kinds of good: responsible work and careless joy. Gösta in his farewell speech to his friends declares that the greatest problem in life is to know how man can be both gay and good. He would seem at first glance to have renounced a life of pleasure at last, and chosen the way of poverty and penance. He reserves, however, at least a small corner in his life for beauty. He will have done some good, he thinks, if he can play the polka at weddings and at Christmas, teach country fiddlers the old tunes, and give the shepherd children a few songs to sing along the woodland paths.

Selma Lagerlöf's style is as breathlessly romantic as the story itself. The language is lyrical, even rhythmical, occasionally breaking out into poetry. Repeatedly the author steps out of her story to apostrophize the characters or her beloved province. Exclamations and rhetorical questions abound. The influence of Carlyle is too heavy for modern taste. In her later writing she achieved an artless simplicity more suited to her themes.

Gösta Berling's Saga achieved immediate popularity. It has been translated into many languages and remains one of the best-loved Swedish novels. Miss Lagerlöf wrote many other novels, largely on themes of peasant life. American children probably know her best as the author of a child's story, *The Wonderful Adventures of Nils*.

The Author

Selma Lagerlöf was born in 1858 in Värmland, the Swedish province which she immortalized in her principal work. She grew up on the family manor of Mårbacka. A delicate child, she suffered at the age of three from an illness which was probably infantile paralysis. It left her permanently lame, so that much of her childhood was spent in sanatoriums or at home. When she was in her early twenties, her father died, leaving the family so straitened that the estate had to be sold. She studied for a time at a teacher's seminary in Stockholm and then was assigned as a schoolmistress to Landskrona in the north of Sweden. Here she studied peasant life with the same affectionate interest that she had in the south.

Miss Lagerlöf's first book was her greatest; it originated in stories told her by her grandmother about life in Värmland half a century earlier. The first five chapters were published in a magazine and won a prize. The entire saga appeared in 1891, and made her the most popular author in Scandinavia since Hans Christian Andersen. During the next twenty years, many honors came to her: in 1895 she won a fellowship to travel in southern Europe; in 1904 she was given a medal by the Swedish Academy; in 1909 she received an honorary doctorate; in 1909 she was awarded the Nobel Prize for literature; and in 1914 she became a member of the Swedish Academy.

The Nobel Prize money made possible the realization of Miss Lagerlöf's fondest dream. She bought back Mårbacka, remodeled it, and lived there as lady of the manor, presiding over some fifty tenants and employees. The property was commercially profitable, and the grain raised there was made into a popular breakfast food. She never married, lived quietly, and expressed no strong opinions on religion or partisan politics. Her last months were darkened by the outbreak of war and the German occupation of neighboring Norway. She died of peritonitis in 1940.

Buddenbrooks

by

THOMAS MANN (1875–1955)

The Characters

Johann Buddenbrook, Sr.—A robust old man who wears the stamp of the eighteenth century in dress and thought.

Josephine—Beloved first wife of Johann, dies in childbirth.

Antoinette Duchamps—Johann's second wife. They are not deeply in love, but she is a loyal and able companion.

Gotthold Buddenbrook—Josephine's son, who marries in defiance of his father and sacrifices his share in the family business.

Fräulein Stüwing—Gotthold's wife. After his death, she keeps up the family feud.

Consul Johann Buddenbrook—Johann's second son, an honorable businessman, deeply pious.

Elizabeth Kröger (Frau Consul Buddenbrook)—Wife of the younger Johann. Accustomed in her youth to the lordly style of the Krögers, she occupies her position with conscious dignity.

Clothilde—A poor relative living with the family, good-natured, simple, hungry, constantly teased by the rest.

Thomas Buddenbrook—Eldest son of the Consul and heir to the firm. In his youth he is ambitious in business and politics, but without the toughness of his father and grandfather; in the end, overcome by frustration and emptiness. He is fastidious in dress, scrupulously correct in manner and rather reserved.

Christian Buddenbrook—The second son of the Consul, indolent, bohemian, hypochondriacal.

Antonie Buddenbrook (Tony)—Third child of the Consul, emotionally immature, with a childish sense of her own importance and of the wrongs done her.

Clara Buddenbrook—The fourth child, rather harsh and demanding in manner, austerely religious.

Gerda Arnoldsen—Thomas's wife. Her musical interests make her an outsider among her prosaic in-laws.

Bendix Grünlich—Tony's first husband, a fortune hunter.

Alois Permaneder—Tony's second husband, amiable but uncultivated and unambitious.

Sievert Tiburtius—Clara's husband, a clergyman.

Aline Puvogel—Christian's mistress, later his wife, never accepted by the family.

Fredericke, Henriette and Pfiffi Buddenbrook—Gotthold's daughters, bitter, jealous spinsters.

Hanno (Justus Johann Kaspar Buddenbrook)—Thomas's only child, delicate, sensitive, and passionately fond of music.

Erica Grünlich—Tony's daughter, patient and submissive.

Hugo Weinschenk—Erica's husband, sent to prison for sharp business practice.

Justus Kröger—Brother of Elizabeth, a dapper man with expensive tastes.

Jacob Kröger—Elder son of Justus. He is guilty of dishonesty in business and emigrates to America.

Jurgen Kröger—Second son of Justus. Not very bright, he fails as a law student and gets a job in a post office.

Consul Lebrecht Kröger—Consul Johann Buddenbrook's father-in-law, tall, distinguished, politically conservative.

The Hagenstrom Family—The principal business and political rivals of the Buddenbrooks, who look on them as parvenus.

Von Throta—A young lieutenant with musical tastes, suspected of being Gerda's lover.

Morten Schwartzkopf—A young medical student whom Tony loves before she marries Grünlich, a serious young man with liberal political opinions.

Anna Iwersen—The wife of a florist who lives opposite Thomas's house; in her youth, his mistress.

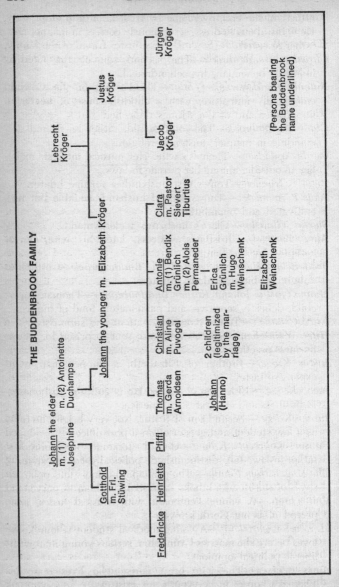

THE BUDDENBROOK FAMILY

(Persons bearing the Buddenbrook name underlined)

Johann the elder
m. (1) Josephine
m. (2) Antoinette Duchamps

Gotthold
m. Frl. Stüwing

Fredericke   Henriette   Pfiffi

Johann the younger, m. Elizabeth Kröger

Thomas
m. Gerda Arnoldsen

Johann (Hanno)

Christian
m. Aline Puvogel

2 children (legitimized by the marriage)

Antonie
m. (1) Bendix Grünlich
m. (2) Alois Permaneder

Erica Grünlich
m. Hugo Weinschenk

Elizabeth Weinschenk

Clara
m. Pastor Sievert Tiburtius

Lebrecht Kröger

Justus Kröger

Jacob Kröger   Jürgen Kröger

Herr Marcus—Senior clerk in the firm, later partner; dry, cautious, pedantic.

Therese Weichbrodt (Sesemi)—A spinster friend of the family, and a humpback. She keeps a boarding school attended by Tony.

Kai Mölln—Hanno's only friend; a shabby and neglected child with a keen imagination and a talent for making up stories.

Herr Pfühl—A church organist; Hanno's music teacher, a strict exponent of traditional musical form.

The Story

The theme of *Buddenbrooks* is the decline and fall of a merchant dynasty, accomplished not by any pressure of outward circumstance, but by psychological forces: chiefly by the emergence, with increasing force in each generation, of an antibourgeois spirit which saps the energy and self-confidence of the various members of the family. In some, it takes the form of loose living, in others of artistic talent; it ranges in intensity from mere laziness to a passionate yearning for death.

The Buddenbrooks are grain merchants of Lübeck, then a small, autonomous city-state on the Baltic Sea. The firm is a century old, and its owners are solid, responsible citizens, prosperous, prominent in civic affairs, and justifiably proud of their position. In temperament, they are vigorous, practical, and unimaginative, sure of themselves and of the values they represent.

When the story opens in 1835, the family has just moved to Meng Street into a large house which had formerly belonged to another merchant family, but was now decayed. The first ten chapters are devoted to describing the housewarming party at which friends gather to congratulate the family on its solid good fortune. At the head of the Buddenbrooks stand father and son, Johann senior and junior, cut from the same cloth, with the virtues of their class and clan.

The happiness of the occasion is marred, however, by one rebel. The eldest son, Gotthold, has married for love against his father's wishes, and his wife is from a tradesman's, not a merchant's family. Shut out from the family business by his disobedience, Gotthold becomes a failure by Buddenbrook standards. After his death, his three daughters hover on the edges of the story as perpetual poor relatives, ugly, jealous, and embittered.

The story concerns itself mainly with the four children of Johann the younger: Thomas, Christian, Antonie and Clara. Thomas, as the eldest and ablest, becomes head of the firm. He is not, however, of so sturdy a fiber as his father and grandfather. Even as a child, his delicate features, slender fingers, and poor teeth suggest a decline in physical vigor. Furthermore, he causes the townsfolk to raise their eyebrows by marrying Gerda Arnoldsen, a girl whose exotic appearance, remote bearing and musical interests make her seem "queer." At first, however, all goes well. Thomas expands the business, builds a luxurious new house, and is elected to the municipal senate. These successes he achieves at great cost. Inwardly Thomas feels empty and frustrated; he loses his self-confidence and begins to fumble in business matters. By forty he is burnt out. He dies suddenly, seemingly from shock following the extraction of a tooth, but his will to live had died first.

The second son, Christian, does not even try to be a Buddenbrook; he is a bohemian from the start. More imaginative than Thomas and with a touch of the artist in him (he is an excellent mimic and raconteur), he is never able to settle down to any business for long. He becomes the black sheep of the family, spends his inheritance, sires several illegitimate children, and quarrels intermittently with Thomas. He also becomes a hypochondriac, and finally a patient in a mental hospital.

The third child, Tony, makes a bad marriage. In her teens, she falls in love with a young medical student, Morten Schwartzkopf, whose father is captain of one of the company's ships. Her parents, however, expect her to marry someone with good business prospects, and force her to accept Bendix Grünlich from Hamburg. But Grünlich is a fortune hunter who counts on the credit of the Buddenbrook house to save him. When his affairs end in bankruptcy, Tony obtains a divorce and returns with her daughter, Erica, to the family house in Meng Street. Her second husband, Alois Permaneder, is a businessman from Munich, amiable and extroverted, even if his speech and manners embarrass the fastidious Buddenbrooks. A short stay in Munich convinces Tony that she will never take to Bavarian ways. The marriage comes to an end when Alois returns home one night a little drunk and tries to kiss the maid. Tony and Erica return to Lübeck, this time for good.

The fourth child, Clara, plays only a minor part in the story. She marries a clergyman from Riga and dies of tuberculosis.

By the fourth generation, the family has narrowed to two children: Thomas' little son, Hanno, and Tony's daughter, Erica Grünlich. Erica makes as bad a marriage as her mother. Her husband is sent to jail for dishonest business practice, leaving her with a small daughter, Elizabeth. Hanno is a sickly child who shrinks from the demands of life, from the roughness of the children in school, and from his father's expectation that he will carry on the family business. His one passion is music, for which he displays a precocious talent, frowned on by everyone except his mother. At sixteen, he contracts typhoid fever and dies much as his father did, from sheer lack of the will to live.

As the family dwindles, the outward signs of its wealth and position drop away. After a series of business reverses, Thomas sells the house into which the family had moved so proudly a generation before. To the dismay of all, it is bought by the head of a rival firm. When Thomas dies, the company is liquidated at a considerable loss and the second house is sold as well. Gerda has no further ties in Lübeck, and returns to her native town. Tony carries on in straitened circumstances with her daughter and granddaughter but the Buddenbrook name is extinct.

Critical Opinion

The literary tradition to which *Buddenbrooks* belongs is that of the realistic and objective nineteenth-century social novel. A score of major characters and a large number of minor ones are sharply individualized in appearance and temperament. Physical details add to the sense of reality; the book is rich in references to food, furniture and dress. In particular, the descriptions of illness and death show the influence of the realist movement, although Mann does not offer his reader unpleasant details merely for their shock value, as Zola would have done. (Hanno's death is described in the dryly clinical manner of a medical textbook to spare us from its full impact.)

More important even than its realism in physical details is the novel's social realism. Here is an exhaustive study of a certain class at a particular time and place in history, at work, in public life, in society, and at home. We see it in relation to other classes: paternalistic toward employees, aloof toward tradespeople, uneasily defensive toward the aristocracy, relaxed with doctors and professional men generally. Even within the Buddenbrooks' own circle we note certain social distinctions between the poor relatives and the rich, between the old families and the newcomers, between those who may be invited for dinner and those who may only come for afternoon coffee. In short, *Buddenbrooks* is a portrait of a whole society.

On the other hand, if we read the novel in the context of Mann's later work it seems not so much an exercise in literary objectivity as an expression of a personal problem which always fascinated Mann: the rival claims of the bourgeois and the artist. To this theme he was to return repeatedly in later works: in "Tristan," "Tonio Kröger," "Death in Venice," *The Magic Mountain,* and *Doctor Faustus.*

In *Buddenbrooks,* this conflict is presented almost entirely from the bourgeois point of view—or so it seems at first. The world of the merchant families is the standard of health, order, and normality. The successive heads of the Buddenbrook firm are allowed to defend their system of values fully and persuasively. With the possible exception of Gerda Arnoldsen, no one is strong or articulate enough to defend any other system. Mann does not criticize his characters directly. He simply allows us to see how many lives can be warped or ruined in the attempt to live as they do. Consider, for example, the effects of the taboo against marrying outside of one's social class. Tony, obviously, should have married Morten rather than the businessman her parents chose; it should have been no disgrace for her to be the wife of an up-and-coming doctor, even if his father was only a pilot. Gotthold's life was ruined because he made an unsuitable marriage, and even Tom, who never dreamed of defying his family, might have been happier if he could have married Anna, whom he really loved.

In the Buddenbrook world there is no place for the artist. The town has its society poet who is accepted because his poems are graceful trifles celebrating the virtues of the leading citizens. Pfuhl plays a useful role as organist at Saint Mary's church, but nobody in the congregation understands his art except Gerda and Hanno. By and large, the potential artist winds up as an outcast. In another society, Christian, instead of becoming a neurotic and a ne'er-do-well, might have found success and personal fulfillment as an actor. Hanno's friend Kai is another frustrated artist whose one defense is the scorn he feels for his teachers and schoolmates. The most poignant failure of all is of course Hanno himself. Hanno loves music with an intensity which suggests that his entire libidinal drive has been channeled into this one outlet. Yet he is surrounded by adults who tell him not to take the piano too seriously, and who urge him to memorize the names of the ships that sail between Lübeck and Copenhagen. It is small wonder that Hanno refuses to accept life on these terms.

The one who feels the conflict most acutely, however, is Tom, because in him the opposing forces are most evenly matched. So long as the family business challenges his imagination and gives him the opportunity to create, he is happy and successful. Then, at the height of his success, he loses his nerve, and none of his achievements give him any satisfaction. His son, he realizes, will never be a merchant, and his wife can give him no strength. Instead, she withdraws from him into a world of music where he cannot follow. For a time he holds together his self-respect by an obsessive concern for appearances, especially in grooming and dress, but the effort costs him more each day. In this mood, he reads Schopenhauer on death, and the experience is a revelation. Death now presents itself as a deep joy, an alluring sweetness, a loosening of chains, a correction of a sad mistake. Soon after, death claims him. With his fur coat and his fastidiously groomed mustache, he falls face down in a pool of slush.

The Buddenbrook family, it is clear, have maintained their position at fearful cost to themselves. And yet it would be a mistake to read the novel as a simple attack on the bourgeoisie such as a Marxist would have written. Mann feels love, compassion, and respect for the characters he has created. The portrait of old Johann Buddenbrook and of his generation is basically sympathetic. Admittedly Johann forfeits our sympathies somewhat for his treatment of Gotthold, but in general he strikes us as level-headed and vigorous, the least neurotic character in the book, whose chief strength is the fact that he is not at war with himself. Mann seems to be telling us that the life of the artist is good, and that of the merchant is good too, or would be if only each man might follow his own native bent without being made to feel guilty for his choice.

In a novel that traces the fortunes of the same people for forty years, the author must suggest both continuity and change. Many minor characters remain static. Their unchanging quality is signaled by certain unchanging traits: Clothilde is always hungry, Therese Weichbrodt always makes the same kind of punch at parties, the family doctor always prescribes the same diet, and Christian always enters rubbing his left side, where "the nerves are too short." Poor Tony, through all her vicissitudes, changes very little. At fifty she still repeats opinions which she heard from Morten Schwartzkopf in her teens, and though Mann does not explicitly call attention to the fact, yet we realize with a surge of pity that her emotional and intellectual growth has been cut short by her unwise marriage.

On the other hand, the rhythm of the generations is marked by the births, weddings, and deaths duly noted in the family journal; by the Christmas parties, lavish or stinted as the family fortunes permit; by the fall of old merchant families and the rise of new ones; by the successive moves from one house to another, from the fine mansion which Tom builds in Fisher's Lane to Tony's little apartment in Linden Place. Finally one should not overlook the background of European politics, which determine the changing fortunes of the city and its business firms. In the opening chapters, Johann and his guests are reminiscing about the Napoleonic Wars, only twenty-five years before; at the end Lübeck has become part of a united Fatherland and a Prussian schoolmaster has taken charge of the high school. The town has prospered and grown with the times, and yet, as one compares 1875 and 1835, one wonders if the net gain has been so very great after all.

The Magic Mountain

by

THOMAS MANN

The Characters

Hans Castorp—The hero, a young man from a prosperous middle-class family in Hamburg, trained as a maritime engineer. Outwardly placid and conventional, he has a passion for observation and experience which leads him to explore obscure and even illicit areas of spiritual life.

Joachim Ziemssen—Hans' cousin, simple, unintellectual and honorable, with a strong sense of military duty.

Consul Tienappel—Hans' guardian, a solid, common-sense bourgeois.

Louisa Ziemssen—Joachim's mother, strong, capable, and unemotional.

Hofrat Behrens—The director of the Berghof sanatorium, a doctor with a scientific and unsentimental view of life. As a rule his manner is brusquely jovial, though he sometimes breaks out in fits of temper or falls into spells of melancholy.

Dr. Krokowski—Behrens' assistant, a psychoanalyst who believes that all illness is psychogenic. His manner is somewhat ambiguous and faintly sinister.

Adriatica von Mylendonk—The directress of the Berghof, an unsentimental administrator with an abrupt style of speech.

Ludovico Settembrini—A patient at the sanatorium, and Hans's self-appointed mentor, an Italian man of letters, a humanist, a liberal, a Freemason, a believer in progress, and at times a windbag.

Naphta—A Jewish convert to Catholicism, a short, ugly man with a brilliant mind and incisive tongue. His character has been warped by a childhood trauma. He is now a fanatical believer in violence and despotism.

Pribislav Hippe—A schoolboy for whom Hans once experienced a teen-age crush.

Clavdia Chauchat—A Russian with whom Hans falls in love. She is a sensual woman with faintly oriental features and a lax, careless manner which Hans, with his conventional upbringing, finds strongly appealing.

Pieter Peeperkorn—A Dutch coffee planter from Java, and Clavdia's acknowledged lover; forceful, if inarticulate, the embodiment of strong feeling and vital energy.

Marusja—A pretty young girl with a tendency to giggle; loved by Joachim Ziemssen.

Caroline Stöhr—A patient who sits at Hans's table; a vulgar, silly woman given to malapropisms.

Ferdinand Wehsal—A young man from Mannheim; a prominent masochist.

Anton Karlovich Ferge—Another patient, a mediocrity whose one claim to distinction is having undergone surgical shock.

Ellen Brand—A Danish girl with strongly developed powers as a physical medium.

The Story

In the years immediately before the First World War, Davos, Switzerland, was a health resort where tubercular patients went to take advantage of the high mountain air. The sanatoriums were run as luxury hotels, and relatives were allowed to stay with the patients as visitors. To one of these establishments, the Berghof, comes Hans Castorp, a sober, undistinguished young man from Hamburg. Apparently in good health, he plans to stay a few weeks visiting his cousin Joachim, a young military officer who is rather ill. Hans finds himself unexpectedly attracted by the sanatorium life. He also becomes interested in one of the patients, a Russian woman named Clavdia Chauchat. To his satisfaction, he develops mild symptoms of tuberculosis himself. He now has a good reason for staying at the Berghof as long as he wishes, something which his private income makes possible. He remains for seven years, until the war breaks out and he leaves to enter military service. *The Magic Mountain (Der Zauberberg)* is a record of his experiences during those seven years, of his mental and emotional development, and of the insights which he achieves into the psychological and spiritual meaning of illness.

The opening chapters are devoted to recording Hans's first impressions of the Berghof. The atmosphere is febrile. The patients who are not seriously ill are stimulated by their chronic fever, and for the most part are interested only in flirtation. The hospital itself is dedicated to disease rather than health. The patients take pride in their illness, the director is possibly tubercular himself, and, since the place is run for profit, there is some question as to how eager the owners are to see the patients cured. Hans's whole life has prepared him for a healthy, responsible, constructive and conventional career, and yet he finds this hospital, with its heady mixture of illness, sensuality, and moral freedom, irresistibly fascinating. One of the patients, Settembrini, urges him to leave before he surrenders to the spirit of the place. But Hans feels that he cannot understand life and love unless he approaches them by the unorthodox roads of sickness and death.

In Hans's spiritual education, love plays a major role. Years before, as a schoolboy, he had had an adolescent attachment —unspoken and unexpressed—for another boy in his school. Reminiscences of this episode begin to appear in his dreams, and are powerfully stirred up by Clavdia who strikingly resembles the boy and, like him, is a Slav. Hans's chronic fever is actually the organic expression of his love for Clavdia, at first concealed, then openly declared. The love is consummated only once during a Mardi Gras carnival. The next day Clavdia leaves to rejoin her husband.

In the hothouse atmosphere of the Berghof, Hans's intellectual capacities burgeon. He reads avidly, especially scientific literature, becomes fluent in French, and undergoes psychoanalysis. Two men in particular fight for his intellectual allegiance, the liberal humanist, Settembrini, and a Jesuit named Naphta, whose philosophy is a strange blend of all the authoritarian currents in European culture: Fascism, Communism, and Catholicism. Hans listens to both, but commits himself to neither. His own vision of life comes during a solitary excursion in a blizzard, an experience that is also a flirtation with death, since he nearly freezes. The vision is in two parts: one of an idyllic Mediterranean world, alive with youth, health, happiness, and love; the other of an archaic temple in which two horrible women are dismembering and eating a child. This double vision—actually a kind of racial memory—teaches Hans that death and life belong together, that both must be accepted, and that one must expose oneself to the initiatory experience of death in order to align oneself on the side of light and life. The climactic statement of the book is this: *For the sake of goodness and love, man shall let death have no sovereignty over his thoughts.*

After this epiphany, Hans's education continues. His cousin Joachim dies and is invoked in a spiritualistic séance. Clavdia returns in the company of Pieter Peeperkorn, a Dutch planter from Java, a powerful, vital man with a Dionysian capacity for eating, drinking, and feeling. He regards his sexual drive as the expression of a cosmic life force through which God achieves self-awareness. As his strength fails—for Peeperkorn is sick like the others—he gives his blessing to the love of Hans and Clavdia and then commits suicide.

Meanwhile, the rising war fever of Europe is reflected in the little world of the Berghof. Tempers crackle, there is an ugly outbreak of anti-Semitism, and a mood of reckless violence is in the air. Naphta and Settembrini can no longer tolerate their differences, and fight a duel in which neither shoots the other; Settembrini fires into the air and Naphta kills himself. At length, war breaks out, and Hans, who has never been seriously ill, is called up. The spell which kept him for seven years on the enchanted mountain is finally broken. We last see him taking part in an infantry charge.

Critical Opinion

Part of the fascination of *The Magic Mountain* is the fact that it must be read on several different levels at once. No one approach suffices to reveal its manifold richness. On a superficial level, it may be read simply as an entertaining picture of sanatorium life or as a naturalistic study of tuberculosis.

On another level, it can be understood as a social and political novel. It is obviously a picture of a particular class, the upper middle class of Europe on the eve of the First World War, a prosperous, stable society accustomed to solid meals and regular dividends. Of this society, the Berghof is a microcosm, sheltering under its roof citizens of every country in Europe plus a sprinkling from other continents. The sickness of its inmates is a symbol of the sickness of Europe. In this little world, Hans and his cousin represent Germany with its two faces, Joachim the soldier and Hans the civilian. Joachim follows his destiny without question, but Hans is torn between two poles: the orderly, respectable life represented by his family and his work in Hamburg, and the less rationally structured and more instinctual world of the East, represented by Clavdia, the unconventional Russian with Tartar eyes. Similarly, he must decide between the claims of his two self-appointed teachers, the humanist Settembrini and the proto-fascist Naphta. Hans belongs to the generation of Germans who would be middle-aged during the Weimar Republic, and the decisions he faces are to be theirs also.

The Magic Mountain may also be read as a *Bildungsroman,* a psychological novel tracing the formation of a young man's character. Mann's contribution to this familiar genre is to suggest that Hans's experiences are a ritual initiation in the course of which, like other neophytes in the occult arts, he asks and is asked questions, submits to dangerous ordeals, and emerges with vastly heightened powers of mind and spirit. The title is a clue to the magical symbolism of the novel. It suggests another magic mountain, the Hörselberg, where the knight Tannhäuser was held prisoner by the enchantment of Venus. The magic number seven is also important. There are seven tables in the dining room with seven seats at each. Clavdia's room is number seven. Hans stays for seven years. The novel has seven chapters.

Naphta, in one of his pedagogical conversations with Hans, explains the occult meaning of his pupil's experiences in symbols taken from alchemy and Freemasonry:

> The learner must be of dauntless courage and athirst
> for knowledge. . . . The grave, the sepulchre, has always
> been the emblem of initiation into the society. The
> neophyte coveting admission to the mysteries must al-

ways preserve courage in the face of their terrors. . . . The path of mysteries and purification was encompassed by dangers, it led through the pangs of death, through the kingdom of dissolution, and the learner, the neophyte, is youth itself, thirsting after the miracles of life, clamoring to be quickened to a demonic capacity of experience, and led by shrouded forms which are the shadowing forth of the mystery.

Here in a paragraph is Hans's story.

Psychoanalysis is another form of initiation, and in this Dr. Krokowski is Hans's guide, although the author gives us no clue as to what happens in the semidarkness of the doctor's office. The novel, however, shows that Mann had studied Freud's writings and had obviously learned a great deal about the unconscious and the psychological components of illness.

The Magic Mountain is a novel of ideas, and its mood is generally ironic. Typically, the author establishes two opposing points of view and allows each to undercut the other, as do Settembrini and Naphta. At times, he deliberately throws us off the track; for instance, although Mann seemingly accepts Krokowski's view of illness rather than Behrens', he makes Behrens the much more likable of the two. Sometimes he surprises us with unexpected turns of mood, as when he describes Hans's tears at Joachim's death and then proceeds to analyze them chemically. He quotes the opinions of his characters and seems to agree with them, with only the slightest hint of tongue-in-cheek. He will discuss his hero and pretend to have no knowledge of his inner thoughts, or will complain about the difficulty of capturing a nuance of mood or feeling. All these are highly self-conscious devices which maintain an air of playful detachment toward the subject, and remind us of its many-sided complexity. In this ironic play of ideas, there is a great deal of highly intellectual and sophisticated wit.

Amid these ironically shifting points of view, the best guide to the author's intention is often his use of symbols. For instance, Settembrini, as the apostle of reason, is associated with light, and his first act on entering Hans's bedroom is to turn on the light switch. Krokowski, who deals with the unconscious, dresses in black and maintains darkness in his consultation room. Peeperkorn is regularly described as a pagan priest.

His characteristic mannerism is a ritual phallic gesture. For Hans, a stiff white ruff symbolizes the solemnity of death, and a three-hundred-year-old christening bowl speaks of the continuity of the Castorp family. These symbols are more subtly used than in *Buddenbrooks*. In the earlier book, symbols were merely identifying tags which served to introduce the actors. By contrast, consider the slamming door which signals the entrance of Clavdia into a room. This motif is not a simple identification; it is an expression of her character, just as Hans's irritable reaction to the slamming is an expression of his. Such a symbol is capable of considerable, expressive variation. Later when Clavdia returns in the company of the masterful Peeperkorn, she enters silently, because her lover now shuts the door himself. Finally, these motifs can be woven together in a rich texture for which the music of Wagner provides the best analogy.

Somewhat to the surprise of the author, *The Magic Mountain* was an immediate success, despite its length and complexity. In his autobiographical sketch, Mann suggests that the book was well received because it spoke to the condition of postwar Germany. This suggestion is, however, too modest. It does not do justice to the richness and universality of the book nor does it explain why it was so well received in other countries as well, and why it is universally rated as one of the indisputably great novels of our century.

Joseph and His Brothers

by

THOMAS MANN

The Characters

NOTE: *Where the author has added little or nothing to the information given in Genesis, no characterization has been provided here, except to indicate family relationships.*

ABRAHAM AND HIS DESCENDANTS

Abraham (formerly Abram).

Sarah (formerly Sarai)—Wife of Abraham.

Hagar—Handmaiden of Sarah.

Ishmael—Son of Abraham by Hagar.

Isaac (Yitzchak)—Son of Abraham by Sarah.

Eliezer—Slave of Abraham, and thereafter the name in each generation of a trusted elder servant.

Rebecca—Isaac's wife and cousin; sister of Laban.

Laban—Nephew of Abraham dwelling in Haran; a tight-fisted man.

Esau—Elder son of Isaac; a hunter, rough, crude, impulsive, but not disposed to harbor a grudge.

Jacob (Yaakow, Yekew, Israel)—Younger son of Isaac; in his youth, shrewd and not always scrupulous; in old age, a venerable patriarch.

252

Leah—Older daughter of Laban, Jacob's first wife.
Rachel—Younger daughter of Laban, beloved by Jacob.
Bilhah—Rachel's handmaiden, concubine of Jacob.
Zilpah—Leah's handmaiden, concubine of Jacob.

THE FAMILY OF JACOB

Reuben—The eldest, a tall, heavy man with a certain clumsy dignity. As compared with the rest, he is well disposed toward Joseph.
Simeon and Levi—Called the twins; violent quarrelsome men.
Judah (Jehudah)—A strong man with leonine features and an imperative sexual drive. He is ridden with feelings of guilt for his brothers' conduct toward Joseph.
Dan—Sly and malicious.
Naphtali—Glib and articulate, a messenger for the others.
Gad—A rough, sturdy man.
Asher—"Sweet-toothed."
Dinah—A pathetic young girl, abducted by Sichem.
Zebulun—Fond of ships and travel.
Joseph (Yashub, Yehosiph, Josephja, "Dumuzi," known in Egypt as Osarsiph)—Elder son of Rachel, a beautiful and charming youth, clever and articulate and too conceited for his own good.
Benjamin (Benoni, Beni, "Turturra")—The youngest child, innocent, affectionate, and deeply attached to Joseph.
Manasseh and Ephraim—Sons of Joseph and Asenath. By upbringing and temperament, they are well-to-do Egyptian gentlemen.
Serah—Daughter of Asher, a singer.
Tamar—A Canaanite woman, daughter-in-law of Judah.

OTHER CANAANITES, ETC., NOT OF THE HOUSE OF ISRAEL

Melchizedek—Priest of Salem (Jerusalem) in the time of Abraham.
Jepshe—A traveler entertained by Jacob.
Hamor—King of Schechem.
Sichem (Schechem)—Son of Hamor, in love with Dinah.
Rimanni-Bel (Rimut)—A soothsayer at Harran.
The Guide—A stranger with a peremptory, irritable manner,

who gives instructions to Joseph and Reuben; presumably an angel.

The Midianite (no name given)—A traveling merchant who buys Joseph, a shrewd man of the world.

EGYPTIANS

Neb-mat-Re-Amun-hotpe (abbrev. as Nebmare; known to history as Amenhotep III)—Pharaoh of Egypt, an old and ailing man.

Hor-waz—Captain of the fortress of Thel.

Petepre (Potiphar)—A courtier with many honorific titles but no authority, also a eunuch. Despite the difficulties of his position, he is a man of personal courage and dignity.

Mont-kaw—Steward of Potiphar, a modest and simple man, devoted to his master's interests.

Dudu—The keeper of Potiphar's wardrobe, a dwarf and a spiteful, self-important little man.

Bes (Bes-em-hab, Shepses-Bes, Sa'ankh-Wen-nofer-Neteruhotep-em-per-Amun)—Another dwarf, friendly toward Joseph and opposed to Dudu.

Huia and Tuia—Brother and sister, the aged parents of Potiphar.

Beknechons—High priest of Amun, a theological conservative and a chauvinist.

Mut-em-enet—Wife of Potiphar, a reserved and aristocratic woman passionately in love with Joseph.

Nefer-kheperu-Re-Amenhotempe (known to history as Amenhotep IV, popularly Neb-nef-nezem, familiarly "Meni"; later changes his name to Ikhnaton)—Pharaoh after Amenhotep III, an unstable, impulsive boy, and a devotee of the god Atun.

Tiy—Ikhnaton's mother, a firm-willed woman somewhat resentful of being displaced from her regency.

Nefertiti (Nefernefruaton)—Ikhnaton's consort.

Tabubu—A Negro slave of Mut-em-enet, a sorceress.

Mai-Sachme—The imperturbable governor of Joseph's prison, interested in literature and medicine.

Mersu-Re (Mesedsu-Re)—A nobleman, Pharaoh's chief baker, a suspicious, sly and conspiratorial man.

Nefer-em-Wese (Bin-em-Wese)—Pharaoh's butler, fat, genial and talkative.

Petepre (Potipherah, Potiphar)—High priest of On, father of
Asenath. Not to be confused with Potiphar the eunuch,
Joseph's master.
Asenath—Joseph's wife, a charming, sweet-tempered, obedient
girl.

GODS AND DEMIGODS
(SEMITIC)

Yahweh (Yahu, Elohim, El Elyon, El Shaddai)—God of Abra-
ham, Isaac and Jacob.
Marduk—The head god of the Babylonian pantheon.
Baal—A Canaanite deity equivalent to Marduk.
Tiamat—A Babylonian goddess, personification of darkness
and chaos, overcome by Marduk.
Gilgamesh—The mythical hero of a Babylonian epic.
Utnapishtim—The Babylonian equivalent of Noah.
Tammuz (Adonis)—Syrian god of vegetation, whose death
and rebirth were annually celebrated.
Ishtar (Ashtaroth, Astarte)—Lunar goddess worshipped in
Syria and Canaan.
Ereshkigal—Queen of the underworld in the Syrian religion.
Asherah—A goddess in love with the hero Gilgamesh.
Shalim—A solar deity worshipped at Jeru-shalim (Jerusalem).

(EGYPTIAN)

Geb and Nut—Earth god and heaven goddess, parents of
Osiris and Set.
Osiris—Lord of the underworld and judge of the dead.
Isis—Sister and consort of Osiris.
Set—Brother and rival of Osiris.
Nephthys—Sister and consort of Set.
Anubis (Anpu)—A jackal-headed god, son of Osiris and
Nephthys.
Amun (Amon, Amun-Re)—A solar deity, identified with the
sun-god Re, and represented as a ram; worshipped in Thebes
as the supreme god and associated with a conservative,
xenophobic spirit.
Aton (Atun, Atun-Re, Atun-Re-Horakhte)—A solar deity, also
identified with Re and represented as the solar disk; wor-

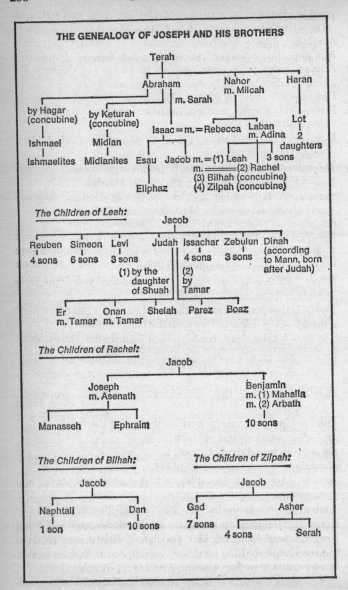

THE GENEALOGY OF JOSEPH AND HIS BROTHERS

Terah

Abraham — Nahor m. Milcah — Haran

Abraham m. Sarah

by Hagar (concubine) — Ishmael — Ishmaelites

by Keturah (concubine) — Midian — Midianites

Isaac = m. = Rebecca

Laban m. Adina — 3 sons

Lot — 2 daughters

Esau — Eliphaz

Jacob m. = (1) Leah
m. = (2) Rachel
(3) Bilhah (concubine)
(4) Zilpah (concubine)

The Children of Leah:

Jacob

Reuben — 4 sons
Simeon — 6 sons
Levi — 3 sons
Judah
Issachar — 4 sons
Zebulun — 3 sons
Dinah (according to Mann, born after Judah)

(1) by the daughter of Shuah

(2) by Tamar

Er m. Tamar — Onan m. Tamar — Shelah — Parez — Boaz

The Children of Rachel:

Jacob

Joseph m. Asenath

Manasseh — Ephraim

Benjamin m. (1) Mahalia m. (2) Arbath — 10 sons

The Children of Bilhah:

Jacob

Naphtali — 1 son
Dan — 10 sons

The Children of Zilpah:

Jacob

Gad — 7 sons
Asher — 4 sons — Serah

shiped at On as supreme god of a religion with syncretic and monotheistic tendencies.

Api (Hapi, Apis)—The Nile, represented as a bull.

Hathor—A cow-goddess representing the sky.

Horus—A sky god represented as a falcon, son of Osiris.

Thoth—Patron of scribes and inventor of writing.

Djehuti—An ape-god, scribe of Thoth.

Ptah—God of artists and craftsmen represented as a bull.

Sakhmet—Wife of Ptah.

Nefertem—Son of Ptah.

Bastet—Cat-god worshiped at Per-Bastet.

Sopdu—A local god worshiped at Per-Sopd.

The Story

Joseph and His Brothers (Joseph und seine Bruder) is based on the second half of the book of Genesis. The hero of course is Joseph, but his father, Jacob, with whose death the book closes, is almost equally important. As the story opens, Jacob, a dignified and venerable patriarch, is living with his twelve sons at Mamre, near Hebron. Most of Volume I is devoted to retelling the family legends about Jacob and his ancestors: how Jacob stole the paternal blessing from his brother Esau, the vision at Bethel, Jacob's service with Laban, the wooing of Rachel, the flight from Laban, the reconciliation with Esau, the seduction of Dinah, the sack of Schechem, the rivalry between the wives and the death of Rachel.

In Volume II Joseph becomes the center of the story. He is seventeen, extraordinarily beautiful and quick-witted, but vain, quick to capitalize on his position as the favorite son, and dangerously insensitive to his brothers' jealousy, which he inflames by his talebearing. To the familiar story of Joseph's two dreams, predicting his ascendancy over his brothers, Mann adds a third dream, more presumptuous still. Jacob in his fatherly indulgence is persuaded to give Joseph a magnificent cloak, which Mann neatly identifies as Rachel's wedding dress. Enraged by this mark of favor, the brothers seize and bind Joseph, intending to kill him. Judah and Reuben try secretly to save Joseph, but the most they accomplish is that he is sold to some passing traders who carry him off to Egypt.

Volume III takes advantage of the terseness of the original

(only one chapter in Genesis) to introduce much new material. Joseph is taken by the traders into Egypt, travels up the Nile to the capital at Thebes, and there is sold for a good price into the household of Potiphar, a courtier of King Amenhotep III. Potiphar is a eunuch who enjoys many titles, although they carry no substantive power. He also has a nominal wife, the beautiful and aristocratic Mut-em-enet, a priestess of Hathor. Joseph quickly learns to adapt, despite the difficulties that surround him, for he has learned from his recent brush with death that tact is important. He makes an enemy of a household dwarf Dudu and a friend of another dwarf, Bes, who play the roles of good and evil angels, comically reduced in scale. His closest friend and protector is Mont-kaw, Potiphar's chief steward, who discovers his talents and advances him to a position of responsibility. Mont-kaw is devoted to his master, and swears Joseph to a like loyalty. In time Joseph comes to the attention of Potiphar himself, becomes his personal secretary, and, upon Mont-kaw's death, his chief steward.

As a foreigner, Joseph is especially vulnerable. Among the many forms of religious worship in Egypt, the most important is the cult of Amun, which expresses itself in rigid conservatism and xenophobia. Jealousy toward Joseph can therefore disguise itself as religious devotion. The dwarf Dudu is of this faction. To dislodge Joseph, he appeals on religious and patriotic grounds to his mistress, Mut-em-enet. She has never noticed Joseph hitherto, but now she does. In her enforced celibacy as Potiphar's wife, she is attracted by his extraordinary charm and beauty. She struggles against her passion for three years, at first silently, but in the end openly and without shame. Dudu now encourages her since Joseph can be destroyed in this way. Joseph plays a dangerous game since he cannot afford to anger either his master or his mistress. At times, he is tempted into flirtation, but maintains his chastity, chiefly out of loyalty to Potiphar and the oath he swore with Mont-kaw. At length, Mut-em-enet makes a direct overture; Joseph escapes, leaving his cloak in her hands. In her rage and frustration she denounces him for attempted rape. Potiphar is obliged to commit Joseph to prison, but his chief wrath falls on Dudu, whom he suspects of being the true villain. For a second time, Joseph descends into the pit.

Volume IV tells of Joseph's climb back to power. The governor of the prison, a thoughtful and considerate man, like

Mont-kaw recognizes Joseph's abilities and puts him in a responsible position. During his imprisonment, Joseph performs his famous feat of interpreting the dreams of two fellow prisoners, an achievement which eventually brings him to the attention of the young Pharaoh. (Mann pleasantly and plausibly identifies this ruler with Amenhotep IV, or Ikhnaton.) The king is also troubled with dreams, which Joseph skillfully interprets, or rather, like a good psychoanalyst, encourages the king to interpret for himself. Seven years of plenty will come, he predicts, followed by seven years of famine. It behooves the government to lay in stores. Ikhnaton, with youthful impulsiveness, appoints Joseph to supervise the project. When the lean years come, Joseph, as custodian of national granaries, gives the grain free to the poor and sells it to the nobles at such a price that they are reduced to the level of tenants of the king. The result is a radical change in the system of land tenure and a great increase in royal power. Since the famine also extends into Palestine and Syria, the surplus of grain in Egypt is a strong diplomatic weapon to reduce the kings of that area to subjection.

Eventually Jacob and his family feel the pinch, and the ten older sons are sent to Egypt to buy food. Benjamin, as the favorite, is kept at home. Joseph has been expecting his brothers and proceeds to play an elaborate trick on them. He pretends to regard them as spies, and, keeping Simeon as hostage, allows the others to go home on condition that they return with Benjamin. Jacob is reluctant to let Benjamin go, but in the end starvation forces the brothers to return to Egypt. This time Joseph receives them all courteously, but, when they leave, he hides a valuable cup in Benjamin's luggage and has him arrested as a thief. This is the crucial test for the brothers which determines Joseph's subsequent treatment of them. Will they stand by Benjamin or abandon him as they did Joseph? All ten return with the youngest and plead his innocence. Judah declares impressively that their present misfortunes are a retribution for their treatment of Joseph years before. He now offers to bear Benjamin's punishment so that the favorite child may return to his father. Joseph, seeing that their hearts have been touched at last, reveals himself and the family is united again.

In the last chapters, Jacob is persuaded to join his sons in Egypt and settle in Goshen, on the eastern frontier of the

country. He dies at a great age, blessing his children and proclaiming Judah, the sinning but repentant son, heir to the
blessing inherited from Abraham and Isaac.

Critical Opinion

Everyone knows the story of Joseph which is told in the book
of Genesis in about one hundredth of the space that Mann
requires for his version. Despite this enormous expansion,
however, *Joseph and His Brothers* sticks closely to its original
and rarely contradicts or omits anything that the Bible mentions. The extra material comes from many sources. Since the
Joseph story is one of the most popular in all literature, there
are many post-Biblical variants which provide much supple-
mentary matter, notably the Koran, the Midrash, and the
poetry of Persia. It was from these sources, for instance, that
Mann drew the account of the banquet given by Potiphar's
wife at which the female guests were so smitten by Joseph's
beauty that they absentmindedly cut themselves with their
knives. Most of the concrete details, however, of daily life in
ancient times are derived from Mann's encyclopedic reading
in Biblical criticism, Egyptology, and the archeology of the
Near East. Without the work of hundreds of scholars over the
past century and a half, Mann would not have been able to
re-create life in the fifteenth century BC in such convincing
and circumstantial detail. The most brilliant of these recon-
structions is Mann's picture of Egypt in the time of Amenhotep III, a picture which goes far beyond external details
and actually tries to capture the spirit of Egyptian culture, its
social attitudes, its religious aspirations, and even the cadence
of its prose style.

Because of the sheer weight of its erudition, this novel has
struck some impatient readers as needlessly pedantic. However, for Mann, who is after all a storyteller and not an
archeologist, all this learning is only a preliminary to the
creation of character. And it is here that we can most readily
take the measure of Mann's originality. For example, Potiphar
is a shadowy figure in the Bible; in the novel, he emerges as
a fully drawn character, pathetic in his impotence, but courageous and dignified. Pharaoh, about whom the Bible tells
us next to nothing, comes alive as the young Ikhnaton, an

unstable and emotional boy of seventeen. Esau becomes a Semitic equivalent of the Greek god Pan, complete with goatskin, pointed ears and panpipes. There is nothing in the traditional literature about Dudu, the self-important dwarf, or the modest, loyal steward Mont-kaw, or Mai-Sachme, the placid prison governor who spends his leisure hours writing novels. Nor should we overlook Rimut, the soothsayer of Harran, a delightful vignette of a self-confident professional man.

In short, this is more than an ordinary historical novel. It is not, for instance, comparable with Flaubert's *Salammbo,* which in some ways it suggests. Even the elaborate show of scholarship is undertaken with tongue in cheek. As Mann explains, this is a bantering pseudo-exactness very close to persiflage, "for scientific treatment of wholly unscientific and legendary matters is pure irony." Mann's interest lies in what he terms "the typical, the eternally human, eternally recurring, timeless—in short, the mythical." Not that Mann meant his characters to be unreal, or that he allows them to evaporate into insubstantial abstractions; rather he presents them as actual, very real human beings who think of themselves in mythical terms and conform their lives to mythic patterns, as actors in a drama which repeats itself generation after generation. Thus the rivalry of Cain and Abel is renewed in Ishmael and Isaac and again in Jacob and Esau. In Egypt it appears in the myth of Set and Osiris. In Jacob's household, a wise old servant named Eliezer (a name which has been borne by men in the same position in every generation, back to the days of Abraham) can speak of himself as if he were the same man who went to seek the hand of Rebecca for Isaac, and when he dies his eldest son assumes the same role. This manner of speaking is made possible by a certain vagueness, common to the entire culture, about the boundaries between one personal ego and another. The result is a foreshortening of historical perspective, which condenses the experience of many centuries into one generation. Perhaps we can compare it to a photographic plate on which a succession of similar images has been registered until all merge as one.

The fundamental myth in which Joseph participates is common to all eastern Mediterranean cultures: the myth of death and resurrection, a myth rooted originally in the cycles of the sun, the moon, and vegetation. Thus Joseph's descent into the pit is symbolically a descent into Sheol, corresponding to the three dark days of the lunar month. It also follows the myth of Tammuz, the beautiful young god who dies each year, is mourned by his worshipers, and is annually reborn. It is like the story of Osiris, killed by his brother Set. When Joseph enters Egypt he takes a name which identifies himself with this god: he becomes Osarsiph, that is, Osiris-Joseph, or the dead Joseph. In Egypt, his prison sentence, which lasts for a symbolic three years, is a similar descent into the grave followed by a second resurrection.

The most familiar instance of the dying and resurrected god is, of course, Christ, and Mann has not hesitated to parallel or anticipate the Gospel story. The three days which Joseph spends in the pit correspond to the three days from Good Friday to Easter, and the rolling away of the stone from the mouth of the well reproduces a detail from the Resurrection. Joseph is not really a Christ figure, of course, and the only salvation he can offer his brothers is material. There is another side to his character. At times, he is the clever rogue, the contriver whose trickery verges on mischief, and in this he suggests both the Egyptian god Thoth and the Greek god Hermes, patron of thieves and all those who live by their wits.

Joseph and His Brothers may also be read as a *Bildungsroman*, the story of the education and maturation of a young man. Joseph at seventeen is an exasperating puppy who deserves a thrashing. His experience in slavery teaches him tact and diplomacy and an understanding of human nature. Others undergo development too. Jacob begins his career with an act of fraud practiced on his blind father, yet ends his days full of patriarchal dignity. Judah, a guilty and tormented man, learns repentance through suffering, and becomes the heir to the promise made first to Abraham. Finally, this story is also a *Bildungsroman* about God himself. Beginning as Yahu, a violent desert demon or kobold, he grows in stature and dignity as his worshipers grow in ethical sensitivity. The covenant between Yahweh and Abraham is a covenant for their *mutual* sanctification.

Like *The Magic Mountain*, *Joseph and His Brothers* was first conceived as a novella. As it progressed, it developed a will of its own which would not be satisfied until Mann had written a tetralogy. When Hitler came to power, Mann was abroad. The manuscript was rescued by his eldest daughter from their confiscated home in Munich. Continued in exile, the story became by its very subject a rebuke to the anti-Semitism of Nazi Germany. The last volume was completed during the forties under what Mann calls "the Egyptian skies of California," and bears the stamp of the author's American experience. Joseph as a servant of the Pharaoh displays a combination of political skill, social idealism, and imaginative practicality, together with a humanistic confidence in the ability of men to master their environment and control their economic destinies, that distinctly suggests the New Deal.

This novel strikes a note of optimism which goes beyond anything Mann had so far written. The Buddenbrooks family decayed. Hans Castorp faced death and defied it, but his fate remains unclear. Joseph, on the other hand, goes down to death and emerges as a conqueror, having played his part in shaping the destiny of his people. The story is sometimes serious but never tragic. Joseph plays his role with the lighthearted and confident abandon of the actor who knows that the play is going to have a happy ending. This book is Mann's *Divine Comedy*.

The Author

Thomas Mann was born in 1875 in the old Hanseatic port of Lübeck in northern Germany. Lübeck had once been a self-governing city, and was still dominated by its wealthy merchant families who formed a burgher aristocracy. Mann belonged to this class. His father was a prominent grain merchant and senator, who anticipated that his sons would continue the century-old family business. From this background, Mann acquired his understanding of and respect for bourgeois values, and also his feeling that an artist in a middle-class world is engaged in something suspect or illicit, perhaps even decadent or criminal. The artistic strain in the family came from the mother who was of mixed German and Brazilian stock. The children, besides Thomas, were Heinrich, who became a novelist in his own right, Viktor, and two sisters, Julia and Carla, both of whom were to die by their own hands.

Mann was a student at the Lübeck Realgymnasium, a school run on Prussian principles, where he was thoroughly unhappy, and where he was made to feel like an outsider because he liked literature and wrote poetry. In 1891 his father died unexpectedly, the business was liquidated, and his mother moved to Munich. Mann stayed in Lübeck long enough to finish school, and then followed the family. He attended the University of Munich for a time as an auditor, but took no degree. For a while he worked as a clerk in a fire-insurance company.

The decade of the nineties was a formative period during which Mann read extensively, especially Nietzsche, Schopenhauer and the Russian novelists, traveled in Italy, did editorial work for a humorous magazine, and tried his hand at writing stories. His first major work was *Buddenbrooks* (1901), a long novel based on his own family and set in a town which is recognizably Lübeck. This work established his reputation. It soon became a best seller and some years later won Mann the Nobel Prize. It was followed in 1903 by *Tristan*, a collection of tales including the famous "Tonio Kröger." This, too, is autobiographical; Tonio is Mann himself, and most of the incidents actually happened. Like so many of Mann's stories, its theme is the position of the artist who is shut out by his gifts from participating in the normal, healthy life around him.

In 1905, Mann married Katja Pringsheim, a member of a wealthy and cultivated family and the daughter of a professor of mathematics at the University of Munich. His happiness at this time is reflected in his next novel, *Royal Highness (Königliche Hoheit,* 1909), a rather lightweight production with a happy ending. There were six children by the marriage, of whom two, Klaus and Erika, became writers, too, and another, Golo, an historian. The Manns are thus the most distinguished and productive literary family in German history.

Another early work of major importance is "Death in Venice" ("Tod in Venedig," 1912), based on impressions gained during a stay in Venice in 1911. This novella is a study of the relation between art and disease, love and death. Its protagonist is a distinguished writer, Gustav von Aschenbach, who has lived a life of rigid discipline and self-denial. On a vacation in Venice he falls in love with a beautiful boy who so bewitches him that he remains in the city in the face of a cholera epidemic. In surrendering to love and shame, von Aschenbach surrenders to death as well, for he dies of the cholera. The story is a classic, marvelously told, and rich in philosophic and psychological insight.

In the same year, Frau Mann contracted a touch of pulmonary trouble and had to be hospitalized at a sanatorium in Davos. While Mann was visiting his wife there, he collected the impressions that he used in *The Magic Mountain* (Der Zauberberg, 1924). This novel was originally intended as a comic sequel to "Death in Venice," and was to explore the same themes of sickness, love and death, but from an ironic point of view. Eventually, the novel took its own course and overshadowed the earlier story.

Mann did not serve in the First World War because an army doctor who had read his books decided that he should be left alone. During the war, he thought much about the role of Germany in European culture, and embodied his reflections in a work entitled *Reflections of a Non-Political Man* (*Betrachtungen eines Unpolitischen*, 1918). This was an ultraconservative statement of romantic German nationalism. His nationalism at this time led him to a sharp and painful break with his brother Heinrich, whose values were more international and western European. In the years after the war, however, Mann moved steadily toward a more liberal and democratic position. During the twenties, he supported the well-intentioned if ineffectual Weimar Republic, and in 1930 he took a firm stand against Fascism, in two works: an address to the German people entitled "An Appeal to Reason" and a story set in Mussolini's Italy entitled "Mario and the Magician" ("Mario und der Zauberer"). When Hitler seized power in 1933, Mann was traveling abroad. He stayed away for sixteen years. In 1936, the Nazi government deprived him of citizenship and the University of Bonn withdrew an honorary degree which it had given him. Mann's reply on this occasion is a famous piece of polemic writing. In 1938 he settled in the United States, living first in Princeton and then in California. In 1944 he became an American citizen.

The greatest of Mann's later novels is *Joseph and His Brothers*, a tetralogy which appeared from 1933 to 1943. This is a vast expansion of the Biblical story of Joseph, told with great erudition and embodying Mann's thoughts on early religion and mythology. *Doctor Faustus* (1948) is a modern treatment of the Faust theme, set against a background of war and Fascism. The hero, Adrian Leverkühn, is a composer of genius and one more in Mann's gallery of sick artists. *The*

Adventures of Felix Krull (1954) is a comic tale of a rogue and confidence man, an elaboration of a shorter story written many years before.

Mann returned to Germany briefly in 1949 to accept prizes at Frankfurt and Weimar. He refused, however, to settle in Germany permanently, preferring to retain his American citizenship and to live on neutral ground in Switzerland near Zürich. He died there in 1955.

The Immoralist

by

ANDRÉ GIDE (1869–1951)

The Characters

Michel—A young man, by profession an historian. He suffers from the effects of a childhood in which he was emotionally constricted and intellectually forced.

Marceline—His young wife, a frail, devoted girl.

Young Arab Boys at Biskra—Bachir, Ashour, Lassif, Lachmi, Moktir.

Bocage—The bailiff of Michel's estate in Normandy, honest, plodding and unimaginative.

Charles—Son of Bocage, a serious, responsible adolescent.

Alcide—Another son of Bocage, a poacher.

Huertevent—A timber merchant.

Bute—A laborer.

Pierre—A farm hand.

Ménalque—A friend of Michel, a sophisticated and articulate hedonist.

A Coachman at Sorrento.

A Coachman at Taormina.

Ali—A young boy at Touggourt.

Characters in the Frame Story—Denis, Daniel, and an unnamed narrator.

The Story

The Immoralist (L'Immoraliste) is a story within a story;
it is a *récit*, or first-person narrative, set in a frame which
bounds it at the beginning and the end. In the frame story,
four friends have made a compact in their youth to come to
the help of any one of them who requires it. Now one of them
has summoned the rest, and, though he lives in a remote
Algerian village, they drop their affairs and hurry to his side.
On arrival, they find that there is not much to be done for
their friend. All he wants is to tell them the events of his life
since they last met together. So the story is launched; and
what the three friends hear distresses them deeply.

The object of their concern is a young man in his twenties
named Michel. After the untimely death of his mother, he
was raised by his scholarly father, under whose discipline his
mind was precociously forced. Michel is already a historian of
considerable ability, but the academic seclusion of his life,
reinforced by a strain of austere Huguenot piety, has turned
him into a bloodless, inhibited intellectual. At twenty-four, in
obedience to his father's dying wishes, he has married a girl
named Marceline whom he respects but does not love.

For their honeymoon, the couple go to North Africa, where
Michel wishes to explore some ruins. They have hardly arrived, however, when he becomes gravely ill with tuberculosis.
Marceline nurses him devotedly, and, as soon as he can travel,
takes him to Biskra, in the Saharan Atlas, to convalesce. In
her spare time, she takes a motherly interest in the swarms
of young boys who live in the town, and, while Michel is
recuperating, she occasionally brings some of them into his
room to divert him with their play and their talk. The joy
Michel finds in their beauty and their health inspires him to
recover. When he is stronger, he walks about the town taking a sensuous delight in the shady gardens of the Biskra
oasis and striking up friendships with the children who pas-
ture their flocks there. A special favorite is a handsome
youth named Moktir. One day, while Moktir is alone with
Michel, he furtively takes a small pair of scissors belonging
to Marceline. Michel sees the theft but makes no effort to
stop it. In fact, he feels a sudden, fierce delight as if, in con-

doning this mildly criminal act, he is releasing himself from conventional morality.

Leaving Algeria, the couple return home by way of Sicily and southern Italy. After his brush with death, Michel finds his outlook on life changed. He no longer cares for history. His only concern is to live fully in the present. He fears that his real self has become buried under the dust of centuries and throttled by the conventions of civilized life, that all his values are false and secondhand. Now, he discovers the importance of mere physical life, of health, of the free play of the muscles, of animal joy. He shaves his beard, lets his hair grow, and takes a pagan delight in bathing naked under the Italian sun. One day, in his newfound strength, he fights and beats a drunken coachman whose reckless driving has endangered Marceline, and that night he possesses her sexually for the first time.

A happy life now begins for both. Marceline becomes pregnant. For a time, they settle in Normandy, where Michel has inherited an estate. The property, unoccupied for some time, is in the hands of an old and trusted bailiff named Bocage. The bailiff's sixteen-year-old son, Charles, is studying farm management. Michel strikes up a friendship with Charles, whose judgment he respects, and on his advice makes a number of reforms in the way the estate is run. He also takes an expensive apartment in Paris, as if to bind himself to his new life by a multitude of possessions and obligations. Finally, he accepts an appointment at the Collège de France. His lectures on the fall of Rome display an unexpected sympathy with the barbarian Goths whose savagery destroyed the effete and ancient Roman civilization.

Michel's new life is upset, however, by the appearance of an old friend, Ménalque. A traveler and man of the world, this articulate hedonist declares that the pleasure he takes in an act is enough reason for doing it. He is involved in a public scandal and lawsuit, never quite made clear. Ménalque too has been to Biskra and has heard stories from Moktir about Michel's sojourn there, including the episode of the scissors. He is puzzled to find his friend in Paris living such a respectable married existence. As Ménalque is going on a long journey, he invites Michel to spend the night with him in intimate conversation. They pass the hours drinking rare wines while Ménalque expounds his philosophy of self-fulfillment through pleasure. When Michel returns home, he finds that Marceline has had a miscarriage and is gravely ill. A long and precarious period of sickness follows: phlebitis, involvement of the lungs, and heart trouble. As soon as Marceline can travel, she and Michel return to his estate in Normandy. This year, however, instead of studying farm management with Charles, Michel strikes up a friendship with Charles's disreputable brother Alcide, who is a poacher. Together they poach Michel's own game, setting snares which Bocage discovers and removes without suspecting that his own master is responsible. Michel finds a keen, illicit delight in this ridiculous situation. When the truth comes out, Charles rebukes Michel, protesting that he and his father can no longer stay with so irresponsible an employer. Michel responds by selling the farm.

Marceline now shows serious symptoms of tuberculosis. Michel, who does not want to admit that she may have contracted it from him, tries to deny the evidence. In search of a suitable climate, he takes her to Switzerland though she is quite happy in Normandy. When Michel becomes bored with the dull, honest Swiss, they head for Italy, retracing their honeymoon and always heading south. In Sicily, the peasant boys remind Michel of the shepherds of Theocritus. At Taormina he flirts tentatively with one of them. Marceline is now too weary to oppose Michel's insistence that they continue, though she sees that his newfound philosophy of life is a ruthless selfishness which has no pity for weaklings like herself.

From Sicily, the couple push on to Africa again, getting farther each day from European civilization. At Biskra, they pause long enough to look up the children they knew a few years before. Most of them are now dirty, dull, and ugly. Only Moktir (who is just out of jail) is still handsome. Suddenly Michel is seized with a desire to see Touggourt, a town far out in the desert. With Moktir as their companion, they press on, though Marceline is exhausted. At Touggourt, they find quarters in a shabby hotel where Marceline tumbles into bed, too tired even to eat. Michel spends the evening strolling through the streets with Moktir, finally entering a Moorish café where Moktir has a mistress. Together they go to her room, and Michel makes love to the woman while Moktir sits on the bed beside them. When he returns to the hotel, he finds that Marceline has had a hemorrhage and is dying.

As the *récit* ends, we are brought back to the present, in which Michel is speaking to his friends. Three months have now passed, he tells them. He is living in a native mountain village where his food and quarters cost him almost nothing. He has a mistress, a handsome native girl, and she in turn has a younger brother named Ali who is Michel's devoted and affectionate servant. The girl likes to make fun of Michel, telling him good-naturedly that it is really Ali whom he wants. Perhaps, Michel admits, she is not altogether wrong.

Critical Opinion

The Immoralist is strikingly autobiographical, built upon many of Gide's actual experiences. Here he has written about his own bookish childhood, his Huguenot training, his family estate in Normandy, his trip to North Africa in 1893 and the illness that overtook him there, his passion for brown-skinned, sensual Arab urchins. Ménalque, both in his philosophy and his manner, is an obvious portrait of Oscar Wilde. Madeleine Gide was very unlike the wearily passive Marceline, yet details from her life have been used: the honeymoon in Switzerland, an illness in North Africa, a carriage accident, etc. All this material, however, has been used objectively, without any attempt at self-justification. Gide here achieves the detachment of a major artist.

Gide's objectivity shows itself especially in the ironic treatment of his hero. Since Michel tells his own story, he has every opportunity to state his own case; nevertheless, he reveals more of himself than he realizes. He sees himself as a man reborn, seeking a new and authentic personality. At the same time, he gives us glimpses of how he looks to others. To Charles he seems criminally irresponsible. To Marceline he seems inhuman. And to his friends of the frame narrative, he is a lost or nearly lost soul. Ménalque, more perceptive than the rest, suggests that Michel is unfitted to be a successful egoist. He should leave such dangerous pursuits to others.

The novel's central moral issue is the conflict between freedom and responsibility (not quite the same as the conflict between evil and good). Michel is right in thinking that his youth has been misdirected and that life is passing him by. He is right in wanting physical exuberance and sexual fulfillment. Ideally, he should be able to accomplish these ends without destroying himself or others. The bailiff's son, Charles, gives him a clear object lesson in this. There is an unbroken colt on the estate which no one can handle. With care, Charles is able to tame the animal. It is just as beautiful and strong as before, but its strength is no longer dangerous. Michel cannot profit by this example. His childhood has been so constricted that the new personality can be achieved only at the cost of shattering the old, and this means rejecting his history, culture, social restraints, property, prudence and consideration for others. The symbolic action which he adopts is theft. He looks the other way while Moktir steals the scissors, poaches on his own land, subverts the honest administration of his property. All this is perhaps forgivable, but his treatment of Marceline verges on homicide. Because she is no longer healthy and therefore no longer desirable, because she is associated with his former self, he drives her to certain death. The momentum of destruction carries him still further. One senses that he is destined to be his own next victim. Thus *The Immoralist* is not to be read as a defense of ethical individualism, such as one might expect from Gide, perhaps not even as an attack on it, but certainly a critique of individualism and an exposition of its risks.

Psychologically this novel shows remarkable insight and realism. Written before Freud became influential, its understanding of repressed sexual drives is thoroughly Freudian. The first serious, mature treatment of homosexuality in modern fiction, it anticipates by about ten years Thomas Mann's in "Death in Venice." Like von Aschenbach, the subject of Mann's novella, Michel is not a practicing pederast; his homosexuality lies just below the surface, and he does not clearly recognize it until the last sentence. The reader, of course, understands Michel long before he understands himself, so that the speaker's willful blindness is rich in dramatic irony.

Despite the autobiographical element, we must not confuse Michel with Gide, who once observed that although his characters were often based on his own experience, they were driven by their folly and blindness to tragic ends which he was able to avoid. Michel is a failure both as an individualist and as a homosexual. His cry for help to his three friends is his confession of failure. He has not learned how to live with the contradictions within him, and he lacks what his creator finally achieved: wisdom and serenity.

The Counterfeiters

by

ANDRÉ GIDE

The Characters

THE PROFITENDIEU FAMILY

Albéric Profitendieu—A magistrate, a prosperous, pompous, self-righteous bourgeois.
Marguerite Profitendieu—His wife.
Bernard—Marguerite's illegitimate son whom Albéric has raised as his own child.
Cécile—Albéric's daughter.
Charles (Caloub)—Albéric's young son.
Antoine—A manservant.

THE MOLINIER FAMILY

Oscar Molinier—A colleague of Albéric Profitendieu.
Pauline Molinier—His wife.
Edouard—Pauline's halfbrother, a bachelor and a novelist.
Vincent—Oscar's oldest son, a doctor.
Olivier—The second son, just graduated from the lycée, with literary ambitions.
George—The youngest son, a schoolboy.

THE VEDEL AZAÏS FAMILY

Pastor Azaïs—An elderly Protestant pastor, the proprietor of a boarding school.
Pastor Prosper Vedel—His son-in-law.
Mélanie Vedel—His wife, a rather foolish sentimentalist.

Rachel—Vedel's oldest daughter; responsible for the business management of the school.

Laura—Vedel's second daughter; an old friend of Edouard, married to Félix Douvier, in love with Vincent Molinier.

Félix Douvier—Laura's husband, a professor in England, a well-intentioned mediocrity.

Alexandre—Vedel's older son, now in Africa.

Sarah—Vedel's youngest daughter.

Armand—Vedel's younger son, a bitter, self-tormenting boy.

OTHERS

Comte Robert de Passavant—An author, a poseur, and a charlatan.

Gontran de Passavant—His younger brother, a student at the École Vedel-Azaïs.

Lady Lillian Griffith—A friend of Robert, and Vincent Molinier's second mistress.

La Pérouse—An elderly music teacher.

Mme. La Pérouse—His wife who suffers from senile paranoia.

Boris—Grandson of La Pérouse.

Mme. Sophroniska—Boris's psychoanalyst.

Bronja—Daughter of Mme. Sophroniska and Boris's playmate.

Solomon Dhurmer—A friend of Olivier.

Victor Strouvilhou—Formerly a boarder with the Vedels, now engaged in counterfeiting and blackmail.

Leon Ghéridanisol—Strouvilhou's nephew, a pupil at the Vedel School.

Philippe Adamanti—A schoolboy.

Justinien des Brousses—Editor of a literary magazine.

Alfred Jarry—An actual figure, author of *Ubu Roi*.

Lucien Bercail—A writer.

Cob Lafleur—A writer.

Séraphine—Servant in the Passavant family.

The Story

Bernard Profitendieu is a youth in his late teens living in Paris just before the First World War. He is—or believes himself to be—the son of a highly respected judge, Albéric Profitendieu (prosper in God). An attractive boy, he has lively intelligence, independent spirit, and much enthusiasm. The story begins with Bernard reading some letters, uncovered in a secret drawer, which reveal that he is not the son of the judge at all, but the fruit of a clandestine love affair of his mother's. As Bernard is not on good terms with his father, the news comes as a great relief. Realizing that he has no ties to keep him at home any longer, he writes his father a needlessly dramatic and insulting farewell letter and leaves to make his way in the world alone.

Bernard's closest friend is a schoolboy named Olivier Molinier, the son of a colleague of Judge Profitendieu. Bernard's first move is to hunt up Olivier and stay with him until he can decide how he will support himself. That night, in Olivier's bed, the two boys talk over their plans, discussing, among other things, women. In this connection, Olivier reveals one of the skeletons in his family closet. His older brother Vincent has a mistress. Olivier does not know who she is, but he does know that Vincent has jilted her. He also tells Bernard about his Uncle Edouard, his mother's halfbrother, whom he vastly admires. Edouard is an author, and has given Olivier perceptive criticism of his youthful poetry. The next morning Bernard wakes early and steals out of the house to look for work. He is ready, he feels, to do anything.

The story now shifts its focus to Vincent—a young doctor with a promising future who has become entangled in a love affair. Now his mistress is pregnant, and Vincent wishes to help her. Unfortunately, he does not have enough money, and he has friends who give him bad advice. One such friend, a writer, the Comte Robert de Passavant (get ahead), introduces him to a gambling club where Vincent loses what little money he has. Passavant extricates him, and in repayment, asks for an introduction to Olivier. He is starting a new magazine, he says, and would like Olivier to be editor, and though Vincent thinks the offer suspicious, he agrees. His other corrupting friend is Lady Lillian Griffith, a friend of Passavant who becomes Vincent's new mistress. She is ruthless and selfish, and advises Vincent to be the same. At her suggestion, he abandons his former mistress and goes off with Lillian, thus passing outside the purview of the story until almost the end of the book.

Next we meet Olivier's Uncle Edouard. He has just been summoned from England to Paris by a letter from an old friend, Laura Douvier, with whom he was once inconclusively in love. Now she is asking for help. Earlier, at Edouard's suggestion, she had married a man whom she respected rather than loved, Félix Douvier. Then, while staying in a sanatorium in Pau, she fell in love with another man by whom she became pregnant. Now that her lover has abandoned her, she is without money, and is ashamed to return to her husband. Arriving in Paris, Edouard is met in the station by Olivier, checks his baggage, and goes off with his nephew to lunch.

Bernard, still roving at random about the city, runs into Olivier lunching with his uncle. During the conversation, Edouard absentmindedly drops his baggage check which Bernard quietly pockets. He is hungry and getting desperate. He goes off to the station to claim Edouard's property. There is a good sum of money in the luggage. Bernard appropriates it, but what really interests him is Edouard's journal and private papers, including the letter from Laura Douvier. She, Bernard realizes, must be Vincent's cast-off mistress. Excited by the intrigue, of which only he knows the complete story, he resolves to help Laura. Though he is a complete stranger, he goes to her hotel and quixotically offers her his services and Edouard's money. At that moment, Edouard also arrives and recognizes Bernard as Olivier's friend. He also realizes that it is he who has stolen the valise. He does not, however, take the theft too seriously and seems more amused than annoyed by it. He even agrees to engage Bernard as his secretary.

Meanwhile, Olivier has, through Vincent, made the acquaintance of Passavant. The Comte has just written a flashy and meretricious novel which is enjoying great popularity. Now he is launching a literary magazine. But since its chief purpose will be to praise his books, he prefers to hide behind a dummy editor. He offers Olivier this post—a dazzling temptation for a boy who has only just come up for his baccalaureate. He also suggests that Olivier should spend his vacation with him so that they can plan the magazine together. It is obviously homosexual seduction that Passavant has in mind, though Gide does not go into details. Olivier accepts.

Edouard is distressed by Olivier's behavior, not on grounds of sexual morality, but because he considers Passavant a bad writer and a charlatan. But he has other problems on his hands. There is another old friend of his in Paris, an elderly music teacher, La Pérouse, unhappily married to a querulous, nagging wife. The one person whom La Pérouse really loves is a thirteen-year-old grandson, Boris, whom he has never seen. Boris is the illegitimate child of La Pérouse's only son and his Polish mistress. Now the boy's father is dead and La Pérouse has no communication with the mother, but he yearns to meet the grandchild. He is staying in Switzerland. Will Edouard go there and find out what he can? Edouard agrees since it occurs to him that it would be a good idea for Laura to go to another country during her pregnancy. Posing as Laura's husband, and taking Bernard along as his secretary, Edouard sets out for the Swiss Alps.

In Switzerland, Bernard has no duties whatever, and passes his time sightseeing and talking to Edouard about the book which Edouard is writing, a novel entitled *The Counterfeiters* (*Les Faux Monnayeurs*). Olivier, vacationing in Corsica with Passavant, assumes that Bernard is enjoying the same kind of relationship with Edouard, and, since he is more than a little in love with them both, becomes intensely jealous. Actually, Bernard has fallen in love with Laura, though in a boyishly worshipful and thoroughly Platonic spirit. Laura, however, does not stay in Switzerland to deliver her child, for her husband generously offers to take her back and accept the baby as his own. Bernard is moved by this; he recognizes that this same relationship must have existed between his mother and her husband.

Edouard, meanwhile, has located little Boris. He is a badly disturbed child, subject to neurotic obsessions and tics. His mother has placed him in the care of a Polish psychoanalyst, Mme. Sophroniska, who is now staying with Boris at Edouard's hotel. Under her probing therapy, the cause of Boris's behavior emerges. He is suffering from guilt over secret masturbation which has become associated in his mind with guilt and grief arising from his father's death. With analysis, the outward signs of neurosis vanish, though Edouard suspects that the problem has merely been repressed. Since the patient is apparently cured, Edouard proposes to Mme. Sophroniska that Boris be united with his grandfather. There is a Protestant boys' school in Paris, the École Vedel-Azaïs, run by the father and grandfather of Laura Douvier, where old La Pérouse is a teacher. Edouard had studied there himself as a boy and now Olivier's younger brother George is a student. Bernard could undoubtedly find a post there; both he and La Pérouse could keep an eye on the boy.

These arrangements are made and Edouard returns to Paris, where more opportunities await him to meddle in other people's affairs. His brother-in-law, Judge Molinier, informs him that there is a scandal afoot involving schoolboys who have been regularly visiting prostitutes and conducting orgies. Some of the boys are from highly respectable families. Judge Profitendieu has had the girls arrested, after waiting until the school vacation so that the boys' names will not appear on any record. Molinier imagines that Bernard is involved. He does not realize that his own son George is one of the ringleaders.

Bernard, now settled at the school, has become friendly with Laura's family, especially her brother, Armand, and her sisters, Rachel and Sarah. Relations with Olivier are somewhat strained, though Olivier is beginning to suspect that Passavant is a fraud, and yearns to resume his friendship with Bernard and Edouard. The circle is reunited at a literary dinner attended by Olivier, Edouard, Passavant, Bernard, and Laura's younger sister, Sarah. Edouard takes the opportunity to warn Olivier that he is in bad company. As the party progresses, it becomes more drunken and abandoned. One of the guests fires a pistol loaded with blanks at his neighbor. Passavant flirts violently with Sarah, not because he cares for her, but simply to maintain his reputation for heterosexuality, and Olivier gets into a drunken brawl. Edouard finally takes the boy under his protection and carries him back to his own apartment. Olivier is quite drunk, but blissfully happy at being restored to Edouard's good graces. He is resolved to break off with Passavant at last. Bernard meanwhile takes Sarah home to her parents' school where Armand locks them into a bedroom so that they are obliged, with her brother's connivance, to sleep together.

The next morning when Edouard wakes, there is a smell of gas in the apartment. During the night Olivier has attempted suicide. His motives spring from a jumble of emotions: his shame over his behavior during the summer, his embarrassment for his drunken quarrel, his penitence at having been alienated from Edouard, and his joy at being restored to his uncle's love. Edouard nurses him back to health, rocking him in his arms like a child. They are both idyllically happy.

George meanwhile is in serious trouble. Now that their brothel has been closed by the police, he and his nasty circle of friends turn their energies to passing counterfeit ten-franc gold pieces. The leader of the ring is a vicious boy named Ghéridanisol but the brains of the operation is Ghéridanisol's uncle, the sinister Strouvilhou, who has now replaced Olivier as editor of Passavant's magazine, and who in his spare time engages in counterfeiting and blackmail. Among other things, he encourages the boys to steal compromising letters from their parents to be used in case the families threaten him with exposure. Judge Profitendieu discovers that George is involved and fears Bernard may be also. He asks Edouard to investigate. Edouard does so, and the young counterfeiters, in fear of the police, throw their coins down a sewer.

Time now hangs heavy on the hands of the gang at the École Vedel-Azaïs, and for amusement, they turn to tormenting little Boris. Their game is especially cruel. Under Ghéridanisol's leadership they form a club the members of which must be brave enough to do anything whatever. At first, Boris is excluded, then as a great favor, reluctantly admitted. The test of courage is that one of them must commit suicide in front of the entire school, using a pistol stolen from Boris's grandfather, La Pérouse. They draw lots which are so manipulated that Boris is chosen. The joke is that the pistol is to be empty though Boris does not know it. Only Ghéridanisol, of all the conspirators, knows that there is one live cartridge in the pistol. This La Pérouse has been saving for himself. Boris bravely accepts his fate, driven by a desire to prove himself a man, and also by hidden, unexorcised feelings of guilt. Before a horrified school, and in the presence of his grandfather, he takes the pistol from his desk, stands up, and blows his brains out.

This sudden tragedy shocks George back to his senses. His former admiration for Ghéridanisol gives way to horror, and he returns to his parents, shaken but reformed. The school is so rocked by the scandal that it has to close. Bernard, finally reconciled with his foster father, returns home. Indirectly, we hear word of Vincent. He has drifted with Lillian Griffith to Africa and murdered her under obscure circumstances. Now he is intermittently insane, and believes himself to be the Devil. The story has ended happily for Bernard, happily after serious trouble for Olivier and George, and tragically for

Boris and Vincent. There is one more boy who is too young to
have figured prominently up to this point: Bernard's younger
brother Caloub (Charles). In the last sentence of the book,
Edouard remarks, "I feel very curious to know Caloub."

Critical Opinion

The Counterfeiters is an extraordinarily complicated story.
Critics had accused Gide of lacking ingenuity in plot construction, and *The Counterfeiters* was his answer. It was written over a number of years and was slowly and painfully ham-
mered into shape. The story was assembled from a number
of sources. At one point, Gide visualized it as a continuation
of an earlier novel entitled *Lafcadio's Adventures (Les Caves
du Vatican)*, with Lafcadio as the central figure. Later as the
story became richer and more complex, Lafcadio became Bernard. Other characters were drawn from life: Armand Vedel
is a portrait of a friend, and La Pérouse is La Nux, Gide's
former music teacher. Several of the episodes came from the
daily papers. In 1906, a group of students and artists in Paris
were caught passing counterfeit money. In 1909 some schoolboys in Clermont-Ferrand formed a club in order to trick one
of their number into committing suicide. The shooting at the
literary dinner is based on a famous incident involving an
actual author, Alfred Jarry. As Gide worked these elements
together, he recorded the progress of the novel in a commonplace book entitled "Journal of the Counterfeiters." In some
editions, it is printed as an appendix.

This novel is of great technical interest to novelists and
critics for its manipulation of many complex and overlapping
points of view. It is told by an anonymous narrator, presumably Gide speaking *in propria persona;* at times he steps out
of his story in the eighteenth-century manner to comment
directly on his characters or even to talk about himself. Of the
actual characters, the central one is Edouard, the author who
knows everyone else in the story and comments on them
perceptively. The narrator tells us that Edouard represents
himself, but it would be naïve to accept the identification
without qualification. Edouard, like Gide, is writing a novel
called *The Counterfeiters*, and, like Gide, he is keeping a journal of its progress. The situation is like a series of toy boxes

each of which contains a smaller one. The novel within the novel, however, is not to be confused with the novel itself; it has different characters and a different story. Edouard, for instance, decides not to use Boris's death in his novel: it is unanticipated, inexplicable, too brutally real for him. Furthermore, if we can judge from one or two short extracts, Edouard's novel is rather weak. We may seriously doubt if it will ever get written. This device of the novel within a novel is used by Huxley in *Point Counter Point;* it also recalls the play-within-a-play in *Hamlet.*

The flashback is a common device used by authors to establish a backward perspective in time. Here the same function is served by back entries from Edouard's diary. Edouard and Olivier provide still further perspectives, especially through their letters to each other. Since Bernard has a bad habit of reading other people's papers, we are able to see incidents filtered through two points of view, theirs and his.

As the points of view shift, so does the tone. The different voices speak in a variety of accents: sentimental, ironic, witty, intellectual, pathetic, or horrified. At times (the improbable first interview between Laura and Bernard being one) the story seems to be written with tongue in cheek, as if Gide were merely playing at constructing a plot, and did not expect to be taken seriously. The stolen letter or diary, for example, was a favorite device of eighteenth-century writers, a bit naïve in the twentieth, yet Gide uses this creaky piece of machinery no fewer than four times.

So much for technique. What is the novel about? The central, unifying symbol is the counterfeit ten-franc gold coin Bernard has received from a butcher. Gradually these coins are traced to the gang of boys at the École Vedel-Azaïs, but these children are only the most honest of the counterfeiters, for everyone in the story is to some extent involved in deception.

The most blatant counterfeiter is Robert de Passavant: a complete charlatan, a minor author pretending to be great, who launches a magazine to get himself favorable reviews. Most of his bons mots are plagiarized. He fools no one but Olivier, and him only for a few months. A more complex counterfeiter is Pastor Azaïs, kindly and well intentioned, but committed to a sentimental brand of moralistic piety which cannot take the measure of evil in the world. He is so rigid that he can accept people only on his own terms. Consequently his family and students are forced to lie to him. Though he imagines he is dealing with people openly, he never hears anything but the echo of his own voice. Besides these two, almost everyone else has some shameful secret, usually sexual. Mme. Profitendieu has tried to keep Bernard's illegitimacy secret. Judge Molinier has a mistress whom he scrupulously conceals from his wife, and she conceals from him the fact that she knows all about it. Laura has her lover, while Edouard, for appearances' sake, pretends to be her husband. Pastor Vedel is in the grip of some obsession, presumably sexual, and records his struggles in his diary as an attempt to give up smoking. George Molinier wears a yellow ribbon in his buttonhole which identifies him as a patron of a schoolboy brothel, yet he convinces Azaïs that it is the badge of a society for good deeds. Boris's repressed guilt expresses itself in tics and obsessions which are explained only after extensive analysis.

The characters have been forced into their manifold dishonesties by the pressures of society, religion, and conscience, and they must extricate themselves if they are to discover their authentic selves. Only the boys are sufficiently plastic; there is some hope for them. Their elders are committed to their hypocrisies. Bernard states the problem thus:

> I should like all my life long, at the very smallest shock, to ring true with a pure authentic sound. Nearly all the people I know have rung false. . . . One wants to deceive people, and one is so much occupied with seeming that one ends by not knowing what one really is.

In this struggle Vincent fails, George and Olivier succeed with difficulty, and Caloub is an open question. Bernard succeeds best, possibly because his illegitimacy frees him of the need to emulate his false father, and enables him to penetrate the fictions of society.

Among many other matters, *The Counterfeiters* deals with homosexuality though somewhat differently from *The Immoralist*. There, sexual inversion was presented as a selfish and destructive passion; here it is shown sympathetically. The love of Edouard and Olivier is a love like any other, with its jealousies, estrangement and happy reconciliation. There are passages in it that are almost cloyingly sweet. On the other hand, Gide does not disparage heterosexual love, and is especially sympathetic of Bernard's feelings toward Laura. *The Counterfeiters* is not another *Corydon;* it is not an apology for homosexuality so much as a plea for integrity.

The Author

André Gide's honorary doctorate from Oxford in 1947, and his subsequent Nobel Prize for literature, the first honors he had ever received, came very belatedly. His distinguished literary career lasted for sixty years, beginning in the nineties, in the age of Wilde and Mallarmé, and continuing into the atomic era. He was born in Paris in 1869 of an upper-middle-class Protestant family. His father was a professor of law at the University of Paris. Puritan piety continued to influence Gide even after he had rejected it, providing the moral background for much of his writing. Because of illness, he was educated largely by tutors.

Gide fell in love with his future wife when he was only thirteen and she two years older. She was his cousin, Madeleine Rondeaux, an unhappy, troubled girl whom he married when he was twenty-six. The marriage was marked by serious friction, yet Madeleine never ceased to occupy the center of his affections. Their maladjustment was largely sexual: she was erotically inhibited, he was, by this time, an overt homosexual. He married her expecting to be cured of his perversion, but the hope was disappointed. Gide's homosexuality first manifested itself on a trip to North Africa where he was initiated by a young Arab boy; it was reinforced by the influence of his friend Oscar Wilde. This burden continued to torment him for years until he finally resigned himself to "allowing the contradictions to live in him." In 1924 he wrote *Corydon,* a reasoned defense of homosexuality which hurt his reputation and prevented his work from receiving the attention it deserved.

Apart from these private agonies, Gide's life is largely a record of his literary activity. As early as 1891, he began to frequent the famous Tuesday salons of Mallarmé and to enjoy the friendship of Paul Valéry. His own writing is strongly autobiographical. With searching psychological insight he treats sexuality and marriage, self-denial and self-realization, love and egotism, and the need for honesty in human relationships. He recorded his experiences and reflections also in his *Journals,* an interesting personal document which provides a useful commentary on the stories. Although he moved painfully away from the Protestant piety of his youth, Gide always remained a moralist, albeit a moralist of a lonely, nonconforming type. His style matured from a richly lyrical manner, derived from the symbolists, to an austere and unadorned prose in the French classical tradition.

Despite the urging of his friend, the poet Claudel, that he become a Catholic, Gide moved in the opposite direction. For a while in the mid-thirties, he believed himself to be a convert to Marxism, although characteristically it was not Marx that brought him to this position but the Bible. A tour of Russia as guest of the Soviet government cured him. He found there the same mindless conformity that had already appalled him in the Fascist countries. When the Second World War came, he was too old to be anything but an anguished spectator. In 1942, he went to North Africa, where he stayed till the fighting was over. In his last years, he achieved a philosophical serenity far different from his tormented youth. He died peacefully in 1951 after a short illness, and was buried next to his wife.

Jean-Christophe

by

ROMAIN ROLLAND (1866–1944)

The Characters

Ada—Christophe's first mistress, a rather vulgar and deceitful
  working girl.
Amélie—Manageress of a creamery, one of Olivier's circle of
  left-wing friends.
Arnaud—A schoolteacher living in Christophe's apartment
  house, intelligent, hardworking, honest.
Mme. Arnaud—His wife, a lonely, quiet woman who is one of
  Christophe's principal confidantes.
Aubert—A self-educated journeyman electrician.
Bäbi—The Brauns' meddlesome servant.
Count Berény—Grazia Buontempi's husband, a diplomat.
Aurora Berény—Grazia's daughter.
Lionello Berény—Grazia's son, a petulant invalid.
Berthe—Mistress of Joussier.
Dr. Erich Braun—A Swiss friend of Christophe who shelters
  him; a kindly mediocrity.
Anna Braun—His wife, a pious and repressed woman who
  falls in love with Christophe.
von Brombach—An official who marries Minna von Kerich.
Grazia Buontempi—Cousin of Colette Stevens and a student

of Christophe. She grows up to be a serene and gracious woman.

Pierre Canet—A middle-class revolutionary.

Commandant Chabran—A retired army officer, an ultraconservative and an anti-Semite.

Mlle. Chabran—His daughter. She marries André Elsberger.

Sylvain Cohn—A schoolmate of Jean-Christophe, now working for a Paris publisher. He has changed his name to Hamilton and is posing as a French sophisticate.

Sebastien Coquard—A revolutionary.

Corinne—A French actress, a gay but superficial girl.

Abbé Corneille—A modernist priest, under censure for his opinions.

Otto Diener—A boyhood friend of Christophe, the son of a prominent local citizen.

Lucien Ehrenfeld—One of the staff of the literary magazine, *Dionysus*.

Élie Elsberger—An engineer living in the same apartment with Christophe and Olivier, a passionate Dreyfusard.

Mme. Elsberger—His wife.

André Elsberger—Brother of Élie, and also an engineer. He marries Mlle. Chabran.

Emmanuel—Grandson of Feuillet, a hunchback. He is a talented and sensitive boy who becomes a writer.

Justus Euler—The Kraffts' landlord, an honest but narrow-minded bourgeois.

Euphrat—A conductor who deliberately mangles one of Christophe's compositions.

Feuillet (La Feuillette)—A cobbler, a veteran of the Commune, grandfather of Emmanuel.

Cécile Fleury—A musician and a friend of Christophe; healthy, practical, phlegmatic.

Sabine Froehlich—A tenant of Euler, an easygoing, lazy, sensual young widow.

Bertold Froehlich—Sabine's brother, a farmer.

Arsène Gamache—An editor.

Alcide Gautier—A revolutionary.

Mme. Germain—A widow, grieving in seclusion for her husband and daughter.

Raphael Goldenring—One of the group of Jewish intellectuals on the staff of *Dionysus*.

Uncle Gottfried—Brother of Louisa Krafft, a gentle, saintly peddler.

Théophile Goujart—A music critic.

Graillot—A revolutionary.

Grünebaum—A wealthy family which Antoinette serves as governess.

Guérin—An upholsterer.

François-Marie Hassler—A celebrated composer.

Daniel Hecht—A publisher of music. Though coarse and brutal in his manner, he appreciates Christophe's talents.

Manousse Heimann—A Russian refugee.

Hurteloup—A friend of Olivier, a postman of an old Burgundian family.

Antoine Jeannin—Olivier's father, a bankrupt.

Antoinette Jeannin—A French girl working as a governess to finance the education of her beloved brother Olivier.

Georges Jeannin—Olivier's son, a playboy.

Lucie Jeannin—Wife of Antoine.

Olivier Jeannin—Antoinette's brother, a gentle and affectionate boy who becomes a writer and Christophe's closest friend.

Casimir Joussier—A revolutionary leader.

Josepha von Kerich—A widow and a neighbor of the Kraffts; she befriends Christophe in a cool and faintly patronizing manner.

Minna von Kerich—Her daughter, a pupil of Christophe.

Ernest Krafft—Christophe's ne'er-do-well younger brother.

Jean-Christophe Krafft—The hero, a musician of genius, fiercely independent, honest, intensely emotional. He is Melchior's eldest son.

Louisa Krafft—Christophe's mother, a simple and long-suffering peasant woman.

Melchior Krafft—Christophe's drunkard father, a talented musician.

Jean Michel Krafft—Christophe's grandfather, a gruffly affectionate old man, a musician and minor composer.

Rodolphe Krafft—The second son of Melchior, who becomes a businessman, steady, quiet, slyly ambitious.

Jacqueline Langeais—A wealthy girl who becomes Olivier's wife, rather superficial and self-centered.

M. and Mme. Langeais—Her parents.

Marthe Langeais—Jacqueline's aunt, a sober spinster.

Grand Duke Leopold—Ruler of the Rhineland state where Christophe lives, an arrogant autocrat.

Lucien Lévy-Coeur—A minor writer and critic, witty and cynical.

Lorchen (Elenor)—A peasant girl on whose behalf Christophe gets into a brawl with some soldiers.

Adolph Mai—One of the staff of *Dionysus*.

Franz Mannheim—The son of a Jewish businessman, interested in literature and the editor of *Dionysus*.

Lothair Mannheim—Father of Franz, a banker.

Judith Mannheim—Sister of Franz, a subtle, intelligent woman.

Modesta—A blind girl befriended by Gottfried.

Taddée Mooch—A Jewish photographer, an original and independent thinker.

Myrrha—Friend of Ada, mistress of Ernest Krafft.

M. and Mme. Alfred Nathan—Friends and protectors of Antoinette Jeannin.

Siegmund Ochs—Second *Kapellmeister* of the grand-ducal orchestra.

Françoise Oudon—A famous actress who becomes Christophe's mistress. She is a self-made woman who has been badly hurt by life.

Philomela—Nickname of Cécile Fleury.

Poppetschmidt—A friend of Peter Schulz, a singer.

Poyet—Married name of Mme. Jeannin's sister.

Rainette—Grandniece of Trouillot, a crippled girl, friend of Emmanuel.

Herr and Frau Reinhart—Academic friends of Christophe. They are warmhearted, unconventional people.

Roussel—A workman living in Olivier's apartment house.

Achille Roussin—A socialist politician.

Mme. Roussin—His wife.

Peter Schulz—An elderly conductor and professor of music, an ardent admirer of Christophe's music.

Sidonie—A servant in Christophe's apartment house, a kind peasant girl.

Colette Stevens—A student of Christophe, a clever girl who flirts with him and confides in him.

Uncle Theodore—A stepson of Jean Michel Krafft, a vulgar, bullying, successful businessman.

Trouillot—An old revolutionist, a neighbor of Feuillet.

Vogel—Son-in-law of Justus Euler, a hardworking hypochondriac.

Amalia Vogel—His wife, a self-righteous, graceless, duty-
ridden housewife.

Leonard Vogel—Their son, destined for the priesthood, a
gentle, indolent, unintelligent, unquestioning youth.

Rosa Vogel—Their daughter, a plain-looking girl in love with
Christophe.

Adalbert von Waldhaus—A young nobleman who finances
Mannheim's review.

Watelet—An elderly radical, formerly a communard, now
living in retirement with his adopted daughter.

Felix Weil—A distinguished Assyriologist, an intelligent, distinguished, kindly man who has taken refuge behind a wall
of ironic and aristocratic reserve.

Mme. Weil—His wife.

The Story

1. DAWN

Jean-Christophe Krafft, the hero of this novel, is born some
time in the late nineteenth century in a provincial capital in
the German Rhineland. His father, Melchior Krafft, a talented
musician but a chronic drunkard, has a precarious tenure with
the local grand-ducal orchestra. His mother is a simple woman
who works about town as a cook. She gives him the love his
father cannot. Two younger brothers play a very minor part
in the story. The most formative influences in Christophe's
youth are his grandfather, Jean Michel Krafft, himself a
musician and minor composer, and his maternal uncle Gottfried, a simple peddler, but remarkable for his gentle, loving
and natural disposition.

The family love of music shows itself in Christophe while
he is only a child; he loves to play on an old piano, to listen to
chamber music, and to attend the theater with his grandfather.
His love of music is reinforced by a meeting with the most
distinguished living composer of the day, F. M. Hassler, who
kisses him and promises him a glorious future. When it dawns
on Melchior that his son has extraordinary, precocious talent,
he sets Christophe to practicing with the aim of turning him

into an infant prodigy, a second Mozart. Christophe's first composition, a collection of airs arranged and harmonized by his proud grandfather, is played before the grand duke and his court. It earns him the title of *Hof Musikus,* or Court Musician, and a small stipend, even though the boy is not yet in his teens.

2. Morning

Christophe finds his honors more tedious than gratifying; he is sturdily independent and unimpressed by conventional dignity. After Jean Michel dies, Melchior becomes too much of a drunkard to manage his own affairs, so that Christophe is forced to become the responsible head of the family, even though he is only fourteen. He has little time for normal boyish activities. But he strikes up a friendship with Otto Diener, a boy his own age, pouring into it all the intensity of his thwarted emotions. The boys maintain an ardently sentimental relationship and exchange letters couched in high-flown language. Then Christophe's brothers discover the correspondence and draw the obvious, if unjustified, conclusion from it. In shame and revulsion, Christophe and Otto break off their friendship.

A second and equally sentimental relationship springs up with Minna von Kerich, the teen-age daughter of a widow who lives next door. Christophe is her piano teacher. The mother displays a kindly interest in the talented boy and looks after him in a good-natured if slightly patronizing manner. Christophe senses only her kindness and responds by falling in love with the daughter. Frau von Kerich, considering her young friend a most unsuitable son-in-law, discourages Christophe. He writes her a passionately angry letter. She replies with contemptuous courtesy, and the love affair comes to an end.

3. Youth

Melchior Krafft dies, and Christophe moves with his mother to modest rooms near the center of town. Their landlord is Justus Euler. He and his children and grandchildren form a little circle of honest, industrious, narrow-minded, self-righteous, lower-middle-class personalities whom Christophe finds stifling. The granddaughter, Rosa, a kind, plain-featured girl, is slightly in love with him, but Christophe cannot return her love. He succumbs to Sabine, another tenant in the same building, an easygoing, indolent widow who keeps a linen-draper's shop. Christophe is infatuated with her, much to the irritation of the Eulers who have counted on his marrying Rosa. The affair has almost reached its natural consummation when Sabine contracts influenza on a country outing and unexpectedly dies.

Christophe's next romance is with a shopgirl named Adelheid, or Ada, whom he meets while walking in the fields on a holiday. The two are drawn to each other, spend the day in the open air until they miss their boat back to town, and are obliged to spend the night in a country inn. This is Christophe's sexual initiation. His attentions to his new mistress are soon common gossip and embroil him with his musical colleagues, his landlord, and even his mother. The romance is brought to an end by the meddling of his younger brother Ernest, the accepted lover of Myrrha, Ada's closest girl friend. One day, the two brothers go on a country outing with the two girls, in the course of which Ernest contrives to switch partners and go off with Ada, leaving Myrrha to make advances to the innocent Christophe. He is horrified by the casual insensitivity of the exchange and the semi-incestuous relationship into which the others have tricked him. In a shudder of revulsion, he falls out of love with Ada as quickly as he had fallen in.

4. REVOLT

Once free of sentimental entanglements, Christophe turns to the maturation of his art. His early compositions now strike him as false. In fact, most of the recognized giants of German music, especially Wagner and Brahms, seem to him pretentious and bombastic, sentimental and dishonest. Since he makes no attempt to hide his opinions, his own reputation suffers. A symphony of his is greeted with silent incomprehension, and he quarrels with a distinguished soprano who insists on bellowing his lieder. At this juncture, he is offered the post of music critic on a local magazine called *Dionysus*, edited for the most part by a group of young Jewish intellectuals. This review is devoted to deflating established reputations, but Christophe's criticism is so outrageous that even his colleagues try to make him more temperate. When he disregards their advice, they quietly rewrite his articles, knowing that he never reads them once they are published.

Still another imbroglio arises when a friend mischievously gives Christophe a ticket to a performance by a company of French actors. This ticket had actually been promised to a wealthy merchant named Grünebaum, who is indignant at missing the show. To make matters worse, Christophe meets a shy French girl in the lobby and offers to share his box with her. She proves to be the governess in the Grünebaum family, who assume that she is Christophe's mistress and dismiss her peremptorily. She returns to Paris before Christophe can even learn her name. Far from being interested in the governess, he is attracted to one of the actresses, a gay, flighty girl named Corinne who flirts with him and arouses his interest in things French.

Meanwhile, Christophe continues to write, but without winning recognition. An opera of his is a failure and involves him in a quarrel with his librettist. When he discovers that his magazine articles have been doctored, he quarrels with his friends and leaves the staff of the review. Other articles are printed unexpurgated in a Socialist paper and lose him his job as court musician. There follows an angry exchange of shouting with the grand duke which causes a scandal. Once he has lost his official position, everyone tries to drag him down. A symphony of his is performed and deliberately mangled. A published collection of his works remains unsold. When he strikes up a friendship with an amiable professor and his wife, the only people in town who are unconventional enough to befriend him, the three are made miserable by poison pen letters. The only ray of sympathy is an appreciative letter from an obscure conductor named Peter Schulz, which Christophe hardly bothers to acknowledge.

In desperation, Christophe seeks out Hassler, the composer who spoke kindly to him as a child. The great man lives in Berlin and is not easy to reach. When Christophe finally gets an interview, Hassler listens to his compositions with rude indifference at first, shows interest for a moment, but finally dismisses his guest irritably. He does not really mean to be unkind; it is simply one of his bad days. Christophe is thoroughly discouraged. On his way home, he decides on the spur of the moment to visit Schulz, the one man who has so far shown him any appreciation. He finds that his correspondent is an elderly widower, a retired professor of music, who lives alone except for a small circle of musical friends. They greet him with delight, and Christophe spends a happy two days in their company. Shortly afterward Schulz dies.

Christophe, now tired of Germany, is eager to try his fortune in France, but his mother is reluctant to let him go. Then fate forces his hand. He is spending an evening at a dance hall in a country village not far from town where he has become interested in a peasant girl named Lorchen. Nearby is stationed a detachment of soldiers who take pleasure in insulting and terrorizing the local country folk. On this particular evening, a brawl breaks out in which Christophe, who hates tyranny of any kind, joins. When the fight is over, three soldiers have been seriously wounded, one fatally. Christophe, identified as the ringleader, is obliged to make a break for the French border. He takes the next train west and barely reaches the frontier ahead of the police. A new chapter in his life now begins.

5. The Market Place

In Paris, Christophe is unknown. He looks up his old friend Otto Diener and receives a cold, embarrassed reception. Another old friend, Sylvain Cohn, is more obliging and introduces him to the musical and literary circles of Paris, particularly to a publisher named Hecht who grudgingly gives Christophe odd jobs arranging music. Christophe, with his honesty, passion and idealism, is out of place among the sophisticated, ironic, disillusioned French: he alienates them by his bluntness and bad manners, while they strike him as shallow and decadent. He does make some superficial acquaintances, all of whom disappoint him in one way or another: Colette Stevens, a wealthy, spoiled Franco-American girl to whom he gives lessons; Lévy-Coeur, a clever but superficial critic; Roussin, a socialist politician; and many others. The one who admires him most is Grazia Buontempi, a cousin of Colette who is, however, too young to make much of an impression on him. His attempts to secure a hearing for his music are as unsuccessful in France as they were in Germany.

Roussin arranges for one of his works to be performed, but only in order that his mistress may have the leading part. When Christophe takes a dislike to the lady's voice, Roussin withdraws his support. The work is publicly hissed, and Christophe exchanges insults with his audience across the footlights.

When his fortunes are at their lowest ebb, Christophe accidentally encounters Antoinette Jeannin, the little French governess whom her employers had dismissed on his account. He sees her for a moment in a street full of traffic, but, by the time he can fight his way across, she has been swept off in the crowd and he never meets her again. He does, however, meet her brother Olivier at the home of his pupil Colette, and with this young man he strikes up an immediate friendship.

6. ANTOINETTE

Through Olivier Jeannin, Christophe learns the full story of Antoinette and her family. She is the daughter of a prosperous provincial banker who was ruined by imprudent investments and who committed suicide, leaving his family penniless. Mme. Jeannin and her children find life intolerable in their native town and come to Paris where they are barely able to make ends meet. Soon after their move, the mother dies suddenly, leaving Antoinette and Olivier to face life alone. He is the younger and frailer of the two, so Antoinette must work to support them both and help him finish his education. Her self-sacrifice even obliges her to turn down a tempting offer of marriage that would take her out of France and away from her beloved brother. Finally she accepts a post in Germany as governess to the Grünebaum family in Christophe's hometown. Here the encounter with Christophe takes place and leads to her unjust dismissal. She returns to Paris and continues the struggle until Olivier finally passes his crucial examination for admission to the École Normale, an examination which will guarantee him a position for the rest of his life. For the first time in years, the brother and sister feel happy and secure. They celebrate by taking a vacation in Switzerland. Soon afterward, and soon after her chance meeting with Christophe, Antoinette contracts tuberculosis and dies, leaving Olivier in despair.

7. THE HOUSE

After meeting Olivier, Christophe seeks him out in his rooms
and strikes up a warm friendship. The two take an apartment
together and become inseparable. Olivier is the more passive
and more feminine of the two, shrinking from combat with
the world as much as Christophe invites it. But each is able
to offer something of spiritual and emotional value to the
other. Christophe now realizes that he has never known France
or the French. The chattering crowd of Parisian critics and
society women are not truly representative of the country;
there is also a strain of sober integrity and ardent idealism,
which has made the country great in the past and which can
still be found in people like Olivier and his sister.

In the same apartment house are a number of other tenants
who lead quiet lives and go their separate ways. Christophe
now sets out to meet them. A Jewish scholar and an anti-
Semitic army officer, a modernist priest and an old communard,
an engineer, a teacher, an electrician and a widow—all are
out of the swim of public or fashionable life, and each labors
in obscurity according to his ideals. They do not form a
community, however, and Christophe, once he has come to
know them individually, tries to persuade them to be friends
with each other. He is so successful that in time the revolutionary is hobnobbing with the priest and the army officer is
respectfully reading the books of his Jewish neighbor.

Christophe's friendship with Olivier is darkened only once.
Inevitably minor frictions arise between them, as always happens with roommates, and Olivier innocently mentions them
to Colette. She passes the story on to the critic Lévy-Coeur
who makes it public. Christophe is enraged, and thinks Olivier
has betrayed him. In a fury, he insults Lévy-Coeur publicly
and is challenged to a duel. The fight ends with neither party
hurt. Afterward Christophe and Olivier are closer than ever.
They collaborate in their work, and even the growing tension
between France and Germany does not separate them. When
Christophe's mother is on her deathbed, both young men hurry
to her side. After her death, because Christophe is still wanted
by the police, he leaves Olivier to arrange for the burial.
Christophe hurries back across the border, bearing in his heart

a grateful memory of his mother, along with Gottfried, Sabine, and Antoinette, as one of the beloved dead whose influence has become a permanent part of him.

8. LOVE AND FRIENDSHIP

At length Christophe becomes famous and much sought out for dinners, concerts, and the like. The bachelor quarters with Olivier have to be broken up when Olivier finally marries. His wife is Jacqueline Langeais, an heiress. At first, she is half in love with them both, but when Christophe discovers her interest in Olivier, he does all he can to further the romance. After his marriage, Olivier goes off to the obscurity of an academic post in the provinces. Meanwhile Christophe finds other friends to fill his life: his neighbor, Mme. Arnaud, who serves as a quiet, kindly confidante; a pianist named Cécile Fleury, who brings some stability into his life; and Françoise Oudon, a celebrated actress who for a time becomes his mistress.

About this time, Christophe is mystified at evidences that his career is being quietly helped by unknown benefactors, the Count and Countess Berény, whose kindness he cannot explain. Thanks to their influence, he is allowed to return briefly to Germany to visit his mother's grave and see some of his old friends. The mystery is solved when the countess proves to be Grazia Buontempi, the cousin of Colette Stevens, to whom he had given piano lessons when she was a child. Her husband is now a diplomat and a man of influence. The reunion is brief since Berény is about to be tranferred to a post in Washington, but it gladdens Christophe.

Meanwhile Olivier's marriage collapses. He and Jacqueline have returned to Paris where she turns into a jaded woman of society, tries to flirt with Christophe, falsely suspects Olivier of having an affair, and finally leaves him for another man. Olivier returns brokenhearted to Christophe with a baby boy named Georges whom Cécile Fleury undertakes to raise for him.

9. THE BURNING BUSH

The humanitarian concern of Christophe and Olivier now involves them in the social agitations of the time, bringing them in contact with socialists and revolutionaries of all kinds. One of these is a cobbler named Feuillet whose grandson, a hunchbacked boy named Emmanuel, displays an unexpected taste for books. Olivier takes the boy under his protection, teaches him and helps his imagination to expand so that he develops into a talented writer.

Soon their dabbling in revolutionary agitation takes a serious turn for both friends. A general strike is called by the trade unions, and Olivier and Christophe turn out to watch the demonstrations. Violence and street fighting break out. Olivier is fatally stabbed and Christophe kills a policeman with his own bayonet. Christophe's friends do not dare tell him what has happened to Olivier. They hustle him away from the fighting and put him on a train for Switzerland, telling him that Olivier will follow soon. He is safely across the border before he receives a warning, in the form of an apparition of his friend, that Olivier is dead. When a letter arrives confirming his fears, he almost goes insane with grief.

For the second time in his life, Christophe is a refugee from the police. Fortunately he has a friend in Switzerland, a Doctor Braun, who gives him shelter until he can recover his health and emotional stability. Braun is helpful and kind, but busy with his practice, so Christophe is left much of the time with Braun's wife Anna. Eventually a guilty liaison springs up. Anna is a pious woman, inhibited by a strict Calvinist upbringing, but she blossoms emotionally in the warm and unfamiliar climate of love. Christophe is overwhelmed with shame at betraying his benefactor, but is unable to leave Anna. They finally hit on suicide as the only way out of the impasse. Their pact never is consummated, however; twice the pistol misfires, and the psychological moment passes. Anna becomes mentally ill, and Christophe finds a plausible pretext to leave abruptly, without even saying good-bye to Anna or to the man he has wronged.

In a turmoil of despair, he buries himself in a remote corner of the Swiss Jura where he spends the winter physically and emotionally shut in upon himself. When spring comes, he gradually recovers his equanimity. Although he has long since rejected religious faith, he now discovers God as a voice within himself which speaks of life and resurrection. Out of despair and grief Christophe is born again.

10. THE NEW DAWN

Christophe is now old and his hair white. For many years he lives in Switzerland until he is so famous that he may travel where he wishes without being arrested. His music is bolder and more experimental than ever. In addition to the passionate delight in life which it has always expressed, it now voices a new faith and serenity. Once again he meets Grazia. She is a widow with two children, Aurora and Lionello. Time has not changed her. She is a lovely, gracious, serene woman who has only grown the wiser as she has grown older. For Christophe, she is the last and most perfect of the many women he has loved, and in their relationship he finds a ripe, autumnal peace. Christophe would like to marry her, but Grazia is tied to her invalid son, who jealously opposes the match. Christophe must be content with her friendship until she dies.

Christophe's last years are spent happily in the serene mastery of his art. He has the pleasure of watching the growing-up of Olivier's son Georges, and of Grazia's daughter Aurora. The hunchback Emmanuel becomes a good friend. Christophe is even reconciled with Lévy-Coeur, with whom he once fought a duel. He, who has been a rebel all his life, is now one of the older generation against whom the young crop of composers are rebelling. He, however, resists the temptation to defend his art against attack, knowing that his struggles have made possible the achievements of the younger men. At the wedding of Georges and Aurora, he contracts pneumonia, and he dies hearing within himself the sound of mighty music promising him a new birth.

Critical Opinion

Jean-Christophe is ten volumes and fifteen hundred pages long. Obviously it cannot be judged by conventional standards. It is first of all the life story of a musical genius. In this respect it superficially resembles Thomas Mann's great novel *Doctor Faustus*. Secondly, it is a social and intellectual picture of Europe during the years just preceding the First World War. Finally it is a testament of faith, an affirmation of the spiritual unity of Europe, and a hymn to the creative human spirit.

Although this is not, in any strict sense, a *roman à clef*, Rolland has drawn his material so freely from the great men of his times that we can identify familiar features in his cast of characters. Jean-Christophe is modeled largely on Beethoven, at least in his early life: both are of Flemish descent, living in the Rhineland, and both have as their parents a drunkard and a peasant girl. The letter which Christophe writes to the grand duke is modeled on a similar letter written by the young Beethoven to the elector of Bonn. Other aspects of his personality are drawn from other musicians. From the life of Hugo Wolf, Rolland took Christophe's dislike of Brahms, his career as a music critic, the fiasco of his first opera, and the visit to Hassler (originally Wagner). Rolland's biographer, Stefan Zweig, also professes to find traces of Mozart, Gluck, Handel, Schumann and Wagner. Olivier may be Rolland himself. We note in particular his provincial middle-class origins, his studies at the École Normale, his gentleness, idealism, and pacifism. Lesser characters have also been tentatively identified, like Françoise Oudon, for whom Eleonora Duse has been suggested as the possible model. Finally, a number of actual figures hover in the background: Maeterlinck, Debussy, Charpentier, and Bernhardt among others.

The reader should not overlook the symbolism of the names of the principal characters. The hero bears the name of Saint Christopher, the giant who offers to carry the Christ child, and who discovers that he is bearing the weight of the whole world. In Rolland's symbolism, the holy child is the day that is about to be born, the new generation that will arise on the shoulders of the old. Christophe's surname Krafft is also significant; it means "strength" in German. Grazia's name, of course, means "grace," a meaning which Christophe underscores when he addresses her as "tranquil Grace." As for Olivier's name, its meaning is clear if we remember that he is a self-portrait of the author, for who was the best friend and alter ego of Rolland if not Olivier? These three are representative national types as well, Christophe embodying the strength and courage of Germany, Olivier the intellectual clarity of France, Grazia the graciousness of Italy. These were the three peoples Rolland knew and loved best. To these we should add a fourth, the Jews, an international people who play a very large role in the novel and who contribute their vigorous, critical intelligence as a leaven to the culture of Europe. Out of these four strains, Christophe forms his art which rises above all parochial differences of nation or group.

Rolland is well aware of the vices of these countries as well: the stodginess of middle-class Germany and the arrogance of her military men, the compulsive morality of the Swiss, the ugly anti-Semitism of the Dreyfus era in France. He is opposed to whatever in each national culture stands in the way of international understanding, and this novel is written to demonstrate the possibility of a truly international European culture. The principal spokesman for internationalism in the story is Olivier, himself a thoroughgoing Frenchman. During a period of diplomatic tension, when it appears that war may break out between France and Germany, Olivier realizes sadly that his friend would, if necessary, fight on his own country's side, even against his adopted country, France. Olivier's convictions are different:

> It is a terrible thing. . . . I love my country as you do. I love France; but could I slay my soul for her? Could I betray my conscience for her? That would be to betray her. How could I hate, having no hatred, or, without being guilty of a lie, assume a hatred I did not feel?

In these lines, we clearly hear the voice of Rolland, foreshadowing the position he would take in 1914.

Jean-Christophe could only have been written by someone who was himself musical. Rolland, as a professional musicologist, is able to give us a convincing picture of musical Europe in the generation of Debussy and Richard Strauss, its singers, conductors, professors, critics, and performers. Christophe's own music, at least in its later phases, clearly anticipates the experiments of our own age. An unfriendly critic complains that it has "no melody, no meter, no thematic workmanship: a sort of liquid core, molten matter which has not hardened, . . . a glimmering of light in chaos." Music exerts its influence on Rolland's writing itself. The novel may be compared to a vast symphony, in which Christophe, Olivier, and Grazia are the three principal themes, carried with many variations through a succession of movements. At certain points, the novel actually breaks out into real music; for instance, during the courtship of Olivier and Jacqueline, Rolland, apparently unable to suggest in words the sweetness of their first kiss, sets down instead a liquid, swooning melody in six flats. There are at least four such passages. This is perhaps the only novel ever written in the G clef.

Religion also plays an important role in *Jean-Christophe*. Both Christophe and Olivier are lapsed Catholics who, despite their loss of formal belief, remain fervent idealists. Christophe is sustained through his troubles by many things: his creative urge, his love of life, his love of humanity. Eventually he recovers religious belief in the period of dumb agony after his separation from Anna. The God who then speaks to him is not the transcendent, omnipotent deity of Christianity, but the inner life and creative urge within man, constantly at war with the forces of nothingness and death.

There are several unresolved problems in the novel. One is the time scheme, which seems unduly compressed. There are almost no dates anywhere. The year 1909 is mentioned once, but otherwise we must guess at the chronology indirectly. The *terminus a quo* is the Franco-Prussian War, which is always alluded to in the past tense. The *terminus ad quem* is 1913, when the novel was finished. Between these lie only forty-two years, and yet at the close, Christophe is spoken of as a white-haired old man. One wonders if Rolland, who did not anticipate the war, projected his hero's life into the 1920's, not realizing how soon the European scene was to be transformed.

Had Rolland been twenty years younger, his treatment of sex would probably have been different. As it is, there is a certain pre-Freudian innocence about the story which distinguishes it from the work of Rolland's contemporary, André Gide, for instance. The modern reader has no trouble seeing incestuous feelings in the affection of Olivier and Antoinette, and homosexuality in the friendship of Olivier and Christophe, yet Rolland presents both these relationships as sympathetically as a nineteenth-century author would. He is almost the last major writer to treat such subjects without at least a knowing wink to the reader.

The chief critical problem in *Jean-Christophe*, however, is to appraise the long sections in which Rolland practically lays aside his story to discourse on the cultural state of France, on German music, on socialism, on the role of the Jews, in short, on virtually every topic that interests him. Much of the story is undramatic, as if Rolland had found it easier to talk about things than to present them. The novel constantly threatens to turn into an essay. It is rich in ideas and—as befits the subject—rich in sounds, but it is starved for visual images. We read for pages without ever being made to see anything. Furthermore, the cultural debate belongs so obviously to the age that is past, even though recently past, that we do not yet know how much there remains in all these pages that will prove of permanent and universal value. For instance, Brahms no longer dominates German music, so that Christophe's detestation of that composer seems cranky and unnecessary. The whole problem of anti-Semitism has taken on a new dimension since Hitler, and so on. Perhaps the permanent merit of the novel will prove to be its lively portrayal of character, and here Rolland's achievement is impressive. Certainly Jean-Christophe Krafft is one of the most vigorously alive characters in twentieth-century fiction.

The Author

Rolland was born in 1866 at Clamécy, a small village in Nivernais, of a respectable provincial family of lawyers and magistrates. His father was a notary. From his mother he inherited a love of music, a subject which interested him as much as literature. The family decided to move to Paris in order that their son could profit by better education, and after studying at the Lycée Louis le Grand, he went on to the École Normale Supérieure for advanced training. Among his teachers were the historians Lavisse, Monod, and Brunetière. The poets Claudel and Peguy were good friends, and Tolstoi honored him with his correspondence and influenced his thought.

In 1889, Rolland won a scholarship to study in Rome for two years. Here he met and was befriended by Malwida von Meysenburg, a social liberal of the preceding generation who had known Wagner, Nietzsche, Mazzini, and Herzen. She remained his close friend and correspondent for the rest of her life. In 1895, he returned to the École Normale to teach the history of fine arts, and in 1897 he went on to the Sorbonne where he taught the history of music. A history of the opera appeared in 1895, followed by a series of plays inspired by the

French Revolution. *Jean-Christophe* was conceived in Rome, but the first volume did not appear until 1904. The last was published in 1913. With it Rolland's reputation as a major author was firmly established. During these same years, he also produced a series of heroic biographies of great men: *Millet* (1902), *Beethoven* (1903), and *Michelangelo* (1906).

The outbreak of the First World War found Rolland in Switzerland. He was by now forty-eight and too old for military service, and so remained in Geneva to work for the Red Cross, helping to trace invalids, prisoners, and refugees. As a liberal and a man who considered himself the product of a pan-European culture rather than of one country, he was revolted by the war and unmoved by the tide of patriotic feeling which swept over France. In the fall of 1914, he published a series of antiwar articles which were later collected under the title *Above the Battle* (*Au dessus de la Mêlée*). He also did his best to rally intellectuals from America to Russia to the cause of peace, but succeeded only in making his name hated in his own country.

After the war, Rolland remained in Switzerland until 1938. During these years, he continued his peace activities and strenuously opposed the rise of Fascism. He also became interested in the Orient, numbered Gandhi and Tagore among his friends, and produced biographies of Gandhi, Ramakrishna, and Vivekananda. When the second great war broke out, he was living at Vézelay in his native province. Because of his opinions the Vichy government placed him under house arrest, but his work was not interrupted. He died on December 30, 1944.

Pelle the Conqueror

by

MARTIN ANDERSEN NEXÖ (1869–1954)

The Characters

NOTE: *The standard English translation of* Pelle *is inconsistent in the treatment of names; thus* Per *is sometimes Anglicized to* Peter, *and married women are variously referred to as* Fru *(Danish),* Frau *(German) or* Madame *(French), while* Kapelvej *must be understood to be the same as* Chapel Street.

THE KARLSSONS

Pelle—The hero, a sturdy, healthy, self-reliant peasant boy.

Lasse Karlsson—Pelle's father, a Swedish immigrant, hard-working, slow-thinking, and devoted to his son.

Mother Bengta—Pelle's mother, now dead. In life she was rather sharp-tempered.

Kalle Karlsson—Lasse's brother, a peaceable and good-natured man.

Maria Karlsson—Wife of Kalle, in her youth one of Kongstrup's conquests.

Grandmother—Maria's mother, about eighty and blind.

Maria's children, cousins to Pelle—Albert, Alfred, Albinus, Anton, Anna, and eight others.
Due—A carter married to Anna Karlsson.

THE KONGSTRUPS

Kongstrup—Master of Stone Farm, notorious for his promiscuity.
Kongstrup's Wife—At first a melancholy, complaining woman, she later becomes hard and possessive.
Jomfru (Miss) Koller—A young relative of Fru Kongstrup.

FARM WORKERS IN VOL. I

The Bailiff—The hard-fisted manager of Stone Farm.
Hans Peter—An agricultural student and a petty bully.
Erik—A burly farm hand, later a half-wit.
Karna—A dairymaid, about forty, kind to Pelle.
Johanna Pihl ("The Sow")—A prostitute.
Rud—Johanna's son by Kongstrup.
Others—Bodil, Per Olsen, Long Ole, Anders, Karl Johan, Mons, Bengta, Sara, Maria, etc.

VILLAGERS IN VOL. I

Fris—The schoolmaster, an ignorant and pathetically ineffectual man.
Fru Olsen—A sailor's wife, believed to be a widow.
Niles Köller—A fisherman, haunted by guilt for the death of his illegitimate child.

THE KOFODS

Master Jeppe Kofod—An old-fashioned cobbler, proud of the traditions of his craft.
Master Andres Kofod—His son, fatally ill with consumption.
Master Jörgen Kofod—Jeppe's brother, a baker.
Sören Kofod—Jörgen's weakling son, pious and sexually timid.
Marie—Sören's wife.

OTHER TOWNSFOLK IN VOL. II

Anker—A mad watchmaker, obsessed with millennial expectations.

Bjerregrav—An old tailor whose hobby is attending funerals.

Peter Jörgensen ("The Great Power")—A powerful stonecutter, bitter against the economic system that has ruined him.

Fru Jörgensen—His meek, intimidated wife.

Grandmother Jörgensen—Peter's mother, the only person who can control him.

Morten Jörgensen—Peter's son, Pelle's closest friend.

Karen Jörgensen—Peter's daughter, worn out by hard work and abuse.

Monsen—A wealthy shipowner, stingy and dishonest.

Sjermanna (Manna)—A teen-age girl who flirts with Pelle.

Garibaldi—A traveling cobbler.

Sort—A traveling cobbler.

Marie Nielsen—A pretty young widow who feeds and cares for Pelle.

PELLE'S RELATIVES IN VOLS. III AND IV

Stolpe—A mason, an old unionist grown prosperous.

Otto and Frederick—His sons.

Ellen—His daughter, a quiet, aloof girl with middle-class ambitions, who marries Pelle.

Lasse Frederick—Pelle's eldest son.

Anna—Pelle's daughter.

"Boy Comfort"—Son of Pelle by Marie.

THE RESIDENTS OF THE ARK

"The Family"—Marie, a girl of thirteen who acts as substitute mother to her brothers and to Pelle; Peter, a worker in a tinplate factory; Karl, who peddles papers.

Vinslev—A mad dwarf.

Pipman—A drunken cobbler.

Mme. Johnsen—A widow.

Hanne—Her daughter, a high-spirited girl who dreams of being a princess.

Johanna—Hanne's illegitimate daughter.

Ferdinand Frandsen—A street boy of about eighteen, later a criminal.
Widow Frandsen—His devoted mother.

OTHERS IN COPENHAGEN, VOLS. III AND IV

Meyer—The court shoemaker, a sweatshop operator.
Petersen—Head of the shoemakers' union.
Hansen—A unionist turned strikebreaker.
Queen Theresa—A streetwalker.
Brun—An elderly librarian, a rich man turned socialist.
Peter Dreyer—An anarchist.

The Story

I. BOYHOOD

Bornholm, an island belonging to Denmark, is in the Baltic Sea off the southern tip of Sweden. Its sailors, fishermen, and farmers are Danes, but Swedes were formerly imported as laborers on the larger farms. Pelle is the son of one such laborer, Lasse Karlsson, who comes to Bornholm in 1877. Lasse is a widower, and the eight-year-old Pelle is his sole love and care.

Stone Farm, where Lasse and Pelle work, is a gloomy place ruled by a stern bailiff, a philandering master, and an alcoholic mistress. The work is hard, and the men have few diversions except fighting, hard drinking, and occasional joyless lovemaking. Lasse is put in charge of the cattle, and Pelle becomes his helper. Life is bewildering, and Pelle is made the butt of all sorts of heartless practical jokes. Fortunately, his youthful spirits and good health keep him uncorrupted by the sullen mood of the farm. He enjoys long hours by himself tending the cows, and finds a playmate in Rud, the illegitimate son of the farmer.

As Pelle grows older, he attends school where he learns to read and write and sing hymns. There the children lead a robust, confident life which Pelle tries with partial success to enter into. His relation to his father changes as Lasse grows older and Pelle more self-reliant. On one occasion he is able to save Lasse from an angry bull.

The farm owners and farmhands, whom Pelle observes half-comprehendingly, provide most of the excitement. Nearly all have love affairs, with incidental rivalries or pregnancies. Even Father Lasse tries to court a certain Fru Olsen, a plump and cozy woman whose husband has disappeared at sea. The romance is blighted when Olsen returns unexpectedly after many years' absence. The most dramatic episode, however, involves the farmer, Kongstrup, who is notoriously unfaithful to his wife and has sired bastards all over the island. She, in turn, wearies him with reproaches, drinks herself sodden, and fills the farm with her weeping. At length, after a particularly outrageous affair in which Kongstrup seduces a young relative of hers, she avenges herself fearfully by castrating him. Thereafter she takes firm possession of her farm and her husband, who sinks into broken, driveling helplessness.

As Pelle enters early adolescence, he faces a choice: shall he take service on the farm like his father, or try to leave and better himself? He decides to try his luck in the world. His education, such as it is, is finished, and he has proved his mettle by whipping most of the boys in the school. Saying good-bye to Lasse, he leaves to seek his fortune in the town.

II. Apprenticeship

In the town (presumably Rönne, on Bornholm), life is busier and more sophisticated than on the farm, and Pelle learns to shed his country ways. He finds work as a cobbler's apprentice. The other apprentices haze him at first, but finally accept him as one of them. Pelle learns the trade, and acquires a knowledge of its traditions and a pride in his craft. He is now on his own, growing rapidly in self-reliance and experience. The town is full of interesting and eccentric people: Master Andres, a gentle young man dying of tuberculosis; old Anker, a crazy watchmaker who dreams of building a clock that will not tell time but *be* time; Bjerregrav, an old tailor who enjoys funerals; Sören, a youth too timid to have a child by his own wife; and Jörgensen, a stonecutter, half-crazed by his failure to establish himself as an independent contractor. Pelle listens and begins to form ideas about the world. In his spare time he has some experiences with girls.

In particular, Pelle comes to a fuller awareness of social and economic injustice. On Stone Farm, poverty was part of the

established order of things, and injustice was no more to be
questioned than rain. In the town, on the other hand, hardworking and ambitious people are ground into poverty for
reasons beyond their control. The cobblers are being put out
of business by the factories. Jörgensen is defeated by a combination of business competitors and bankers. Even Pelle has a
taste of class privilege when he thrashes a rich man's son and
is publicly whipped at the town hall. Some manage to rise on
the backs of others. Pelle's cousin Alfred, for instance, marries
a rich merchant's daughter, and Pelle, at the wedding, sees his
uncle Kalle snubbed by the bride's family and ignored by his
own son as being too rustic and unfashionable.

Lasse, meanwhile, is having his own struggles. He has
rented some rocky, inaccessible land to clear for a farm. The
work proves too much for him. He defaults on his payments, is
dispossessed, and has the bitterness of seeing another tenant
take over.

For the first time, Pelle understands that these injustices are
curable; everywhere he finds eager hopes of a better world
for the poor and oppressed. Some men remember the constitutional reforms and revolutionary agitation of 1848. The
shoemaker Garibaldi, who has wandered through Europe, tells
the men they should strike for shorter hours. Pelle is interested,
but has no idea what a strike is. Finally, there is confused talk
of political agitation in Copenhagen by the Social Democrats,
though no one knows what they stand for.

At length, Pelle loses his place when his employer has to
sell his business. Bornholm holds no prospects for him. Again
he says farewell to Lasse and sails for the capital.

III. The Great Struggle

In Copenhagen, Pelle meets, for the first time, capitalism
in its classic form. The shoe industry is dominated by a few
large manufacturers who have pushed their competitors to the
wall as ruthlessly as they have exploited their workers. He also
encounters urban poverty. Back on the farm, no one had
money, but at least no one starved. Here, he finds people
living from one meal to the next. Pelle finds lodgings with a
family of three orphan children; the eldest, Marie, is a girl of
thirteen who mothers the rest. Their quarters are a ramshackle
tenement called the Ark, where the walls are green with

mold and the stair rails have been pillaged for firewood. The inmates, more pathetic than the people of Rönne, are rag-pickers and scavengers, drunkards and hardworking widows, and a delicate child named Hanne Johnsen who dreams of being a princess but ends up by bearing an illegitimate child to a sailor.

Pelle, who has never even heard of a trade union, now joins the Shoemakers' Union, and finds an outlet for his talents for organization and public speaking. Rising rapidly to leadership in the movement, he meets an old veteran unionist, the mason Stolpe, who has achieved something like middle-class comfort and respectability. His daughter Ellen is a quiet and rather distant girl. Pelle woos and marries her. They set up housekeeping and have two children; at the same time, Father Lasse comes to the capital to join them.

At first the happiness of his marriage keeps Pelle from his union work, but as the children increasingly fill Ellen's life, he returns to the movement and becomes president of his union. He leads a strike which drives one of the more unscrupulous manufacturers out of business. Next, he organizes a National Federation of trade unions and establishes contacts with leaders in other countries. He is temporarily deflected from this career when the management of his shop offers him a post as a draftsman. This advance is a great satisfaction to Ellen, for Pelle is now a white-collar worker and may rise into management. She dreams of buying new dresses and sending the children to a middle-class school. These hopes are shattered when a strike breaks out in the shop, and the office staff are ordered to act as strikebreakers. Rather than break faith with his old friends, Pelle resigns and aids the strike.

The workers are at a disadvantage, for their resources have been depleted by a bitter winter, and the employers take the opportunity to crush the whole movement with one blow by declaring a general lockout covering all factories in the city. Pelle holds his forces together at great cost. Lasse is reduced to scavenging and even Ellen, her hope and patience at an end, prostitutes herself to buy food for the children. Pelle sees her act not as a sacrifice but as a betrayal. He leaves her bitterly and throws himself entirely into the struggle. The unions finally win when the municipal garbage collectors join the strike and public opinion forces the manufacturers to capitulate.

The story comes to an end in a crowded climax. Lasse dies on the eve of the great victory. The Ark, a symbol of the exploitation of the masses, burns down. The unions stage a great victory parade and lead their forces to the very gates of the royal palace. Pelle, now without a home, seeks out his old friend from the Ark, Marie, and spends one night with her. He is in deep trouble, however, for on the day after the victory celebration he is arrested on a false charge of counterfeiting. The unions have emerged into the full stream of the national life, but the prison doors shut on their leader.

IV. Daybreak

Several years later, Pelle is released, paler and grayer, but unbroken in spirit. His first step is to seek out Ellen, who loyally welcomes him home. There are three children now: Lasse Frederick, who works on a milk truck; the girl Anna; and a baby called "Boy Comfort," who is Pelle's child by Marie. The mother died in childbirth and Ellen has taken him in. Pelle now looks up his old friends, especially an old companion from Bornholm named Morten. Now a free-lance writer and an intellectual with revolutionary convictions, Morten has adopted the daughter of Pelle's old friend Hanne Johnsen. Pelle's old associates in the unions have largely forgotten him, however, and the movement itself has changed. The workers are a political power and the better-paid craftsmen are on the way to bourgeois security and comfort, but capitalism is as well entrenched as ever. There still remains a group of outcasts and unemployed whom the unions do not help, and whom the state keeps alive without giving them self-respect. Some of the more articulate of these have lost patience with unionism and become anarchists.

Meanwhile, Pelle tries to reestablish himself. He and Ellen try unsuccessfully to run a boardinghouse. He is offered another job in management, but turns it down out of conscientious scruples. He moves his family to the outskirts of the city, hoping to try his hand at gardening, but Ellen shows no great talent for the life. Finally, opportunity comes in the form of Herr Brun, an elderly librarian with a capitalist's income and a socialist's convictions. To Brun, Pelle unfolds his dream: a cooperative workshop, owned by the workers, in which each man will enjoy the same share of the profits, regardless of his skill or responsibility. With Brun's capital, Pelle buys a small factory, staffs it with like-minded workers, and builds up a flourishing shoe business. When competitors combine to deny him access to leather, he branches out into tanning and cattle-raising, until the enterprise is self-contained and impregnable. The cooperative even buys land and builds model homes for the workers.

Pelle is now convinced that workers' cooperatives offer the best hope for a reconstructed society. His ideas are opposed by one of his foremen, an anarchist named Dreyer, who proposes more revolutionary programs. Pelle respects Dreyer as a man, but argues that his plans are shortsighted and doomed to fail. Dreyer has planned a demonstration in front of the royal palace at which he hopes, by a show of mob strength, to precipitate some kind of crisis. At the last moment, the police come to arrest him; he shoots it out with them and is killed. Pelle takes Dreyer's place at the rally, addresses the mob, preaches the gospel of workers' cooperation and persuades them to disperse. Now he is truly a conqueror. He has found peace and fulfillment with his family and he is working creatively at the task of social reconstruction. This is only the dawn of a new day, but Pelle is confident that he is building for the future.

Critical Opinion

Pelle the Conqueror can be read both as a proletarian novel, analyzing the evils of society and prescribing a cure for them, and as a *Bildungsroman*, that is, a story which traces the development of the character of a young man. For many of the details, Nexö drew on his own memories of his childhood as a herdboy, cobbler's apprentice, and slum dweller. The story, however, is not closely autobiographical, since the author's experiences have been distributed between two characters, Pelle and Pelle's alter ego, Morten. For the nonpolitical reader, the personal side of the novel is perhaps the more interesting, but Nexö himself would have wished it to be judged principally as a social document, a book with a message.

The novel's historical background is the trade union movement which, in Europe, first achieved effective strength and legal recognition after 1870. A second element, more distinctively Scandinavian, is the cooperative movement which began in the early eighties. A third element is the rise of left-wing parliamentary parties such as the Social Democrats, who won their first seats in the Danish legislature in 1882. All these developments are chronicled in this novel. The temper of the movements was liberal and moderate in that they stressed progressive reforms within the framework of the existing political structure. The rise of the Third International, or Comintern, was still a decade away when Nexö began writing. Consequently the extreme revolutionary sentiment in the story is voiced, not by Communists, as one might expect, but by anarchists like Peter Dreyer.

The events of the story take place in a country where some traces of the medieval order still linger on. At Stone Farm, the workers, though nominally free agents, are little better than serfs, and nobody dreams of questioning the existing order. The farmer even enjoys a kind of feudal *droit de seigneur* with the farm girls. In the town, a guild economy prevails, in which small employers live and work at home with their apprentices and journeymen. Here, however, the old order is being weakened by technological change. In the city, the development of capitalism has progressed furthest: handcraftmanship is an anachronism and profits are possible only for owners of large shops with expensive machinery. The workers compete for a dwindling number of jobs, and wages are forced down as sturdy peasants and once-independent craftsmen are degraded into an urban proletariat. The classic symptoms of labor unrest appear: strikes and boycotts by the workers, countered by lockouts and blacklists by the employers.

Volume III, "The Great Struggle," admirably catches the spirit and mystique of the labor movement in its early phase. Nexö presents it as almost a secular religion, the members of which are united in bonds of mutual charity and sustained by the hope of the imminent social millennium. Biblical symbolism is freely used. The tenement which shelters Pelle while he is trying to establish himself is appropriately called the Ark, and the great strike in Volume III brings on a long period of Lenten hardship followed by a glorious victory at Easter time.

Artistically, the book's chief flaws appear at the end of Volume III and throughout Volume IV. The story grows melodramatic and relies too heavily on coincidence. For instance, the charge that leads to Pelle's arrest depends on a casual accident, something that could just as well not have happened. Again, the story of Hanne's illegitimate daughter, her discovery, adoption and eventual death, reveals a shameless manipulation of coincidences more appropriate to Dumas than to a naturalistic novelist. Brun is a blatant *deus ex machina*.

Brun's role presents ideological problems as well. Pelle can lay the foundations of his ideal society for two reasons: he is able to find a rich man who will give him capital, and he is ready to dismiss from his cooperative every worker who disagrees with him. A workers' cooperative existing only on these conditions contains a built-in contradiction. Nexö was not wholly sure of his ground at this point, and the prominence in the last volume of the two revolutionaries, Dreyer and Morten, suggests the direction in which the author himself was moving. In fact, the whole of "Daybreak" voices dissatisfaction with the achievements of the Danish Social Democrats, who had managed to raise large numbers of workers to the level of the petty bourgeoisie without radically transforming the structure of society or improving the lot of those at the bottom.

In America and western Europe, the proletarian novel is now outdated, along with the intellectual and political milieu that nurtured it. Thus it is now irrelevant to criticize *Pelle the Conqueror* (as was done thirty years ago by Harry Slochower and even by Nexö himself) on the grounds that it is imperfectly revolutionary. Its survival as anything more than a period piece must be on artistic rather than ideological grounds. Certainly its breadth, its truthfulness, and its deep humanity transcend political issues. Yet even here we must discriminate, for the four component volumes are of unequal value and appeal to us on different grounds:

"Boyhood" has a charm that derives from elemental things: the soil, the sea, and the unfolding of a child's awareness of the world. Father Lasse is drawn with loving sympathy, and the sturdy little Pelle wins our affection quite legitimately, without melodrama or sentimentality. A counterpoint to Pelle's innocence is the somber tragedy of the Kongstrups, which might have come out of a Bergman movie.

"Apprenticeship" effectively captures the turbulence and

aimlessness of an adolescent trying to find his way. The subordinate characters include a whole portrait gallery of well-drawn personalities, some of whom, like Anker and Bjerregrav, suggest eccentrics out of Dickens.

In "The Great Struggle," ideology takes over. A social novel in the full sense of the word, at times it waxes too explicitly didactic. Nexö's human sympathies, however, rise above the claims of ideology, as when, for instance, he presents with compassion the plight of Hansen, the strikebreaker, who puts the welfare of his family above that of the union, and when he makes it clear that Ellen, though she would much rather see her husband a manufacturer than a labor leader, is still the source of the love and strength that make possible Pelle's achievements. This volume is clearly derived from Zola's *Germinal,* and at times invites explicit comparison with it. The fiery destruction of the Ark, a symbol of the old social order, is formally analogous to the violent destruction in the older novel of Le Voreux, the coal mine. In spite of the awkward coincidences with which it closes, "The Great Struggle" is still moving and usually convincing. The reader who has gotten so far will wish to continue to the end for completeness' sake, but the last volume is an embarrassment.

The Author

Martin Andersen Nexö was born of peasant stock in Copenhagen in 1869, his father being a former quarry worker from the island of Bornholm. The name is from the village of Nexö (or Neksø) on that island. His mother, the daughter of a blacksmith, worked as a charwoman. The fourth of eleven children, Martin was a delicate child, terrorized by his father whose drunken rages suggest those of Jörgensen, the "Great Power" of the novel. Nexö attended school but disliked it. He taught himself to read from street signs. While he was still a young child, his family returned to Bornholm, where he worked for a time as a herdboy, like Pelle. In his teens, he was apprenticed to a shoemaker in Rönne (the principal town of the island), read books at night, and began to become interested in social problems. These years are recorded in Volume II of *Pelle the Conqueror.*

In 1892, Nexö became the protégé of the widow of a Danish poet, Molbach, who took an interest in his career, lodged him, and saw to his education. When he was ill, she sent him to Spain and Italy to recuperate, like Pelle's friend Morten. In 1898, he became a schoolteacher and began to write seriously. After 1901, he devoted himself wholly to literature. *Pelle the Conqueror* appeared in four volumes from 1906 to 1910 and attracted wide attention. His second proletarian novel, *Ditte,* tells the story of a child of even humbler origins than Pelle who is crushed by her life and dies in her twenties without ever having known happiness.

When Nexö wrote *Pelle,* his political position was still reformist and evolutionary, rather than revolutionary. After the Russian Revolution and the establishment of the Third International, he became a committed Communist, traveled much in Russia, and enjoyed the friendship of Lenin. Unlike Silone and others, he never recanted. In 1940, when the Germans occupied Denmark, he was placed in a concentration camp. In 1949 his eightieth birthday was celebrated as a national holiday. In 1951 he left Denmark to live in East Germany. He died in Dresden in 1954.

Swann's Way

by

MARCEL PROUST (1871-1922)

The Characters

NOTE: *The following list includes only those characters who figure prominently in* Swann's Way; *it omits characters, like Bloch and Charlus, who first appear there but do not become important until later, and it gives only a minimum of information about the later adventures of the characters who are listed. For a full index, with complete references, see P. A. Spalding,* A Reader's Handbook to Proust (*London: Chatto and Windus, 1952*).

1. THE COMBRAY CIRCLE

Marcel—The narrator. During *Swann's Way* he is a small boy, emotional and hypersensitive, deeply attached to his mother, interested in books and the theater.

Marcel's Father—A government official, rather stern toward his son, though occasionally and unpredictably indulgent.

Marcel's Mother—Tender and affectionate toward her son, submissive and admiring toward her husband.

Uncle Adolphe—Marcel's great-uncle, one of Odette's lovers.

Curé of Combray—A worthy if unimaginative parish priest, interested chiefly in the history of place-names.

Eulalie—A retired servant of the Combray household and a regular visitor of Aunt Leonie's.

Françoise—The cook at Combray, a devoted and privileged family retainer.

Grandfather—An old friend of Swann's father.

Grandmother—A sweet, modest old woman, fond of good literature.

Legrandin—A friend of Marcel's father, by profession an engineer and by avocation a man of letters; a clever if somewhat affected talker, and a snob.

Aunt Léonie—Owner of the house at Combray, a chronic invalid who stays in her room receiving a few friends and gossiping about the neighbors.

Vinteuil—An old music teacher living near Combray, so modest and old-fashioned in his ways that his associates do not realize he is a genius. He is the author of a sonata which deeply moves Swann.

Mlle. Vinteuil—His daughter, a lesbian.

2. The Verdurin Circle

Mme. Verdurin—The leader of a salon at which Swann meets Odette. She is jealous for her hegemony over her "little group," and she affects artistic and musical tastes which she does not actually possess. (After her husband's death she becomes Princess de Guermantes.)

M. Verdurin—Her husband.

Master Biche—Nickname of the impressionist artist, Elstir; a member of the Verdurin circle where he is conspicuous for loud talk and coarse joking. (Later he becomes a very distinguished painter.)

Dr. Cottard—A friend of the Verdurins, stupid, ill-bred, socially inept, and fond of bad puns.

Dechambre—Pianist at the Verdurins' salons.

Comte de Forcheville—A member of the Verdurin circle, a vulgar and aggressive man. (After Swann's death, he marries Odette.)

Odette de Crécy (also appears as the Lady in Pink, Miss Sacripant, Mme. Charles Swann, and the Comtesse de Forcheville)—A prostitute and occasional lesbian, mistress and later the wife of Swann. She is vulgar in her tastes and feelings, and an incurable liar.

Saniette—A distinguished paleographer, a friend of the Verdurins, a modest, timid man.

Brichot—Professor at the Sorbonne, a rather vulgar pedant.

3. The Swann Circle

Charles Swann—The son of a wealthy stockbroker of Jewish
ancestry, a man of great charm and taste, who, despite his
middle-class origins, moves in the highest social circles.

Gilberte Swann—Daughter of Swann by Odette. Marcel is in
love with her as a child.

Bergotte—A distinguished writer and friend of Swann, much
admired by Marcel whose friend he later becomes.

Duchess Oriane de Guermantes, Princess des Laumes—Member of a noble family of Combray, a witty and aristocratic
woman, admired at a distance by the young Marcel whose
friend she later becomes.

Remi—Swann's coachman.

The Story

Swann's Way (Du côté de chez Swann) consists of a novella
entitled "Swann in Love" ("Un Amour de Swann") preceded
and followed by long sections of reminiscence by the narrator,
Marcel, the whole forming a prelude to the vast expanse of
*Remembrance of Things Past (À la Recherche du Temps
Perdu)*.

In Part I ("Overture"), Marcel recalls scenes from his
childhood, especially holidays spent at Combray, a pleasant
small town not far from Paris, together with his parents,
grandmother, aunts and uncles. It is a stable, cultivated
middle-class family with bookish tastes, which Marcel shares.
Among the family friends is a M. Swann, a faithful visitor
whom they accept as one of their class and circle of acquaintances. Actually, unknown to them, he is also at home in
the highest levels of society, an intimate of the Prince of
Wales and the President of the Republic. He is reputed to
have made a bad marriage, and his wife is not received in
Combray. On the occasion of one such visit, Marcel is sent
to bed early, and so does not receive from his mother his
treasured and accustomed good-night kiss. The omission leaves

him heartbroken. When the company has left, he is still so upset that his mother consents to stay with him during the night, a concession which he believes was responsible for confirming his habit of emotional self-indulgence and neurotic dependence. These memories, however, are fragmentary and isolated, since the past cannot be recovered by an effort of the will alone. Then one day, when Marcel is a grown man, his mother serves him some sweet cakes, or madeleines, which he dips in his tea to soften. The flavor evokes a rush of memories. The past now floods back in its entirety, enabling him to re-create his life as a child in Combray.

Part II ("Combray") explores these memories further. Marcel remembers his Aunt Léonie, a fretful hypochondriac, and her faithful servant Françoise. He recalls his Uncle Adolphe who was something of a roué, and a lovely lady in a pink dress whom he once met in his uncle's apartment. He recalls his early admiration for the writer Bergotte, and his awed admiration for Swann and his daughter Gilberte who counted Bergotte among their personal friends. In particular, he recalls two walks into the countryside which his parents were accustomed to take. Leading in different directions, each had its own character, and, in Marcel's mind, they came to represent two distinct ways of life. One, the Méséglise way, led across the plains in the direction of Swann's estate. The other, the Guermantes way, led along the river to the property of a distinguished noble family named Guermantes. The Duchess of Guermantes figures in his imagination as the embodiment of aristocratic distinction. It is a great moment when he sees her in the flesh in the parish church at Combray. Finally, among other memories, he is moved to tell at greater length a story, dating back before his birth, of a love affair in which Swann had been involved, and which was destined to have its influence years later on Marcel's life.

Part III ("Swann in Love") is the story of this romance. It begins in a rather seedy Parisian salon conducted by a M. and Mme. Verdurin. The guests include an obscure painter, an unknown pianist, a young doctor of some talent but no sophistication, and—since the Verdurins pride themselves on being open-minded—a handsome demimondaine, Odette de Crécy. Odette has met Swann through a mutual friend, and is eager to pursue the acquaintance further. She arranges for him to be introduced to the Verdurin circle. Ordinarily Swann would have found the Verdurins not worth his attention, but he is intrigued by Odette's style of beauty and joins the group to be near her. Hitherto, he has had many mistresses without ever being seriously in love. This time he succumbs, not because of any special merits of Odette, who is thoroughly commonplace, but because she is able to make him jealous. The more Odette deceives him the more passionately he is tied to her, suffering all the agonies of a jealous lover, reading her mail and lurking outside her windows at night to see if she has other callers. An anonymous letter arrives denouncing Odette for all sorts of vice, including lesbianism. His investigations show that the accusations are in their general tenor true. In time, Odette transfers her loyalty to another member of the Verdurin circle, the Comte de Forcheville, and the Verdurins turn against Swann. Gradually his passion diminishes, until he is able to see that he has lavished all the wealth of his heart on a woman who is not really to his taste at all.

In the last section, Marcel returns to his reminiscences. He recalls that as a child he played with Swann's daughter, Gilberte, in the Champs Elysées. Gilberte's mother is none other than Odette, whom Swann has finally married for the sake of the daughter though he is no longer in love. Years later, Marcel as a grown man revisits the scenes where he had known Gilberte and her mother. The automobile has replaced the more stylish carriage and women wear short, shapeless dresses. Marcel is saddened by the changes that have taken place and by the way in which people, places, and events, and even our memories of them, are swallowed up by time.

The volumes that follow continue the reminiscences of Marcel, which expand to include not only Swann and Odette, but many others who are not mentioned in *Swann's Way*. The titles of these volumes, with their standard English translations, are *Within a Budding Grove* (À *l'Ombre des Jeunes Filles en Fleur*), *Guermantes' Way* (*Le Côté de Guermantes*), *Cities of the Plain* (*Sodome et Gomorrhe*), *The Captive* (*La Prisonnière*), *The Sweet Cheat Gone* (*Albertine Disparue*), and *The Past Recaptured* (*Le Temps Retrouvé*). Together they form a vast and detailed panorama of Parisian society of the upper and upper middle classes during Proust's lifetime.

Within a Budding Grove shows us Marcel in adolescence. He is still in love with his childhood playmate, Gilberte, and becomes a frequent guest of her parents, who are much drawn to him. At their home he meets the author Bergotte, whom he has always admired, and is able to study Odette at close range. Gilberte has tired of him, however, and Marcel decides to give her up. For his health, he is sent to a seaside resort named Balbec where he makes new acquaintances. One of these is the great painter Elstir who years before had been a member of the Verdurin circle. Another is the Baron de Charlus, a clever, eccentric, and somewhat sinister nobleman who makes tentative homosexual advances to Marcel, advances which Marcel does not at the time recognize as such. A third friend is Charlus's nephew, Robert de Saint-Loup, a handsome and talented young man with whom Marcel becomes intimate. There is also a group of some half a dozen young girls who play on the beach. Marcel first falls in love with them collectively, and then singles out for his special attention Albertine Simonet.

In *Guermantes' Way* Marcel is living in Paris, a tenant and close neighbor of the same Duchess de Guermantes whom he had admired from a distance as a child. Socially, however, they are still worlds apart, and Marcel longs to enter the exclusive society in which she moves. Thanks to his acquaintance with Charlus and Saint-Loup, who are relatives of the duchess, he becomes first her guest and then her friend. He discovers, however, that the aristocracy are not as he had imagined them. The duchess, though brilliant and witty, proves to be a calculating, manipulative, self-centered woman. In the closing episode, Swann, now seriously ill, comes to tell his old friend the duchess that he is dying. She and the duke, however, are about to leave for a party, and are more preoccupied with the slippers she should wear than with Swann's troubles.

Cities of the Plain is an examination of homosexuality, male and female. Charlus's perversion now becomes clear. He falls in love with a young violinist named Morel, who is a mere boor but who, thanks to Charlus's sponsorship, becomes a fashionable attraction. Albertine is now Marcel's mistress, but Marcel is tormented with jealousy when he suspects that she is the lover of one of the girls from the group at Balbec. From this point on he undergoes the same grief that Swann felt years before with Odette. To protect Albertine from lesbian attachments, he decides to marry her, and induces her to come and live with him in Paris.

In *The Captive*, Marcel has installed Albertine in his apartment and keeps her there virtually a prisoner, so jealous is he. There is a quarrel, an apparent reconciliation, and then quite unexpectedly Albertine vanishes, leaving Marcel in anguish.

The Sweet Cheat Gone deals with Marcel's reaction to the loss of Albertine. After several unsuccessful attempts to lure her back, he sends her a telegram begging her to return on any terms. This is answered by a telegram from her aunt, saying that Albertine has been killed in a fall from a horse. Marcel next begins to investigate her past life. He discovers that the accusation of lesbianism had been at one time true, but that at the time she left him she was in love with another man whom she hoped to marry. Gradually he roots the memory of her out of his mind as he recognizes that he has never loved a real woman, but only a fantasy of his own creation.

Marcel is now disillusioned with love and even friendship, his erotic life is completely divorced from his emotions, and he is satisfied with purely casual encounters with women. Sometime thereafter he receives a telegram, apparently signed by Albertine, announcing her marriage to Saint-Loup, but by now he is so indifferent that he does not even answer it. Later he discovers that it was from Gilberte, whose bad handwriting was responsible for his misreading the signature.

The final volume, *The Past Recaptured*, brings the story to a close during the years of World War I. Many changes have taken place. Marcel is a semi-invalid, living much of the time in a nursing home. Robert has gone to war and requested duty in the front lines where he meets a hero's death. Charlus has degenerated sadly. He now pays young men in a male brothel to beat him with chains, and finally ends up driveling and insane. The last episode is a reception given by the Princess de Guermantes, actually the vulgar and ambitious Mme. Verdurin, who has risen to this dazzling height by a subsequent marriage. This marriage, like that of Gilberte to Saint-Loup, proves how far the aristocracy has been infiltrated by the bourgeoisie. Many old friends are present at the reception, but they are sadly changed, and their children are now grown up. In front of the house, Marcel stumbles over an uneven paving stone, which unlocks another flood of memories, much as the madeleines and tea had done in the first volume. He realizes

that the past, vanished though it appears to be, can be recovered by memory and preserved by art. He resolves to devote his few last years to writing a great book which will
achieve this purpose.

Critical Opinion

It is the diverting, if not very profitable, pastime of some
scholars to speculate on how far the events and characters in
Proust's novel are based on real life. Combray is obviously
much like Illiers, though the details are different. Proust has
projected much of himself into Swann and Marcel, who divide
between them the author's double racial heritage. Charlus is
generally agreed to have been drawn from Count Robert de
Montesquieu, Proust's friend, who also served Huysmans as
the inspiration for Des Esseintes of *Against the Grain (A Re-
bours);* the difference between the two fictional characters
suggests how far both may be from the original. It has often
been noted that the women with whom Marcel falls in love
—Gilberte, Albertine and Andrée—have names that are simply boys' names with feminine endings, and that about Albertine in particular there hovers a certain sexual ambiguity.
One of her models may have been Proust's chauffeur and secretary, Alfredo Agostinelli. Odette has been identified with
Léonie Closmesnil and Laure Hayman, two celebrated cour-
tesans of the day. In fact, Laure Hayman protested when
Swann's Way was published, largely on the grounds that she,
like Odette, lived on the Rue La Pérouse. Guermantes is an
actual name, but the duke and duchess are composite figures,
as are Elstir, Bergotte, and Françoise.

Whatever the identity of the characters, it is universally
agreed that Proust gives us a picture of French society at the
end of the nineteenth century rivaling, and in some ways sur-
passing, that painted by Balzac fifty years before. It was a
time when the aristocracy still clung to their traditions and
their social prestige, though they had lost their power. At
the same time, the upper bourgeoisie were infiltrating the
ranks of the nobility. Swann and Marcel are received by the
Guermantes clan, and Gilberte actually marries into the family. Regardless of who is at the top of the pyramid, snobbery
and social climbing are everywhere. Legrandin, Gilberte, the

Verdurins, and Marcel himself are all infected. In the background, we catch the echoes of the great social and political upheavals of the day, like the Dreyfus affair which rocked France in the nineties, while in the last volume the World War sums up all the forces which were demolishing the world into which Marcel was born.

This picture is composed with great architectonic skill, by no means apparent to the reader who goes no further than *Swann's Way*. This has led critics to compare the whole book, with its elaborate detail carefully subordinated to a vast overall plan, to a Gothic cathedral. There are incidents in the first volume which do not yield their full significance until the very end of the story. Thus there is no clue at first to tell us that the Lady in Pink whom Marcel meets in his uncle's apartment is actually Odette, or that the raucous Master Biche of the Verdurin salon will become the great Elstir. Nor can we realize, except in retrospect, how one incident will echo another; how closely, for instance, Swann's love for Odette will repeat itself in Marcel's love for Albertine, or how Marcel will in later years develop the same traits which he found laughable in his Aunt Léonie. Finally there is the symmetry that begins and ends the story in a flood of images triggered by a slight accidental stimulus, the madeleine in one case and the paving stone in another.

Proust as a psychologist stands in a very old tradition of French letters that goes back to Montaigne and La Rochefoucauld. Perhaps no one has ever examined with such minute care the exact nuance of implication in a word, a gesture, a revealing act. To take only two examples, how does a young bride act when she is approached by an elderly general who is in fact drawn to her by her beauty, but whom she takes to be an old and respected friend of her husband's family whose name she should know but cannot for the moment remember? How does a princess carry herself when she is trying, out of courteous consideration to her hostess, to look inconspicuous at a party given by a mere countess? Proust can tell us.

However, it is love in its various forms that most concerns Proust as a psychologist. Love in these novels is virtually synonymous with jealousy. It brings no happiness. It is a disease which men contract because of an inner compulsion to suffer. The loved ones like Odette, Gilberte, and Albertine are inferior to their lovers and treat them cruelly; that is their chief attraction. In homosexual affairs where there is no hope for conventional, domestic happiness, the element of cruelty is still more obvious, as in the relation between Mlle. Vinteuil and her friend, or Charlus and Morel. The one form of love that is not corrupt is filial or maternal, as in Marcel's feeling for his mother and grandmother. Yet even this has its morbid side; and the fact that Marcel was able to trace the whole course of his later emotional instability back to the night when his mother consented to leave her husband's bed and sleep in her son's room shows how close Proust was to the insights of Freudian psychology.

Proust's concern with the processes of remembering and forgetting also reveals his psychological sophistication. The past is constantly vanishing, not only materially, but in our minds as well. Marcel, meeting Gilberte after many years, does not even recognize her, so completely has he lost his old infatuation. Time, which destroys everything, is the real villain of the story. Nevertheless, the past remains locked up in the unconscious, awaiting the touch that will release it—a cup of tea, or the sound of a creaking gate. But even this recovered past is not the truth or, at most, is only a fragment of it, since each man's truth is always relative to the beholder. Which, for instance, is the true Odette: Marcel's lady in the pink dress, Elstir's painting of Miss Sacripant, Swann's beloved mistress, Swann's unloved wife, or the Countess de Forcheville? Like the three steeples which the boy Marcel sees in constantly shifting perspective from a rapidly moving carriage, and which inspire him to his first piece of creative writing, so the characters in the story keep shifting, and it takes seven volumes, extending over many years, to explore their relationships.

Life for Proust is a stream of moments, of memories, or feelings, which shift and vanish even as we observe them. It is sad, too, for even our most precious experiences are three parts pain. Neither philosophy nor religion affords any real consolation. Only art is able to stop the flow of experience and transmute the suffering into beauty. It is no accident that three of the most important characters in the story are artists: the painter Elstir, the writer Bergotte, and the musician Vinteuil. Of these, Vinteuil is perhaps the most important. He is an obscure provincial music teacher whose life has been made hideous by the realization that his beloved daughter is a lesbian. Nevertheless, out of his suffering he creates great music: a sonata with a haunting theme, and a great septet whose strains echo through the book, providing Swann and Marcel with their one authentic glimpse of an ideal and unchanging loveliness.

The Author

The author of *Remembrance of Things Past* is so overshadowed by his one great book that it is easy to confuse him with his hero Marcel. He was born in 1871 at Auteuil, near Paris, and spent his holidays at Illiers, near Chartres, where his family originated. His father was a successful doctor, a Catholic married to a Jewish woman. Marcel, the elder child of the marriage, was nominally a Catholic though actually of no religion. In his novel he displays his sympathy for his Jewish inheritance by his treatment of Swann and his discussion of the Dreyfus case. Always a frail child, he began to have serious attacks of asthma by the time he was nine, an illness which he later recognized was psychosomatic in origin. Despite this handicap, he was able to acquire a standard education and even to complete his military service.

During the nineties he was nominally employed in the Bibliothèque Mazarine, but actually engaged in writing, in travel, and in social climbing. In this latter activity his sponsor was Count Robert de Montesquieu who introduced him to some of the more distinguished aristocracy. Being a charming and intelligent young man, Proust was in demand socially, despite his rather self-centered, infantile, and hypochondriacal personality. His emotional problems, largely caused by an excessive dependency on his mother, manifested themselves in crippling attacks of asthma and hay fever, as well as a series of homosexual attachments. His many close friendships with women were all platonic.

After the death of his parents, Proust moved into the celebrated apartment in the Boulevard Haussman, a chronic invalid who devoted himself with heroic dedication to his work. His study was lined with cork to keep out noise, the windows were never open to keep out dust and pollen, and food was sent in from the Hotel Ritz to avoid the danger of cooking odors. Occasionally, he would venture out, usually in the middle of the night, to put in an appearance at a late party, or he would receive old friends in his room and question them about happenings of years before, how such and such a duchess had been dressed, or what had been said at a certain dinner party. These memories, tirelessly recovered and examined, form the inspiration, though not the literal content, of *Remembrance of Things Past*. Virtually the last third of Proust's life was spent trying to recapture and record the first two thirds.

The great work was begun about 1907 and the first version finished in 1912. *Swann's Way* was published in 1913 after some difficulty. One publisher's reader who rejected it was André Gide. The last two volumes appeared posthumously. In 1919, Proust received the Prix Goncourt in recognition of *Within a Budding Grove*. He died in 1922 of asthma and overwork. It is said that on his deathbed he found strength and determination to dictate a description of the death of the author Bergotte.

Growth of the Soil

by

KNUT HAMSUN
(KNUT PEDERSEN HAMSUND) (1859–1952)

The Characters

Isak—Proprietor of Sallenraa, a stolid, laconic, hardworking peasant, devoted to his land.

Inger—His wife, as unpretentious as himself, disfigured by a harelip.

Eleseus—Elder son of Isak, a restless, semi-citified young man with no taste for farming.

Sivert—Younger son of Isak, a hardworking, good-natured farm boy.

Os-Anders—A migrant Lapp.

Oline—Housekeeper for Isak and others, an envious, querulous gossip.

Geissler—The district *lendsman*, or sheriff's deputy, a restless, self-confident man, interested in schemes and speculation.

Brede Olsen—Proprietor of Breidablick and jack-of-all-trades; rather ineffectual and shiftless.

Heyerdahl—Lendsman after Geissler, a petty clerk turned official.

Fru Heyerdahl—A feminist with advanced opinions.

Leopoldine—Elder daughter of Isak and Inger.

Axel Ström—Proprietor of Maaneland.

Barbro—Wife of Axel, Brede's daughter, a girl whose simplicity has been corrupted by city life.

Uncle Sivert—An old relative of Inger, reputedly rich.

Jensine—The blacksmith's daughter, serving girl at Sellenraa.

Aron Aronsen—A speculator who opens a store in the district.

Gustaf—A Swedish miner.

Rebecca—Youngest child of Isak and Inger.

Andresen—Aronsen's chief clerk.

The Story

Growth of the Soil (Markens Grud) is set in the wilderness of northern Norway where public lands are open to settlement by any resolute homesteader. Isak, a heavy-set, homely peasant of few words and simple thoughts, comes here to clear a farm. In time, he finds a woman to share his life. She is Inger, a peasant as simple as himself, whose harelip has hitherto prevented her from marrying. Together they build a comfortable farm; first a cow, then a horse, together with carts, farm tools, a loom, and even a few luxuries. Sellenraa, as the place is called, becomes prosperous and self-sufficient.

Inger has two boys, Eleseus and Sivert, who grow into healthy lads. A third child, a daughter, has a harelip, and Inger, who knows how unspeakably her own deformity has made her suffer, strangles the baby before it is ten minutes old and buries it without telling Isak. A neighborhood gossip named Oline ferrets out the crime, and Inger is eventually sent to prison in Trondhjem for several years. When she returns, she has been somewhat corrupted by the experience, not so much from consorting with criminals, but in subtler ways. She has learned to read and write and wear city clothes. So simple is life at Sellenraa that even a prison is more sophisticated, and for several years Inger is restless on the farm. In time she settles down again to her quiet routine.

Gradually, civilization penetrates the wilderness. Other settlers follow Isak until eight or ten farms are spread out between Sellenraa and the nearest village. A telegraph line is run over the mountains. Then copper is discovered; and with the assistance of Geissler, a local promoter, Isak sells a portion of his land to a mining company for several thousand kroner. These developments do not deflect Isak from developing and working the land, but Eleseus, the elder son, grows restless and leaves to become an engineer's assistant in Bergen. There he adopts city ways, sports a cane, and goes to theaters. His father hopes to lure him back to the country, and, when it is quite clear that Eleseus will never make a farmer, buys him a store. For a time, Eleseus takes to the work, but he proves a bad manager, sells out, and emigrates to America. Sivert, the younger brother, stays behind to continue his father's work.

The subplot deals with Isak's neighbors, especially another peasant named Axel Ström, whose experiences are rather similar, though he is less successful in his ventures. He, too, clears land and takes a girl, Barbro, to live with him. Barbro has lived in Bergen and has been vulgarized by city life. When Eleseus returns to the district, she sees in him the nearest thing the district has to offer in the way of a city gentleman, and flirts with him. By now, however, she is pregnant by Axel, and, like Inger, she kills the baby lest it tie her to Axel permanently. The indefatigable Oline ferrets out this infanticide as well. There is a trial and Barbro is acquitted. Eventually she returns to Axel—there being no other place to go—and marries him.

There is no decisive end to the novel: Eleseus is gone, Axel and Barbro are settled, Isak and Inger are getting older, and Sivert will manage the farm. Life is good at Sellenraa. The final judgment on it is pronounced by Geissler, who tells Sivert:

> Listen to me, Sivert: you be content! You've everything to live for, everything to believe in; being born and bringing forth, you are the needful on earth. 'Tis not all that are so, but you are so; needful on earth. 'Tis you that maintain life. Generation to generation, breeding ever anew; and when you die the new stock goes on. That's the meaning of eternal life. What do you get out of it? An existence innocently and properly set towards all. That's what you get out of it.

Critical Opinion

Growth of the Soil has often been compared to an epic because of the dignity and elemental quality of the theme. The hero is Isak, the sturdy, inarticulate man of the soil, with few ideas, but those generally sound. Isak is almost too primitive to have a clear personality, and yet his simplicity bespeaks a fundamental worth and dignity such as perhaps Adam had before the fall. He too has his Garden of Eden: the *allemenning* or common lands, which must be converted from a wilderness into a productive farm. This process is not a warfare but a wooing, a symbiotic collaboration of man and nature, and the fruit of the wooing is Sellenraa. As the title indicates, the cultivation of the land is the basic theme of the book.

If there is a villain in the story, it is no single person, but a force, the city, Bergen or Trondhjem: in the broader sense, all the tendencies of our age which deracinate man and alienate him from the soil. The culture of the cities is restless (Eleseus cannot hold a job); it is exploitive rather than productive (mining, not farming, is one of its activities); it leads to false or cheapened values (as in Barbro's yeasty dreams of gay life); it makes for pretenses (like Eleseus's umbrella handle, which he pretends is a cane); it leads men to think in windy abstractions (like Fru Heyerdahl in her speech before the court). Barbro is the most deeply tainted by these values, and consequently the most vicious, but Eleseus, Aronsen, and the others are contaminated as well.

Inger belongs basically with the country, and so is sound at heart. To be sure, she has murdered her child, but she does so out of pity for its deformity, and not, like Barbro, to be rid of an unwelcome responsibility. Her stay in prison allows all sorts of modern ideas to enter her head, where they prove temporarily unsettling, but in time she settles down with Isak again.

The system of values which Hamsun advances here stems straight from the primitivism of the romantic movement. Isak is perhaps not a noble savage, but he does have much in common with Michael and the Cumberland Beggar of Wordsworth's poetry. All are simple, sturdy, self-reliant folk who, in their isolation, achieve an almost patriarchal gravity. So timeless is Isak that at first we have no clues to locate him in history. He is an archetypal figure who might have lived at any time. Only when we read about telegraphs and mowing machines do we realize that Hamsun is writing about his own day, and addressing the restlessness of modern man. Indeed, the book calls into question the value of our entire modern scientific and liberal culture. The world of telegraphs and mining machinery and feminism, Hamsun seems to say, is only transient. The world of Isak and Inger is fundamental and permanent.

The promoter Geissler is hard to place. He stands somewhere between the two camps. His activities align him with the modern exploiter, as does his rootlessness. On the other hand, his sympathies are with Isak. His final words to Sivert in praise of the country are something more than the easy sentimentality of a city dweller dreaming of the simple life. They contain a serious judgment. Hamsun has chosen Geissler —one of the few articulate characters in the story—to be his spokesman.

The style of this novel calls for special attention. Hamsun does more than write about peasants; he writes as if he were one; that is, he adopts a simple style and speaks not as a detached observer but as the characters themselves do. Consider, for instance, the following passage:

> A wonder of a child! Isak made no objection to his being called Sivert, though he would rather have preferred Jacob. Inger could hit on the right thing at times. Eleseus was named after a priest of her parish, and that was a fine name to be sure; but Sivert was called after his mother's uncle, the district treasurer, who was a well-to-do man, with neither wife nor child to come after him. They couldn't do better than name the boy after him.

The thoughts here are clearly Isak's, a kind of interior monologue. Inasmuch as Isak's speech is limited pretty much to words like *h'mm* and *ho*, such passages are a useful form of character presentation. For another instance of characterization through style, turn to the speech which Fru Heyerdahl makes at Barbro's trial. The *lendsman*'s wife is a graceless, unfeminine character whom Hamsun obviously detests. Her speech is full of the clichés of the orator or pamphleteer.

More than anything else her style enables us to form a judgment about the woman.

A gentle humor sometimes lights up the story. We detect it in the mild vanity of Isak as he makes improvements on the property, or brings Inger gifts, or tries to make out the directions for assembling his mowing machine. In one characteristically humorous passage, Isak spends most of the day trying to move a boulder, while Inger—rather to his secret satisfaction—stands admiringly by. When the stone is pried up at last, it proves unexpectedly to be quite flat on the under surface.

"A fine door slab," says he proudly.

And Inger, simple creature: "Why! Now how on earth could you tell that beforehand?"

"H'm," says Isak. "Think I'd go here digging about nothing?"

This is a gentle, kindly, understated kind of humor; there is no malice in it, and we like Isak all the more for his little pretenses. In the last analysis, however, Isak is not comic but heroic. Critics have especially noted the dignity of the opening and closing passages of the novel, which set him against the vast backdrop of sky, mountains, and fruitful soil. Isak is not just one man; he is an archetype, a Tiller of the Soil; he is Man.

The Author

Knut Hamsun came from Gudbrandsdal in central Norway. His family were small yeomen landholders. The name Hamsun was actually the name of the ancestral farm. He had almost no formal education of any kind and was always somewhat sensitive on this score. At the age of four, he moved to the Lofoten Islands in the far north and worked for some years for an uncle, a harsh and even brutal man. In his teens, he held various odd jobs as a store clerk, traveling salesman, cobbler's apprentice, sheriff's deputy and schoolteacher. He also wrote and published several stories before he was twenty.

As a young man, Hamsun came to Kristiania (Oslo) to attend the university, but found himself unable to study, write, and support himself all at once. After a variety of jobs, ranging from journalism to highway labor, he emigrated in 1882 to the United States. Here he settled among the Scandinavian communities of Wisconsin, Minnesota and the Dakotas, again doing odd jobs, writing and lecturing when he could, and serving as an assistant for a Unitarian minister in Minneapolis. In 1884, fearing that he was ill with tuberculosis, he returned to Norway. Finding no work there, he came back to the United States, and from 1886 to 1888 worked for a time as a streetcar conductor in Chicago and as a fisherman on the Grand Banks. The fruit of these experiences was a book entitled *The Cultural Life of Modern America* (1889), a sharp attack on the materialistic values of America in the gilded age.

Soon thereafter Hamsun achieved sudden fame with the publication of *Hunger (Sult,* 1890), a novel based on his own experiences. From then on he became a prolific writer, turning out novels by the dozen, not to mention plays, short stories and poetry. *Growth of the Soil* (1917) was translated into a score of languages and won him the Nobel Prize in 1920.

Hamsun's politics are an embarrassment to Norwegians. In the First World War, he sympathized openly with German militarism. In the Second World War, he was the only Norwegian writer to welcome the invasion of his country by the Nazis, and in 1943 he visited Hitler. His countrymen responded by sending him copies of his own writings. They poured in by the thousands, well worn and once treasured, but now repudiated. In 1945, he was arrested as a collaborator, together with his wife, and most of his personal fortune was confiscated. In respect of his great age, he was spared a prison sentence and placed instead in a mental hospital. He died in 1952.

There have been various explanations for Hamsun's German sympathies. Some have suggested that he was merely senile, others that he was taking his revenge on Norway and America, the countries that let him starve as a young man, while still others have suggested that the romantic primitivism of *Growth of the Soil* is itself anti-liberal and anti-intellectual, and has some affiliation with Nazism. Hamsun's actions in 1940, however, need not prevent us from enjoying what he wrote in 1917. The novel is greater than the man.

The World's Illusion

by

JAKOB WASSERMANN (1873–1934)

The Characters

CHRISTIAN'S FAMILY

Albrecht Wahnschaffe—Christian's father, a wealthy German industrialist.

Frau Wahnschaffe—Christian's devoted mother.

Christian Wahnschaffe (Eidolon)—Eldest son of Albrecht Wahnschaffe, a handsome, charming and pampered youth.

Wolfgang Wahnschaffe—Christian's jealous younger brother.

Judith Wahnschaffe—Christian's sister, spoiled and self-centered.

Felix Imhof—Judith's first husband, a wealthy businessman of unknown origins.

Edgar Lorm—Judith's second husband, a celebrated actor.

LETITIA'S FAMILY

Febronius—A childless nobleman, Crammon's friend.

Else von Febronius—His wife, Letitia's mother.

Letitia von Febronius—Charming, self-indulgent daughter of Else von Febronius and Crammon.

Bernard Gervasius von Crammon—A middle-aged bachelor with epicurean tastes, a close friend of Christian.

Countess Brainitz—Letitia's aunt, formerly an actress.

Hilde Stojenthin—Another aunt of Letitia, the widow of a judge.

Stephen Gunderam—Letitia's first husband, a German from Argentina.

Georgette and Christina Gunderam—Letitia's twin children.

Egon Rochlitz—Letitia's fiancé after her divorce from Stephen.

OTHERS

Miss Aglaia—A relative and housekeeper of Crammon.

Ivan Michailovich Becker—A Russian revolutionary.

Bradshaw—A wealthy American.

Jean Cardillac—A French financier.

Adda Castillo—A lion tamer, admired by Christian.

Miss Constantine—A relative and housekeeper of Crammon.

Grand Duke Cyril—A member of the Russian imperial family, lover of Eva Sorel.

Karen Engelschall—A prostitute taken care of by Christian.

Widow Engelschall—Karen's mother, a greedy fortune teller.

Niels Heinrich Engelschall—Karen's worthless, vicious brother.

Cornelius Ermelang—A poet, a member of Eva Sorel's circle.

Mlle. Sinaide Gamaleja—Mistress of Prince Szilaghin.

Willibald Girke—A private detective.

Gisevius—A workman with whom Christian lives.

Herr von Grunow-Reckenhausen—A Brandenburg noble, grandfather of Botho von Thüngen.

The Gunderams, Family of Stephen Gunderam—Gottlieb, his father, a lawyer; Dona Barbara, his mother; Riccardo, Paolo and Demetrius, his brothers; Esmeralda, his sister; Eleutheria, a nurse.

Molly Gutkind—A prostitute who shelters Michael Hoffman.

Heinzen—A crippled machinist with reputed powers of healing.

Joachim Heinzen—Heinzen's son, the half-witted friend of Niels Engelschall.

Emmanuel Herbst—Lorm's manager.

David Hoffman—An impecunious traveling salesman.

Ruth Hoffman—His sixteen-year-old daughter.

Michael Hoffman—Ruth's brother.

Roderick Kroll—A workman who tries to kill Albrecht Wahnschaffe.

Frau Kroll—His wife.

M. Labourdemont—Eva Sorel's secretary.

Lamprecht—A student, tutor to Michael Hoffman.

Dennis Lay—A wealthy and talented Englishman.

Beatrix van Leer—A Flemish sculptress.

Brother Leotade—A monk who attempts to rape Eva Sorel.

Count Maidanoff—Incognito of Grand Duke Cyril.

David Markuse—A jeweler.

Alfred Meerholz—A friend of Christian, killed in a motoring accident.

Friederich Pestel—A naval officer in love with Letitia.

Angiolina Pratti—An Italian peasant girl, admired by Christian.

Lucas Rappard—Ballet instructor to Eva Sorel.

Susan Rappard—Eva Sorel's companion.

The Ribbeks—Employers of Amadeus Voss.

Isolde Schirmacher—A neighbor in Christian's tenement.

Johanna Schöntag—Daughter of a Viennese banker, in love with Christian.

Eva Sorel—A celebrated dancer. Originally a brilliant and gracious woman, she becomes corrupted by success and wealth.

Randolph von Stettner—A friend of Christian, an officer who resigns his commission rather than fight a duel.

Fräulein Stöhr—Attendant of Countess Brainitz.

Stübbe—A drunken inmate of Christian's tenement.

Prince Fyodor Szilaghin—A corrupt young friend of the Grand Duke Cyril.

Marquis Vincente Tavera—A Spanish diplomat.

Botho von Thüngen—A Westphalian nobleman, under the spiritual influence of Christian.

Dr. Voltolini—A physician.

Amadeus Voss—A friend of Christian, a religious hypocrite, warped by his poverty and jealous of Christian's fine qualities.

Dietrich Voss—Brother of Amadeus, a deaf-mute.

Walpurga—A prostitute, sheltered by Voss.

Weikhardt—A painter.

Franz Lothar von Westernach—A friend of Crammon, a diplomat.

Clementine von Westernach—His sister.
Prince Alexis Wiguniewski—A friend of Eva Sorel.
Andrei Gabrilovich Yaminsky—A Russian scholar, a lover of
    Eva Sorel.
Katherine Zöller—A young girl.

The Story

The World's Illusion (Christian Wahnschaffe) takes place
around 1905, a time of international tension and social unrest. For the upper classes, it was the one decade in European
history when one could simultaneously enjoy the satisfactions
of inherited feudal privileges amid the luxury of twentieth-
century technology. The hero, Christian Wahnschaffe, the
son of a German steel millionaire, has been indulged by a
loving mother and pampered with every luxury conceivable
to a fastidious and ingenious taste. Young, handsome, and
captivating, he is, however, coolly self-centered and detached.
He can be casual when a friend is killed by his side in a
motoring accident or when his mistress (a circus performer)
is mangled by a lion, and he instinctively shrinks from any
kind of poverty or unhappiness. His most brilliant success is
to win the love of a dancer named Eva Sorel, for whom he
buys a diamond worth half a million marks.

Gradually Christian comes to realize how sheltered and
selfish his life is. His eyes are opened by a dedicated Russian
revolutionary, Ivan Michailovich Becker, as well as by the
unpleasant young Amadeus Voss, who has been warped by
poverty and jealousy of those more fortunate than himself.
Christian's first attempts to atone for his sins of omission are
quixotic. He gives Voss large sums of money, presses a
diamond ring on the wife of a poor workman, and buys
several cartloads of mackerel at an exorbitant price to dis-
tribute among the poor on the waterfront. Not much comes
of these gestures: Voss becomes a gambler, the woman spends
her money foolishly, and Christian is made sick by the smell
of mackerel.

Gradually Christian comes to understand his vocation. He
is not to be a practical reformer or philanthropist. His duty
is to share the life of the poor, doing what good he can by
force of personal influence. Despite the protests of his

scandalized family, and of an old friend, the worldly Bernard von Crammon, he surrenders most of his income, sells his castle and settles in a shabby Berlin slum. To become useful, he enters medical school, though he realizes he can never accept fees for his services.

Two women occupy his life at this time. One is Ruth Hoffman, a young Jewish girl who lives with her brother Michael in the same tenement. A delicate, lovely child, her unselfish good nature brings happiness to everyone. The other, Karen Engelschall, is a degraded prostitute whom he meets in a tavern. He rescues her from the blows of her pimp, finds her shelter and medical care, and even some luxuries. He talks to her like an amateur psychiatrist or social worker, urging her to tell about her past history. These sessions are not especially therapeutic. At times, however, he lapses into conversation about himself, and these moments are the most human part of his relationship with her.

Karen has a brother, Niels Heinrich, a thoroughly vicious young man. For some time he has cast lustful eyes on Ruth Hoffman, whose obvious purity presents a constant challenge. One day he entices her into a cellar, rapes her, and then murders her, fixing the blame on a half-witted friend of his, Heinzen. Christian has never shown any aptitude for police work hitherto, but now he turns detective, and guided largely by intuition and clairvoyant visions identifies Karen's brother as the true murderer. Finally he brings the murderer to such a state of repentance that Niels confesses his crime. Heinzen is set free.

Christian's family, meanwhile, are so appalled by the social circles in which their son now moves that they consider committing him to an asylum. Christian spares them the trouble; he offers to disappear. What becomes of him we do not learn for sure, although we hear rumors of him in German mining communities, in the East End of London, and in New York's Chinatown. His memory remains with a few friends, notably the aging epicurean Crammon who still cherishes, not the saintly and ascetic Christian, but the Christian of old, the beautiful, extravagant, vital, bewitching youth.

Critical Opinion

If good intentions can keep a book from oblivion, then *The World's Illusion* should be immortal. Here is a novel that obviously tries to do for German literature what Dostoevski did for the Russian. Both in plot and in ideas it is very much in the Russian manner: long, sprawling, crowded with characters and tangled with many lines of plot. Several scenes are actually laid in Russia, complete with conspirators, mobs, and a wonderfully sinister grand duke. The hero is a Christ figure in modern dress, a composite of Prince Myshkin and Alyosha Karamazov. Christian's proposal to deal with evil on its own ground, by sinking into the lowest depths of degradation, is something Dostoevski would have understood. Finally, the scene in which Niels and Christian kneel before each other in mutual penitence and forgiveness reminds us of Father Zossima bowing to Dmitri or Raskolnikov kneeling before Sonia. It is a thoroughly Russian gesture and utterly un-German.

A second source of inspiration for Wassermann is undoubtedly the life of Saint Francis of Assisi, whose name runs through the novel like a leitmotiv. Here was a young man of wealth and position who, like Christian, forsook his worldly life and his family for a career of poverty, humility, chastity, and good works. Wassermann particularly stresses in Christian the quality of gentleness and courtesy which also characterized Saint Francis. Another possible hagiographic influence is the story of the Buddha, which Wassermann was studying at the time.

In short, Wassermann has tried to draw a picture of a saint in twentieth-century costume, a saint so modern in his views, in fact, that he no longer believes in God. Christian's name is deliberately symbolic, like that of Bunyan's hero. However, for a saint he seems a bit too chilly and distant. He always retains an air of fastidiousness, and even his finest benefactions seem to be performed more out of duty than love. Christian is supposed to have extraordinary power for touching men's hearts, yet he is unconvincing. For instance, at one point Karen, the prostitute whom he tries to redeem, decides that the one thing in life she craves is a string of pearls belonging to Christian's mother, the finest pearls in all Germany. Christian agrees that the pearls would be good for Karen's morale, or, as he puts it, a "symbol of compensation, of moral equilibrium." He asks his mother to lend them for a time, and she, shuddering, with averted face and outstretched arm, hands him the pearls. It is clear that Wassermann is trying to show that even the most depraved of beings can be redeemed if only one respects their human dignity. It is hard, however, to see how these pearls, which are such a spiritual burden to Christian and his family, can be a means of grace for Karen, while to her mother and brother they are a dangerous provocation to theft.

This episode of the pearls, with its theatrical posturing, its melodrama, and its moral pretentiousness, is the sort of thing that mars a promising book. To take another example, the dancer Eva Sorel early in her career unfortunately inspires the lust of a young monk, Brother Leotade. Trapped alone with him in a ruined tower, she takes refuge on the topmost parapet. The would-be rapist crouches below her, knowing that if he advances one more step she will leap to her death. For hours, they stand tensely until finally Brother Leotade throws himself on his face, begins to pray, and then quite sensibly vanishes down the stairs. This sort of thing is delicious in the gothic novels of the eighteenth century, but in the twentieth century it is just too much.

The same lack of reality infects most of Wassermann's scenes of fashionable life. He never convinces us that he really knew anything about the very rich. His scenes of luxury sound like the superheated fantasies of a poor boy.

The plot of *The World's Illusion* is both loose and leisurely, embracing a large number of characters whose only connection is that they are more or less acquainted with one another, or that their lives touch Christian's. One story line traces the two marriages of Christian's sister Judith, and another follows Eva Sorel to Russia, where she dies when her palace is sacked by a revolutionary mob. A great deal of space is devoted to that charming man of the world, Bernard von Crammon, and the marital misadventures of his daughter Letitia. One does not resent this wealth of material, much of which is more interesting and more credible than the main plot. However, in 1932 Wassermann issued a revision, shorter than the original by a seventh, omitting many passages and generally tightening the structure. Some of the speeches became less florid. Still, in either version the novel is not a masterpiece, only the raw material out of which a masterpiece might have been carved.

The Author

One of the chief problems to which Jakob Wassermann constantly turns in his writing is the problem of being a Jew in a Gentile world. The torment of Michael Hoffman in *The World's Illusion* is written out of the experience of the author whose early years were made ugly by anti-Semitism, and who died a year after Hitler came into power. Wassermann was born in southern Germany near Nuremberg, the son of an unsuccessful businessman whose life was a constant struggle against bankruptcy. He lost his mother when he was nine, and his stepmother proved harsh and unsympathetic. His chief consolation was in writing stories, but even this escape was punished. His stepmother would tear up or burn his papers, so that he was obliged to write secretly at night, sitting by his window in the moonlight.

At sixteen, Wassermann was sent to Vienna to work for his uncle, a manufacturer of fans. He disliked the job and ran away, only to be termed by his family a wastrel and a ne'er-do-well. The next few years he spent aimlessly, as a hobo, in the army, or at odd jobs, from one of which he was discharged on account of his religion. Sometimes he would tell stories to children in country villages in exchange for food, or pick up a few coins by copying. At length he found his way into newspaper work and attracted the attention of authors and editors. Some of his stories and poems were published in *Simplicissimus*, the humor magazine. Wassermann himself found a post there as editor. His first novel, *The Jews of Zirndorf*, appeared in 1897.

Wassermann now began to make his way in literary circles and became friendly with such men as Hofmannsthal, Schnitzler, and Thomas Mann. In 1901, he married the daughter of a well-to-do Viennese manufacturer named Speyer. She bore him two sons and two daughters. The marriage was difficult and resulted in a separation in 1919, followed by a divorce in 1926. His second wife was Marta

Karlweiss, herself an author, by whom he had a son. With the help of his literary admirers, he was able to buy a house at Alt-Aussee in Austria, where he spent the rest of his life.

Wassermann's reputation was at its height during the 1920's and 1930's, when he enjoyed a worldwide audience and was well known as a lecturer in university communities everywhere. At least one reviewer hailed him as equal or superior to Tolstoi, Dostoevski, and Balzac.

Politically Wassermann was a liberal, and an outspoken opponent of the forces of hate that were rising in the world. After Hitler came to power, he was expelled from the Prussian Academy of Letters. He died, fortunately, before the Austrian *Anschluss*.

Wassermann's writings include some two dozen or more novels and novellas, two plays, and a number of biographical and autobiographical works. The best known is *The World's Illusion (Christian Wahnschaffe*, 1918; published in English, 1928); others are *Caspar Hauser* (1908; English, 1928); *The Goose Man (Das Gansmännchen*, 1915; English, 1922); *Gold (Ulrike Woytick*, 1923; English, 1924); *The Maurizius Case (Der Fall Maurizius*, 1928; English, 1929); *Dr. Kerkhoven* (1934). Wassermann's life is told in *My Life as a German and a Jew (Mein Weg als Deutscher und Jude*, 1921; English, 1933).

The Castle

by

FRANZ KAFKA (1883–1924)

The Characters

K.—The principal character, a land surveyor; stubborn, determined, unimaginative.

Count Westwest—The Lord of the Castle, a mysterious personage who is named but does not appear.

Klamm—An important member of the Castle hierarchy. Although he is sometimes seen, his true nature remains obscure.

Frieda—Barmaid at the Herrenhoff Inn, mistress of Klamm and later of K.

Arthur and Jeremiah—K.'s surveying assistants, a pair of grotesque incompetents.

Barnabas—A messenger from Klamm to K., a well-intentioned and obliging young man.

Olga—Sister of Barnabas, much interested in K.

Amalia—Younger sister of Barnabas, who has disgraced the family by refusing the advances of Sortini.

Sortini—A Castle official.

Gardana—Landlady of the Herrenhoff, formerly Klamm's mistress.

The Village Superintendent—A fussy, disorganized bureaucrat.

345

Momus—The village secretary.
Hans Brunswick—A twelve-year-old boy, son of the cobbler, who befriends K.
The Schoolmaster.
Fräulein Gisa—The schoolmaster's assistant.
Erlanger—A secretary from the Castle.
Bürgel—A Castle official, serving as "liaison secretary."
Peasants, servants, villagers, etc.

The Story

The Castle, originally written in the first person, was later recast in the third person, but the story is still limited to the experience and point of view of the protagonist, a surveyor named K. K. has been hired to survey an estate or small principality ruled by a certain Count Westwest. Its principal features are an undistinguished village inhabited by shop-keepers and artisans, and a nearby hill with a castle occupied by government offices. Presumably the count lives there, too, but we hear no more of him. K.'s problem is to go to the Castle and find out what he is expected to do. Normally this should be a simple, routine matter, but he meets with a maddening succession of checks and obstacles. His struggles to reach his goal and to prove that he has been engaged as surveyor makes up the story.

Arriving at the village on a winter day, K. first makes in-quiries at an inn. Since the villagers greet him suspiciously and evasively, K. decides to set out on foot in the direction of the Castle. However, he loses his way. The Castle appears to recede before him, and the road never takes him in the direc-tion it appears to lead. Finally he hails a driver who refuses to take him to the Castle but is willing to drive him back to the inn. There two men announce themselves as his assistants. They are a grotesque, clumsy, comic pair, always tumbling over each other in their eagerness to help. Next K. telephones the Castle for instructions, but gets confusing and exasperating answers. When he pretends to be his own assistant and asks when he may come to the Castle, a voice replies, "Never."

No sooner has he hung up the telephone than a messenger arrives from the Castle with a letter from a department head, an important official named Klamm, welcoming K., promising him assistance, and assigning him to work under the village superintendent. The messenger, a pleasant young man named Barnabas, is helpful. He takes K. home with him and offers him lodgings with his own family. Instead K. goes to a second inn, the Herrenhoff, which is used by officials from the Castle. There he meets the barmaid, Frieda, who proudly announces herself as Klamm's mistress. Klamm is at the inn at the moment, she tells K., allowing him to catch a glimpse of the great man through a peephole. K. sees Frieda as a means of getting at Klamm, and proposes that she transfer her affections to him. Frieda is unexpectedly obliging. That night the two make love under the bar amid puddles of beer while the assistants settle down in the taproom. The next morning, the landlady has a serious talk with K. He is presumptuous in expecting that he can ever speak to Klamm, she tells him. Furthermore, he is being inconsiderate to Frieda, and does not realize how much she has sacrificed in leaving Klamm for him. The landlady herself was once Klamm's mistress many years before, and, though Klamm deserted her after three nights, she still lives in the memory of the dizzying privilege that was once hers.

K. now begins to see himself not as a professional man engaged to do a job, but as someone whose very right to exist is suspect. His struggles to obtain recognition become more desperate. He consults his superior, the village superintendent, who rummages futilely through a mass of documents, denies that K.'s letter has any official standing, and suggests that the whole confusion may be due to administrative errors. Even the telephone call proves nothing, for there is no central exchange at the Castle. Anybody may answer a ring. The reply may have been given in ignorance or even in jest.

Until his position can be officially regularized, K. is offered a post as the janitor of the village schools. There is no salary, but he and Frieda may sleep in the schoolroom. Though Frieda urges him to accept, K. is insulted and refuses. Going back to the inn, he installs himself in the Klamms' coach, expecting to speak to Klamm before he returns to the Castle. Instead, another official appears and orders him out. When K. refuses, the horses are simply hitched to another coach, leaving him fuming and helpless. Another interview follows with the village secretary, Momus, who wishes to make an official report on K.'s claim to be a surveyor. Klamm may never read it, he admits, but the procedure is authorized by him, "and how can anything have Klamm's assent that isn't filled with his spirit?" K., still on his dignity, refuses to answer questions. A letter arrives from Klamm congratulating K. on the progress of his survey. At length, K. agrees to accept the janitorial post, and sets up housekeeping in the school with Frieda and the two assistants. Next morning they oversleep and are still in bed when the students arrive, much to the horror of the teacher. When an attempt is made to dismiss him, K. refuses to leave. When he, in turn, tries to get rid of his useless assistants, he meets with no better luck. Meanwhile Frieda quarrels with him, saying he is merely using her for his own ends.

Next, K. begins to learn more about his messenger Barnabas, who is not to be blamed for seeming unreliable. His tasks are assigned him unexpectedly and capriciously; he may wait for days and then be told to deliver a letter that is months overdue. Although he has entry to the Castle, he is a novice there and is not even sure who it is who gives him orders. His position is made the more difficult because his entire family is in disgrace. The story is a shocking one. Three years before, his father, an official in the fire department, was taking part in a ceremony involving the acquisition of a new fire engine. An official from the Castle, Sortini, was also present, and was attracted to Barnabas's younger sister Amalia. Soon afterward he sent her a letter couched in obscene terms summoning her to a rendezvous at the inn. When Amalia refused, although neither she nor the family was actually punished, the villagers began to ostracize them, the father lost his post in the fire brigade, his business was ruined, and he wore himself out petitioning year after year to be restored to favor.

Barnabas is finally able to secure for K. an interview with an official named Erlanger who is staying at the Herrenhoff. When K. arrives, Erlanger is asleep and no one will waken him. To make matters worse, his assistants have left, and one has taken Frieda with him. Now back at her job as barmaid, she will have nothing more to do with K.

In the first edition, the story ended at this point, cut short by Kafka's death. In the second edition, Brod published another episode from Kafka's manuscript, in which K. is interviewed by an official named Bürgel who assures him that the Castle, far from rejecting K., is actually eager to communicate with him. It is only necessary to try a different approach. This message of hope falls on deaf ears, however, for this time K. has fallen asleep. According to Brod, the story was to end with K. continuing his struggle until he dies of exhaustion. As he lies on his deathbed, word arrives from the Castle saying that although K. has no valid claim to be in the village, yet "taking auxiliary circumstances into account" he will be permitted to continue to live there.

Critical Opinion

It is obvious to any reader that *The Castle* is symbolic, yet the critics cannot agree upon what it symbolizes. The symbols are ambiguous and do not have simple equivalents, as in an allegory. There is no key which enables us confidently to decode the story and assign explicit meanings to each character and episode. Instead, Kafka builds up his story with a multitude of concrete details and makes no reference to any structure of meaning beyond these details. In older, more traditional types of fiction the author was assumed to be omniscient and to know facts about his characters which even they did not know, so that he could if he wished take us behind the scenes and tell us what was really going on. Kafka, on the other hand, confines us to the partial insights of the characters themselves, and since these insights conflict, we do not know which to trust. Who, for instance, is able to say which of the many descriptions of Klamm is the right one? Even Barnabas does not know. And who has made the right choice: Frieda, who accepts Klamm's love, or Amalia, who rejects Sortini's? All we know is that the Castle dominates everyone in the village. Its decrees are declared to be absolutely wise and infallible. Yet to the ordinary mind it appears completely irrational, capricious, unfathomable, and even immoral.

K.'s struggle to get to the Castle should be read as a kind of frustrated pilgrimage, an attempt to enter a realm of being that transcends his own. If he could penetrate the secrets of the Castle, he would achieve that lucid vision which would clarify the meaning of his existence. As it is, the difficulties which he meets are a statement of man's actual condition, his inability to achieve his own salvation. The realms of the absolute cannot be entered from below. Kafka's originality lies in his choice of a metaphor to represent this situation.

As in *The Trial*, he has represented the transcendent order by a typical central European bureaucracy. Thus a serious, perhaps tragic theme is expressed through situations that are rich in comic or satiric possibilities. The administration of the Castle is hardly more arrogant or dilatory than the administration of the old Austrian Empire. The failure of communication between Castle and village was reproduced in scores of communities in Kafka's native Bohemia, where Czech-speaking peasants lived on estates owned by absentee, German-speaking landlords.

But just what is this other realm which K. wants to reach? Most commentators fall into one or the other of two camps, the theological and the psychological, just as they do with regard to *The Trial*. The theological approach sees the Castle as representing the divine order. The ruler, Count Westwest, is so inaccessible that he hardly appears; perhaps he is God the Father. Klamm, however, is sometimes manifest in the flesh; he may be God the Son. Certainly Klamm is treated with adoration, although his exact features are not known. All his servants, however, faintly resemble him. This suggests God's immanence in the world. The ways of the Castle (the workings of Providence) are a mystery to human intelligence, especially to the surveyor K. (the analytic reason); in fact, the Castle cannot be surveyed and needs no surveyor. The workings of its administration are painstaking, omniscient, and unhurried, although its decrees, as recorded in the files of the village superintendent, are disorderly, obsolete, or not available for ready reference. Communication between the two realms is unreliable and capricious. Messages addressed to the village (revelation) are obscure and do not seem to apply to the recipient, while messages for the Castle (prayer) may not reach their destination.

There are many roads to the Castle. Sometimes one is popular while another is unaccountably deserted (shifts in doctrine and religious usage?). When K. tries to get there on his own initiative, all roads lead him equally astray. Barnabas is an angel; his clothing is shining white, and he is specifically described as a messenger (in Greek, *angelos*). The Castle officials will accept bribes (sacrifice), but there is no evidence that their decisions are affected thereby. At times, the will of the Castle seems cruel, though not more so than Jehovah's command to Abraham to sacrifice his firstborn son. The happiest are those who, like Gardana and Frieda, submit their wills gratefully to Klamm's. Amalia, who tore up Sortini's letter and threw it in the face of the messenger, is rather like the Virgin Mary if she had given such an answer to the Angel of the Annunciation. She is not actually punished, but destiny has passed her by, and thereafter, so far as Castle and village are concerned, she no longer exists.

If we accept this interpretation, we will place Kafka in the company of those theologians, from Paul and Augustine down to Kierkegaard and Barth, who stress the absolute otherness of God, the incommensurability of the human and the divine.

The psychoanalytic interpretations differ according to the school of the interpreter. One Freudian reading sees the Castle as the mother figure and Count Westwest as the father, while K.'s quest is actually an Oedipal wish. A Jungian critic sees the life of the Castle as representing the unconscious, a realm which is inaccessible, illogical, imperious, and amoral, yet charged with life, power and mystery. K. is therefore striving to achieve a harmonious relationship between the conscious intellect and the unconscious. Until he can do so, he is alienated from himself. His best hope lies in Frieda who is at one with the unconscious (she is Klamm's mistress). In Jungian language she is K.'s *anima*, the incarnation of the repressed, other side of his personality. Like Dante's Beatrice, she is a guide, and her name means "peace" (in German, *Frieden*).

Whether one adopts the theological or the psychological interpretation, it is clear enough why K. does not reach his goal. In the first place, he relies too much on reason. He is trying to force the transcendent world into his own limited categories of understanding. In this he is both blind and arrogant. In fact, the German verb which means "to survey" (*vermessen*) also means "to be presumptuous." His second sin is that he uses other people for his own ends, rather than as ends in themselves. He is insufferable with the villagers, and he exploits Frieda. Both these faults are repeatedly pointed out to him. His failure to understand is the willful blindness of invincible ignorance. His punishment is simply to be left to his own impotent devices.

One last question: what does the village represent? The traditional interpretation, advanced by Thomas Mann and Max Brod, is that the village is the ordinary life of mankind, the normal healthy existence of family and community. If K. can learn to live in the village, he will achieve a state of grace and discover that in some mystical sense the life of the village is the same as (or at least participates in) the life of the Castle. Against this view others have argued that the village is never represented as a desirable place. Its citizens are, for the most part, coarse, surly, and uncomprehending, and cut off from the ordinary world outside quite as much as from the Castle. These two points of view can be reconciled if we recollect that the reader sees the village only through K.'s eyes, and therefore must subject himself to K.'s limitations. The village represents society well enough, but society as it must appear to a man like K., who is so obsessed by his quest for spiritual absolutes that he no longer has any feeling for the rest of mankind. In any event, the village is the closest that K. ever gets to his goal, for he dies, like Moses, in sight of but forever outside of the promised land.

The Trial

by

FRANZ KAFKA

The Characters

NOTE: *There is really only one character in* The Trial: *the protagonist, Joseph K., whose struggles make up the entire story and who is "on stage" at all times. Most of the other actors are nameless and almost faceless, and may simply be projections of certain aspects of K.'s own unconscious. The most sharply defined characters are the following:*

Joseph K.—A thirty-year-old bachelor and a successful bank official. He is a colorless person, without conspicuous vices or virtues or close personal attachments.

Frau Grubach—K.'s landlady, a respectable woman who adopts a motherly attitude toward him.

Fräulein Bürstner—A typist who lives in K.'s boardinghouse.

Huld—A lawyer whom K. consults. He boasts of his influence with court officials, but accomplishes nothing.

Leni—Nurse and housekeeper to Huld. A sensual woman, she makes advances to all her employer's clients.

Titorelli—A painter who offers to help K.

The Chaplain—A priest in the cathedral who tries to explain to K. the gravity of his situation.

Other Characters—An inspector, two guards, an examining magistrate, various clerks and court officials, the wife of a court attendant, a law student, a friend of Fräulein Bürstner, a nephew of Frau Grubach, K.'s uncle, a manufacturer, a client of Huld's, a client at the bank, a crowd of teen-age girls, two executioners, and others.

The Story

The Trial takes place in an unspecified city with no distinguishing features; it could be Prague in the first decade of this century. The details do not matter, however, for in this psychological and spiritual allegory the real scene is the soul.

The protagonist is Joseph K., thirty years old, who has a good job at a bank and is well thought of. He lives in a boardinghouse, eats at quiet cafés, and works till nine at night. He is a gray, empty person, a bachelor with no close friends.

One morning his tidy routine is shattered by the appearance of two men who tell him that he is under arrest. K. is aware of having committed no crime, and it takes him some time to realize that he is in the hands of no ordinary civil court. Everything is bewildering. He is never told what offense he is guilty of, or what code of law applies in his case. His guilt is always assumed by those he meets, and yet he is free to come and go about his usual occupations. Proceedings are conducted in squalid, out-of-the-way places. The most unexpected people turn out to be officials of the Court, or familiar with it. The procedure is involved and complicated, so that nobody, not even the court officials themselves, can grasp it all. The lesser officers are corrupt. The most powerful judges are so remote that no one is sure that they even exist. And, worst of all, though cases drag on for years, no one is ever acquitted.

The novel is the record of K.'s attempt to clear himself of the charge, or at least to discover what the charge is. For a whole year, he goes for help from one person to another, without success. The first is his neighbor in the boardinghouse, Fräulein Bürstner, a typist. He tries to explain what has happened, but she is not interested. When he tries to make advances to her, she puts up with him wearily for a time, then dismisses him. He is summoned to a hearing set for the following Sunday, which proves to be disorderly and confused. He makes a windy speech in his defense and supposes that he has won the sympathy of the audience in the courtroom. They all turn out to be agents of the Court. The next week he returns, but this time the room is empty. He takes the opportunity to look at the books of law, which turn out to be full of childishly obscene drawings.

By now, K. is obsessed with the proceedings against him, so much so that his work at the bank begins to suffer. His Uncle Karl takes him to a lawyer named Huld who has a reputation in such cases. The lawyer is an invalid, and while he discusses the case with the uncle, K. leaves the sickroom to make love to the lawyer's nurse, Leni. Afterward, his uncle warns him that he has seriously jeopardized his case. K. proposes to submit a petition to the court, but his lawyer tells him that it may not be read. In fact, it is a question whether the Law even recognizes the right of the accused to defend themselves.

Acting on a tip from a business associate, K. seeks out a painter named Titorelli who lives in a squalid tenement surrounded by a swarm of rowdy and impertinent girls. Titorelli is the official portraitist of the court, and professes to wield great influence. He tells K. that there are three possibilities for the outcome of his case: a definite acquittal, which never happens, a provisional acquittal, which will leave him open to subsequent arrest, and an indefinite postponement, which results neither in acquittal nor in sentence. K. is disheartened and leaves, after buying a number of paintings he does not want.

Next, feeling that his lawyer has been neglecting the case, K. tries to dismiss Huld. He meets another client of Huld, a ruined businessman named Block, whose case has dragged on for years with as little success as K.'s. He too complains of neglect, and has been consulting other lawyers on the sly. Huld is indignant that K. should presume to dismiss him, and to demonstrate his grip over his clients he calls in Block, forces him to kneel, and humiliates him.

The last interview takes place in the cathedral of the city, where K. has gone on other business. The church is dark and empty. Suddenly a voice speaks from the pulpit addressing K. by name. It is a priest who identifies himself as a prison chaplain, and therefore a servant of the Court. He tells K. that his case is going badly, that he does not yet understand the nature of the Court, that he relies too much on the help of others, especially women.

The climax of the interview in the cathedral is an ambiguous and disturbing parable which the priest tells K. A certain man begs for admission to the Law. At the gate is a doorkeeper who tells him that he cannot be admitted at the moment. For year upon year, the man waits before the door. He tries to bribe the guard, who takes his money but still does not admit him. At last, he dies. On his deathbed, he asks the guard why, since all men seek to attain the Law, no one else has come to seek admittance. The doorkeeper replies, "No one but you could gain admittance through this door since this door was intended only for you. Now I am going to shut it." K.'s instinct is to protest that the man has been deceived. But the priest proceeds to comment on the story with such casuistry that K. becomes confused about the real issue and the application of the parable to himself.

The last chapter is set a year after the first, on the eve of K.'s thirty-first birthday. Two plump men in top hats and frock coats come to K.'s door and lead him away unresisting. He suspects that they are his executioners, but he has lost the will to fight back. He even refuses to hail a policeman who might save him. At the last moment, a window in a nearby house flies open, and silhouetted against the light, he sees a figure leaning out with hands stretched, perhaps in sympathy or to offer help. Whatever it means K. never discovers. One man holds him by the throat while the other stabs him in the heart.

Critical Opinion

The Trial must be read on several levels, and does not yield its full meaning at once. There are two principal interpretations which, however, do not necessarily exclude each other: the psychological and the theological. The psychological interpretation takes for its starting point the facts of Kafka's life and his sense of inadequacy before his overpowering father. All his life Kafka felt judged and found wanting. These feelings were expressed in the plight of Joseph K., pursued by an all-powerful court of justice, in vindication of a law which he does not understand and cannot possibly obey. Because the world of men torments him, K. tries to find solace in the company of women, but with them he is generally fumbling and ineffective. He clings as long as he can to the public, rational world of business and banking, but these defenses crumble as the trial goes on. In the end, the court destroys him.

Another psychological approach sees *The Trial* as if it were a nightmare and interprets it accordingly. There are many scenes that are particularly dreamlike: scenes in which trivial or mysterious acts seem pregnant with some ominous meaning, or scenes which blend and shift so that commonplace events become suddenly charged with terror. K. may open an ordinary door at his bank or boardinghouse or in some tenement house, and discover behind it a different world in which the Court carries on its work. Such episodes suggest the way in which repressed anxieties may break through the defenses of ordinary life, and open a door into unsuspected depths of the unconscious.

Some psychological interpreters go further than this, and propose detailed symbolic meanings for each episode. According to one, the bank where K. works is the conscious mind, the boardinghouse is the preconscious, and the Court, with its irrationality, infantilism and obscenity, is the unconscious. K. is said to be an anal personality, plagued by castration anxiety. Huld, the lawyer, symbolizes a psychoanalyst; Frau Grubach is a mother figure; the two warders who guard K. on either side are his testicles; and so forth. Whether the reader accepts these identifications will depend largely on his attitude toward psychoanalytic theory in general.

The theological reading of the book does not necessarily rule out the psychological, though it goes beyond that. It suggests that Kafka saw in his own inadequacy and guilt a parallel to the human condition, and that the story is actually a parable about man's attempt to find grace at the hands of a God who remains forever hidden. In this interpretation, *The Trial* is the most impressive indictment of God since the book of Job. K. is accused before the Law, in the eyes of which, as Saint Paul argued, no man can be justified, since all have fallen short of the glory of God. The Law expresses the will of a Court so unutterably beyond man that the highest judges are never seen, and their decrees, once they have been adapted to human ears, seem mysterious and even irrational. Man's contact with this Court is through a hierarchy of functionaries (representing organized religion) who are stupid, narrow, and corrupt. The Court's proceedings promise great things but accomplish little. Beyond these functionaries, to be sure, there lies the possibility that divine grace may break through, that man may find acceptance and justification from the highest judges themselves. But this possibility depends, it seems, on being able to accept the fact of one's guilt, and this K. is to the very end unable to do.

If this latter interpretation is valid, then K.'s failure is doubly tragic, for it is God's failure also. The Court, for all its omnipotence and omnipresence, leaves K. alone to carry on his daily routine. That is, it does not interfere with the freedom of his will. Rather it leaves him to work out his salvation as best he can amid the conflicting counsels of his many advisers. The Court cannot or will not penetrate K.'s mind, making him understand his true situation. At one crucial point the chaplain exclaims, "Can't you see anything at all?" and his cry is described as "the involuntary shriek of one who sees another fall." Man cannot save himself nor can God save him either. God and man reach out to one another, but they are so far apart that they cannot communicate.

A third and subordinate line of interpretation is possible: Kafka may be attacking the ponderous and authoritarian bureaucracy of the old Austrian Empire, smothered in self-importance and red tape. Kafka, as a minor functionary himself, was familiar with the ways of government. *The Trial*, however, is not an attack on the courts in the way *Bleak House,* for instance, clearly is. The details of court procedure in the novel may have been suggested by actual models, but they are only the symbols of the truth that Kafka is concerned with, not the thing itself.

The richness of this book makes it susceptible of many interpretations. Whether we read it in psychological, religious, or political terms, there is probably no book which so effectively explores the anxiety of our own age. Its critical reputation and its influence have continued to grow steadily. For the general reader who wishes to characterize a real-life situation that is a mixture of anxiety, frustration, dreamlike unreality, or sheer horror, it is sufficient to say that it is like something out of a novel by Kafka.

The Author

Franz Kafka was born in 1883 in Prague, then part of the Austro-Hungarian Empire. His family was Jewish though not conspicuously religious, and it was not until later in life that he felt any great interest in his Jewish heritage. In language and in culture, he belongs to German literature.

His father, Hermann Kafka, was a self-made businessman, robust, successful, blustering, and, in comparison with his son, rather coarse and insensitive. In Kafka's eyes, his father represented a kind of animal vitality and normality which he envied but could never achieve for himself. His feelings toward his father are most explicitly stated in a long (15,000-word) letter which he wrote in 1919, explaining with a wealth of anecdote and much psychological probing his sense of inadequacy in the presence of so overwhelming a personality.

Kafka was educated in the German-language schools of Prague and at the University, where he took a degree in law simply to postpone making a decision about his life's work. After graduating in 1908, he found a post in a semi-governmental office that handled insurance claims. Its chief attraction was that his work was over by two in the afternoon. His one real vocation was writing. To this he devoted all his spare time, becoming part of a literary circle which included Franz Werfel and Martin Buber.

Kafka wished to marry, but never did, partly because he

feared that marriage would distract him from writing, but more fundamentally because his relation with his father had crippled him emotionally and left him a prey to neurotic indecision. In 1912, he met a certain Felice Bauer with whom he contracted a tortured engagement which lasted, off and on, for five years. Then in 1917 he developed tuberculosis, an illness which he believed to be psychological in origin and intended to save him from marriage.

The war did not touch Kafka directly; he was exempt from military service by his official position and his illness. By 1918, he was spending much time in the country, trying to recover his health. He also began to study Hebrew and to investigate the world of Eastern European Jewry, with which he (as an urban and German-speaking Jew) was unfamiliar. His friend and biographer, Max Brod, insists that a more hopeful and affirmative spirit began to show itself about this time, but other critics, pointing to the unrelieved gloom of Kafka's writing, have accused Brod of wishful thinking. In the early twenties, Kafka had freed himself from his family ties sufficiently to go and live in Berlin. In 1923, he met and fell in love with Dora Dymant, a young girl whose family were Orthodox Polish Jews. Both families opposed the marriage, but Franz settled down to live with Dora in Berlin.

Kafka was thoroughly happy at last, but by this time his disease was entering its last fatal stages. Indeed, his euphoria may have been in part a symptom of the disease. On one level of his mind he wanted to live; on another the prospect of death seems to have given him some relief, as if it were easier to suffer in his body the struggle which had hitherto been raging in his spirit. In 1924 he returned to Prague and was placed in a sanatorium near Vienna. In June he died, and was buried in Prague.

Kafka in his life was known only to a few friends. His present great reputation is wholly posthumous. His instructions in his will were that the manuscripts of most of his stories, including *The Trial*, were to be burned. However, since his executor, Brod, had already warned Kafka that he would disobey his wishes, and since Kafka still retained Brod, we may wonder how serious the instructions were. At any rate, the stories were saved, and remain as a monument to a powerful and tormented genius.

Steppenwolf

by

HERMANN HESSE (1877–1962)

The Characters

Harry Haller—The hero, a man of about fifty, divorced and living alone on a modest independent income. He is torn between the rival claims of two sides of his personality, the one represented by the orderly life of a civilized and intellectual man, the other represented by the *Steppenwolf* (wolf from the steppes, or lone wolf), which is freedom-loving, savage, and at odds with society. His intellectual doubts and his spiritual despair have led him to the verge of suicide.

The Landlady—A motherly, bourgeois housekeeper.

The Landlady's Nephew—The author of the preface. A conventional person who has found his place in a bourgeois world. He is much attracted by Haller despite their differences in temperament.

The Professor—A former friend of Haller, a militarist and a nationalist.

Erica—A friend of Haller whom he meets rarely, and then only to quarrel.

Hermine—A call girl who befriends Haller. She is sympathetic, vital, and authoritative, and teaches Haller how to enjoy the simple, natural pleasures of life.

Maria—A prostitute who instructs Haller in love.

Pablo—A handsome saxophonist, an inarticulate and unintellectual sensualist who is bisexual and takes drugs.

The Man with a Signboard.

Figures out of Harry's memories and hallucinations:

  Rosa—A girl whom Haller loved as a boy.

  Hermann—A childhood friend whom Hermine resembles.

  Gustav—Another boyhood friend.

  Goethe.

  Mozart.

  Attorney General Loering.

The Story

The central figure of *Steppenwolf* is Harry Haller, a man approaching fifty, who lives a lonely life moving from one rooming house to another. He is gifted and sensitive, but melancholy, disillusioned, and antisocial. The preface describes Haller as he appears to the outsider, the nephew of his landlady: a quiet but eccentric boarder, who calls himself a *Steppenwolf,* or wolf from the steppes (freely translatable as "lone wolf"). His loneliness is not a private misery, however. It is an expression of the spiritual malaise of the times, the alienated and fragmented quality of modern life.

One day Haller pays his bills and disappears, leaving in his rooms a bundle of papers which the nephew examines and (convinced that they are of general interest) decides to publish. These records make up the remainder of the book. They bear the title "For Madmen Only."

Haller begins by describing his lonely, disorderly life, contrasting it with the comfortable routine of ordinary domestic existence for which he feels nostalgia but which he can no longer accept. Much of his time is spent in a quiet tavern, frequented by men like himself. One night as he is returning home after an evening of moderate drinking, he passes a door which he has never noticed before. It bears a sign *MAGIC THEATRE: ENTRANCE NOT FOR EVERYBODY; FOR MADMEN ONLY.* He tries the handle, but the door is locked. Wandering on, he meets a man carrying a sign on a pole displaying the same message. He runs after the sign carrier to get more information, but the man merely thrusts a little pamphlet into his hands and then disappears. The pamphlet is entitled "Treatise on the Steppenwolf. Not for Everybody."

The treatise proves to be still another account of Haller, written by a detached, impersonal, unidentified observer. We are told that Haller feels himself a double personality: man and wolf, the civilized human being and the freedom-loving outlaw from society. So great is this inner tension, we learn, that Haller has often been on the point of taking his life, and indeed is able to keep on living only because he has promised himself the luxury of committing suicide on his fiftieth birthday. This suffering, nevertheless, marks him as a superior being set apart from the ordinary run of human beings; he is the type from which spring artists, intellectuals, and social critics. Haller is wrong, however, in supposing that he is a twofold person. Actually all men have manifold potentialities, and the common notion that each of us is a single ego is quite false. The road to enlightenment or the "way of the immortals" is to surrender the idea of a central ego, to accept the multiplicity within us, and to expand the soul until it includes not less than everything. The best way to this condition is through laughter, the one force which embraces all the polarities of life and at the same time transcends them.

This treatise could only have been written by one of the "immortals" themselves, since no one else could assume such a lofty point of view. And having made this diagnosis of Harry's condition, it proceeds to the following prognosis:

It is possible that Harry will one day be led to this latter alternative. It is possible that he will learn one day to know himself. He may get hold of one of our little mirrors. He may encounter the Immortals. He may find in one of our magic theatres the very thing that is needed to free his neglected soul.

These prophecies are soon fulfilled, and just in time, for Haller's fiftieth birthday is at hand, the day on which he has promised himself release from life. As the moment approaches, however, the thought of death fills him with fear. While wandering through the streets, he again meets the sign carrier of some days before, and asks him with a wink if there will be another entertainment that night. The man, misinterpreting the question, suggests that he go to the Black Eagle, a dance hall frequented by prostitutes.

At this juncture an episode occurs which demonstrates to Harry how far he has become alienated from respectable society. By chance he meets an old acquaintance, a professor of comparative folklore with whom he once studied. The professor greets him gladly and invites him to dinner. The meal is painful; Harry is forced to behave courteously and exchange social lies with his host and hostess. Worse still, the professor, who is a right-wing nationalist, produces a newspaper article written, as he supposes, by a namesake of Haller, an article attacking the Kaiser, the army and militarism generally. Never dreaming that his guest is the author, he holds the article up to ridicule. Haller can stand it no longer; he declares angrily that he is tired of keeping up a polite pretense, that he is the author of the offending article, that he cares nothing for the professor, his scholarship or his politics, that he is a schizophrenic and that he is no longer fit for human society. With this outburst he leaves; the lone wolf in him has decisively triumphed over the bourgeois.

Wandering through the city by night in a turmoil of wretchedness, and still foreseeing suicide as the only cure for his pain, he finds himself by chance in the Black Eagle, the dance hall to which he was recommended earlier in the day. A pretty girl named Hermine takes him in hand, and seeing that he is depressed, cheers him up, gets him to eat something, and offers to dance. When Haller confesses that he cannot dance, she taunts him for wasting his time in study and neglecting the simple, natural pleasures of life. Haller is by now quite weary; as he sits in the restaurant he drowses off, and the dream that comes to him speaks the same message. He dreams that he is speaking with Goethe, who proves to be, not the solemn Olympian that he is usually represented as, but a playful, roguish old man, who fondles a woman's legs and tells Harry that he is too solemn.

The following week Harry has a rendezvous with Hermine. Teasing him kindly, she offers to take him in hand, to teach him how to dance, to manage his life and to make him love her. In return he must someday perform her one last request: when she desires, he must kill her. Haller dismisses this last condition as a piece of unlikely melodrama, and gladly accepts the rest of the bargain. A new life now begins for him.

Hermine brings fresh air into his life and teaches him to enjoy each moment as it comes, without being pompous or philosophical. Although he has always worshiped Mozart as the greatest of composers, he now buys a gramophone with jazz records and learns to fox-trot. He also makes new friends. One is a call girl named Maria, who at Hermine's suggestion becomes his mistress and instructor in the art of love. Another is a jazz saxophonist named Pablo, a handsome young man with a languorous, caressing manner and no morals. Pablo is a versatile sensualist with extensive experience both in sex and drugs. He generously puts himself at Harry's disposal for either purpose. The two also discuss music. In reply to Harry's defense of Mozart, Pablo answers that the qualitative difference between *Don Giovanni* and dance-hall music is of no importance since the only important thing for a musician is to play as well as he can and give pleasure to his hearers, whatever their tastes.

Under the instruction of these three friends, Harry learns rapidly. The climax of his new life comes a few weeks later at a fancy-dress ball. Hermine attends in a man's costume. Harry at first takes her for his old friend Hermann. After the dance, Pablo invites the two to his quarters for a little entertainment. It is, he explains, for madmen only, and the price of admission is Harry's mind. At last, Haller is to enter the magic theater which he has repeatedly heard of. The ticket of admission is one of Pablo's narcotic preparations: opium or hashish. When all three have come under its influence, Pablo holds up to Haller's gaze a small mirror in which Haller sees himself in a double vision, as a man whose features blend with those of a shy, beautiful, dazed wolf with smoldering, frightened eyes. This is Haller as he has hitherto known himself. Next Pablo leads him into a theater corridor where there is a full-length wall mirror. Standing before it, Harry sees himself in a hundred forms: as a child, adolescent, mature man and oldster, solemn and merry, variously dressed and quite naked. One form, an elegant young man, embraces Pablo. Turning from the mirror, Haller walks down the corridor, off which there open dozens of doors, each with an inscription like a penny peep show, promising a different diversion within.

Each of these doors offers the fulfillment of a thwarted or unrecognized aspect of Haller's personality. The first bears the sign *JOLLY HUNTING: GREAT AUTOMOBILE HUNT.*

Inside, he finds himself caught up in a great war between men and machines. In company with an old boyhood friend, he stations himself by a roadside with a machine gun and fires on each automobile as it comes by, shooting down the drivers and passengers in cold blood. The experience is exhilarating, and Haller exclaims, "Strange that shooting can be so much fun! And to think that I was a pacifist!" The next door reads *GUIDANCE IN THE BUILDING UP OF THE PERSONALITY*. Inside, he finds a man resembling Pablo seated in front of a large chessboard. Each chessman is a fragment of Haller's personality. Quickly and confidently the instructor takes the pieces and plays one game after another with them, running through endless combinations representing all the vicissitudes of life. Then sweeping the pieces from the board he passes them to Haller and tells him to play the game as he pleases. The third door reads *MARVELOUS TRAINING OF THE STEPPENWOLF*. Inside, Haller sees a tame wolf being put through a routine of idiotic tricks like a trained dog, even forgetting his own nature so far as to lie down peacefully with a rabbit and eat chocolate from his trainer's hand. Next, the wolf and the man exchange places. The trainer drops on all fours like a wolf and tears the rabbit with his teeth. In horror, Harry dashes from the room with the taste of blood and chocolate mingling in his own mouth. The fourth door is labeled *ALL GIRLS ARE YOURS*. Passing through, Harry finds himself an adolescent again, in the presence of the first girl he ever loved; but this time, instead of shrinking from each other, the two make love with youthful and natural innocence. Next he meets one woman after another, every girl he has ever loved or desired, if only for a moment, and every unexpressed wish finds its fulfillment at last. Only one woman remains: Hermine. Returning to the corridor to find her, he discovers himself in front of a sign reading *HOW ONE KILLS FOR LOVE*. He feels in his pocket for the chessmen which represent his life. In their place there is a dagger. Wearily he enters the last door. There on the rug lie Hermine and Pablo, naked and asleep in each other's arms. Remembering her command the first night in the dance hall, Haller takes the dagger and drives it into Hermine's breast.

The last scene is entitled *HARRY'S EXECUTION*. Haller stands before a dozen robed judges and a newly erected guillotine, ready to pay the penalty of his murder. Solemnly the prosecutor reads the indictment:

"Gentlemen, here stands before you Harry Haller, accused and found guilty of wilful misuse of our magic theatre. Haller has not alone insulted the majesty of our art in that he confounded our beautiful picture gallery with so-called reality and stabbed to death the reflection of a girl with the reflection of a knife; he has in addition displayed the intention of using our theatre as a mechanism of suicide and shown himself devoid of humor. Whereupon we condemn Haller to eternal life, and we suspend for twelve hours his permit to enter our theatre. The penalty of being laughed out of court may not be remitted. Gentlemen, all together, one—two—three!"

On the word "three" all who were present broke out into one simultaneous peal of laughter . . . a frightful peal of laughter of the other world that is scarcely to be borne by the ears of men.

At last Harry realizes how much he must still learn about life before he can accept himself; he has been ready to suffer and if need be to die, but he is not yet ready to live. "One day," he promises himself, "I would be a better hand at the game. One day I would learn to laugh."

Critical Opinion

Steppenwolf is not a novel of action or character in the ordinary sense, but a novel of ideas, in which philosophical and psychological truths are presented dramatically and symbolically. Since the main action is internal, dreams and hallucinations are as significant as "real" happenings. The theme is nothing less than a diagnosis of the spiritual state of modern Western society. According to the "Treatise on the *Steppenwolf*" (written presumably by one of the immortals, and therefore authoritative), the dominant type of man today is the *Bürger*, which may be translated as "citizen" or "bourgeois." The key to his character is that he stands in the middle ground between all extremes; he is equally incapable of asceticism or profligacy, and he achieves the preservation of his rudimentary self at the cost of all intensity of feeling. Consequently he is ready to conform and easily led.

In this bourgeois world the *Steppenwolf* is a perpetual outsider, the man who is potentially both a saint and a profligate, the man who longs for absolutes and responds to the claim of the unconditioned. Nevertheless, because of inertia or cowardice, he cannot break completely with the world, but makes some kind of uneasy compromise with it. Consequently he never rises to the dignity of tragedy. His destiny is more ignoble: to live in an atmosphere where he cannot flourish, and to penetrate all the disguises of the world without any compensatory counterrevelation.

Beyond both the *Bürger* and the *Steppenwolf* are the immortals, the few who have risen to a state of unified life in which the polar opposites of this world are no longer reciprocally exclusive, a state in which it is possible to affirm all aspects of life, flesh, mind and spirit without compromising any. Such men no longer cling to their personal egos. They are beyond self-affirmation. Instead, they have expanded and multiplied themselves until they have merged in the All. They include the saints and also the great artists like Goethe and Mozart. These men have discovered the secret of cosmic laughter, of an eternal gaiety which both affirms and transcends the world. As Goethe explains it to Haller, while the latter is dozing in his booth at the Black Eagle:

> You take the old Goethe much too seriously, my young friend. . . . We immortals do not like things to be taken seriously. . . . Seriousness, young man, is an accident of time. It consists, I don't mind telling you in confidence, in putting too high a value on time. . . . In eternity, however, there is no time, you see. Eternity is a mere moment, just long enough for a joke.

For Harry to rise to this condition he must learn to accept the part of himself that he has hitherto denied: the sensual and unintellectual. In this, his guides are Hermine and her friends. Another man might have found wholeness of spirit by other roads and other mentors. Harry's act in killing Hermine—or rather in fancying that he has done so—is an attempt of the old, unliberated Harry to crush his own sensual nature. It is a proof that he has only partly learned his lesson.

The reader may be of two minds as to the nature of Haller's visions. How are we to explain the unfamiliar door in a familiar wall, the man with the sign board, and the printed treatise which so unerringly diagnoses Haller's condition? Do these represent the supernatural intervention of the immortals? Or do they have a natural explanation as hallucinations stemming from Haller's unconscious understanding of his condition, released during a state of emotional stress and alcoholic intoxication? The question is ultimately irrelevant, since the meaning is the same in either case. Similarly Pablo's magic theater may be only an opium dream, yet it is nonetheless a source of valid insight.

Of all Hesse's novels, this is the most nearly autobiographical. The hero's initials are the same as the author's, and Hesse has also given his name to the heroine, the ambiguously bisexual Hermann-Hermine. Like Hesse, Haller is an intellectual approaching fifty, and he is divorced from his wife, who has been mentally ill. He is also a pacifist, and his writings have attracted the wrath of the German right-wing press. These parallels, however, are of no importance in assessing the value of the book; the reader will respond to it to the extent that he recognizes himself there.

The Author

Though he is one of the major figures in modern German literature, Hermann Hesse was cnly ambiguously a German. His grandfather was a Russo-German, a subject of the Czar living in Estonia. His maternal grandmother was a French-speaking Swiss. His father was a Swiss citizen, a Protestant missionary who had returned from service in India to settle in the Swabian town of Calw where he worked for a missionary publishing house. Hesse himself was a German citizen only from 1891 to 1923, when he resumed his Swiss nationality. His childhood was spent mostly in Calw, where his parents lived a simple, quiet, pious life, graced by a humanistic love of learning and a cosmopolitan experience of many countries and cultures.

Hesse was educated in Protestant schools in Switzerland and South Germany, but soon showed that he was not suited for a religious or academic career. A rebellious student, he went through a period of deep depression and even attempted suicide while still in his teens. After a brief apprenticeship to a clockmaker in Tübingen and then to a bookseller, he decided on a literary career and began to write in his spare hours. In 1904, he married and settled with his wife on a farm on the shores of Lake Constance, writing, raising his own food, and associating with the other writers and artists in the vicinity. From 1907 to 1912, he was an editor of and contributor to a weekly magazine *März*, which adopted a liberal and anti-militaristic policy, in sharp contrast to the prevailing temper of imperial Germany. In 1911, he visited the Far East, Ceylon, Singapore and Malaya, a trip which inspired a book of travel (*Aus Indien*, 1913) and which reinforced the interest in Oriental civilization which he had acquired from his father.

When the war came, Hesse was exempted from service on medical grounds and assigned to the German embassy in Bern to work on behalf of German prisoners of war. As the conflict continued, Hesse's disapproval of it grew, and he became increasingly outspoken in his demands for peace. Most of his German readers turned against him, and only the support of a few sympathetic pacifists like Romain Rolland saved him from complete isolation. Private difficulties multiplied as well. His son was seriously ill, his father died, and his wife entered a mental hospital. In desperation he sought psychiatric help himself and underwent a partial Jungian analysis, with the result that psychoanalytic insights and imagery began to appear in his writing. After the war Hesse settled in Switzerland at Montagnola in the Ticino. His first marriage ended in divorce in 1923; a brief second marriage was no more successful, but a third in 1931 proved happy and lasting.

Hesse's first writing was in the tradition of nineteenth-century romantic and impressionistic fiction. Two of his early books, *Peter Camenzind* (1903) and *Knulp* (1915), deal with the familiar theme of the youthful wanderer who finds himself at odds with the life around him. After the war Hesse adopted a new manner. *Demian* (1919) appeared under the pseudonym Emil Sinclair, and deals symbolically with the search for integration of personality. *Siddhartha* (1922) reflects Hesse's interest in the Orient; it describes the spiritual quest of an Indian in the days of Gautama Buddha. *Steppenwolf* (1927) deals with the efforts of a tormented intellectual to come to terms with the many aspects of his divided personality. *Narcissus and Goldmund* (1929-1930) is an allegory, set in the middle ages, of the conflicting claims of the ascetic and the worldly life. The last major novel was *The Bead Game (Das Glasperlenspiel)* or as it is called in the English version, *Magister Ludi* (1931-1942). This is set in the year 2400, and envisions a pedagogical community dedicated to the restoration of the unity of culture as part of the transcendent unity of God. Various ideas and cultural activities are symbolized by glass beads strung on wires and their many combinations form the "game" of the title.

The rise of Hitler and the Second World War left Hesse deeply embittered, the more so as his wife's family was largely wiped out in the Nazi extermination camps. After the war, he began to find recognition again in Germany as well as in the world at large. In 1946, he received the Nobel Prize for literature. His popularity in India and Japan grew rapidly, largely on the strength of *Siddhartha*, which has been translated into many Oriental languages. In the United States, he has enjoyed a steadily increasing reputation, although he has never found so many readers as Mann or Kafka. In 1962 he died suddenly and quietly in his sleep at his home in Montagnola.

And Quiet Flows
the Don

by

MIKHAIL ALEXANDROVICH SHOLOKHOV
(1905–   )

The Characters *

THE MELEKHOVS

Prokoffey—A Cossack veteran of the Russo-Turkish War, married to a Turkish woman.

Pantaleimon Prokoffievich—His son, a sturdy old peasant with a hot temper.

Ilinichna—Pantaleimon's corpulent wife.

Piotra Pantalievich—Pantaleimon's elder son, stocky, fair-haired, good-natured.

Gregor Pantalievich (Grishka)—The younger son.

Dunia—Pantaleimon's daughter and favorite child.

Daria—Piotra's wife.

THE KORSHUNOVS

Grishaka—An old veteran, respected for his honesty and hospitality.

Miron—His son, a well-to-do farmer.

---

* See Note on Russian Names, p. 173.

Maria Lukinichna—Miron's wife.

Mitka Mironovich—Miron's son, shifty and quarrelsome.

Natalia (Natashka, Natiushka)—Miron's beautiful young daughter, later wife of Gregor Melekhov.

THE ASTAKHOVS

Stepan—Neighbor of the Melekhovs, brutal to his wife.

Aksinia—Stepan's wife, hot-tempered and sexually passionate.

Tania—Aksinia's illegitimate daughter by Gregor.

OTHER PEASANTS AND VILLAGERS

Boyarishkin—A technical student, one of the local intelligentsia.

David—A mill worker, later a Bolshevik.

Filka—A shoemaker.

Getka—Servant of Miron Korshunov.

Ivan Alexievich Kotliarov—Engineer at Mokhov's mill.

Lukieshka—Stockman's landlady.

Fyodor Manitsov—Village ataman.

Sergei Mokhov—A wealthy merchant and landowner.

Anna—Mokhov's second wife, a childless, irritable woman.

Vladimir Sergeivich—Mokhov's son, a sullen, vindictive boy.

Elizabieta—Mokhov's daughter, an undisciplined adolescent.

Timofei—A mill hand.

Valet—A scalesman at Mokhov's mill, later a Bolshevik.

Aunt Vasilisa—A matchmaker, cousin of Ilinichna.

Father Vissarion—The village priest.

Yemelin—Mokhov's coachman.

Servants in General Listnitsky's household—Benyamin, Lukesia, Nikitich, Tikhon.

BOLSHEVIKS AND OTHER REVOLUTIONARIES

Abramson—An organizer.

Ilia Bunchuk—A machine gunner and a dedicated Bolshevik.

Members of Bunchuk's Machine-Gun Detachment—Bogovoi, Gievorkiantz, Khvilichko, Krutogorov, Mikhalidze, Rebinder, Stepanov.

Garanzha—A Ukrainian soldier whose revolutionary talk greatly influences Gregor.

Golubov—A captain in the Don Revolutionary Army, a hectoring, bullying disciplinarian.

Mikhail Krivoshlikov—Secretary of the Don Revolutionary Committee.

Ivan Lagutin—A member of the Don Revolutionary Committee.

Mrikhin—A Cossack.

Fiodor Podtielkov—Chairman of the Don Revolutionary Committee.

Anna Pogoodko—A Jewish student, in love with Bunchuk.

Stockman—A locksmith and a Bolshevik agitator; patient, persuasive and self-possessed.

Officers and Counterrevolutionaries

General Mikhail Vasilievich Alexiev—Chief of staff under Kerenski, later a supporter of Kornilov.

General Zakhar Akimovich Alferov—Regional ataman of the upper Don.

Colonel Chornetsov—Executed by Golubov and Podtielkov.

Captain Izvarin—A Cossack nationalist.

General Alexei Maximovich Kaledin—Ataman of the Don Cossacks.

General Lavr Georgyevich Kornilov—Leader of a putsch against Kerenski, subsequently a commander of the counter-revolutionary army.

Fiodor Dmitrievich Likhovidov—District ataman at Migulinsk.

General Nikolai Alexievich Listnitsky—A retired officer and hero of the Russo-Turkish War, living as a widower near Tatarsk, a forceful, old-fashioned type.

Eugene Listnitsky—His son.

General Nazarov—Provincial ataman at Novocherkass.

General Popov—Successor to Kaledin as ataman of the Don Cossacks.

Sidorin—Popov's chief of staff.

Lieutenant Spiridonov—The officer who executes Podtielkov.

Others—Lieutenant Atarshchikov, Lieutenant Chubov, Captain Kalmikov, General Krimov, Captain Malmikov, Lieutenant Merkulov.

COSSACKS

Griaznov—A notorious horse stealer.

Avdeich Senilin—A boaster.

Alexei Shamil—A one-armed man, but a powerful fighter.

Simion—A Cossack of Sietrakov, who defies a detachment of Bolshevik soldiers.

Uriupin—A cold-blooded killer.

Other Cossacks—Anikushka, Fiodot Bodovskov, Bogatriev, Nikita Dugin, Emelian Groshev, Mikhail Ivankov, Matvei Kashulin, Zakhar Koroliov, Kozma Kruchkov, Martin Shamil, Prokhor Shamil, Shchegolov, Christonia Tokin, Ivan Tomilin, Yegor Zharkov, Prodhor Zikov.

The Story

The Cossacks were descendants of outlaws and refugees who fled from serfdom in the sixteenth and seventeenth centuries, settling in outlying parts of the Russian empire where they maintained a semi-independent status under their atamans or elected leaders. The government respected their autonomy and used them as a privileged and professional military caste, allowing them to serve in the Russian Army under their own officers and to maintain their own proud traditions. When their term of service was over, they would return as farmers to their villages where they kept themselves apart from the Russian peasantry. In the early days, they were leaders in many popular revolts under Stenka Razin, Pugachev, and others. Later they became conservatives and a major prop of a reactionary government. During the Civil War, many supported the counterrevolution. Afterward they lost their privileged status. Sholokhov's novel is centered around the experiences of a young Cossack from the Don basin named Gregor Melekhov. The events cover some five or six years, ending in 1918.

PART I. PEACE

Part I begins just before the First World War and shows the life of a typical Cossack village, Tatarsk, a life which, as in most peasant societies, is archaic and changeless. Gregor Melekhov lives on the ancestral farm with his parents, sister, and married brother. He is carrying on an affair with Aksinia, the wife of his neighbor Stepan Astakhov, who is away on military service. His father, Pantaleimon Melekhov, arranges a marriage between Gregor and Natalia, the daughter of a wealthy Cossack farmer. Natalia is a loyal wife, but cold and sexually unawakened, and after a few months of marriage, Gregor drifts back to Aksinia. Matters become tense when Stepan returns home, threatening vengeance on Gregor. The lovers run away and take service in the household of General Listnitsky, a retired army officer. Here Aksinia bears Gregor's child. Natalia, meanwhile, unable to win back her husband, attempts suicide with a scythe, but only succeeds in severely wounding herself. Gregor is called up for military service as the Russian Army mobilizes for the struggle with Germany.

Part II. War

The Cossacks of Tatarsk see active service very quickly. Gregor is revolted by his first engagement, a cavalry charge in which he kills an Austrian officer, but in time he becomes hardened to scenes of violence. He is wounded several times and once is erroneously reported dead. While he is convalescent, his illegitimate daughter, Tania, dies of diphtheria, and Aksinia, lonely and miserable, allows herself to be seduced by Eugene Listnitsky, the son of the general. When Gregor recovers, he returns home on leave, breaks with Aksinia, gives Eugene a beating, and is reconciled with Natalia. After he returns to his regiment, Natalia bears twins.

As the war continues, discontent spreads through the army, which becomes a fertile field for revolutionary propaganda. One of the Bolshevik soldiers, a volunteer named Ilia Bunchuk, has joined the army to learn the art of war as a machine gunner. He hopes to use his knowledge when, as he anticipates, the war with Germany turns into a civil war. There are many signs of unrest. Surreptitious leaflets calling for peace begin to appear. Gregor becomes disillusioned with a war which seems to benefit only the wealthy classes.

PART III. REVOLUTION

In 1917 the Czar abdicates and Kerenski comes to power. As unrest spreads, some groups, like the Bolsheviks, call for immediate peace, while conservatives like General Kornilov call for continuing the war. A three-way struggle begins between Kornilov, Kerenski, and the Bolsheviks (Sholokhov never mentions the Mensheviks) in which the loyalties of the Cossacks become confused. Kornilov orders the Cossack regiments to march on Petrograd. Bunchuk is able to persuade them not to advance. The Kornilov putsch loses its impetus, while, in the capital, where the Bolsheviks are strongest, the Cossack guard outside the Winter Palace leaves its post. Revolution breaks out in Petrograd. In the Don basin the Cossack leaders hope to take advantage of the turmoil by establishing an independent Cossack republic. Gregor is by this time an officer, confused in his loyalties, but weary of the war and inclining to the Bolshevik side.

PART IV. CIVIL WAR

The war has now turned, as Bunchuk predicted, into a civil conflict. In the south, a counterrevolutionary army under General Kaledin, ataman of the Don Cossacks, advances on Rostov, which is held by a Revolutionary Committee. Bunchuk is now in Rostov organizing a machine-gun unit. One of his trainees is a Jewish girl, Anna Pogoodko, who combines pure revolutionary ardor with the courage of an Amazon. She is obviously the perfect match for Bunchuk, who falls in love with her. Most of the Cossacks, meanwhile, care neither for revolution nor counterrevolution. They simply want to go home. Gregor is by this time serving with the revolutionary forces, though he is not a party member. He is, however, revolted, even after three years of war, by the cruelty and violence which he witnesses. In particular he is shocked when Podtielkov and Golubov, members of the Don Revolutionary Committee, kill a group of captured officers in cold blood. Finally he leaves his unit and returns to Tatarsk, where Natalia and his children make him welcome.

The Don area is now in chaos. General Kaledin commits suicide, the Germans advance on Rostov, and undisciplined bands of Bolsheviks wander through the country. One such band comes near Tatarsk and is wiped out by the local Cossacks, who set up an autonomous local administration. Gregor takes part in this effort, and his brother Piotra serves as captain of the Tatarsk detachment. Meanwhile, Anna Pogoodko, who is pregnant, is killed in a skirmish outside Rostov, leaving Bunchuk almost demented with grief.

The situation in the Don is now extremely critical for the Soviet government as the Red forces continue to retreat eastward from the Ukraine before the advancing Germans. Podtielkov, in command of a detachment of Red Cossacks, meets a group of Whites. He is outnumbered and his men have no will to fight further. No sooner have they been disarmed than they are treacherously executed. Gregor sees a retributive justice in this, but he takes no part in the killing. Bunchuk is shot, and Podtielkov is brutally and clumsily hanged, but before he dies he predicts the victory of the Soviet system throughout Russia.

Critical Opinion

And Quiet Flows the Don immediately invites comparison with Tolstoi's epic novel *War and Peace*. Both are long, panoramic works, set in a time of invasion and unrest, and heavy with their authors' social philosophy. Both are acclaimed by Russian readers as works which have recorded crucial moments in the Russian national experience in a classic and definitive way. The American reader will turn to Sholokhov for an opposite reason, because the events of the book are not familiar. Most people understand the main outlines of the Russian Revolution, but outside of Russia the average person has only the vaguest ideas about the bloody Civil War which raged in that country from 1917 to 1920. Sholokhov presents these events as they were experienced at the time by an ordinary soldier who was swept up by history, confused about the issues, and tried to live through the conflict without the clarity of vision which historical hindsight confers.

Sholokhov writes, of course, as a Communist, which means that he accepts the dictum that art must have a didactic purpose. A criticism of this novel might therefore begin by considering how far Sholokhov's handling of his material has been controlled by ideological considerations, and whether the book has been strengthened or weakened thereby.

At least four characters in the story are conventionally heroic Bolsheviks who, with their firm jaws, clear eyes, and purposeful stance, resemble the stereotypes in official Soviet art. Stockman, the patient and persuasive agitator; Bunchuk, the fanatically dedicated machine gunner; Anna, the emancipated revolutionary woman and finally Podtielkov, the courageous martyr, are obviously meant to be inspirational figures. Yet they are the weakest in the book, not because of their politics, but because they have no existence apart from their politics. Here, for instance, is a love scene:

> She stared with misty eyes at the snowy expanse . . . and her voice was low and crooning in timbre like a violoncello:
> "And besides, how poisonous and petty seems any care for the achievement of one's own individual little happiness at the present time! What does it signify in comparison with the uncompassable human happiness which suffering humanity will achieve through the revolution? . . . we must fuse with the collective group and forget ourselves as isolated parts."

Perhaps young lovers really do croon like that in times of revolution; if so, one feels sorry for them.

On the other hand, the four chief revolutionists are not organically related to the central plot, which deals with the Melekhov family and its fortunes. Pantaleimon and his children are real people, and, since their ideas lack the ideological clarity of Bunchuk's, the issues they face seem more complex and confused with the ambiguity of life itself. We see them at first in their daily lives, divided by parochial jealousies from the Russian and Ukrainian peasants around them. We see them go off to war with no great eagerness but sustained by their professional sense of honor. We see the community bled to exhaustion and eager only to return to normal life. We see their bewilderment during the Civil War, in which families are divided in loyalty, and atrocities are committed on both sides. Gregor sums up all these ambiguities: he is an ordinary person, capable in peacetime of treating his own dependents rather shabbily, but rising in wartime to unexpected heroism. He comes from a class which has many real virtues, and for which Sholokhov feels genuine affection, a class which history has made an anachronism. Gregor stands between the old order and the new, and actually fights on both sides of the Civil War. In the end, he wants only to be left in peace. That Sholokhov could create such a character is proof of his artistic integrity.

One difference between Sholokhov and the older Russian novelists is that he spends less time on the inner life of his characters, who interest him as sociological rather than psychological types. Consequently, there is a certain sameness about all the Cossacks. Piotra, Gregor, Stepan and the rest are all carved from the same block. Their lives offer little scope for individuality. True, one expects all peasants to look and act much alike, yet the same criticism holds true at all levels of society. One need only compare Listnitsky with Bolkonsky, or Kornilov with Kutuzov, to see how much more fully rounded and individualized are Tolstoi's characters in *War and Peace*. Similarly, Aksinia is a far less interesting adultress than Anna Karenina.

One should not overlook the significance of the title. Sholokhov has portrayed the life of the Cossacks and the violence of war against the background of strong, unchanging, elemental nature, which makes its mute commentary on the anguish of revolution and counterrevolution. The epic scale of the book is suggested by the spaciousness of the steppes and the sky above them, and by the Don itself, sometimes shimmering in the sun, sometimes swollen with flood, but always dominating the picture as it does the life of the Cossacks themselves. The Milky Way, hanging in the sky like a silver Cossack belt, is another image which appears often, suggesting that whatever else may happen, the processes of nature still go on. The novel closes on this note. The last scene describes the grave of a Bolshevik who has been executed by the Cossacks and buried on the steppes:

Later on . . . two bustards fought around the shrine. They beat out a little bare patch in the blue wormwood, crushing the green flood of the ripening speargrass, fighting for the female, for the right to life, for love and fertility. And again, after a little while, right by the shrine, in the shaggy shelter of the old wormwood a female bustard laid nine speckled, sky-blue eggs and sat on them, warming them with her body, protecting them with her glossy wings.

This image is both a summary of the book and a prophecy for Russia; at the same time it is universal enough to speak to all mankind as well.

The Author

Sholokhov knows intimately the area and people which he describes in his novel. He is himself a Cossack from the Don, and, like his hero, Gregor, he has a streak of Turkish blood in him, his great-grandmother having been a war prisoner. His father was a farmer and small mill owner. His mother was illiterate for much of her life. He was educated at state schools in Voronezh and Moscow from which he returned to his village at the age of fifteen, intending to become a school-teacher. Russia was then in the midst of civil war, and Sholokhov was caught up in it. He was given a clerical post by the Bolsheviks and finally became a member of the executive committee for his district. In 1922, he helped to fight the bandits who then infested the Don basin.

Sholokhov began to write at eighteen. His first book was *Tales of the Don* (1925), a collection of short stories. His chief work appeared in four stages: 1928, 1929, 1933 and 1938. It was hailed as an achievement of major importance from the start, and is undoubtedly the most popular work of Soviet fiction, inside of Russia and out. In 1933, he followed it with *Seeds of Tomorrow,* a study of traditional farm life giving way to a collective economy. In 1937, he was elected deputy to the Supreme Soviet. During the Second World War he served as a war correspondent.

For most of his life, Sholokhov has chosen to live quietly with his family in his native district, maintaining his contacts with the simple people he knows best. Recognition has come to him from everywhere. In Russia and abroad he is accepted as a novelist in the classic tradition, the heir of Gogol and Turgenev, Tolstoi, and Gorki.

Kristin Lavransdatter

by

SIGRID UNDSET (1882–1949)

The Characters

THE FIRST GENERATION

Lavrans Björgulfssön—A country gentleman; deeply religious, he had hoped as a boy to enter the Church, but was married at eighteen to a woman older than himself. Though he is a good husband, the marriage is not entirely happy. A gentle and affectionate father, he is forced by his moral principles to judge Kristin harshly for her affair with Erlend, and to oppose her marriage.

Ragnfrid Ivarsdatter—Lavran's wife, a moody woman, frustrated by Lavran's sexual unresponsiveness.

Aasmund Björgulfssön—Lavran's brother at Oslo, happily married with two children.

Lady Aashild Gautesdatter—A noblewoman, formerly close to the royal court at Oslo, a woman of great determination and force of character, she has real skill in medicine and reputed skill in magic.

Sir Björn Gunnarssön—Lady Aashild's husband; in his youth a fine and handsome man, but now listless in retirement.

Ulf Haldorssön—The illegitimate child of Sir Baard Peterssön and henchman to Erlend Nikulaussön, his first cousin once removed, a rough diamond, loyal to Erlend and a strong support to Kristin.

Trond Ivarssön—Brother to Ragnfrid, with whom he is on distant terms.

Sir Andres Gudmundssön of Dyfrin—A local magnate, father of Simon.

THE SECOND GENERATION

Kristin Lavransdatter—Daughter of Lavrans Björgulfssön and the heroine of the novel. Though deeply in love with her husband, Erlend, she resents his thoughtless irresponsibility. She judges him harshly and is never able to forgive or forget any injury.

Erlend Nikulaussön—Kristin's lover and husband, handsome and dashing, but impulsive, irresponsible and improvident. In his marriage he often wounds Kristin, but more through thoughtlessness than malice. He is quick to apologize and to forgive.

Ramborg Lavransdatter—Kristin's sister, married to Simon Darre.

Ulvhild Lavransdatter—Kristin's youngest sister, who dies in childhood.

Gunnulf Nikulaussön—Erlend's brother, a priest who acts at times as Kristin's confidant. He sacrifices a promising ecclesiastical career to serve as a missionary in Lapland.

Simon Andressön (Simon Darre)—A young man betrothed to Kristin, who finds him rather fat and prosaic for her taste. Later he marries Ramborg.

Sir Munan Baardssön—Son of Lady Aashild by her first husband, a somewhat ill-bred and loose-living man, but intelligent and influential at court. His wife is Lady Katrin; his mistress, Brynhild Fluga.

THE THIRD GENERATION

Orm Erlendssön—Erlend's illegitimate son by Eline Ormsdatter, a gentle boy who dies at sixteen.

Margaret Erlendsdatter—Orm's sister, a self-centered girl who knows how to wheedle her father.

Nikulaus Erlendssön (Naakkve)—Kristin's eldest son, a healthy, high-spirited boy. Out of loyalty to his brother

Björgulf he becomes a monk, although he is too insubordinate to make a very good one.

Björgulf Erlendssön—Kristin's second son. He goes blind and enters a monastery.

Gaute Erlendssön—The third son, who inherits the manor at Jörundgaard.

Ivar and Skule Erlendssön—Twins, Kristin's fourth and fifth sons, boisterous, adventurous, and undisciplined.

Lavrans Erlendssön—Kristin's sixth child.

Munan Erlendssön—Kristin's seventh child, the baby of the family, who dies in childhood.

Erlend Erlendssön—The eighth son, who dies at three months.

Andres Simonssön—The small son of Simon and Ramborg, a gentle and attractive child who has religious visions.

Arngjerd Simonsdatter—Illegitimate daughter of Simon by Jorunn, a servant.

CLERGY

Sira Eirik—Priest at Jörundgaard. Like many of the medieval clergy, he has a family. In his youth, he was a fighting man; in his old age he is a venerable and respected figure.

Sira Eiliv—House priest at Husaby and Kristin's principal confessor.

Brother Edvin Rikardssön—A Franciscan friar, a gentle and deeply religious man who is Kristin's spiritual counselor in her youth.

Sira Solmund—Sira Eirik's successor at Jörundgaard, a man of mediocre abilities who spreads scandal about Kristin.

Bishop Halvard of Nidaros—A venerable and intelligent prelate. He rejects the accusation which Sira Solmund makes of Kristin.

Lady Groa Guttormsdatter—The abbess at Nonneseter, a stout elderly woman, a firm administrator, but kindly toward Kristin.

Lady Ragnhild—Abbess at Rein, an unremarkable and somewhat peevish old woman, who conducts herself during the plague with great piety and firmness.

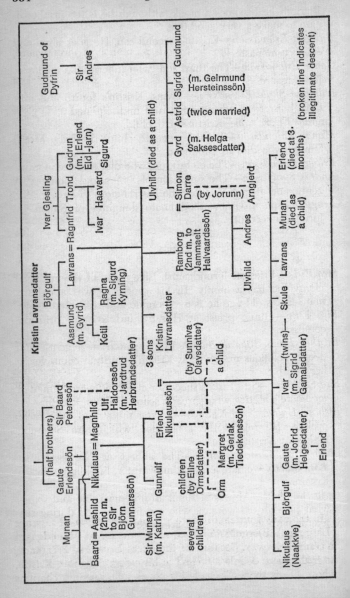

Kristin Lavransdatter

(broken line indicates illegitimate descent)

OTHERS

Arne Gyrdssön—A boy living on the manor at Jörundgaard, and Kristin's childhood playmate.

Bentein Priestson—Grandson of Sira Eirik, a coarse, violent man who tries to rape Kristin.

Ingebjörg Filippusdatter—Kristin's best friend at Nonneseter, a flighty adolescent.

Erling Vidkunssön—A powerful nobleman, formerly regent during the childhood of King Magnus.

King Magnus VII of Sweden and Norway (ruled 1319–1343) —A self-confident and autocratic young man, more concerned with his Swedish than with his Norwegian possessions.

Jardtrud Herbrandsdatter—Ulf's wife, an ill-natured shrew.

Eline Ormsdatter—Erlend's mistress and mother of two children by him, a handsome, passionate woman, driven desperate by Erlend's refusal to marry her.

Sunniva Olavsdatter—A married woman with whom Erlend has a brief affair.

Jofrid Helgesdatter—The pretty young daughter of a Bergen nobleman whom Gaute abducts, a strong-willed, hard-working girl.

Sir Baard Peterssön—An old knight, half brother to Erlend's grandfather. Ulf Haldorssön is his illegitimate son.

Brynhild Fluga—A loose woman in Oslo, at whose house Erlend has a rendezvous with Kristin. She is mistress of Sir Munan Baardssön and bears him several children.

Haakon Eindridessön—The lover of Margaret Erlendsdatter, whom Erlend wounds and cripples for life.

The Story

I. THE BRIDAL WREATH

In the early fourteenth century a gentleman named Lavrans (Laurence) Björgulfssön lives on his manor at Jörundgaard in central Norway. Because his three sons have died in infancy, he is the more deeply attached to his eldest daughter, Kristin, whose life is the subject of this novel. The opening chapters are devoted to her childhood: her life on the manor; her friendship with an older boy named Arne; a trip into the woods where she is frightened by a strange woman, believed to be an elfmaiden; a trip to Oslo, on which she meets a kindly and devout frair named Brother Edvin; the birth of her sister Ulvhild; and an accident in which Ulvhild is seriously injured by a bull. In general, despite occasional misadventures, her childhood is happy, and the atmosphere in Lavrans Björgulfssön's home is affectionate, orderly, peaceful, honorable, and devout.

When Kristin is fifteen, her father betroths her to Simon Andressön of Dyfrin, five years older than she. It is a promising match, though Kristin neither loves nor hates her fiancé. Her affections lie, if anywhere, with her childhood playmate, Arne, who is deeply in love with her, but is too poor to aspire to her hand. Arne is leaving the manor anyway. They meet, for the last time, in tears and say their farewells. On the way home Kristin encounters Bentein, the brutal young grandson of the parish priest, who tries to rape her. Kristin manages to break away unhurt and strikes Bentein down with a stone. A few days later, the news comes that Arne and Bentein have fought and that Arne is dead. Kristin realizes that he has died in defense of her honor. In her anguish, she asks permission to enter a convent school for a year or so, and Simon, who wishes to give her time to recover from her grief, readily agrees to postpone the marriage. Accordingly, Kristin goes to Oslo to stay in a convent at Nonneseter.

Kristin forgets Arne soon enough. In fact, she takes the money she has set aside for masses for his soul and spends it on a pair of gaudy shoes. Life at the convent school is pleasant, the girls are her own age and they are allowed to go about the town. On one of these innocent excursions, Kristin becomes lost and is helped home by a stranger, a handsome young man with winning ways named Erlend Nikulaussön. Erlend has a shady past. Born to wealth and good family connections, he has already squandered his inheritance and reputation. At eighteen he had an illicit affair with Eline Ormsdatter, the wife of a noble whose guest he had been. The king dismissed Erlend from court, and the two lovers escaped to Holland, where two children were born. Now Erlend and Eline are estranged, and, though his mistress has become a widow, Erlend refuses to marry her. Instead, he woos Kristin, who falls deeply in love with him and readily allows herself to be seduced. Then to her father's burning humiliation, she breaks off her engagement. Simon realizes what has happened, but honorably conceals the facts for the sake of Kristin's reputation. He soon consoles himself by marrying a wealthy widow.

Getting Lavrans' permission to marry Erlend is difficult, and Kristin mopes at home for many months. At last Erlend proposes that they elope, and enlists the cooperation of his aunt, Lady Aashild, a neighbor of Lavrans. Kristin obtains permission to visit Aashild for a few days, planning not to return home. While she and Erlend are leaving, they are interrupted by Eline, Erlend's mistress. There is an angry confrontation during which Eline tries to poison her rival. Erlend tries to force her at dagger's point to drink the potion she has offered Kristin. In a frenzy Eline seizes the dagger and stabs herself. The tragedy is hushed up and Kristin returns to her unsuspecting family.

Lavrans is finally won around to allowing Kristin to marry the man of her choice, though he considers Erlend completely unsuitable. Kristin celebrates her engagement by becoming pregnant, and the wedding takes place none too soon. Lavrans realizes bitterly that his beloved daughter has deceived him, made a bad match, and dishonored herself in the bargain.

II. The Mistress of Husaby

Kristin and her husband settle on Erlend's manor at Husaby near Nidaros (Trondhjem), and, thanks to her prudent management, the badly run-down property begins to prosper. Her new life is difficult. She is often homesick, and the neighbors gossip about her obviously early pregnancy. Erlend's two illegitimate children come to live with them, and Kristin manages to win the affection of the boy, a frail, quiet lad named Orm. After a difficult and dangerous pregnancy, her first child is born Nikulaus (Naakkve). When Erlend fetches Lavrans to visit his daughter, the two men are reconciled. Meanwhile, Kristin finds spiritual consolation in the company of two priests, Erlend's brother Gunnulf, and Sira Eiliv, the incumbent on the estate. As soon as Naakkve can travel, she goes on a pilgrimage alone and barefoot to Nidaros to obtain absolution for her sins, especially for her part in Eline's death. Her piety, however, cannot free her of bitterness against Erlend, who is a heedless, irresponsible husband with no understanding of her sacrifices for him. Their life is marred by bickering. Kristin's soul becomes a tangle of love and hate, guilt, fear, and stubborn resentment.

As the years go by, more sons arrive: Björgulf, who has weak eyes; Gaute, who is sickly as an infant; Ivar and Skule, the twins; Lavrans; and Munan. Orm dies of scarlet fever. Erlend serves for two years as governor of a military post in Lapland where his brother Gunnulf becomes a missionary. Simon, Kristin's old fiancé, now a widower, marries her younger sister Ramborg. Her father, Lavrans, grows old and dies a Christian death. Margret, Erlend's illegitimate daughter, becomes unruly, begins to receive lovers (one of whom Erlend attacks and cripples for life), and finally is married off to the son of a rich but unfashionable silversmith in Nidaros. Kristin and Erlend, though still in love, live stormily together.

After a time, Erlend falls into serious trouble. A number of the nobility are dissatisfied with the constitutional arrangement by which a mere boy, Magnus VII, has inherited the crowns of both Norway and Sweden. Under his rule a political vacuum has developed in Norway and the land is exposed to foreign domination. Erlend leads a rebellious conspiracy, with the ambiguous encouragement of a powerful noble, the historical Erling Vidkunssön. The plan is to force Magnus to divest himself of his Norwegian possessions in favor of his half brother Haakon. Unluckily, Erlend ruins his plan by carelessly showing his correspondence to Sunniva Olavsdatter, a married woman with whom, during a period of estrangement from Kristin, he has been having a brief and unsatisfying affair. When he finally breaks with Sunniva, she denounces him to the crown. Erlend's only explanation for his incredible carelessness is that he never knew his mistress could read. Erlend is arrested on a charge of high treason and tortured to make him reveal his associates, but he proves unbreakable on the rack. Finally he is released, thanks to the intervention of Simon and Erling, but his lands at Husaby are forfeited to the crown. He and Kristin must now live on the manor at Jörundgaard which she has inherited from Lavrans. The arrangement dismays Simon who, after saving his rival's life, now sees him and Kristin settle down as near neighbors. He realizes that he has never ceased to love Kristin.

III. The Cross

At Jörundgaard, Kristin again takes charge of an estate. Her seven sons grow up as sturdy, boisterous lads who worship their charming but shiftless father. Simon and Ramborg have two children, one of whom falls seriously ill. Kristin, now considerably skilled in home remedies, nurses the boy, and, when all else fails, cures him at the risk of her soul by means of a prohibited pagan ceremony. Erlend saves Simon's life during a brawl with some neighbors. Although the two men are now free of obligation to each other, Simon remains resentful of his rival, and the two become estranged.

Erlend's position is now especially hard; without lands or influence, and resented by the local folk as an outsider and a traitor, he must endure the humiliation of living on his wife's land. Kristin does not make matters easier. She forgives and forgets nothing and can never accept Erlend's sincere if facile expressions of remorse. One day after a bitter quarrel, she taunts him by saying that he is unfit to sit in her father's seat. Deeply wounded, he leaves the manor, vowing never to live on his wife's bounty again. Instead, he moves to a small farm high in the mountains, the one property he still owns, and lives there in lonely pride. With equal stubbornness, Kristin stays at Jörundgaard, although the boys from time to time steal away to meet their father.

Meanwhile, Simon continues to be troubled by his old love for Kristin, which he does not reveal to her, though he struggles with his feelings in the confessional. His wife, Ramborg, suspects and becomes sullenly jealous of her sister. One day, Simon is caught in a tavern brawl and receives a light flesh wound while trying to part two fighters. Infection sets in, and Kristin is summoned to tend him. The sickness rapidly becomes grave. Knowing that he is about to die, Simon speaks openly with her at last, and begs her for his sake to become reconciled to Erlend. Accordingly, after the funeral, Kristin goes back to Erlend on his mountain farm and is reconciled sufficiently to become pregnant once again. However, she refuses to live there permanently, and Erlend is no less stubborn about returning. He will not come down, even while his eighth son, named for him, is born and then dies at the age of three months.

The birth of Erlend Erlendssön starts gossip among the local folk who have not forgotten Kristin's earlier unchastity. The rumor goes around that the real father is one of Erlend's henchmen, an old and trusted retainer named Ulf. Charges are made by the parish priest; the bishop investigates, and the boys are provoked into armed violence in defense of their mother's honor. Erlend is summoned and comes to his wife's side at last. As he rides into the courtyard at Jörundgaard, he finds a hostile knot of neighboring farmers standing guard over Gaute, who is under house arrest. Words are exchanged, then blows, and Erlend is fatally wounded. Kristin tries to call the priest, but Erlend will not receive the sacrament from the man who has slandered his wife.

During her last years, Kristin devotes herself to her boys, but they are nearly grown now, and one by one they leave home. Munan dies. Ivar and Skule find service in other parts of the country. Björgulf goes blind and enters a monastery near Nidaros. Naakkve has until this time looked forward to a career of adventure as some knight's squire. Now, out of loyalty to his brother, he follows Björgulf into a monastic life, though he is temperamentally unsuited to it. Gaute remains on the farm and finds a wife, Jofrid, the daughter of a powerful noble from Björgvin (Bergen), whom he carries off without her father's consent. After a child is born, Jofrid's father is forced to accept the marriage, just as Lavrans had consented to Kristin's. Jofrid proves to be a thrifty and hardworking wife, but the inevitable tensions arise between her and her mother-in-law, so that Kristin begins to feel she no longer belongs on her own manor.

Her responsibilities to her husband and her children discharged at last, Kristin enters a convent at Rein as a lay sister. She wears a habit and takes vows though she does not make her final profession as a nun. In the quiet routine of the convent she finds a kind of peace, and begins to come to terms with her past life.

Then the Black Death—the bubonic plague—comes to Norway. The country is decimated. Naakkve and Björgulf die in their cloister, and many of the sisters at Rein as well. Those that remain on their feet spend their strength tending the sick and burying the dead. In a desperate attempt to avert the plague, many of the people revert to the old dark superstitions of pagan times. Word reaches the convent that a group of peasants are planning to conduct a human sacrifice: to bury alive a small child whose mother has just perished. Kristin and the abbess venture out by night, defy the would-be murderers, save the child, and bury the rotting body of the mother. Possibly from contact with the corpse, Kristin contracts the plague herself and falls fatally ill. As she reviews her past, she realizes that for all her misery, she has loved it all, and that there is not a day in it which she would willingly have foregone. She realizes, too, that God has not deserted her despite her willfulness and waywardness. She dies in peace.

Critical Opinion

Kristin Lavransdatter is a massive and ambitious achievement, tracing the lives of some forty major characters over four generations, against the background of medieval Norway six centuries ago. Of course, historical novels of the Middle Ages are no rarity—the English reader thinks at once of Scott—but as a rule such novels, though often very popular, have not been unqualified successes. The medieval novel of the last century was a product of the romantic movement. Consequently, it did not create a true picture of the Middle Ages so much as an ideal, imaginary world which was by implication a criticism of the ugly, prosaic present. Many of these books were populated by gentle knights, fair damsels, jolly friars, romantic outlaws, swarthy Saracens, *et al.*, all acting as if they had stepped out of some romance of chivalry. *Kristin Lavransdatter*, on the other hand, is a convincingly realistic picture of medieval life which is richly detailed but never strains after merely picturesque effects. Its characters, though unmistakably men of their own time, are driven by the same forces that we recognize in ourselves.

To be sure, Sigrid Undset had the advantage over the romantic generation in having access to the fruits of a century of historical research between Scott's time and her own. The daughter of a distinguished archeologist, she wrote with authority of the marriage customs of medieval Norway or its political institutions or church architecture. These matters, however, are not what we remember; the erudition is solid, but not showy or conspicuous. In the background, we are remotely aware of stirring political events—the union of the thrones of Norway and Sweden, the regency of Erling Vidkunssön, the scheming of the Danish adventurer Knut Porse—but they reach Kristin's ears only as rumors which she scarcely understands.

One reason that *Kristin Lavransdatter* seems so contemporary is that it dwells on those aspects of life which have altered least with the centuries. The life of the European peasant has changed far less than the life of the city dweller. Furthermore, Norway, even in the fourteenth century, never had a fully developed feudal system or court nobility. It was a society of sturdy country gentry, living on their farms surrounded by free yeomanry and self-respecting tenants, participating in their local political assemblies, and jealously opposing any attempt to impose an autocratic central rule. Lavrans Björgulfssön, descended from kings, is not ashamed to cultivate his fields with his own hands. This is not twentieth-century democracy, but in some ways it is closer to it than what existed at the time through most of Europe. Finally, of course, Kristin's role as a daughter, wife, and mother—the real theme of the story—is timeless. Women have always nursed their children, quarreled with their husbands on occasion, and worried over their sons' marriages. No reader needs historical footnotes to understand what Kristin experiences.

The realism of the book is not archeological but psychological, though the psychology is Catholic rather than Freudian. It does not probe too deeply into the unconscious. It assumes the freedom of the will, and it regards people as morally responsible for their actions. Within this framework the psychological analysis is searching. It spares us nothing of the emotional storms, the excruciating guilt, and the hard pride which Kristin feels. It certainly does not underestimate the importance of sexuality in human life. The characters are anything but static. We see Kristin in four dimensions, so to speak, over many years: a happy child, a rebellious daughter, then a bitter and estranged wife, and finally a woman who, while hardly a saint, nevertheless achieves real heights of Christian heroism.

The moral framework of the book is unequivocally Christian. The reader must be prepared to understand the Christian doctrine of sin in its full seriousness. Men are unhappy because they are sinners; this is the moral thesis of *Kristin Lavransdatter*, and if the novel seems somber, it is because sin is the habitual condition of natural man. We will not understand the novel unless we can recognize that Kristin and Erlend have sinned gravely. Their fault is not unchastity alone, so much as all the evil consequences that unchastity entailed: disobedience to Lavrans, stubbornness and deceit, cruelty to Simon, estrangement from Ramborg, involvement in the death of Eline. Even Kristin's love for Erlend, for which she sacrificed so much, is tainted by a hard, undying resentment which ultimately drives them apart. And finally, she has the bitterness of seeing her own son Gaute imitate his father's folly, telling her that she is in no position to blame him for it.

If this picture of life is somber, it is not ignoble. If all men are sinners, their sin is not the ultimate fact about them. The human scene is lightened from time to time by precious moments of godliness, true repentance, and divine grace. Lavrans, despite his occasional melancholy, remains a sane, kindly, honorable man largely because of his genuine, deep piety. Although Gunnulf, the priest, undergoes periods of spiritual drought, he seems a better and happier man than his turbulent brother Erlend. Kristin repents slowly indeed, but she yields at last, and her heroic death proves how far she has come from her willful, disobedient youth. Finally, there is the gentle, winning figure of Brother Edvin, who may or may not be a saint, but who certainly embodies the ultimate possibilities of human goodness.

Sigrid Undset chose to set her story in pre-Reformation Norway in part because the Catholic system could there be displayed in its unchallenged authority. In matters of religion, her spokesmen are Gunnulf, Sira Eilif, and Brother Edvin. Their lengthy conversations with Kristin provide the moral and theological framework by which her life is measured. Norway in the fourteenth century was only recently and somewhat imperfectly Christianized. Not only were Finns and Lapps in the North still heathens, but a number of pre-Christian customs still lingered on among the countryfolk, and men still remembered the pagan beliefs. Thus when

Kristin meets the elfmaiden in the woods, her father crosses himself but he is not enough of a Christian to disbelieve what she has seen. When Kristin goes to the graveyard by night to get earth to cure her sick nephew, she is observing a pagan ritual at the risk of her soul. Even the clergy are incompletely Christianized. In Sira Eirik and Naakkve we sense the untamed spirit of the Vikings under their clerical garb. The saint whom Kristin especially venerates is Olaf, the king who Christianized Norway, but who personified the heroic paganism against which he warred. Erlend dies unshriven, rather than admit into his house a man who has slandered his wife; he dies as an unrepentant pagan, rather than as a child of Christ. In short, if the Christianity of the novel seems at times austere, we must remember that the spirit of the old Norse days was still alive, and so robust that only an equally stern and heroic Christianity could subdue it.

Kristin Lavransdatter is not to be read quickly or lightly. A thousand pages long, it is also deliberate and slow-paced. The action covers forty years, leaving out very little. We experience the novel as we experience life itself: as a steady accumulation of events, the pattern of which gradually becomes clear in retrospect. The days go by in all their detail: Lavrans breaking in a colt, Kristin washing Naakkve's diapers, pilgrims gossiping on the road to Nidaros. Occasionally an episode occurs which explains at last the meaning of events of years before, occasionally the story rises to heights of emotional intensity, but the pace neither hurries nor slackens. As the reader shuts the book at last and tries to look back over the many chapters, he feels as if he were looking back over an actual life.

The Author

Sigrid Undset was born in Denmark on May 20, 1882, the eldest of three daughters. Her father was Martin Undset, a native of Trondhjem in Norway and a noted archeologist. Her childhood was spent largely in Oslo (then Christiania) where her father lectured at the University. She was not especially happy at school where the prevailing atmosphere—liberal, feminist and Socialist—was uncongenial to her conservative temperament. Her teachers hoped that she would go on to the University and distinguish herself in science or history, but Sigrid, who at this time had ambitions to be a painter, refused. Unfortunately, her father's untimely death left the family in difficult circumstances, and obliged her instead to attend a commercial school and take a job in the office of an electrical engineer. In her spare time, she began to write stories.

In 1911, she married an artist, A. G. Starsvad. He had three children by a former marriage and she bore three of her own. Two of the children—one stepchild and one of hers —became mentally ill, and the marriage ended in divorce in 1922. Of this difficult period she writes simply, "I wrote books, kept house, and took care of the children."

During these years she became increasingly skeptical of liberal culture, with its faith in progress, political reform, women's rights, pacifism, socialism, and national self-determination. The mild liberal Protestantism in which she had been reared had left her an agnostic, and offered her no support. Her study of history convinced her that liberalism was in error because it had misread the facts of human nature and underestimated the power of evil in men's souls. This frame of mind was not uncommon at the time on the continent, where other Protestants like Karl Barth were turning from liberalism to neo-Calvinism. Sigrid Undset turned instead to Roman Catholicism, and in 1924 was received into the Church.

Kristin Lavransdatter was written during the period of her conversion and is, among other things, a statement of her convictions as a Catholic. Men and women should not expect to be allowed to do as they wish in this life since for the most part they wish for the wrong things. Nothing can safely guide the shifting passions and the willfulness of sinful men except the will of God expressed in the teachings of the Church. In varying degrees, the characters of the novel illustrate this belief. Edvin and Lavrans accept it at all times, Erlend never does, while Kristin achieves it only with great suffering at the end of her life.

Sigrid Undset was awarded the Noble Prize for literature in 1928. Her next major work was *The Master of Hestviken* (1928–1930), a tetralogy set, like its predecessor, in medieval Norway. Her subsequent writings were a disappointment to her critics who felt that the didactic and moralistic element in her writing had come to dominate the artistic.

When war came to Norway in 1940, her home town of Lillehamar was devastated and her twenty-six-year-old son killed by the Nazis. She escaped to Sweden, was sheltered for a time by friends in Stockholm, and eventually made her way to the United States. In 1945, she returned to Norway and thereafter lived quietly in retirement. She died in 1949 of a paralytic stroke at the age of sixty-seven.

All Quiet on the Western Front

by

ERICH MARIA REMARQUE (1897–   )

The Characters

Paul Bäumer—The narrator, a German soldier nineteen years old.

Albert Kropp—A lance corporal and "the clearest thinker among us." He suffers a leg amputation.

Müller—A bookish soldier who carries his school texts with him.

Leer—The most experienced sexually of the group.

Tjaden—A locksmith in civilian life.

Haie Westhus—A peat digger. After the war, he plans to become a career soldier.

Detering—A peasant who thinks only of his farm. He deserts and is arrested.

Stanislaus Katczinsky (Kat)—The unofficial leader of the group of friends, about forty years old, with a nose for food and soft jobs.

Kemmerich—A young boy who dies of an amputation.

Himmelstoss—A sadistic corporal who torments Paul and his friends during basic training.

Paul's Family—His father, an office worker; his mother, who is dying of cancer; his sister.

Kantorek—The schoolmaster who persuades Paul and his friends to enlist.

Gerard Duval—A French soldier whom Paul kills.

Peter—A patient in the hospital with Paul.

Sister Libertine—A strong, cheerful hospital nun.

The Story

All Quiet on the Western Front (Im Westen Nichts Neues) relates the experiences of a group of German soldiers during the First World War. Four are straight out of school: Bäumer, Kropp, Müller and Leer; four more are older men of peasant background: Tjaden, Westhus, Detering and Katczinsky. Bäumer is the narrator. The only "plot" is a series of episodes, the experience of a combat soldier in any army: training, combat, furlough, girls, defeat, and death.

In 1914, with the outbreak of the war, Bäumer and his classmates are persuaded by a patriotic teacher to volunteer. The usual ordeal of basic training is made miserable by a sadistic ex-postman turned corporal. Once in active service, they become seasoned not only in combat, but in stealing food, griping about the war, sneering at younger recruits, and finding girls. Certain experiences stand out. Young Kemmerich dies of an amputation in a military hospital while his friends wait by his bed to take his boots, which he will no longer need. There is the joy of stealing two whole geese and surreptitiously roasting them. On the furlough home, well-meaning armchair strategists in the town cafés offer Bäumer drinks and tell him how to win the war. There is the grim time when Paul grapples with a French soldier in a shell hole, wounds him fatally, and then must stay by him for two days while the man dies. The day the Kaiser comes to inspect the unit, the soldiers are issued fresh equipment, only to have it taken away afterward. Little Peter, in the hospital, is carried off screaming to the "dying room," from which no one has ever been known to return.

These experiences isolate the soldiers psychologically from any world but their own. As boys, they have hardly lived, but their youth has receded into the unrecoverable past. Still they are not yet men with wives and families and jobs. Toward adult civilians they feel only resentment and a sense of betrayal: adults have made the war which boys have to fight. With their parents, too, they feel an unbridgeable gap. Even if one could explain to any civilian what combat is like, one would choose out of pity not to do so. Lost as they are in this no-man's-land of the spirit, they are able to create one positive value, the comradeship of shared suffering.

Then, one by one, the comrades drop off. One is shot through the lungs, another receives a Very flare point-blank in his stomach, a third goes insane. As the war drags on, despair deepens. The men have lost all hope of winning and are interested only in staying alive. Paul's best friend, Kat, receives a leg wound, and while he is being carried back of the lines for medical attention, a tiny shell fragment in the skull finishes him. Finally, in the last month of the war, October, 1918, Paul himself dies, on a day so inactive throughout the whole front that the army communiqué confines itself to the single sentence, "All quiet on the western front." On his face is "an expression of calm, as though glad the end had come."

Critical Opinion

The student who thumbs through the standard histories of German literature in the twentieth century for information about *All Quiet on the Western Front* is due for a disappointment. It is hardly mentioned. The critics speak of it patronizingly, if at all, as a poorly written book that became a best seller for reasons having nothing to do with its literary qualities. Nevertheless, this book is without dispute the classic war novel of our time. It is worth considering why.

It is a commonplace that Remarque is interested more in his message than in his art, a judgment which may or may not be true, and which is not necessarily discreditable if it is. Admittedly, bad writing is never to be excused on the grounds that it gives voice to fine sentiments. Nevertheless, there will always be some writers who move their readers less because they have technical craftsmanship than because they have something important to say. If their message becomes dated, their popularity will not long outlive the generation for which they wrote. If their message is of permanent value, they will continue to find readers.

Remarque is such a writer. His achievement was first to describe the experience of the common soldier truthfully and convincingly, and second to give voice to the mood of his generation, its disillusionment, and its longing for peace. Simply as an historical document, this book will always be important; it is still too soon to tell whether future generations will find that it speaks to their condition.

Certainly the novel is not memorable for its plot and structure. Remarque turns on the bloodshed as if he were turning on a faucet. When he reaches the end of a chapter, he turns it off. There is little progression or complication or deepening insight. Instead, the author's attention moves like a searchlight through the dark, lighting up one scene after another, ghastly, pathetic, or comic as the case may be, and then moves on. The episodes could be shuffled around without seriously disrupting the story.

The characterization is not remarkable. The various soldiers are on the whole rather shadowy. One is good at finding food, another is homesick for his farm, a third boasts of his exploits with girls, and so forth. But generally they are as alike as the uniforms they wear. Strange to say, the narrator, Paul Bäumer, is the vaguest of all. We see the war through his eyes but never really see him. Perhaps this featurelessness is to be explained by the circumstances in which the characters find themselves. Here are soldiers so young that their personalities are still unformed, who are first subjected to a training intended to suppress their individuality, and then hurled into a war which strips them of all nuances and subtleties of civilian behavior and reduces their life to the most elementary terms. In a sense, they have never had a chance to become characters. Still, the fact remains that other authors have created soldiers, from Henry Hotspur down to Yossarian of *Catch-22*, who are individually unforgettable. Remarque's soldiers are never more than representative types.

For the most part, Remarque confines himself to a simple, objective account of events, told without much complexity or variety of tone. The conversation moves on the ordinary level of soldiers' talk, purged of most of its characteristic obscenity. At times, the author steps out of his narrative long enough to moralize upon the fate of his lost generation, but these passages, self-conscious rhetoric for the most part, do not say anything about the story which the story does not say better for itself. Occasionally the tone becomes embarrassingly rhapsodic: "O earth, earth, earth"; "O life, life, life!" After such passages one turns with relief to the barracks discussion about whether the Kaiser has to go to the latrine like other men.

Undoubtedly the timing of Remarque's novel helped to make it a success. The Kaiser's Germany was dead and Hitler's Germany was not yet born. It was the era of disarmament and the Locarno Pact. During that short interlude in German history, an anti-military writer like Remarque could make himself heard. Furthermore, Remarque did not write only as a German. The experiences he described were the same on both sides of the battlefront. Paul Bäumer is able to see that the French soldier he kills and the Russian soldiers he guards are men like himself, and this universal sympathy undoubtedly is what makes the book acceptable to non-German readers. In Remarque's view, the war is not a battle between good and evil, or between the fatherland and the enemy. It is simply a tragic part of the common experience.

The Author

Erich Maria Remarque is a German descended from a French family which emigrated after the Revolution and settled in Osnabrück in Westphalia. His father was a bookbinder and the family was Catholic, not Jewish as the Nazis claimed. Remarque was educated in the local gymnasium and drafted at eighteen. During the war, he was wounded five times, the last time seriously.

After his discharge, he taught school for a time, but found the routine intolerable, worked for a while as a stonecutter in a cemetery, and then found more congenial work as test driver for a tire company in Berlin. He wandered into the literary world by the back door, writing advertising copy for his company, contributing articles to a Swiss auto magazine, then acting as assistant editor of an illustrated magazine on sports.

All Quiet on the Western Front appeared in 1929 after having been refused by several publishers. It sold 1,200,000 copies in the first year in Germany alone, was almost as successful elsewhere, and was made into a film still important in motion picture history. The success of the book brought Remarque wealth and fame and criticism. To escape the flood of unwelcome publicity, he settled in Switzerland in a house which he built in 1932 on Lago Maggiore. The rise of Nazism obliged him to stay in exile permanently. His books were condemned as unpatriotic, and in 1938 he was deprived of his citizenship. In 1939 he came to the United States and settled in California; he became an American citizen in 1947 and now lives in New York City. His present wife is Paulette Goddard, the film actress. Among his other novels are: *The Road Back* (1931), *Three Comrades* (1937), *Flotsam* (1941), *Arch of Triumph* (1946), *Spark of Life* (1951), *A Time To Love and a Time To Die* (1954), *The Black Obelisk* (1957), *Heaven Has No Favorites* (1961).

Man's Fate

by

ANDRÉ MALRAUX (1901–   )

The Characters

Gisors—Formerly a professor of sociology at the University of Peking; a man of wisdom and perception, but an opium addict, incapable of action.

Kyo Gisors—His son, half French and half Japanese, a serious and dedicated revolutionary organizer.

May Gisors—Kyo's wife, a doctor of German extraction.

Kama—Brother-in-law of old Gisors, a Japanese painter, serenely dedicated to his art.

Ch'en Ta Erh—A young Chinese, the graduate of a missionary school, now a terrorist in the grip of a lonely obsession with death.

Katov—A veteran of the Russian Revolution and Civil War, formerly a medical student, now an organizer of the Shanghai insurrection.

Baron de Clappique—A dealer in antiques and opium. He likes to invent stories about himself, is a compulsive gambler, and stutters.

Hemmelrich—Proprietor of a record shop, a conspirator who is made cautious by his duties to his wife and child.

Lu Yu Hsüan—Hemmelrich's partner.

Ferral—Head of the Franco-Asiatic Consortium, a financial adventurer with a strong desire for power.

Valérie—Ferral's mistress.

Martial—Chief of police in the French sector of Shanghai.

König—Chiang Kai-shek's chief of police. Being tortured by the Communists has made him vindictive and brutal.

Suan and Pei—Ch'en's accomplices in the attempt to assassinate Chiang Kai-shek.

Tang Yen Ta—An official killed by Ch'en.

Liu Ti Yu—Chief of the Shanghai Bankers' Association.

Vologin—A Russian revolutionary organizer in Hankow.

Possoz—Another Communist at Hankow, of Swiss origin.

Count Shpilevski—A Shanghai police official speculating in food.

Smithson—A Protestant clergyman, formerly Ch'en's teacher.

Others—A Kuomintang officer, a representative of Chiang; an antique dealer, a prostitute, a prison warden.

The Story

China, in 1927, was a nation badly divided. The republic which had been set up fifteen years before had given way to government by war lords, none of whom could dominate the country, though each could prevent the others from doing so. In the South, Chiang Kai-shek, leader of the Kuomintang or Nationalist Party, maintained a center of power which he was expanding northward. He accepted the support of the Chinese Communists and their Russian advisers, but, once Shanghai was taken, he turned against his allies. *Man's Fate (La Condition Humaine)* is set amid these events.

The story begins with an assassination: A terrorist, Ch'en Ta Erh, stabs an official to steal from him a document authorizing the delivery of arms from a European freighter to the local government. The Communists propose to use this document to divert the arms to their own use in an approaching insurrection. The murder accomplished, Ch'en joins his associates: a Russian revolutionary, Katov; a Franco-Japanese, Kyo Gisors; and a small German shopkeeper, Hemmelrich. After conferring with his friends, Ch'en goes off to relieve his tension by conversation with Kyo's father, a wise old man who was formerly a professor at the University of Peking.

Kyo and Katov also leave to arrange for the delivery of the weapons. They use as their middleman a seedy French baron, a smuggler and antiques dealer, Clappique. The negotiations are successful. Using the stolen papers, Kyo and Katov take possession of the shipment, and before morning the weapons have been distributed to revolutionary groups throughout the city.

The following morning we see the maneuvers of the President of the French Chamber of Commerce in Shanghai, Ferral. His task is to safeguard French interests and to see that Chiang Kai-shek, if he wins the revolution, will cooperate with the Europeans rather than with his present Communist associates. Ferral talks with the chief of the French police, negotiates with an officer from Chiang's staff, and extracts money from the bankers of the city to pay off the Kuomintang. His telephone brings him reports that one by one the strategic points of the city have fallen to the revolutionaries. That evening he relaxes with his mistress of the week, Valérie, whom he despises as he does all women. As a prelude to their lovemaking there is a short struggle of wills during which she wishes the light turned off and he prefers it on. He has his way, while gunfire sounds through the darkened city outside.

Meanwhile, Ch'en and his friends have been in the thick of the fighting. Shortly before noon, a general strike begins, followed at one o'clock by an attack on the precinct police stations. Many of these surrender without resistance; at others there is bloody fighting. Ch'en leads a particularly risky attack with hand grenades on one police post where he is caught for a time between the fire of the enemy and of the insurgents. By five o'clock, however, the insurrection has clearly gained the upper hand. The chief remaining pocket of resistance is an armored train manned by government troops. On the following day Chiang's army has entered the city, bringing up enough artillery to wipe out the last resistance. No sooner are the Kuomintang in control, than an officer demands of Kyo and Ch'en that the insurgents hand over their weapons to the regular troops. The Communists balk, fearing to put themselves in the power of their allies. Kyo and Ch'en decide to go for instructions to Hankow, a city up the river from Shanghai, where the Communists control the government and where the representatives of the Third International have their headquarters.

In Hankow, they learn to their dismay that the Communist high command does not wish a break with Chiang at this moment. It has agreed to the surrender of weapons, and the fighters of Shanghai will have to look after themselves as best they can. It is strongly intimated that comrades who do not submit to the judgment of the International have no place in the party. The two return to Shanghai. Kyo plans to keep the revolutionary cadres intact, despite his orders, while Ch'en, realizing that nothing can be done by group action, plans to assassinate Chiang. As they leave, they see a group of stevedores under Communist guard who have rebelled after working for three days without food. Kyo realizes that the parties of the right have no monopoly on injustice.

Two weeks later the Kuomintang, firmly in the saddle, has taken charge of the police system. A policeman, Shpilevski, passes word to Clappique that, because of his part in the seizure of the weapons, he should leave Shanghai within two days. Kyo is also wanted. At Gisor's urging, Clappique sets out to warn Kyo and also to borrow from him the money that will buy him a passage out of China. On the way, he wanders into his favorite night spot and becomes so involved in a game of roulette that he misses his appointment with Kyo and loses what money he has left. Panic-stricken, he manages to stow away disguised as a sailor on a ship bound for Europe.

Ch'en meanwhile has been preparing to assassinate General Chiang. As he waits with his bomb in a briefcase for the General's car to pass, he conceals himself in an antique store and pretends to be interested in old jade. At the crucial moment, he tries to dart into the street, but the shopkeeper, not wishing to lose a sale, holds him back and the moment is lost. Two associates also miss their chance. Ch'en dashes off and tries to take shelter in Hemmelrich's store, but Hemmelrich, with a wife and child to think of, does not dare shelter him. Concluding that a terrorist must act entirely without accomplices, Ch'en makes another attempt. This time he throws himself, bomb and all, in the path of the General's car. He survives the explosion long enough to shoot himself. He never knows the car was a decoy. Chiang has escaped again.

Ferral, meanwhile, is having trouble both with his mistress and with his business interests. Valérie, resentful of his attitude, leaves him for another man, unburdening herself in a scathing letter. Ferral goes to the nearest pet shop, buys every bird in the place as well as a kangaroo, takes them to Valérie's hotel, and, in her absence, releases them in her room. His anger still unassuaged, he engages a prostitute for the pleasure of insulting her. Then he leaves for France in the same ship as Clappique, hoping to find loans there to keep afloat his foundering business interests.

At length, a message reaches Kyo from Hankow that the International has changed its mind; the weapons still held by revolutionary soldiers are to be hidden from the Kuomintang or buried. Though the order is too late to be effective, Kyo goes to notify his associates. Since he has not been warned that the police are looking for him, he is quickly picked up, along with Katov and Ch'en's terrorist associates. The new chief of police, the sadistic König, proposes that Kyo work for him secretly. Kyo refuses and is sentenced to death. While awaiting execution, he manages to take cyanide obtained from Katov and dies quickly. Katov is now left alone between Kyo's body and the two terrorists whose fortitude is failing them. As conspirators against Chiang's life, they will not be shot but burned alive. Katov has cyanide hidden in his belt that will suffice for two men. In an act of heroic renunciation he gives the two precious pellets to the other condemned men and prepares himself for an excruciating death.

The last chapter is an epilogue about the men who survive. Ferral, in Paris, pleads with a syndicate of bankers for a loan which will certainly be refused. Hemmelrich, in Russia, is happy as a Soviet worker. Kyo's father, in Japan, is teaching. He is, however, broken by Kyo's death and finds consolation only in opium.

Critical Opinion

The subject of *Man's Fate* is stated in the English title; it is an examination of the various ways in which men meet their destinies. Its leading themes run through most of Malraux's fiction: the absurdity of life, the likelihood of violence and the certainty of death, the alternate possibilities of humiliation or human dignity, and man's heroic self-affirmation in the face of defeat. Kyo Gisors is probably the central character, but only barely so. He is surrounded by half a dozen other figures of comparable importance, each of whom chooses to meet his destiny in his own way.

Kyo, a committed political activist, has adopted his career gravely and consciously as other men decide to become soldiers or priests. He believes that Communism will make dignity possible for all men, his enemies as well as his comrades. His decision to return to Shanghai and continue resistance is the crucial decision of his life, made so that he will not break faith with those who fought beside him, and it leads directly to his death.

Katov's death is equally heroic. He is defeated, and the cause for which he fought has apparently been defeated as well. Nevertheless, he is able to give meaning to his death by choosing to carry the burden of suffering for two of his comrades. His act is an affirmation of human solidarity.

Ch'en is different. In his youth, he received a Protestant education which left him not with a belief in God, but with a Calvinist sense of man's vileness. Emotionally, he is cut off from his Chinese roots, and, after his first killing, he is plunged into a prison of spiritual isolation where even his friends cannot reach him. Now obsessed with death and torn by inner anguish, he plans his attack on Chiang Kai-shek not only as a blow in the cause of the revolution, but as a suicide.

Gisors is an intellectual who has insight but cannot act. He has a superb mind, and yet his wisdom has led him only to a conviction of the utter emptiness of everything. In different circumstances, he could have been a Buddhist monk. Instead he finds serenity in opium, which relieves for a time the burden of life's absurdity.

Ferral is an adventurer who has at various times been a professor, a politician, a diplomat, and a financier. His deepest need, however, is to dominate people or, failing this, to humiliate them. (His quarrel with his mistress springs from his need to assure himself of his power over her by reading on her face the transformation wrought by the sexual act.) At the end, we see him humiliated in his turn when his pleas for a loan are rejected.

Clappique, a secondary figure, at times almost runs away with the show. He is grotesque, frequently comic, with a need to place himself in the midst of marvelous and wholly fictitious adventures. Malraux calls him a mythomaniac—one who lives in and through his myths. When the myths collapse, he is reduced to near-insanity.

Hemmelrich, also a peripheral figure, is torn between his loyalty to his family and his comrades. He takes no part in the fighting until one day he returns home to find that his wife and child have been killed by Chiang's men. At last, he can fight. Eventually he finds a second and happier life in Russia, the author apparently not feeling that he was important enough to merit a more tragic fate.

Although this story is laid in Shanghai and deals with Chinese politics, the characters are for the most part not Chinese but rootless international wanderers or persons of mixed ancestry. Probably no novel set in China ever had so little local color. Shanghai was of course an international city at the time, but Malraux so strips it of individuality that it might be anyplace. What is local and particular is the historical context. The 1920's were that brief moment in the Communist movement after the Revolution had established itself in Russia and was still confidently expanding, but before it had hardened into the inhuman Stalinism of the thirties. It was still possible for intellectuals like Malraux to argue that Communism stood on the side of human dignity. Later, after the Stalin-Hitler pact, Malraux would claim that he had not deserted Communism, but that Communism had deserted him.

During the thirties, it was customary to read *Man's Fate* as a fairly orthodox revolutionary novel. Once Malraux had turned anti-Communist, it was easy to see what should have been apparent all along: that the cause of the Revolution, in the sense that Kyo and Katov understood it, was destroyed as much by the Third International as by Chiang Kai-shek. Kyo and his friends were pursuing an ideal far purer than the expediencies of practical politics, and when their moment of truth arrived they proved themselves to be, not disciplined party men, but individualists; a Marxist critic might even call them bourgeois individualists. They found themselves committed to something more basic than political success, namely their integrity and dignity as human beings.

The Author

There is no authorized biography of Malraux and a great many legends have accumulated about his name, legends which he has done nothing to dispel. Much of his life was spent in undercover activity in behalf of lost causes in far-off lands, so that naturally not many records survive. One important biographical dictionary even gives a wrong date of his birth. All accounts agree, however, that Malraux has combined the life of the intellect with that of action and achieved distinction in both.

He was born in 1901 in Paris. After a classical lycée education, he turned to the study of art, archeology, and Oriental languages. His father was a civil servant in Indo-China, where Malraux went in 1923 to hunt for ancient Cambodian statues buried in the jungle. The colonial authorities, however, prosecuted him for trying to remove a national treasure from the country, and sentenced him to three years in jail. The charge is often made that the sentence was really given because of his activities on behalf of the Young Annam League, a Communist-influenced political movement seeking political autonomy for the country. Public opinion in France was mobilized to secure his release, after a petition was circulated by a number of distinguished literary men headed by André Gide.

Two months after his release, Malraux was back in Indo-China, up to his neck in politics and operating an opposition newspaper. In 1925, he was in China doing propaganda work for the Communists, who were at that time collaborating with the Kuomintang. By the following year, he was sitting, along with Chiang Kai-shek, on the Central Committee of Twelve of the Kuomintang. In 1927, he was in charge of propaganda in Kwantung and Kwangsi provinces. The capture of Shanghai, however, as described in *Man's Fate*, does not appear to be an eyewitness account, though many have supposed that it is. When Chiang broke with the Comintern, Malraux left China.

He next returned to his old interest in archeology, collecting Greco-Buddhist art in Afghanistan and looking for the capital of the Queen of Sheba in Arabia. When the Spanish Civil War broke out in 1936, he hurried to Spain, helped to organize a

Republican air force, flew on missions himself, and toured the United States to raise funds on behalf of the Loyalists. These experiences inspired a long novel entitled *Man's Hope*. When the Second World War broke out, he enlisted as a private, was captured, escaped, served in the resistance movement, and was wounded in action. After the war he startled the country by transferring his loyalties to General de Gaulle and becoming Minister of Information in de Gaulle's first government. Since then he has written mainly on artistic and cultural themes, notably in *The Psychology of Art* (1949) and *The Voices of Silence* (1951).

Bread and Wine

by

IGNAZIO SILONE
(SECONDO TRANQUILLI) (1900–   )

The Characters

Don Benedetto—An elderly priest, formerly a schoolteacher, now in retirement because of his resolute anti-Fascism.
Marta—Don Benedetto's devoted sister.

FORMER STUDENTS OF DON BENEDETTO

Concettino Ragu—An officer of militia.
Nunzio Sacca—Formerly a youthful idealist, who has com-promised himself to become a career doctor.
Don Piccirilli—A priest, an informer for the ecclesiastical authorities.
Pietro Spina (alias Don Paolo Spada)—A worker in the anti-Fascist underground.

THE GIRASOLE FAMILY

Berenice—Proprietress of a hotel at Fossa dei Marsi.
Bianchina—Her niece, in love with Alberto Colamartini.
Don Girasole—Priest at Fossa dei Marsi.

The Colamartini Family

Don Pasquale—The only patrician in Pietrasecca, now struggling to maintain his ancestral estate.

Alberto—His son.

Cristina—His daughter, a pious girl who wishes to be a nun.

Other Residents of Pietrasecca and Environs

Cardile Mulazzi—A peasant who shelters Spina.

Magascià—A carter.

Sciatàp—An emigrant to America, returned to his village.

Matelena Ricotta—Innkeeper at Pietrasecca.

Cassarola—A "wise woman," *i.e.*, a dealer in herbs and magic.

Signora Patrignani—The village schoolteacher, a Fascist.

Brother Antifona—A Franciscan.

Residents of Fossa dei Marsi

Marco Tuglio Zabaglia (Zabaglione)—A lawyer, formerly a Socialist, now trying to ingratiate himself with the Fascists.

Don Senofonte—A druggist.

Don Genesio—A government clerk.

Pompeo—Son of Don Senofonte, a follower of Mussolini the Socialist, rather than Mussolini the Fascist.

Residents of Rome

Mannaggia Lamorra—A laborer who shelters Spina.

Romeo—A stonemason and underground leader.

Chelucci—A party worker, now in prison.

Luigi Murica—A student and party worker acting as a double agent for the police.

Achilles Scarpa—A con man whose specialty is "protecting" female tourists.

Uliva—A revolutionary disillusioned with revolutionary governments who turns to acts of individual violence.

Annina Pecci—A dressmaker, mistress of Murica.

The Story

In 1935, Italy is on the point of declaring war on Ethiopia.
The Fascist government is firmly in the saddle; all opposition
has been silenced or driven underground. Some enemies of
the regime have gone into exile, others have compromised their
convictions or have been forced out of their positions. One
of these last is Don Benedetto, an elderly priest, formerly a
teacher, who has been expelled from his school for being too
outspoken. Now he lives in retirement with his sister, still outspoken and still suspect.

As the book opens, Don Benedetto is celebrating his
seventy-fifth birthday with some former students. One has
become an officer of the militia, one, a priest, is now the
bishop's stool-pigeon, and a third, Dr. Nunzio Sacca, has
sacrificed his former principles for the sake of a medical career.
Their conversation turns to a fellow student, Pietro Spina,
whom Don Benedetto had especially loved for his independence and idealism. In another age, Spina might have become a saint. As it is, he has not even remained a Catholic.
The rumor is that he has become a Socialist and is now living
in exile in Belgium.

Shortly thereafter, Dr. Sacca has an unpleasant surprise.
He encounters Spina, who has returned to Italy to carry on
subversive agitation against the Fascists. Reluctantly and in
embarrassment, Sacca gives his old friend medical attention
and a disguise to enable him to leave town safely. Spina is
now metamorphosed into Don Paolo Spada, a priest traveling
in the Abruzzi for his health. At Sacca's suggestion, he settles
in the tiny mountain village of Pietrasecca where he can
remain unnoticed.

At Pietrasecca, Don Paolo, as he is now called, comes into
intimate contact with the people. His landlady, Matelena,
expects the presence of a priest to bring good luck to her inn.
Don Pasquale Colamartini, one of the landed gentry, now has
financial difficulties. Cristina Colamartini, a girl of sincere
if somewhat conventional piety, wants to be a nun. Bianchina,
a natural, warmhearted girl, is far from nun-like.

The episodes that follow are rather loosely organized. Some
are pathetic, while others have the robustness of folk humor.

As a priest, "Don Paolo" comes in especial contact with Cristina. He admires the depth of her faith, but chides her for its social irrelevance. To do God's work in the world, he tells her, men should not bury themselves in monastic seclusion. Disappointed in Cristina, Spina looks for a following among the peasantry, but soon realizes that his abstract theories of society mean nothing to the *cafoni,* a swarm of landless peasants who live in poverty, degradation and ignorance, but nevertheless have an earthy sense of reality which is wiser and healthier than the windy rhetoric of Fascist propaganda. The work of reconstruction, he decides, cannot start with propaganda; it must begin with simple, trustful human contacts which will break through the walls of fear and suspicion to form a community based on love.

Now that he understands more clearly what he wishes to do, Spina decides to take an active part in the political struggle. He leaves Pietrasecca for Rome, where he establishes contact with members of the underground who live like early Christians in the catacombs, in daily fear of arrest. Their leader is the stonemason Romeo. Another is Chelucci, who has been jailed for passing out pamphlets and has gone blind during his confinement. A third is Uliva, a disillusioned revolutionary convinced that all revolutions end by perpetuating the tyranny they were meant to overthrow. Uliva has turned from group activity to individual violence, and meets his death when some explosives which he has stored in his apartment go off prematurely. The most tragic figure is a little dressmaker named Annina, in love with another member of the underground, Luigi Murica. Murica was briefly detained by the police, and the experience of interrogation left him severely shaken. After his release he became increasingly agitated and withdrawn. One Christmas, the police broke in on the two lovers in Annina's apartment. Luigi escaped to the roof, while Annina bought his life by allowing the police to sleep with her. When Luigi came down from his hiding place, in his rage and humiliation he denounced her as a whore and abandoned her. Now Annina does not know what has become of him.

Finding his activity in Rome ineffective, Spina resumes his disguise as Don Paolo and returns to the Abruzzi. On the way, he stirs up a hornet's nest in the small town of Fossa dei Marsi by writing "Down with the war" and similar slogans in the streets. Since the country is mobilizing, the townspeople assume that the slogans have been written by someone from a neighboring, rival town in an attempt to discredit the patriotism of the local inhabitants. The only outcome of Spina's activity is that two innocent citizens of the rival community are arrested and nearly lynched.

On the same trip, Spina meets his old teacher, Don Benedetto, and the old man gives him his blessing, recognizing that God's purposes are sometimes better served outside the church than within. Back in Pietrasecca, Spina finds that the local peasants trust him. At their request, he serves as their confessor, even though he is reluctant to act in any unauthorized clerical role. One young man who comes to him is Murica, who deserted Annina in Rome. Overwhelmed with remorse, he confesses to Spina what lies even heavier on his conscience: during his work for the underground he was forced to serve as a double agent for the Fascist police. Despite this sad history, Spina accepts Murica, trusts him, and urges him to continue his work.

The book closes with Spina's plans in collapse. Don Benedetto, outspoken to the last, is poisoned while celebrating mass. Bianchina enters a house of prostitution. Murica is caught by the police and tortured to death under circumstances recalling the passion of Christ. Spina is obliged to flee from Pietrasecca over the mountains in heavy snow. Cristina, in attempting to follow him, is killed by wolves. Nevertheless, even in this defeat, Murica's death becomes both a sacrifice and a sacrament, a pledge that the ideal community of justice and love will someday be established. "If we live like him," says Spina, "it will be as if we were not dead. We must stay together and have no fear."

Critical Opinion

During Mussolini's rule in Italy, the policy of the church was distinguished more for its prudence than for its heroism. Fearing Socialism far more than Fascism, it quickly came to terms with the regime, so that in the eyes of critics like Silone it appeared that the church had not only entered a new Babylonian captivity, but was actually making love to its captors. It was easy to suppose that religion and social justice were incompatible. As Bianchina succinctly put it, "I am for liberty

. . . you as a saint are against liberty, of course." That phrase "of course" is a testimony to the dilemma in which many religious people found themselves, and which some could resolve only by leaving the church.

Spina is one of these. He is by nature intensely religious, hungering and thirsting after righteousness. In a schoolboy essay he once wrote:

> If the prospect of being displayed on altars after one's death, and being prayed to and worshiped by a lot of unknown people, mostly ugly old ladies, were not very unpleasant, I should like to be a saint. I should not like to live according to circumstances, environment, and material expediency, but I should like, ignoring the consequences, in every hour of my life to struggle for that which seems to me to be right and good.

When Spina later turns to politics, he loses none of this sense of vocation. His radicalism is not so much social or political theory as it is concern for actual human beings. He does not see the people as the proletariat, but the proletariat as people, as Magascià, Sciatap, Bianchina, Matelena, Luigi. In his contacts with them, he is trying to create a secular Christianity which in spirit is closer to the primitive Christianity of the first century than to the official ecclesiasticism of the twentieth. His ambiguous disguise suggests this. He is a priest yet not a priest. He exercises no clerical function, and yet Bianchina and the rest feel in him a sacramental presence. Don Benedetto recognizes that Spina has never broken with his boyhood ideals. In fact he suggests that God himself has gone underground:

> In times of conspirational and secret struggle the Lord is sometimes obliged to hide Himself and assume pseudonyms. . . . Might not the ideal of social justice that animates the masses today be one of the pseudonyms the Lord is using to free Himself from the control of the churches and the banks?

The symbolism of the book is an expression of this unbaptized Christianity. The death of Murica, for instance, is described in language strongly suggestive of the Gospels:

So they put a chamber pot on his head instead of a crown, in the yard of the military barracks at Fossa. "That is truth," they told him. They put a broom in his right hand instead of a scepter. "That is brotherhood," they told him. Then they wrapped his body in a red carpet they picked up from the floor. They bound him, and the soldiers kicked and punched him backward and forward among themselves. . . . That was how the judicial investigation began.

The bread and wine of the title are also Christian symbols: the bread and wine of the Eucharist. We first meet them in Chapter II as the food which Cardile brings to Spina as he lies on the straw of a stable, flanked by an ox and an ass. In Chapter XI, after Murica has made his confession to Spina, they eat the bread and wine in their silent meal of communion. And finally, after Murica dies, his father serves the friends of the dead man with the bread and wine made by Murica's labors, saying as he does so, in Eucharistic phraseology, "Eat and drink; this is his bread and this is his wine." Spina's reply makes the symbolism still more explicit, perhaps too much so:

The bread is made of many grains of corn. Therefore it stands for unity. Wine is made of many clusters of grapes, and therefore it stands for unity too. Unity of similar, equal and useful things. Hence also it stands for truth and brotherhood, things that go well together.

As if this were not enough, Murica's father and mother go on to point out that it takes nine months from springtime to the harvest or vintage to make bread and wine, the same nine months that it takes to make a man. In other words, the bread and wine of this meal are the body and blood of Luigi Murica.

The reader should not overlook other symbolic suggestions. Don Benedetto's name means "blessed." Cristina is obviously the Christian of the story, while Bianchina, though a prostitute, has a purity of her own (*bianca* means "white"). She plays the role of Mary Magdalene. The hero's real name, Pietro, and his assumed name, Paolo, are the names of the two great saints and missionaries of the first century, Peter and Paul, both of whom went to Rome and were martyred there. The hero's two surnames suggest his secular role as a political agitator: *spina* means "thorn" and *spada* means "sword."

Fortunately, there is more to *Bread and Wine (Pane e Vino)* than allegory. There are also richly humorous passages, especially in the delineation of some of the minor characters. For instance, there is old Sciatap, who has returned from America knowing only one phrase of English which he uses till it becomes his nickname: "shut up." There is the ironically named Marco Tuglio Zabaglia, the Marcus Tullius Cicero of his community, a windy old hypocrite much in demand for patriotic speeches. There is the no less ironically named Achilles Scarpa, who pays an associate to accost women so that he, Achilles, may win cheap glory in their eyes by rescuing them. He prefers tourists from hard currency countries. There is the patriotic schoolmistress who tries to explain to the skeptical *cafoni* that they have participated in an "agrarian revolution." And finally there are the *cafoni* themselves, whose one act of social rebellion is to urinate defiantly behind a bush hitherto traditionally reserved for the gentry. It may be that, in the long run, *Bread and Wine* will be remembered less for its symbolism than for its affectionate pictures of peasant life.

In 1955, Silone published a rewritten version of the novel in which the ending was considerably softened, especially the parts dealing with the tales of Bianchina and Don Benedetto. The changes were so substantial that Silone altered the title: *Wine and Bread (Vino e Pane)*.

The Author

Ignazio Silone is the pseudonym, and now the legal name also, of Secondo Tranquilli, born in 1900 at Pescina, an impoverished village in Abruzzi, on the eastern slope of the Apennines. His father was a peasant landowner and his mother a weaver. The district (as a character in *Bread and Wine* remarks) was never really Romanized; it speaks its own dialect, so much so that literary Italian was for Silone almost a learned language. The style of his novels shows the influence of the Abruzzese dialect. The language is Italian, but Italian stripped of its rhetorical elegance and reduced to something like the simple bluntness of peasant speech.

The most memorable experience of Silone's youth was the great earthquake of 1915, which devastated the mountain villages and killed fifty thousand people in a matter of seconds. Memories of this disaster appear in *Bread and Wine*, and it became in Silone's mind a symbol of the sort of apocalyptic destruction which, he felt, would have to precede any major renewal of society. Another formative experience was a minor riot against the local carabinieri, in which Silone took part. It afforded him the chance, at sixteen, to make his first political speech. The following year he left for Rome and joined the Young Socialist League. He brought with him a peasant's suspicion of authority, a provincial's resentment of the capital city, and, buried under his newly acquired Marxism, a thoroughly Christian longing for the absolute righteousness of the Kingdom of God.

For the next dozen years, Silone was a dedicated Marxist. When the left wing of the Italian Socialists broke away to join the Third International, he followed. The story of his career as a Communist is told in an autobiographical sketch available for English readers in a collection of similar statements by various authors, *The God That Failed*. There Silone states that his disillusionment with the Communists began in 1927 when, at a party meeting in Moscow, the delegates were asked to condemn a statement by Trotsky, a statement which no one present had read or was allowed to read. The French and Italian delegates refused their vote, and Silone returned, deeply depressed by this glimpse of authoritarian power in action. Some of this disillusion is voiced by Uliva, the embittered and lonely revolutionary in *Bread and Wine*. Despite his doubts, Silone stayed in the party a few years longer, but did so in an agony of inner conflict until he was expelled in 1931.

The most painful sacrifice which Silone's Communism cost him was the life of his younger brother Romolo. In 1928, Romolo was arrested on a completely false charge of trying to assassinate King Victor Emmanuel. The only evidence against him was that his brother was a notorious Communist. Romolo was actually a good Catholic, but in prison he confessed to being a Communist, not out of fear, but as a gesture of solidarity with Ignazio—to act, in short, as he felt his brother would have done. Romolo died after four years' imprisonment, and Ignazio's reluctance to quit the party was due in large measure to a desire to keep faith with the brother who had kept faith with him. There is a tribute to Romolo in the character of Berardo, the hero of *Fontamara*.

After 1928, internal resistance to Mussolini's regime virtually collapsed, and in 1930 Silone took refuge in Switzerland. After breaking with the Communists, he turned to writing fiction. His first novel was *Fontamara*, a powerful story of a mountain hamlet occupied, raped, and massacred by Fascist militia. The hero is a peasant, Berardo, whose political awareness matures under this occupation. Arrested on a charge of vagrancy, he meets in jail the leader of the anti-government underground movement in Abruzzi, the "Unknown Hand." Since police are looking for this man and do not know that they have him, Berardo confesses to being the "Unknown Hand." He dies under torture, while the other goes free to continue his work.

Bread and Wine, Silone's best-known novel, first appeared in Zurich in a German translation. It tells the story of the wanderings, the adventures, and the spiritual maturation of Pietro Spina, a political exile who returns to Italy to work with the underground movement. Its sequel is *The Seed Beneath the Snow* (1941) in which Spina, like Berardo, confesses to a crime of which he is innocent and is executed for it. It continues and develops the Christian symbolism of the earlier book, and gives voice to Silone's ideal of a community united not by self-interest or fear, but by love.

Silone remained in exile during the Second World War, but returned to politics in 1941 when he became secretary of the Foreign Headquarters of the Italian Socialist Party, and edited a party weekly. In 1944, after the Allied invasion of southern Italy, he returned to his own country in a plane provided by the American authorities. The story that he traveled southward down the peninsula disguised, like his own hero Spina, as a priest is a piece of romance.

Once democratic institutions were restored to Italy Silone became an active Socialist, edited the party periodical *Avanti*, and in 1953 ran unsuccessfully for the legislature as the Socialist candidate in his native district. Thereafter, he withdrew from active politics although still describing himself as a left-wing Social Democrat. His later novels are *A Handful of Blackberries* (1953), dealing with a Communist who becomes disillusioned and leaves the party, and *The Secret of*

Luca (1956), another treatment of his favorite theme of the man who suffers for a crime he has not committed. He is also founder of a review called *Tempo Presente*. His writings are internationally acclaimed and have been published in many languages. In general, his own countrymen have been the last to know about him and to recognize his ability.

Nausea

by

JEAN-PAUL SARTRE (1905–   )

The Characters

Antoine Roquentin—The narrator, a lonely intellectual whose disgust with life is the theme of the novel.

Anny—A former mistress of Roquentin, an actress growing middle-aged.

Françoise, "La Patronne" (The Boss)—A café proprietress with whom Roquentin sleeps.

Ogier, "The Self-Taught Man"—A petty clerk with a commonplace mind who tries to educate himself by reading all the books in the Bouville Library.

The Story

To distinguish, as we have done throughout this book, between plot, characters and theme is always arbitrary, but nowhere more so than in discussing Sartre's *Nausea (La Nausée)*. Here the revelation of character is the only plot; we are concerned not with the hero's actions but with his reactions. The novel is in the form of a diary written by Antoine Roquentin, a lonely intellectual without ties of friends or family or even of employment. Only a few facts about him emerge.

He has traveled extensively in Europe, Africa and Asia, taking part in archeological expeditions in India and Indo-China, but has lost his interest in these activities. At one time, he has had a mistress, Anny, with whom he has quarreled and whom he has not seen for years. At present, he is living in a small hotel in the provincial city of Bouville ("Mudville," possibly Le Havre), where he is doing research into the life of the Comte de Rollebon, an obscure eighteenth-century adventurer. His sexual needs are satisfied by a mutually agreeable arrangement with the proprietress of a nearby café, who has to have a man a day and who never says no.

This solitary self-sufficiency is disturbed by increasingly painful attacks of what Roquentin calls nausea: a total disgust with life, not merely with his own life, but with being as such. At first, the feeling comes only in flashes which pass without his understanding what has happened, though he wonders momentarily if he is going insane. Things seem to have a life of their own alien to his. Commonplace objects become strange, and he finds himself unable to pick up a stone or a piece of paper. He is able to dispel this sensation for a time by listening to an old jazz record which by its clean hardness is able to restore his sense of the familiar solidity of things. However, the feeling of strangeness can be held at bay for only a few moments. Soon it extends itself to Roquentin's own body, so that even his hand looks like a strange animal with an autonomous existence, a fish, or a crab wiggling its claws. He is overwhelmed by an intense and novel awareness of his own body which he feels is not the seat of a conscious, integrated personality, but simply a warm, viscous, indeterminate focus of life. At length, he finds that everywhere things have taken on an unexpected, unsettling character, as if they had become divorced from their names and from all their customary uses. The upholstered seat of a streetcar looks like a dead donkey floating on its back with its belly bloated. He murmurs to himself, "It's a seat," by way of exorcism, but the words will not attach themselves to the thing. Every object is nameless, grotesque, and purposeless.

In this world, nothing has any reason to be. No God wills or directs its activity. Things exist with a thick, fat, sensual, bloated, obscene exuberance which revolts Roquentin. Things are absurd. They don't obey any rules. They are *de trop*, superfluous, in the way. In such a world, anything can turn into anything else, since there is no law or logic governing its existence. What would it be like, Roquentin speculates, if a mother staring at a pimple on her child's face should see it turn into a laughing little eye, or a man should feel a scratching in his mouth and open it to find that his tongue had turned into a squirming, clawing centipede? Because the world is lawless and illogical, man is free to be and do whatever he wishes even though there may no longer be any point in doing anything. It is the revulsion against this total but meaningless freedom that underlies the existential nausea.

Despite his isolation, Roquentin's life impinges on that of others who see the world differently. His relation with the proprietress of the café scarcely matters. She is only a physical convenience. On the other hand, he is aroused to fierce anger by the spectacle of the decent citizens of Bouville, all self-respecting, self-important men whose lives are a constant attempt to conceal their true state from themselves. All their social rituals, their words like order and duty and rights, are unreal, an elaborate machinery of deceit. In describing them for the most part as statues in public squares or portraits in the municipal art gallery, Roquentin underlines the deadness and artificiality of their lives.

Another human being who keeps getting underfoot is a painful little pedant whom Roquentin calls "The Self-Taught Man." He is a bailiff's clerk who has humorlessly decided to educate himself by reading all the books in the Bouville Library. He attacks them alphabetically and after seven years has reached the L's, a procedure which Sartre apparently intends as a caricature of all rational systems which try to impose an extraneous order on the rich multiplicity of life. "The Self-Taught Man" constantly buttonholes Roquentin, driving him almost to tears with his tedious platitudes. He claims to be an idealist in love with humanity, though when Roquentin challenges him, he is unable to tell the color of the hair of the person seated next to him. Life catches up with him in a cruel way. It turns out that he is a pederast who gets pleasure from furtively caressing the legs and hands of young boys who frequent the library. The librarian, a fiercely virtuous man, drives him from the room in which he has kept life at bay for so many years. As Roquentin puts it, he now begins his apprenticeship in loneliness.

The one person about whom Roquentin feels any optimism

is his former mistress, Anny. If only she came back to him, his nausea might be dispelled. When he receives a peremptory letter from her requesting a rendezvous in Paris, he obeys, though more out of curiosity than love. In the past, Anny, who is an actress, had taken a rather theatrical view of their relationship. She demanded of it a series of what she called "perfect moments" in which everything—setting, mood and action—combined to make an artistic whole. Roquentin never understood what was needed to create these perfect moments, and she would never explain. She only made abrupt demands and then mocked him when the hoped-for experience did not materialize. Now she is middle-aged and growing plump. She no longer believes that perfect moments are possible. Her disillusion is rather like Roquentin's own, but ironically neither one perceives the change in the other. Existential insight, it would seem, is incommunicable, and all men are alone in their vision of reality. The meeting with Anny fizzles out, and she returns to the man with whom she is living, who means nothing to her.

In this anguished, meaningless life there is one ray of hope, one possibility of salvation: it is suggested by the jazz record which Roquentin regularly plays with such delight. Contrasted with the formless, pulpy, ambiguous, indeterminate existence which so revolts him, this melody is clean, impersonal, and rigorous. It is "washed clean of the sin of existing." The composer and singer have achieved their salvation in the purity of their art, and Roquentin wonders if he cannot do the same. His achievement would be a book, probably a novel, since the Comte de Rollebon and history in general no longer interest him. Perhaps, because of it, he might succeed in accepting himself.

We are left to speculate on what becomes of Roquentin. Does he write his book? Is this diary the book in question? The diary is prefaced by a fictitious "editor's note" stating that what follows was found among Roquentin's papers. What happened? Did he die? Did he commit suicide? Did he go insane? We never know.

Critical Opinion

When Sartre wrote *Nausea,* he did not think of himself as an existentialist since that term was not coined till about five years later. Philosophically, he belongs in the tradition of phenomenalism, a school of thought deriving from German thinkers like Husserl and Heidegger, which is concerned with describing the concrete facts of immediate experience. The phenomenalists are not interested in ideal forms, like Plato, or in things in themselves, like Kant, or in the Absolute, like Hegel; nor do they distinguish between objective and subjective experience, like the positivists. The world that concerns them is the world of things before they have been organized by the rational mind into systematic relationships and assigned names. The formula which sums up this point of view is that "existence precedes essence." In other words, the concrete object is logically prior to its intellectually apprehended nature. For the idealist the converse is true.

This phenomenalist view of the world explains many of Roquentin's experiences. For instance, if his hand appears to him as a fish or a crab, or a cushion as a dead donkey, it is because he is looking at it in its nakedness, so to speak, with no names interposing themselves between him and what he sees. A name forces us to see things in certain ways only, so that we cannot, for instance, think of a seat by that name without also thinking of its normal use as something to sit on; whereas if we see it only as an object by itself, any name is as good or bad as any other. Such an attitude enables us to set aside the ordinary laws of cause and effect which are, after all, only abstractions which the mind imposes on experience rather than facts of experience itself. Consequently, as Roquentin puts it, anything may happen. A pimple may turn into an eye or a red rag into a lump of squirming flesh. (Such transformations are also found in surrealism.)

The realization that life is fundamentally absurd forces Roquentin to reappraise his own past. He concludes that, despite his active life and wide travels, he has never had any adventures, since what is commonly called an adventure is actually the creation of the raconteur. He also gives up trying to write his biography of Rollebon. All he has succeeded in doing thus far, he feels, is to impose a speculative arrangement upon fundamentally incoherent facts. If he cannot resurrect even his own past, how can he do so for a man long dead? A similar insight underlies an ironic scene in which Roquentin sits in a café trying to read *Eugénie Grandet* while two people nearby carry on a conversation. The dialogue in the book is clear, orderly and logical; the words of the two diners are disjointed, elliptical, and almost unintelligible to the eavesdropper. The difference illustrates the function of art and of reason in imposing clarity and order on the brute facts of existence.

Convinced there is no reason why he or anything else should exist or, for that matter, not exist, Roquentin fiercely rejects all the purported answers which men have given the meaning of life. These are all dishonest. They are simply an expression of man's terror at facing an absurd universe where he may do whatever he wishes. Man invents rights, duties, causes and ideals to shield himself from his terrifying freedom. The people who live by these illusions and who lack Roquentin's sad, disabused lucidity, he calls *salauds* (pigs, bastards, finks). But there is surely an inconsistency here. If the existential view is based on immediate experience, the only truth which it can reveal is the truth for each individual observer, and there is no reason to prefer one kind of experience to another. It is obvious that most people do not suffer from disgust over the fact that objects exist. The man of common sense finds himself in an uncertain world and yet manages to get by somehow. Unless the existentialist can persuade us to feel as he does, his views have no claim on us, and a "system" of existential philosophy is a contradiction in terms. For this reason, the most influential productions of the movement are works of the imagination, like plays and novels, rather than philosophical treatises.

The English-speaking reader, who is probably more at home with the positivists than with the phenomenalists, is likely to press his criticism still further. Is not Roquentin merely psychotic? And if so, does his experience have anything more than a clinical interest for us? Certainly, his feeling of dissociation from his own body, his obsession with details rather than whole patterns, his fantasies that border on hallucinations, all sound rather schizophrenic. Some critics with a psychological bent have gone further and speculated about the private traumas or obsessions which may have determined Sartre's nightmarish view of life. To this attack, the existentialist has his own answer. The very attempt to write off Roquentin's nausea as pathological is itself an act of cowardice, an expression of the fear that Sartre might be right after all. Thus each party to the debate may be said to have undercut the other without finding any common ground on which the issue can be resolved.

A final appraisal of *Nausea* must therefore wait until our culture decides what it is going to make of existentialism. Unquestionably *Nausea* is one of the most revealing novels of our time, one which speaks to our present condition. Readers have testified, often against their will, to its compelling imaginative power. Still, the history of literature is strewn with novels once acclaimed as masterpieces that are now only period pieces. Many books which pretentiously enunciated some new philosophy are now read for qualities unsuspected by the author, while the great message is tolerated with a yawn. Sartre's work may be dimmed in another thirty years, and may undergo an eclipse. If it has any staying power, eventually it will assume its permanent place in the literary firmament.

The Author

Needless to say, the definitive life of Sartre is still to be written, and the student who wants to go beyond the ordinary facts available in standard reference works must rely on anecdotes and reports of interviews. Sartre was born in Paris in 1905, his father died when he was two years old, and his mother remarried when he was eleven. He was educated in Paris lycées and at the École Normale Supérieure from which he received high honors in 1929. After graduation, he taught philosophy in the lycées of Le Havre, Laon and Neuilly. He traveled widely in Europe and the Near East. From 1933 to 1934, he studied philosophy in Germany under Husserl and Heidegger. He also studied the works of the Danish philosopher Kierkegaard (1813–1855), perhaps the most seminal thinker of the existentialist movement. In 1935 Sartre settled in Paris, taught at the Lycée Condorcet, and attracted to himself a circle of youthful intellectuals. Largely through them,

Frenchmen became aware of such contemporary American writers as Hemingway and Faulkner. Sartre's first important work, *Nausea*, appeared in 1938, followed by an equally grim collection of short stories entitled *The Wall (Le Mur*, 1939).

When the war came in 1939, Sartre entered the French army as a private, and when France collapsed a year later he was taken prisoner. While interned, he wrote and directed plays for his fellow prisoners. After he was freed, he joined the French resistance movement and wrote for underground publications. The years of occupation saw the appearance of two important plays. *The Flies (Les Mouches)* was produced in 1943, and although its theme is rebellion against tyranny it somehow escaped German censorship. *No Exit (Huis Clos)* appeared in 1944; it is a study of three people in hell, their torment being simply to live with each other for eternity. *Being and Non-Being (L'Etre et le Néant*, 1943) is an exposition of Sartre's philosophy which is helpful in understanding his imaginative works of the same period.

After the war, Sartre emerged as the most conspicuous leader of the existentialist movement, in association with Simone de Beauvoir, Camus, Merleau-Ponty, and others. The movement was not only influential but almost fashionable. The Café de Flore, frequented by Sartre and his friends, became a tourist attraction, and some of his younger disciples threw themselves into the game of being existentialists with an exuberance that sometimes drew ridicule. Sartre's serious work continued, however. From 1945 to 1949 he produced a novel entitled *Roads to Freedom (Les Chemins de la Liberté)* in three parts: I. *Age of Reason (L'Age de Raison)*; II. *The Reprieve (Le Sursis)*; III. *Troubled Sleep (La Mort dans l'Ame)*. Some of his later plays were *The Victors (Morts sans Sépulture)*, *The Respectful Prostitute (La Putain Respectueuse)*, *Dirty Hands (Les Mains Sales)*, *The Devil and the Good Lord (Le Diable et le Bon Dieu)*, *Kean*, and *The Condemned of Altona (Les Sequestrés d'Altona)*.

Though Antoine Roquentin might have disapproved, his creator believed that men should become politically engaged, a faith to which he bore witness during the occupation and later as the founder and editor of the journal *Le Temps Moderne*. His view of history and society is Marxist, despite the fact that Marxism, which professes to find an objective pattern of meaning in history, can hardly be reconciled with phenomenalism. The Hungarian revolt shook Sartre's attachment to the Communist party. He is now described as a neo-Marxist, that is, an independent and unorthodox believer.

Sartre first found an audience in the English-speaking world after the war. *The Flies* and *No Exit* were translated in 1947, *Nausea* in 1949, and later works within a year or two of their first appearance. His influence has been greatest in those circles where Kafka and more recently Camus are appreciated. His plays and novels are more widely known than his philosophical works, which are addressed to professionals. Lovers of French prose will deplore the fact that in his more technical works Sartre has tried to teach the French to write like Germans.

Darkness at Noon

by

ARTHUR KOESTLER (1905–   )

The Characters *

Nicolai Salmanovich Rubashov—An old Bolshevik purged by
Stalin, an intelligent and dedicated revolutionary, capable
of independent thought.

Vassilii—A porter in Rubashov's house, formerly a soldier in
his regiment.

Vera Vassiliovna—Vassilii's daughter, an indoctrinated Communist.

Number 402—A prison mate of Rubashov, a Czarist, a former
officer, given to bawdy conversation, possessed of a rigid
sense of military honor.

Richard—A young German Communist expelled from the
party by Rubashov.

Kieffer "Harelip," Number 400—A young man who denounces
Rubashov.

"Little" Loewy—An organizer in a Belgian port who commits
suicide in 1935.

Ivanov—An old associate of Rubashov, now his jailer; intellectually they are much alike.

---

* See Note on Russian Names, p. 173.

Gletkin—Ivanov's younger associate, more crude, rootless, and uneducated.

Arlova—Rubashov's secretary and mistress, a phlegmatic but devoted woman.

Rip Van Winkle, Number 406—A former Balkan revolutionary who has served twenty years of solitary imprisonment.

Bogrov—An old friend of Rubashov, a naval officer.

Number One—Stalin.

The Story

The year is 1938, the year of the Moscow trials. Nicolai Salmanovich Rubashov, an old Bolshevik, a veteran of 1905 and 1917, formerly a member of the Central Committee of the Party, a commander of the revolutionary army and head of the state Aluminum Trust, a man with a keen and well-stocked mind which for forty years he has placed at the service of his party, has just been arrested. Now, after a night visit from the police and a hurried trip to prison through the sleeping city, he is left to himself and can examine his surroundings. There is only a tiny peephole in the door, but he can communicate with the adjoining cells by tapping on the wall in a code familiar to prisoners. Next to him is a monarchist, a member of an old military family and a defender of the traditional code of values. Though he is inclined to scold Rubashov for his politics, he is friendly and mainly interested in telling smutty stories. On the other side is a former revolutionary from a Balkan state. Released by his government after twenty years in prison, he hurried off to Russia, expecting to find an ideal revolutionary society. Perhaps he talked indiscreetly or tried to speak to men now in disgrace. At any rate he is in jail again. Down the corridor is a prisoner called "Harelip" whose identity is obscure.

Most of the time Rubashov is alone and he thinks back over his life as a trusted party official. In the past, he was ruthless himself. Once in 1933, after Hitler had come to power in Germany, he disciplined a young German party worker named Richard who did not follow orders from Moscow closely enough. Richard's expulsion from the party deprived him of the protection of his associates, and virtually condemned him to death at the hands of the Nazis. Rubashov himself had been taken by the Nazis, tortured, and then returned to Russia. Almost at once, he returned to Western Europe on a new assignment. Italy was at war in Ethiopia and the Russians were shipping war materials into the Fascist countries. The dock workers, who supported the party because they were anti-Fascist, tried to put an embargo on the shipments of gasoline and strategic raw materials, and Rubashov's job was to persuade them to let the Russian ships dock. An old party member named Loewy opposed him, was publicly denounced, and committed suicide. Next, Rubashov became the leader of a trade delegation in Berlin. His secretary and mistress, Arlova, was devoted to him. When the purges began, she was denounced as a conspirator. She appealed to him to exculpate her, but to save himself he remained silent. Now, he is awaiting the same fate.

After some days, he is called up for his first hearing. His interrogator turns out to be an old college friend named Ivanov who presents the case against him. He is to be accused of an attempt on the life of Number One (Stalin). Confessions from other conspirators are already in hand. However, these are only details. Fundamentally, his crime is that he is suspected of being less than enthusiastic about the present leadership. He no longer speaks of himself and the party as "we"; he says "I" and "you." Rubashov, incredulous that Ivanov believes the first charge, admits his growing suspicion that Communism has betrayed the Revolution. Ivanov proposes a partial confession, denying the main charge but accepting the accusation of antiparty convictions. There will be a trial, imprisonment, and eventual rehabilitation. He leaves Rubashov to think over this proposal, convinced that he will recognize it as inevitable.

Ivanov has a subordinate, Gletkin, a younger man who has grown up since the Revolution without the education and intellectual roots of Rubashov and Ivanov. Gletkin's methods are more brutal and direct. He has an old friend of Rubashov, a naval officer named Bogrov, tortured for three days and then led past Rubashov's cell on his way to execution. Hitherto Rubashov has thought of executions in abstract terms. Now he begins to see them in terms of human suffering. Arlova, he realizes, must have died like this. All the arguments which he had used to justify the political use of force and terror begin to weaken. The old logical equations

no longer balance out now that the human element has
entered. This development upsets Ivanov's carefully planned
program of psychological warfare. He quarrels with Gletkin
and tells him he deserves to be shot. Gletkin says nothing,
but remembers the words and bides his time.

Returning to the interrogation, Ivanov now argues with
Rubashov as one intellectual to another. He chides Rubashov
for his newly discovered humanitarianism. The party, he
argues, is the agent of historical necessity, and it will do what
it must do. Ruthlessness is necessary for the Revolution to
continue, as Rubashov, who has always been ruthless himself,
recognizes. Left to himself again, Rubashov decides to
capitulate. His ideal of a just, humane government, the ideal
that led him to join the party forty years before, is not to be
realized at the present juncture in history. Until it is, it is
reasonable to bow to necessity, to suppress one's own beliefs,
to set aside personal shame and pride as weaknesses, and to
do the one thing that may still be of service to the party.
He sends a note to Ivanov indicating that he is ready to sign
a confession.

There is a long wait. When Rubashov is next interviewed,
he finds that Gletkin has taken over. In fact, Ivanov has been
shot because of his lenient handling of the case. The investigation now becomes more brutal, and the old agreement
with Ivanov no longer holds. Rubashov must confess in
detail to a complex plot to murder Number One. The
principal witness against him is the prisoner called "Harelip,"
the son of an old friend of his. Rubashov must confess everything in open court. Rubashov's resistance is now aroused,
but after days of interrogation under glaring lamps, without
sleep and without letup, he gives in, point by point. He
admits to treasonable conversations with German diplomats
to surrender Russian territory, he confesses to trying to slip
poison into Number One's lunch, and so forth. Often a tiny
and innocent scrap of real fact is worked into the picture to
lend plausibility. Apart from these fictions, Rubashov admits
readily enough that his silent disapproval of the dictatorship
is a threat to the state, intolerable in a time of crisis and
approaching war. Gletkin makes one promise. If Rubashov
does the party this last service, once the victory has been
securely won, his name will be cleared. Again Rubashov
assents.

The end comes quickly. Rubashov is tried and abjectly confesses. His death is quick and without drama or dignity. "Harelip" precedes him by about ten minutes. While Rubashov waits for the guards to come back for him, Number 402 taps cheerfully through the wall to keep up his spirits. Then come the guards, a stumbling march down to the cellar of the prison, a bullet in the back of the head, and silence. After forty years of pilgrimage, he, like Moses, is unable to enter the promised land. But, unlike Moses, he does not even know if it exists.

Critical Opinion

Darkness at Noon has a unity, an intensity, and an economy of action that suggest the art of the theater. Actually, it was turned into a popular Broadway play. The story focuses on the experience of one man, in one place, during the last few days of his life. The secondary characters exist only insofar as they illuminate this central situation. In fact, it could be argued that Ivanov and Gletkin are not really separate characters, so much as voices in Rubashov's inner dialogue with himself. They conquer him by turning his own thoughts against him. The result is a novel of extraordinary concentration, which is reinforced by the narrow stage on which it is acted: a solitary cell, a windowless interrogation room, a cellar. Broader, more crowded scenes are presented only as reminiscences or as newspaper reports. The open air does not ventilate the story, and the noise of crowds does not distract us from the solitary agony of Nicolai Rubashov.

Koestler, however, has placed his story firmly in its historical context, and his refusal to use the names of Russia, Stalin, and Communism deceives nobody. The setting is the period of the Moscow trials, and Koestler has provided his hero with a career typical of the older generation of Bolshevik leaders, some of whom he knew personally. As a member of the old intelligentsia, who remembers the original humanitarian ideals of the Communist movement, Rubashov is a bridge between the old society and the new. He is far more complex, sophisticated, and ethical than the younger breed of Communists like Gletkin. He finds Gletkin sub-human, calls him a Neanderthal, and a man without an umbilical cord, and yet he recognizes that Gletkin is the product of the society he, Rubashov, has labored to bring into being.

In part, this book is an attempt to answer the question posed by the Moscow trials: why did the victims cooperate with their accusers? Granted that Stalin needed confessions, could not Rubashov somehow have managed to die in silence, without the ritual of public self-abasement? The answers are various. Some men were moved by physical terror. Others tried to protect their families. The best let themselves be sacrificed as a last service to the party which needed scape-goats. And since no man can govern without guilt, all of them were guilty, if not of the crime charged, then of some other. Each one had an Arlova or a Richard on his conscience. Finally, they were trapped by the logic of their own lives. For years, they had denied individual freedom to themselves as much as to others. They had rejected private scruples as sentimental and private judgment as seditious. Now there was no ground left on which one could stand and make a protest.

Though it is rooted in history, *Darkness at Noon* is basically a novel of ideas, an exploration of the old question of how far a just end can excuse unjust means. Rubashov has re-pudiated the old code of morality, not because he is personally unscrupulous or grasping, but because his philosophy of history demands that he do so. Morality, he feels, does not matter to history, much less good intentions. What matters is to be objectively in the right, that is, to be vindicated by history. "If I was right," he says, "I have nothing to repent of; if wrong, I will pay." But such a philosophy imposes a terrible responsibility, for without morality to guide him, a ruler must rely entirely on his intelligence to teach him how to act so that history will vindicate him. If he fails, he has no excuse and no second chance. And when, as actually hap-pened, the same logic led different men to incompatible conclusions, then a man had nothing left to sustain him but his own subjective belief in his infallibility. Number One has faith in himself, but Rubashov is no longer sure he is in-fallible, and that uncertainty he recognizes is the real reason he is lost.

Deserted by the party he has served, by the rules of logic he has followed, and by the laws of history which he has trusted, Rubashov is now forced to look elsewhere. Alone in his cell, he tries to reach some kind of understanding with himself, the authentic self which he has repressed for forty years, the inner voice that says "I," and which Rubashov has hitherto been inclined to dismiss as a mere fiction of grammar. The party does not recognize the existence of the self. Now Rubashov discovers that, despite its irrationality and its obstinate anachronistic scruples and sentimentality, the individual self is what is left him in the end. Had he been accustomed to using the language of religion, he would have said that he had discovered his soul.

The Author

Many writers have grown up speaking one language and have learned to write in another, but Arthur Koestler is remarkable in that he changed languages twice, from Hungarian to German and then to English. He was born in Budapest, the son of a promoter and inventor. Then, at seventeen, he went to Vienna and studied for four years at the University. After graduation, he became a journalist and served as foreign correspondent in the Near East, Paris, and Berlin. By 1930, he was foreign editor of a Berlin newspaper, and the following year he took part in a polar expedition aboard the *Graf Zeppelin*.

In 1931, Koestler, like many other intellectuals of that decade, became a Communist and traveled extensively in the U.S.S.R. and Central Asia. When the Spanish Civil War broke out, he covered the conflict as a journalist, first from the Revolutionary side of the lines, then from the Loyalist. In 1937, he was captured by the Fascists and condemned to death as a spy, but after three months in confinement he was released as part of an exchange of prisoners. These experiences are recorded in *Spanish Testament*, which appeared in 1938. In the same year, he left the Communists in disillusion over the Moscow trials.

Koestler was in France in 1939 when World War II broke out. He was arrested by the French police and placed in a detention camp for Spanish refugees. He has described this episode in *Scum of the Earth* (1941). After escaping from France, he enlisted in the British army. Since then he has

lived mostly in England. *Darkness at Noon* is his most success-
ful book. Others since then have been *The Yogi and the
Commissar* (1945), *The Age of Longing* (1951), *The
Suicide of a Nation* (1963) and *The Act of Creation* (1964).

The Stranger

by

ALBERT CAMUS (1913–1960)

The Characters

Mersault—The narrator of the story, a small clerk living in Algiers. His life, which is without purpose or conviction, expresses his sense of the basic absurdity of existence.

Perez—An inmate of a home for the aged, who has fallen in love with Mersault's mother.

Maria Cardona—Mersault's mistress, a pretty young girl.

Celeste—The owner of a restaurant, a friend of Mersault.

Salamano—An irritable old neighbor of Mersault. He owns a dog which he abuses and yet is much attached to.

Raymond Sintès—A pimp who strikes up an acquaintance with Mersault and involves him in his quarrels.

Masson—A friend of Sintès.

The Story

The central character of *The Stranger* (*L'Étranger*) is Mersault, a young man living in Algiers. His father is dead and his mother is living in an old people's home. Since they have nothing to say to each other, he visits her infrequently. He holds a minor clerical post, but has no interest in getting ahead. In fact, he refuses a promotion which would require his moving to Paris. He lives alone, has a few café acquaintances, and on weekends sees his mistress, who loves him, though he does not love her. When his mother dies, he takes time off from work to attend the funeral, but he feels no grief and goes through the ritual of mourning perfunctorily. By contrast, he notices another mourner, an inmate of the home named Perez, who has become close to his mother and is sincerely grieving. The funeral over, Mersault returns to Algiers and spends the weekend with his girl, Maria.

Among the other inhabitants of Mersault's rather shabby tenement is Raymond Sintès, suspected of being a pimp. When Raymond approaches him to strike up an acquaintance, Mersault offers no resistance. Raymond needs Mersault's help. He has had a quarrel with his girl, and claims that she is unfaithful to him, although the reader suspects that he is trying to push her into prostitution. Now Raymond wants to teach her a lesson. For this he wants Mersault to write the girl a letter which will lure her back so that he can complete his revenge. Mersault obliges, explaining to the reader, "I wanted to satisfy Raymond as I'd no reason not to satisfy him."

The following weekend there is a furious quarrel in Raymond's apartment, where Raymond is beating his girl, an Arab woman. The police come, Raymond is questioned, and Mersault agrees to testify that his friend acted under provocation. Meanwhile, deciding to take vengeance into his own hands, the girl's brother begins to shadow Raymond. A week later, Raymond invites Mersault and Maria to spend the day at the beach where a friend owns a bungalow. Two Arabs follow them, and Raymond expects an attack. Taking the offensive, he attacks first. In the scuffle that follows, they rout the Arabs. Raymond is nicked by one of them with a knife. Later that day, they meet the two Arabs again, and Raymond proposes to shoot them in cold blood, or at least to provoke a second quarrel in which he can use his revolver. Mersault counsels against such a course and tells Raymond to turn the revolver over to him. Raymond yields, and the Arabs scuttle away.

A short time afterward, Mersault is walking alone on the beach, assuming that the incident is closed, when suddenly he meets one of the Arabs for the third time. The day is now searing hot and the sun on the beach is dazzling. Mersault is interested only in getting out of the heat—he is seemingly on the verge of sunstroke. He advances toward the Arab, not to attack him, but simply to get into a patch of shade. The Arab pulls out a knife, from which the sun flashes blindingly into Mersault's eyes. Suddenly his nerves crack, and taking the revolver, which is still in his pocket, Mersault fires once. Then, after a pause, and for no particular reason, he fires four more shots into the prostrate body.

Mersault is arrested and an attorney is appointed by the court to defend him. Both the lawyer and the examining magistrate are bewildered by his apathy, his lack of remorse, his indifference to his own fate. The magistrate appeals to him as a Christian to repent. The lawyer advises him to say as little as possible for fear of making a poor impression on the jury. At the trial, a great deal is made of his lack of grief over his mother's death. This is cited as evidence of his callous immorality. The verdict is guilty, and Mersault is sentenced to the guillotine.

While awaiting execution, Mersault is visited in his cell by the prison chaplain, who offers him the consolations of the church. Mersault, who has no religion, refuses to be comforted or to feel remorse. Under the priest's prodding, he is finally goaded into shouting out a defense of his life and his behavior. Since all men must die, all lives are equally meaningless and all men equally guilty or innocent. What difference does it make how he passes his life or whom he kills? The outburst affords him relief, and he falls asleep. When he awakes, it is night, and he feels calm at last.

It was as if that great rush of anger had washed me clean, emptied me of hope, and, gazing up at the dark sky spangled with its signs and stars, for the first time, the first, I laid my heart open to the benign indifference of the universe. To feel it so like myself, indeed, so brotherly, made me realize that I'd been happy, and that I was happy still.

Critical Opinion

How is man to live in an absurd universe? This question, which is the central problem of *The Stranger,* is an urgent one for European man generally, perhaps the crucial question of our age. In the past, religion provided Europe with a coherent system of meaning, defining man's purpose in life and helping him to achieve it. As Christianity waned, other systems, from Descartes to Hegel, sought to demonstrate that the world is intelligible and rational. For Camus, this assurance too had died. Man, in his eyes, is destined to find his way without any guideposts or goal. Those men today who feel that God is dead, and with Him all other absolutes, whether moral or intellectual, find that Camus speaks to their condition. There are many such readers now. Almost every teacher of literature discovers that his students are reading Camus with a respectful attention that has nothing to do with a desire to earn a good grade. This is why *The Stranger* belongs to that small category of books that are accepted as classics almost from the moment of their publication.

To say that the world is absurd does not describe the world in itself so much as our reaction to it. Our sense of its absurdity springs from our disappointed expectations, from the discrepancy between what we want from life—notably order and consistency—and what we get. This sense of disillusion, which is at least as old as Ecclesiastes, typically finds expression in certain common attitudes or judgments about life. These include, first of all, a sense of the incoherence of things. Events follow one another, but they do not hang together. There is no necessary connection between them. The world appears alien and absurd, as pointless—to use Camus' own simile—as the spectacle of a man silently gesticulating behind the glass pane of a telephone booth. The same absurdity rules in the intellectual sphere. All philosophical systems become questionable, and, with them, all systems of law and ethics that profess to give absolute standards of behavior. Since general rules provide no guide to specific situations, each moment stands by itself and makes its own laws. The one undeniable and authentic fact is the experience of the immediate moment. Finally, all life is lived under the shadow of death, which reduces saint and sinner, sense and nonsense, to the same level. The man who sees the world in this light may respond in one of three ways: he may take refuge in blind faith, he may commit suicide, or he may choose to go on living with lucid awareness and calm acceptance of his situation. For the man who is capable of it, this awareness is a great liberation, for if there is no God, and any moment is as good as any other, and all men die at last, then a man may do anything he likes.

Such a view of life is best presented, not in a systematic philosophic exposition, for such a treatment would imply the very kind of rational order which the sense of the absurd denies, but in a play or novel which will give us the feeling of absurdity itself. Mersault is a man whom this feeling has penetrated to his very bones. Living as he does moment by moment, he has few memories and no expectations. He makes no demands on others, and allows others to make as few demands as possible on him. His chief virtue is his absolute honesty. Even though his life is at stake, he will not pretend to have ideals or feelings which he does not have.

Mersault is certainly not a criminal. He is incapable of active evil, and, unlike Raymond, has no desire to hurt people. Most of his acquaintances like him well enough, and Maria even falls in love with him. He is generally obliging, not on principle, to be sure, but because he sees no reason not to be. He is neither moral nor immoral. He is simply uninvolved, and, to that extent, innocent. Why then did he kill? Because of the sun, he explains. The courtroom laughs at the explanation. And yet this reason is as good as any. The killing is automatic and involuntary, absurd and unmotivated, and might have been committed by anyone in the same position.

This absurd sequence of events, however, delivers Mersault into the power of a world that believes in absolutes, that has a code of behavior for loving sons, that knows there is a difference between criminals and other people, and that recognizes a code of law with punishments adjusted to the gravity of each offense. Mersault has killed a man, but he could conceivably be acquitted on the grounds of self-defense. The decision depends on the way the court sees Mersault. Does his pattern of life suggest that the homicide was the act of a confirmed criminal? If it does, he is guilty of murder. Unfortunately the court cannot understand the sort of person he is. Everyone expects him to react conventionally and finds it damning that he does not. Consequently, Mersault is right in protesting that he is condemned less for killing an Arab than for failing to mourn his mother.

The last movement of the novel is devoted to Mersault's attempt to come to terms with the judgment of society. At first, his response is as flat and toneless as everything else about him. He regrets the loss of his freedom and the sexual frustration it entails, but he manages to adjust even to that. What lifts him out of his apathy at last is the prodding of the chaplain who goads him into formulating explicitly the insights by which he has always lived:

> From the dark horizon of my future a sort of slow, persistent breeze had been blowing toward me, all my life long, from the years that were to come. And on its way that breeze had levelled out all the ideas that people tried to foist on me in the equally unreal years I then was living through. What difference could they make to me, the deaths of others, or a mother's love, or his God; or the way a man decides to live, the fate he thinks he chooses, since one and the same fate was bound to 'choose' not only me but thousands of millions of privileged people who, like him, called themselves my brothers? Surely, surely he must see that? . . . And all alike would be condemned to die one day; his turn too would come like the others. And what difference could it make, if, after being charged with murder, he were executed because he didn't weep at his mother's funeral, since it all came to the same thing in the end?

This outburst is Mersault's declaration of independence. He is now master of himself and can face death unafraid.

The style and structure of this novel are admirably suited to the presentation of a character like Mersault, particularly in its choice of the first-person narrative technique. Had Mersault been described in the third person, he would have seemed as alien and incomprehensible to us as to the judge and prosecutor. If we are to believe in him, we must see him on his own terms. We get a sense of his personality especially from his style of speech—direct, simple, and quite toneless—a quality achieved by the absence of adverbs and adjectives, and the use of short clauses joined by no connectives except for a noncommittal "and" or "but." The style is starved and abrupt, and shows the clear influence of American writers, especially Hemingway. When conventional rhetoric does appear, it is generally in the mouths of conventional people, like the judge or the prosecutor, and by its falsity it suggests that the speakers too are false.

The Stranger achieves a classic, artistic integrity—the perfect harmony of plot, character, theme, style, and structure. This artistic unity creates, within the little world of the novel, that coherence and intelligibility which Camus cannot detect in the real world. In this sense, any artistic creation is a standing rebuke to life. Mersault does not protest at any time against the absurdity of his existence, but Camus, in the very act of writing the novel, does.

The Author

In some respects Albert Camus was hardly French. Born in Algiers, he was the son of a Spanish mother and an Alsatian father. The family was poor, and doubly so after his father, a farm worker, was killed in the First World War. Camus worked his way through the University of Algiers, receiving his degree in 1936 for a thesis in philosophy. For a short time during his student days, he was a Communist, but he soon left the party. From 1935 to 1938, he was busy in the theater as manager of a company in Algiers.

His writing began with two volumes of essays, *Back and Front (L'Envers et l'Endroit,* 1937) and *Nuptials (Noces,* 1938). In 1939 he became a journalist, and the following year wrote for the *Paris-Soir.* When the war broke out he was excused from military service because of chronic tuberculosis of some years' standing. In 1940, he returned to Algeria and taught school for a time in Oran. Two years later, he published *The Stranger* and *The Myth of Sisyphus,* two of his most important works. When France fell, he returned to Europe, took an active part in the resistance movement, and wrote articles for the underground press, especially for the newssheet *Combat.* After the war, *Combat* appeared as a daily paper, with Camus as editor.

The bleak view of life expressed in *The Stranger* caused Camus to be mentioned in connection with Sartre and other existentialists, whose philosophy in some respects resembles his. However, his novel *The Plague* (*La Peste*, 1947) showed him moving toward a more affirmative position, which could not be called faith, but which might be termed an heroic assertion of human courage in the face of a meaningless universe. It was widely hailed as an attempt to reestablish a humanistic view of life. Camus continued to be interested in the theater and wrote three plays: *Caligula* (1938, produced 1944), *The Misunderstanding* (*Le Malentendu*, 1944), and *State of Siege* (*L'État de Siège*, 1948). In 1957, he received the Nobel Prize for literature. He was about to assume charge of a state-supported experimental theater when he was killed in an automobile accident on January 4, 1960.

Two Adolescents *

by

ALBERTO MORAVIA
(ALBERTO PINCHERLE) (1907–   )

The Characters

I. AGOSTINO

Agostino—A boy of thirteen, of a well-to-do family, deeply attached to his mother.

Agostino's Mother—An attractive young widow.

Renzo—A handsome young man, interested in Agostino's mother.

Saro—The attendant at the Vespucci baths, a homosexual.

Berto, Sandro, Tortima, Homs—A gang of boys at the beach.

II. LUCA

Luca—A boy of fifteen in whom the physical and emotional stresses of adolescence have produced a revulsion against himself and all life. He wants to die.

Luca's Parents—A middle-class couple. They are responsible and affectionate parents to their only son, but in Luca's eyes are too much concerned with money and property. The father is gentler and more generous, the mother stricter.

---

* Published originally as two novellas: *Agostino* (1944) and *Luca* (1948). Both novellas were translated into English as *Two Adolescents*.

The Governess—A woman of thirty-five, not pretty, but
   cheerful and vivacious.
The Nurse—A middle-aged woman, strong, kindly, grave,
   and maternal.
Luca's teacher and classmates.

The Story

1. AGOSTINO

Agostino, a thirteen-year-old boy, and his mother, a pretty
young widow from Pisa, are vacationing at a Mediterranean
resort. There is a close relationship between the two. Agostino,
who takes constant pride and pleasure in his mother's company, is vexed when she begins to flirt with one of the
vacationers, a young man named Renzo. The two begin to
spend much time on a bathing raft without the boy, and
Agostino notices with embarrassment that his mother, usually
so sensible and dignified, is beginning to act like a silly girl.
For the first time in his life, he feels excluded. He wanders
off in tears.

Left to his own devices, Agostino falls in with a group of
boys his own age or older who play daily on the beach. They
are of the working class, and Agostino, who comes from a
sheltered, upper-middle-class milieu, is amazed at their
coarseness and sexual sophistication. The gang taunt him
with very explicit speculations as to what is going on between
Renzo and his mother, using obscenity which Agostino
hardly understands. Though he is hurt and humiliated, he
accepts the company of the others as an initiation which he
must endure. Besides, he suspects that the accusations against
his mother may well be true.

The companion and unofficial leader of the gang is a
bath attendant, a fat man of about fifty named Saro, whom
Agostino finds especially grotesque; he has six fingers on
each hand. Saro has a homosexual friendship with one of the
boys, a Negro named Homs, but now he turns his attentions
to Agostino. One day, he takes the boy out sailing and tries
to seduce him in the boat, but Agostino, though he hardly
knows what is happening, draws away in terror. Homs, who

is desperate with jealousy, assumes that the seduction has taken place, and tells the others.

Agostino is in the painful position of having lost his innocence without having gained experience. He feels that he belongs nowhere. He is not really one of the gang, and yet the children of his own class seem immature and insipid. Now he is accused of a depravity which he scarcely understands. One evening, while his mother is with Renzo, he approaches the oldest boy of the group, a handsome fellow named Tortima, and begs to be taken to a prostitute. Tortima agrees, since Agostino offers to pay for both. But a final humiliation awaits him. Tortima goes in, keeping the money, while Agostino is turned away as being too young. He must content himself with peering in at the windows.

Returning to his mother, Agostino asks to be taken home. "Don't you like being with me?" she asks, and strokes his cheek. Without knowing why, Agostino blurts out, "You always treat me like a child." "Very well," she answers; "from now on I'll treat you like a man . . . will that be all right?" But as Agostino falls asleep, he knows he is not a man yet. "What a long, unhappy time would have to pass before he could become one."

2. LUCA

Luca at fifteen has grown too fast. He has almost attained his full height but is thin and rather frail. Hovering uncertainly between boy and man, he finds himself constantly frustrated in a world of things and events that seem to him absurd or even hostile. His parents, too, though they are affectionate and sensible, represent a world in which he is unable to find his place. A trivial incident during a train journey is typical: Luca wishes to eat in the dining car, but his parents decide to buy a box lunch. Luca is humiliated, not merely because he must eat off a greasy paper spread across his lap, but because his wishes have not been consulted. On another occasion he enters his parents' room one night and finds that they have opened a wall safe and are counting a pile of securities. What outrages him is that the safe is concealed behind a picture of the Madonna before which he has been taught to say his prayers. In other words, he has been made to kneel in worship before his parents' money. Thereafter property is hateful to him, as well as the kind of life which his parents envisage for him: a law degree, a partnership in his father's office, a wife from a good family. If accepting life means accepting it on these terms, then he no longer wishes to live.

It never occurs to Luca to take so decisive a step as suicide. He simply breaks the ties, one by one, which bind him to life. First he gives away his stamp collection, then he sells his books and the toys which his father has given him. He explains that he has done so in order to buy a victrola, for he knows his parents will let him part with one possession only for the sake of acquiring another. Next he disposes of his money, tearing up the bills and burying the coins. Finally, he stops eating more than a mouthful or two at meals.

Luca is an adolescent, however, and the one force strong enough to hold him to life is sex. A woman of thirty-five, the governess of his young cousins, has come to stay for a time with Luca's family. The governess is not pretty, but she is gay and full of life. One day, she takes advantage of a game of hide-and-seek in a darkened room to make unmistakable advances toward him. Later she suggests that he visit her apartment. Luca delays for several weeks, and, when he arrives, he finds her critically ill. A few days later, she is dead. Now even sex is inextricably entwined in his mind with the thought of death, and, though the governess still seems desirable, it is from the grave that she summons him.

Soon after, Luca falls seriously ill. The clinical diagnosis is beside the point; basically he wants to die. Instead he sinks into a terrifying delirium filled with animals with sinuous snouts, and unclean imps that emerge from his medicine bottles. When he comes to himself, he finds that he is being tended by a nurse, a kind woman whose strong motherly care gradually wins him back to life. The same world which had once appeared so hateful now seems "serene, clean, familiar, lovable, and, so to speak, appetizing." The nurse, although she is wrinkled and plain, is comfortable, reassuring, and a source of strength. Luca is content at last to accept life happily, and to accept himself.

Toward the end of the convalescence, the nurse helps Luca out of bed to give him a bath, supporting him in her arms, for he is still weak and dizzy. As she dries him, he experiences an erection, and notices to his surprise that he accepts this

too without shame or vanity as a simple natural fact. The
episode is not mentioned again until the day before the nurse
is due to leave. As they talk quietly, she admits that she has
been attracted to him also, and he accepts the declaration
happily. That night, she comes to his room, and in a grave,
kindly way, without a trace of coarseness, grants him his decisive initiation into manhood. In the darkened room, he seems
to see in an eager vision the life that remains for him to live:
"the places, the human faces, the movements, the meetings. . . .
He saw that this was his life; and that now it only remained
to him to be patient and live it out to the end." Later, as he
travels to the convalescent home where he is to stay, he
realizes that the nurse has served as a second mother who
"had given him a second birth when, in his desire for death,
he had already been dead. But he knew that this second birth
could never have taken place if he had not first desired so
sincerely, so wholeheartedly, to die."

Critical Opinion

1. AGOSTINO

Agostino is a boy whose emotional dependence on his mother
has been unnaturally prolonged by his father's death. The
relationship is innocent in the sense that he has not learned
to think of his mother consciously in sexual terms, and his own
sexuality is incompletely awakened. On the other hand, he
takes pride in escorting his mother in public or lighting her
cigarette. When a rival appears in the form of the young man
Renzo, he reacts exactly as a jilted lover would. For Agostino,
then, the crisis of growing up involves several things: he must
loosen the ties of dependence upon his mother, he must learn
to think of her as a woman, like any other, who is attractive
to other men, and he must explore his own sexual capacities.

In trying to find a woman of his own, Agostino is deliberately erecting a defence against an oedipal attachment which
has at last become too conscious and explicit to be tolerated
any further. The experience is far more brutal and wrenching
than it should have been, but it is effective, and, if the initiation does not proceed to its logical climax, the fault is not his.
Agostino's altered view of his mother shows itself in the fact

that he assumes she and Renzo have really been making love on the raft although, so far as he knows, and we can judge, their intimacy has gone no further than a kiss or two. At the end of the story, his determination to be independent finds expression in his demand that his mother cease to treat him as a child.

Agostino's sexual awakening is also an education in the facts of a class society. Up to this point, he has met only boys of his own class. His new playmates, as he realizes at once, are all proletarians. They, in turn, are keenly aware of his superior status and wealth, and question him closely about the life he leads. Agostino is aghast and at the same time fascinated by the bawdiness of his companions, while they speculate about the sexual activities of his mother and her circle of friends. "They're rich," says one; "not like us; they make love, I suppose." In other words, each class defines the other in erotic terms and expresses its hostility by accusations of sexual promiscuity. Agostino's education progresses far enough so that he is able to pass himself off as a poor boy, at least in the presence of his own class. The boys themselves are not deceived.

Amid all this brutality, Agostino never really tries to revert to his original state of unawakened innocence. He knows he must go ahead, not back. In the back of his mind there hovers the dream of an ideal possibility, the experience of maturation as it ought to be. One day, as he and the boys are bathing, he walks off, naked and alone, along the beach. "There arose in him a vague and desperate desire to ford the river and walk on down the coast, leaving far behind him the boys, Saro, his mother and all the old life. Who knows whether . . . he might not at last come to a country where none of these horrible things existed; a country where he would be welcomed as he longed to be, and where it would be possible for him to forget all that he had learned and then learn it again without all that shame and horror, gently and naturally, as he dimly felt it might be possible." This possibility is only suggested, but it provides the yardstick by which we can measure the suffering Agostino actually undergoes. As we read, we suffer with him, but as we see him accept and embrace life in its actuality we realize that his experience, painful though it may be, is not a tragedy.

2. Luca

If *Agostino* can be read as an examination of the relation between sex and the social structure, then *Luca*, at least in the
earlier sections, is a study of the relation between sex and
property. For the possession of property is one of the ways in
which men grasp at life, and, in a middle-class society, it is one
of the most conspicuous expressions of the libidinal drive.
There is a strong hint of this in the scene where Luca breaks
into his parents' room and finds them before an open safe
counting over their life savings. There is something furtive
and indecent about the spectacle of the father in his pajamas
intent before this secret hole in the wall. It suggests a child's
view of the primal scene, that is to say, parental intercourse.
Luca's mother also senses the impropriety, and rebukes him
for breaking in without knocking.

Luca's parents are people of property, if not exactly wealthy.
They are careful about their money, or, if they are generous,
their generosity is in terms of physical possessions. Luca has
many toys, given always with the injunction not to break them.
In his own way he is a man of property, too. He has a collection of a hundred marionettes, three hundred books, and a
treasured stamp album. Luca's struggle to escape from the
tyranny of property is experienced as a kind of death, but one
which will—though he does not yet realize it—prepare the
way for a mature genital sexuality which welcomes life in a
creative and outgoing embrace.

While Luca lies in his delirium, wishing to die, the hallucinations which he experiences speak to him of life, although in the
agony of his metamorphosis that life seems frightening and
demonic. The creatures of his imagination that surround his
bed have long, probing snouts. One of them lays his snout
between Luca's legs; it grows longer and longer, reaching up
toward his stomach and face, while Luca, weeping and
screaming, tries to ward it off. His struggle expresses his fear
of his own genital drive. Again he sees the medicine bottles
by his bed packed with little misshapen dwarves, like ugly
fetuses, while one of them breaks its way out of an eggshell
that lies on his plate. Here Luca has a vision of sexual life
coming to its fulfillment in birth. This is followed by another
and even more explicit birth fantasy. He sees the naked belly

of a woman, taut as a drum. Then it splits open at the navel and a naked leg extends cautiously from the gash, groping for the floor.

Later, during his convalescence, he has another vision of his own rebirth, this time during a dream. It seems that he is a tree, black, leafless, and numb with cold. Around him stretches a dark horizon above which the sun slowly rises. Under its caressing warmth, Luca feels the sap rising in his veins and his bare branches bursting with a thousand buds. Then all at once he becomes a man, standing upright with his arms stretched toward the sun.

These visions symbolize Luca's entrance into sexual maturity, experienced first under the dominion of death and then of life. The passage from one to the other is the archetypal experience of spiritual death and rebirth; it is the ancient mystery which found expression in the cults of Orpheus and Osiris and Adonis, and which even the Gospels recognize when they declare that unless a seed falls into the earth and dies, it cannot bring forth new life. The nurse who is the guardian of this mystery and who leads Luca through the perilous initiation is also an archetypal figure out of the ancestral memory of the race, a priestess or hierophant, perhaps a goddess, the Earth Mother herself. She is a "deity risen up from the earth for his possession," and he embraces her with "a tremor of veneration." Seen in the light of psychology, rather than myth, she is a mother-surrogate, the first step along the road that leads away from his own mother and toward the woman he will finally choose for himself. For all its pathos, the story of Luca is a triumphant celebration of life.

The Author

Alberto Pincherle, whom his readers know as Alberto Moravia, was born in 1907 of an upper-middle-class Roman family such as he describes in most of his own works. His father was a moderately prosperous architect. Most of his childhood was spent in bed. At nine he developed a serious case of osteomyelitis which kept him in sanatoriums until he was eighteen. There is a picture of such a child in his novella, *A Sick Boy's Winter* (1930). During this long confinement he read for pleasure those literary classics which most schoolboys read as a duty. The result was a precocious stimulation of his literary talent. His first major novel, *Time of Indifference* (*Gli Indifferenti*, 1929), was written partly in bed.

This novel brought the author immediate fame. It is a somber picture of three people, mother, daughter and son, living a purposeless existence, groping ineffectually for life and love, but defeated by moral and emotional apathy. The story displays a sense of the emptiness and absurdity of life which anticipates by some years the existentialism of Sartre and his school. Among Moravia's later works have been *Mistaken Ambitions* (1935), *The Fancy Dress Party* (1941), *The Woman of Rome* (1947), *Conjugal Love* (1949), *The Conformist* (1950), *Bitter Honeymoon* (1951), *A Ghost at Noon* (1954), *Two Women* (1951) and *The Empty Canvas* (1960).* Besides these, he has turned out criticism, journalism, scenarios, and miscellaneous writing in abundance.

During the Fascist era, Moravia was chronically under suspicion by the authorities. *Time of Indifference* was banned as unsuited to the official optimism of the government, and *The Fancy Dress Party* as a thinly veiled satire on Mussolini. At the end of the war, during the German occupation, he and his wife tried to make their way south to Naples, behind the Allied lines. They were held up en route and had to spend nine months of boredom holed up in a mountain shack, an experience which is described in the novel *Two Women*. Moravia's reputation on the continent dates from the thirties, and in the English-speaking world from the forties, when most of his works were translated. Today his position as a writer of international importance is firmly established.

Technically, Moravia is not an avant-garde writer. His style and literary structure are traditional and rooted in the practice of the earlier generation of European naturalists. What marks him as a man of his time is principally his vision of people as defeated or alienated (*Luca*, with its life-affirming conclusion, is an exception). In this dead world, the one source of life and meaning is sex: Moravia's novels are all explorations of the different aspects of eroticism. In this, he is honest and never prurient, avoiding on the one hand the mystical rhetoric of D. H. Lawrence and on the other the clinical jargon

---

* The dates given are for the first Italian edition; the titles are for the English translations, appearing in each case a year or two later.

of the psychiatrist. Finally, he is human and humane. The reader of *Agostino* and *Luca* must be struck by the tenderness and the compassion with which Moravia presents his two tormented adolescents.

The Last Temptation
of Christ

by

NIKOS KAZANTSAKIS (1883–1957)

The Characters

Jesus of Nazareth—Portrayed as a man haunted and driven
by God. In his youth, the divine presence has made it impossible for him to find ordinary happiness in marriage. In
rebellion against his destiny, he tries at first to make himself
unworthy of it. Once he accepts his mission, his message is
at first one of love and brotherhood, and his character is
correspondingly gentle and cheerful. Later, after his meeting with John the Baptist, he becomes more fierce and
denunciatory. The temptations which he faces are real
and weighty, but he meets them with heroic firmness.

Judas Iscariot—A bold, violent, red-bearded man, eager for
the expulsion of the Romans.

Mary Magdalene—The daughter of Simeon, in love with Jesus
since her childhood. Her promiscuity is an attempt to drown
her grief after being rejected in marriage.

The Zealot—A Jewish patriot and descendant of the Mac-
cabees, who meets his death courageously.

The Zealot's Mother—A tall, aristocratic woman, who curses
Jesus.

Rufus—A Roman centurion, blunt in manner, a dutiful soldier.

Simeon—The Rabbi of Nazareth, an old man whose one passionate wish is to see the Messiah before he dies.

Mary—The mother of Jesus, whom she never really understands, and to whose ministry she is never reconciled.

Joseph the Carpenter—Father of Jesus, a paralytic old man.

Peter—A fisherman, a good but weak man, full of generous impulses but quick to change his mind, and a coward in a crisis.

Philip—A shepherd, an excitable person who is often on the verge of action, but generally held back by a prudent concern for his sheep.

Zebedee—A shrewd and grasping landowner, unsympathetic with agitators for national independence.

Jacob (James)—Son of Zebedee, a rough man and, until his conversion, a scoffer at Jesus.

John (the Evangelist)—Younger son of Zebedee, a boy in his teens, gentle and affectionate.

Jonah—Father of Peter and Andrew, a simple-minded old fisherman.

Andrew—In his youth, a handsome athlete, later a follower of John the Baptist.

Thomas—A peddler, shrewd and constitutionally skeptical.

Salome—The wife of Zebedee; more devout than he, she sympathizes with her sons' discipleship.

Jacob (James, the brother of Jesus)—A Pharisee, and a religious maniac subject to periodic seizures during which he mutilates himself.

Joachim—The aged abbot of a desert monastery.

Father Habbakuk—Guest master at the monastery.

Barabbas—The leader of a band of Zealots, violent and fanatical.

Nathanael—A simple cobbler.

Ananias—Village elder of Bethsaida, rich, cruel and dishonest.

Simon of Cyrene—An innkeeper of Jerusalem, a drunkard who, nevertheless, has the courage to carry Jesus' cross when the other disciples have run into hiding.

John the Baptist—A fanatical prophet, preaching the destruction of the existing order in preparation for the coming Kingdom of God.

Mary and Martha—Two sisters, devotees of Jesus, Mary being more absorbed in her Master, and Martha more concerned with household responsibilities.

Lazarus—Brother of Mary and Martha.

Pilate—The Roman governor, scornful of Jesus and of Jews generally.

Caiaphas—The high priest, a grotesquely fat, sensual man.

Matthew—A publican, disliked by the other disciples.

The Story

The Last Temptation of Christ is a fictional life of Jesus in thirty-three chapters, the number corresponding to the years of Jesus' life. The novel begins when Jesus is about thirty, shortly before the start of his public ministry. He is the village carpenter of Nazareth, but he knows that he is not like other people. There were strange portents at his birth, and ever since boyhood he has felt God's hand upon him—not in a metaphorical sense, but as tangible claws grasping his scalp. Jesus shrinks from these visitations and hopes that, if he sins gravely enough, God will leave him alone. Accordingly, when the Roman authorities capture a Jewish patriot and execute him as a traitor, Jesus undertakes to build the cross and set it up at the place of execution. The mother of the condemned man curses him, and wishes that Jesus may be crucified himself. This curse, concretely visualized as a woman with the features of a bird of prey, follows him till his death.

The daughter of the village rabbi is Mary Magdalene, who has loved Jesus ever since the age of three, when the two children engaged in some rather innocent sexual play together. As a young man of twenty, Jesus wished to marry her, but once again the mysterious claws reached down and prevented him. In her grief, Magdalene turns to a life of promiscuity, and Jesus is stricken with remorse for what he has done to her. His torment drives him to seek refuge in the ascetic life of a desert monastery (presumably a community of Essenes, although Kazantsakis does not use that name).

Jesus stays at the monastery only a short time, but long enough for two crucial meetings to take place. One is a long conversation with Simeon, father of Magdalene. The old rabbi has impatiently been waiting all his life to see the foretold liberator of Israel, and he suspects that Jesus may be the one. In this interview, Jesus unburdens his soul to Simeon, confesses his doubts, and gains the determination to start upon his public ministry. The other meeting is with Judas Iscariot, a Zealot who has been detailed by his organization to kill Jesus for his part in the crucifixion of their leader. Jesus accepts the verdict so meekly that Judas is disarmed, and cannot bring himself to kill his victim in cold blood. He decides instead to follow Jesus and watch him. If Jesus should turn out to be a Roman spy after all, he can be killed later.

The central chapters of the novel are devoted to retelling the familiar episodes of the Gospel: the baptism, the temptation, the calling of the disciples, the parables, the works of healing, the woman taken in adultery, etc. The crucial episode is the meeting with John the Baptist, which Kazantsakis places at the middle rather than at the start of Jesus' ministry. Up to this point, Jesus has preached a message of peace and universal love. Thereafter he introduces a sterner note and a conviction that the old order must be destroyed before a new one can be built. Judas is delighted by the change. At last he has found a Messiah after his own heart, and he becomes Jesus' closest and most trusted companion.

Jesus and his followers now turn their backs on the peasants of Galilee and make their way to the center of the enemy's power—Jerusalem. As the Passover celebration approaches, events hasten to their inevitable climax. Jesus reveals to the faithful Judas a dark and difficult secret, his conviction, based on the prophecies of Isaiah, that the Son of Man must die before the Kingdom of God can be made manifest. He orders his friend, as the strongest and bravest of the disciples, to arrange for his arrest. Judas reluctantly obeys, and the crucifixion proceeds substantially as recorded in the Gospels.

The last three chapters contain the most brilliant and daring of Kazantsakis' many interpolations into the familiar story. As Jesus hangs upon the cross, uttering his last words, he faints for a split second and in that moment experiences a vision, or perhaps a dream, which is the last of his many temptations. He dreams that it is spring, that he has not died, and that he is at last married to Magdalene. The two meet and consummate their love, Jesus now accepting his manhood without question and with a sense of glad fulfillment. At last, he realizes that God desires love and life for his creatures, not suffering, fanaticism and death. In time, Magdalene dies, and Jesus marries the other Mary, together with her sister Martha. The three live together happily until the house is filled with children and grandchildren and Jesus is an old man. At length, years later, Jesus meets his former disciples, led by Judas Iscariot. One by one they reproach him for his betrayal of them. He had once given them hope and purpose and summoned them to high sacrifices. Then he deserted his own cause. As their voices fade away, he comes back to consciousness and finds himself alone on the cross. With joy, he realizes that he has been faithful to the end, and that he has resisted the ultimate temptation: to cast off the burden of divinity and be a man like everyone else.

Critical Opinion

Since no one, presumably, comes to *The Last Temptation of Christ* without some knowledge of the life of Jesus, the first question in every reader's mind is likely to be, "Is the author's treatment traditional, critical, or imaginative?" The answer is that the book is above all else a novel, not Scripture and not biography. Kazantsakis has not only filled in the gaps of the Gospel story with material of his own invention; he has boldly changed the story to suit his own purposes. Above all, he has tried to imagine the inner life of Jesus, even his unspoken doubts and desires, to discover the psychological forces which drove him to his destiny. The picture that emerges is not likely to satisfy either the orthodox or the skeptic. A Savior who denounces Saint Matthew as a liar and who dreams on the cross of a bigamous marriage is clearly heterodox. On the other hand, the rationalist may be annoyed to discover that he is expected to take seriously at least some of the miracles, including the raising of Lazarus. Furthermore, Kazantsakis appears to accept the claim of Jesus to be, in fact, the Messiah. This particular messiah is often confused as to what road he ought to take and what God intends for him, but as the story proceeds, his sense of mission becomes stronger and clearer, and, when he dies, it is not as a self-deluded fanatic, but as a hero. In some ways, he resembles the Christ painted by Kazantsakis' countryman, El Greco: transfigured and flamelike.

Now to examine these points in more detail. Kazantsakis, in

defiance of all scholarly opinion, has made Matthew an eye-witness to the events he chronicles, a Boswell among the disciples. He is, however, a very unreliable Boswell who invents the whole story of the birth at Bethlehem, twists events to fit prophecy, reports Peter's dreams as literal fact, and suppresses incidents discreditable to the apostles. His excuse is that he writes at the dictation of an angel who assures him that God's truth and man's are not the same. Even so, Jesus is angry with him.

Having suggested that the Gospel story is corrupt from the start, Kazantsakis is free to change events to suit his artistic purpose, or to invent new ones. The episode in which Jesus builds a cross for the execution of the Zealot is pure invention, and a very bold one. Some readers may feel that the parallel between this crucifixion and Jesus' own has been underlined with too heavy a hand. The love story of Jesus and Mary Magdalene is also an invention, though not a very original one. The role of Judas in the crucifixion is not invention so much as speculation. Some scholars have seriously suggested that the Gospels are not wholly convincing on this point, and that Judas was driven, not by greed, but by a fervent wish to hasten the coming of the Messianic Kingdom. Finally, a number of events mentioned in the Gospels appear here in an unexpected sequence: the Galilean ministry comes before the baptism, the interview with Pilate occurs before Palm Sunday, and the dying Simeon recites the *Nunc Dimittis* on Maundy Thursday.

In spite of these alterations, Kazantsakis is true to the spirit of the Gospels in his insistence that Jesus can be understood only in the light of Jewish apocalypticism, that is, the conviction that the end of days was at hand, and that Israel would soon be purged of foreign tyrants and their domestic collaborators. The opening chapters of the novel quiver with this expectation, and for Jesus himself his role as the Messiah is the one important question, to which all other aspects of his ministry, such as healing the sick, are subordinate. It is his faithfulness to this mission, and not any abstract love of humanity or devotion to doctrinal truth, which nerves him to mount the cross.

In stressing the Messiahship of Jesus, Kazantsakis turns his back on the moral and sentimental view of Jesus popular among nineteenth-century liberals, a view which saw him as the gentle apostle of universal love, and which minimized everything that would stamp him as a man of his own time, race and country. Instead, Kazantsakis gives us a wild, strange, tragic, apocalyptic figure in whom there is a strong element of the Nietzschean superman. We detect this quality in the cry of Jesus while still a child: "God, make me God!" Years before, Kazantsakis had put the same words into the mouth of his hero Odysseus, and, if we are to believe his biographer, they were a cry from his own heart—he himself had uttered them as a boy. Jesus and Odysseus are a curious pair to be associated in this way, but they do have certain qualities in common, notably a capacity for endless endurance and a driving force of will. For Kazantsakis, Christ's best title to divinity lies neither in his moral teaching nor in his works of healing, but in his role as a hero, an athlete of the spirit, a man who wills his own destiny.

The Author

Nikos Kazantsakis was born in 1883 in Heraklion, Crete, then still a part of the Turkish empire. His father was a peasant, a primitive man, taciturn and unsociable. Crete itself was still a land of elemental people and strong passions, where something of antiquity still lingered untouched by the European culture of the past five hundred years. In 1897, the island rose against the Turks, and the Kazantsakis family took refuge on the island of Naxos in the Aegean. Here Nikos attended a school run by French monks and received his introduction to Western European culture. He continued his education at Athens where he took a degree in law in 1906.

In the years that followed, he was influenced by many thinkers. The first was Bergson, under whom he studied philosophy in Paris from 1907 to 1909. The philosophy of vitalism proved congenial, and gave him, among other things, a reasonable basis for rejecting the supremacy of reason. Then, for some months he lived at Mount Athos, the monastic community in northern Greece, engaged in a strenuous life of asceticism, meditation, and Christian devotion. Later, he became a follower of Nietzsche, and learned from him that man may by heroic effort transform himself into a superman. From Nietzsche, too, he learned that a strong man can reject every traditional security offered by religious faith, and yet find in himself the strength to live life joyously. This affirmation of life is the basis of what has been called Kazantsakis' "Dionysian nihilism."

Still another of Kazantsakis' teachers was the Buddha, who strongly attracted him in the early twenties, and whose gospel of renunciation, though very different from Nietzsche's, struck an equally heroic note. During the middle and later twenties, he was briefly converted to Communism, and made three pilgrimages to Russia, in the course of which he covered the entire country from Leningrad to Vladivostok. Communism, however, could not long satisfy a man so impatient of restraint and so distrustful of systems that offer easy answers.

During the twenties and thirties, Kazantsakis was constantly on the move in Switzerland, Italy, Austria, Germany, France, Spain, Egypt and Palestine as well as Russia. He always returned to the island of Aegina, near Athens, where he did much of his writing. The subject who interested him in these years was a traveler like himself, Odysseus. In 1938, he completed his major work, a continuation of Homer's *Odyssey* in 33,333 lines of modern Greek verse. It was a daring act for a modern author to try to write a serious epic poem, a genre which the critics have declared to be dead and no longer usable by a poet of the twentieth century. In this poem, Odysseus, like the Ulysses of Dante and Tennyson, finds himself weary of a peaceful life on Ithaca and sets out on a last voyage of discovery from which he is never to return. The story went through seven different stages of revision and rewriting, during which Kazantsakis expanded it until he had poured into it the sum of his life's thought and experience. His Odysseus is a man like himself, a life-affirming nihilist, who rejects all the gods, yet still lives out a life of heroic self-realization.

At various times, Kazantsakis entered public life for short periods. After the First World War, he served for two years as Director General of the Greek Ministry of Welfare where his principal work was the repatriation of the Greek communities living in the Caucasus. In 1945, during the Greek Civil War, he served as Minister of Education, and later for a few months as Director of the Unesco program of translation. He was twice married. His first wife, Galatea Alexiou, was divorced from him in 1924 after fifteen years of marriage. Years later she wrote a novel (*Men and Supermen,* 1957) which was a thinly veiled account of their relationship. His second marriage, in 1945, was to Eleni Samios, who survived him.

At the close of the war, Kazantsakis, now more than sixty years old, was scarcely known in Europe. He had written a number of plays, an epic, a great many translations and a vast number of ephemeral pieces. His present reputation is the result of a remarkable outburst of creative activity during the last eleven years of his life: *Zorba the Greek* (1946), *The Greek Passion* (1948), *Freedom or Death* (1950), *The Last Temptation of Christ* (1951), *The Poor Man of God* (1953), and *Report to Greco* (1956). These were translated widely, and some were made into films. In 1952, he failed by only one vote to receive the Nobel Prize. This fame cut both ways, however, for *The Greek Passion* was attacked by the Orthodox Church, and nearly resulted in his excommunication. In 1957, he fell ill on a trip to China and died in a hospital in Germany. He is buried in his native Crete.

Doctor Zhivago

by

BORIS LEONIDOVICH PASTERNAK (1880–1960)

The Characters *

YURII'S FAMILY

Yurii Andreievich Zhivago (Yura, Yurochka)—A doctor and poet, the son of Andrei Zhivago.

Andrei Zhivago—A ruined millionaire and a profligate who commits suicide.

Maria Nikolaevna Zhivago—Yurii's dead mother.

Nikolai Nikolaievich Vedeniapin (Kolya)—Yurii's maternal uncle, an unfrocked priest, later a well-known author.

Evgraf Zhivago (Grania)—Yurii's half brother, later a man of influence and a general.

TONIA'S FAMILY

Ivan Ernestovich Krueger—Tonia's grandfather, a wealthy ironmaster in the Urals.

Alexander Alexandrovich Gromeko—Yurii's foster father, a professor of agronomy.

Anna Ivanovna Gromeko, née Krueger—Alexander's wife.

* See Note on Russian Names, p. 173.

Nikolai Alexandrovich Gromeko—Alexander's brother, a professor of chemistry and a bachelor.

Antonina Alexandrovna Gromeko (Tonia)—Daughter of Alexander, wife of Yurii.

Sasha—Son of Yurii and Tonia.

Masha—Daughter of Yurii and Tonia.

LARA'S FAMILY

Amalia Karlovna Guishar—A Russianized Frenchwoman, widow of a Belgian engineer, who runs a dressmaking establishment.

Larisa Feodorovna Guishar (Lara)—Daughter of Mme. Guishar, wife of Pasha Antipov, later Zhivago's mistress.

Rodion Guishar (Rodya)—Lara's brother.

Pavel Pavlovich Antipov (Pasha)—A schoolteacher, Lara's husband, later known as Strelnikov.

Katenka—Daughter of Pasha and Lara.

Tania Bezocheredeva—Daughter of Lara and Yurii, abandoned as an infant in Siberia.

MARINA'S FAMILY

Markel Shchapov—Porter in the Gromekos' house.

Agafia Shchapova—His wife.

Maria (Marina, Marinka)—Markel's daughter, later Yurii's common-law wife.

Capitolina (Kapka)—Daughter of Yurii and Marina.

Claudia (Klazhka)—Daughter of Yurii and Marina.

OTHERS

Victor Ippolitovich Komarovsky—A lawyer, lover of Mme. Guishar and later of Lara.

Averkii Stepanovich Mikulitsyn—Krueger's former manager.

Liberius Averkievich Mikulitsyn (Livka)—Mikulitsyn's son, the leader of the Forest Brotherhood, a band of Bolshevik partisans.

Misha Gordon—A childhood friend of Yurii living with the Gromekos.

Innokentii Dudorov (Nika)—A childhood friend of Yurii.

Lavrentii Mikhailovich Kologrivov—A wealthy manufacturer with revolutionary opinions.

Nadia Kologrivova—Daughter of Lavrentii, a school friend of Lara.

Anfim Efimovich Samdeviatov—A lawyer in Yuriatin who helps the Zhivagos.

Daria Antipova—Pasha's mother.

Pavel Ferapontovich Antipov—A railroad employee and a dedicated Bolshevik; Pasha's father.

Bacchus—A driver at Torfianaia.

Blazheiko—A religious fanatic at Zybushino.

Vasia Brykhin—A peasant boy in the conscript labor corps.

Olia Demina—A seamstress employed by Mme. Guishar.

Emma Ernestova—Komarovsky's housekeeper.

Mlle. Fleury—A Swiss woman, formerly governess in the family of a provincial countess at Zybushino.

Kolya Frolenko—Telegrapher at Biriiuchi.

Gimazetdin Galiullin—Janitor in the Tiverzins' tenement; Yusupka's father.

Fatima Galiullina—A janitress; Yusupka's mother.

Osip Gimazetdinovich Galiullin (Yusupka)—An apprentice at the railroad shops in Moscow, later a leader of the anti-revolutionary forces in the Urals.

Vlas Pakhomivich Galuzin—A grocer in Khodatskoie.

Olga Galuzina—Galuzin's wife; sister of Polia Tiagunova.

Terentii Galuzin (Terioshka)—Olga's son, a coarse stupid boy.

Commissar Gints—An official at Meliuseievo murdered by army deserters.

Zakhar Gorazdykh—A partisan soldier involved in a conspiracy against Liberius.

Grigory Osipovich Gordon—A lawyer; Misha's father.

Kharlam—A villager in Veretenniki who slanders Polia.

Khrapugina—A tenant in the Tiverzins' tenement.

Piotr Khudoleiev—A railroad foreman.

Maxim Aristarkhovich Klintsov-Pogarevshikh—A deaf-mute from Zybushino.

Lipa Kologrivova—Nadia's sister; a pupil of Lara.

Serafima Filippovna Kologrivova—Nadia's mother.

Kornakov—A public prosecutor, unintentionally shot by Lara.

Kostoied-Amursky—A former Social Revolutionary, subsequently a Bolshevik under the name of Lidochka.

Kubarikha—A soldier's wife who practices witchcraft.

Dr. Kerenyi Lajos—A Hungarian doctor with the partisan forces.

Aunt Marfa—Tania's foster mother.

Elena Proklovna Mikulitsyna—Second wife of Mikulitsyn.

Ogryzkova—Rival of Polia Tiagunova.

Olia Domina—A seamstress employed by Mme. Guishar.

Christina Orletsova—Fiancée of Dudorov.

Pamphil Palykh—A partisan soldier who goes insane.

Petia—Son of Marfa and Vasili.

Prokhor Kharitonovich Prituliev—A labor conscript.

Seriozha Rantsevich—A soldier in the White army, wounded by Zhivago.

Goshka Riabikh—A friend of Terioshka Galuzin.

Rzhanitsky—A veteran revolutionary, executed by the partisans.

Shura Schlesinger—An eccentric friend of Mme. Gromeko.

Sivobluy—A partisan soldier, bodyguard to Liberius.

Prov Afanasievich Sokolov—A church singer.

Princess Stolbunova-Enrici—Mistress of Andrei Zhivago, mother of Evgraf.

Colonel Strese—A counter-revolutionary officer.

The Sventitskys—Relatives of Yurii's Uncle Kolya.

Pelagia Nilovna Tiagunova (Polia)—Prituliev's mistress.

Kuprian Savelievich Tiverzin—An engineer on the Brest railway.

Marfa Gavrilovna Tiverzina—A widow; Kuprian's mother.

Avdotia Tuntseva—Mikulitsyn's sister-in-law, a librarian at Yuriatin.

Glafira Severinovna Tuntseva—Mikulitsyn's second sister-in-law; a worker.

Simushka Tuntseva—The youngest of the Tuntseva sisters; a religious enthusiast.

Fadei Kazimirovich Tyshkevich—A cellist, neighbor of Mme. Guishar.

Ustinia—Housekeeper at Zybushino.

Uncle Vasili—Tania's foster father.

Vdovichenko—An old anarchist, veteran of the Revolution of 1905.

Ruffina Onissomovna Voit-Voitkovsky—A woman lawyer, friend of Komarovsky.

Private Voroniuk—A guard in charge of labor conscripts.

Ivan Ivanovich Voskoboinikov—An author, a friend of Yurii's Uncle Kolya.

Nil Feoktistovich Vyvolochnov—A Tolstoian idealist; friend of Uncle Kolya.

The Story

Yurii Zhivago, the son of a wealthy Moscow businessman, is born in 1889. His mother dies when he is ten, and his father, who has been financially ruined, commits suicide a few years later. Arrangements are made for Yurii to live with the Gromekos, a cultivated, kindly family of professional people. He grows up among them almost as a son, attends the university, studies to be a doctor, and writes poetry in his spare moments. In his early twenties, he marries Tonia, the Gromekos' daughter, and they have a son, Sasha. His promising medical career is interrupted in 1914 when he is called up to serve in the Russian army.

Lara Guishar is a young girl also living in Moscow, although, since she and Yurii are from different social levels, their paths do not at first meet. She is the daughter of a Russianized French woman, a widow who runs a dressmaking firm. In her teens, her life is made miserable by a lawyer named Komarovsky, formerly a friend of her father and later a lover of her mother, who finally turns his attentions to Lara. To escape his lovemaking, she finds a post as tutor with the Kologrivovs, the wealthy parents of a school friend. The Kologrivovs treat her as one of the family. When her brother Rodion is seriously in debt, they advance the necessary money. Lara, embarrassed by the generosity of her benefactors, wishes to start her life anew and free of debt. She determines to make her former lover, Komarovsky, pay. When he refuses, she tries to shoot him. Fortunately, she misses, and Komarovsky, to protect himself from scandal, hushes the matter up.

Lara has for a long time been loved by a boy living in a tenement near her home, Pasha Antipov, the son of a railroad worker. After the Komarovsky affair, he is still eager to marry Lara, and she accepts him. Both young people are teachers. After their marriage both find positions in Yuriatin, in the Ural Mountains. Pasha is a fine teacher, a dedicated idealist, and a considerate husband, and yet a certain constraint or malaise creeps into their relationship. Pasha fears Lara may imagine he resents her higher social position or her previous relationship with Komarovsky. He finds a way out by enlisting in the army as an officer.

The war now sweeps across Russia. Pasha is caught in an artillery barrage and is believed by his comrades to be dead. Lara, hearing no news of him, enlists as a nurse and goes to the front, thinking that she may find him in some hospital. Zhivago, meanwhile, sees frontline duty and is wounded by a shell splinter. He is sent to convalesce at a village called Meliuseievo. After his recovery, he stays there as a staff doctor. Here he meets Lara who has given up Pasha for dead. The two are on the point of falling in love when she leaves the hospital to prevent the relationship from developing further. Soon afterward, Zhivago returns to Moscow and is reunited with his wife, Tonia, and his son, whom he barely knows.

It is now 1917, and the war has turned into a revolution. When the new regime takes over Zhivago's hospital, many staff doctors withdraw into private practice, but Zhivago remains at his post out of a sense of social responsibility. Moscow is under siege, there is fighting in the streets, and typhus runs epidemic through a population weakened by starvation. Finally he and Tonia decide to move their family to the country and maintain themselves by farming. They settle in Varykino, not far from Yuriatin where Tonia's grandfather, Krueger, once owned a large estate.

Varykino is not a refuge, since Tonia is everywhere recognized as the granddaughter of a wealthy capitalist. The family, however, is taken in, somewhat reluctantly, by Mikulitsyn, former manager of the Krueger properties. By working hard and living inconspicuously, they are able to keep warm and well fed at least. In his spare time, Zhivago resumes writing poetry.

Pasha and Lara are also back in Yuriatin. Pasha has not been killed, only wounded and taken captive. After escaping, he assumes the name Strelnikov and joins the revolutionary forces, although he is not a Bolshevik. He is now military commander of the Yuriatin area, having cleared the counterrevolutionary armies out of the territory, which he rules with incorruptible strictness. To maintain his incognito, he does not communicate with Lara, who lives in a flat of her own with her daughter, Katenka. Lara respects Pasha's decision, and lives to all intents and purposes as if she were a widow.

When Lara runs into Zhivago on one of his trips into town, their love affair is resumed. Zhivago is tormented by the knowledge that he is wronging Tonia, whom he genuinely loves, and after a struggle with his conscience resolves to break off the affair. At this point, fate intervenes. While traveling back to Varykino, Zhivago is captured by the Forest Brotherhood, a group of Bolshevik guerrillas. Their surgeon has been killed, and Zhivago is drafted at the point of a rifle to replace him.

Zhivago stays with the guerrillas a year and finally escapes. Returning to Yuriatin, he finds that unidentified bandits have raided Varykino, but that his family have made their way back to Moscow whence they have safely emigrated to France. He now is free to resume his life with Lara, and for a time they live in complete seclusion, absorbed only in each other. Existence becomes increasingly dangerous, however, as the Bolsheviks consolidate their power. Antipov, who is not a party member, is too powerful and knows too much to be allowed to continue. He is toppled from his position and Lara is also in danger of arrest. Zhivago, of course, belongs to the former propertied class, and is a deserter from the partisans as well. He too is in danger. At this point, Lara's former lover, Komarovsky, intervenes. Now a person of some influence, he is on his way to Siberia, which the Reds do not yet completely control. He offers to take Zhivago and Lara with him, if Zhivago will leave the country by way of Vladivostok and join his family abroad. Zhivago will not accept his freedom on these terms, and yet he knows that the plan is Lara's only hope for safety. Since she will not agree to leave him behind, he lets it be understood that if she goes ahead, he will follow shortly. Instead, he returns to Moscow.

It is now 1922. Zhivago, who has become seedy and demoralized, gives up medicine and maintains himself by odd jobs. For a time he lives with a young boy named Vasia whom he has met in the Urals, occasionally writing poems which Vasia, who is a book designer, publishes privately. After his friendship with Vasia ends, he takes a common-law wife, a girl named Marina whose father had once been the Gromekos' porter. They have two children. His old childhood friends try to set him on his feet again. With the help of his half brother Evgraf he finds a position on a hospital staff. It is now 1929, and Zhivago is only forty. His health, however, is poor. One day he collapses of a heart attack on a streetcar. His only testament is a precious bundle of poems which are already beginning to circulate privately among his former friends.

An epilogue, set in 1943, carries the story a step further. When Lara left Zhivago, she was pregnant. Her child was born in Siberia, and, in the turmoil of the times, had to be left with foster parents. Lara herself vanishes after Zhivago's death. Presumably she is arrested during the Stalin era and dies in a concentration camp. Meanwhile, the child, Tania, grows up neglected and ill-treated by her foster mother. Then, in a particularly harrowing episode, her foster father and brother are killed by a passing tramp, and Tania becomes a drifting waif. In the Second World War, she turns up on the western front as a laundry girl with the Russian army. Zhivago's half brother, who is now a major general, finally identifies and adopts her.

An appendix to the novel is entitled "The Poems of Yurii Zhivago." The literal English translation does them no justice, of course. There are twenty-four, and although none of them bears directly on any of the episodes of the story, their themes, many of them religious, help to clarify the meaning of Doctor Zhivago's short and unhappy life.

Critical Opinion

In view of the fierce controversy that raged over *Doctor Zhivago*, it will be many years before readers can approach it purely as a work of art rather than as a political document. Both its defenders and its attackers agree in seeing it as an indictment of the Communist state. Pasternak in these pages has portrayed the brutality of the Civil War, the fanaticism of the revolutionaries, the senseless cruelty that sends Lara to the concentration camp, the "political re-education" which Dudorov underwent in prison, and much more. The most serious charges, however, that he levels against his society are not so much its overt cruelty as its subtler crime against the intellect and the spirit. At one point, Lara explains, "The root of the evil . . . was the loss of confidence in the value

of one's own opinion." In other words, the demand for conformity to the mass mind produced an atmosphere in which
thought was vulgarized, language degenerated into clichés,
and authentic communication between men was impossible.
Even for those who stayed out of concentration camps, such
an atmosphere was fatal, and not only in a metaphorical sense.
Zhivago, in one of the closing chapters, predicts his own death
from heart disease, and blames it on the spiritual conflicts
amid which his generation is forced to live:

> Microscopic forms of cardiac hemorrhages have be-
> come very frequent in recent years. . . . It's a typical
> modern disease. I think its causes are of a moral order.
> The great majority of us are forced to live a life of con-
> stant, systematic duplicity. Your health is bound to be
> affected if, day after day, you say the opposite of what
> you feel, if you grovel before what you dislike. . . . Our
> nervous system isn't just a fiction, it's a part of our physi-
> cal body, and our soul exists in space and is inside us,
> like the teeth in our mouth. It can't be violated forever
> with impunity. I found it painful to listen to you,
> Innokentii, when you told us how you were re-educated
> and became mature in jail. It was like listening to a circus
> horse describing how it broke itself in.

This is a terrible indictment, and yet it can be argued
that Pasternak was not so much an anti-Communist as he
was nonpolitical. Zhivago makes no apology for the Czar, or
Kerensky, or Kolchak, or Western capitalism, nor do we have
any clue as to the sort of society he would create if he could.
The charge that society produces outward conformity at the
cost of inward tension is as true of the tyrannies of the right
as it is of the left, and it is sometimes heard in democracies
as well. To some extent, Pasternak was indicting all governments. This is probably the real reason why the Russians
found him subversive. If he had said, in effect, to his country,
"You mean well, comrades, but you are making certain mistakes," he could have been forgiven; but what he said was,
"Your millennium does not interest me; leave me alone." This
was unpardonable.

We shall do well, therefore, to listen to Pasternak when
he insists that his aim was simply to bear witness as an

artist to the agony of his time, and not to write a political tract. This is what it was like, he seems to say, to live in Russia in the first three decades of our century. Pasternak is, after all, describing events which he had witnessed. Zhivago, like Pasternak, was born into an upper-middle-class society where it was possible to cultivate good taste, good breeding, sensitivity, and an honorable conscience—all those necessary luxuries by which a civilized and dignified existence are sustained. Then came the triple trauma of war, revolution, and civil strife. The fabric of life was either torn or sadly coarsened. Families fell apart, friendships were poisoned, men walked in daily fear of arrest. It was a constant struggle merely to keep warm, clean, and healthy. By the time Zhivago is in his thirties, he is thoroughly demoralized, and has turned into a seedy tramp who no longer practices medicine or writes. At forty, he is dead. Outwardly he is beaten, and yet his tragedy ends on a serene note that suggests the author saw Zhivago as a conqueror even in defeat. Above all, he has maintained his integrity. He has not bowed down to false gods or praised something he despised. His fortitude has been sustained by three things. Chief of these is love, especially his love for Lara. Next is literature, especially the poetry which is his real life's work, even though medicine is his profession. The third is nature, especially the wild country of the Urals where Zhivago finds refuge, and which inspires some of Pasternak's most memorable passages.

These themes—art, love, nature, and endurance in the face of hardship—combine in one vivid symbol which is introduced near the heart of the story: the rowan tree, or mountain ash. This is a tree growing near the camp of the forest partisans who have captured Zhivago. Even in winter its branches are heavy with orange fruit which glows against the snow and feeds the hungry birds. The rowan is also an image in a folk song which Zhivago hears, expressing the longing of a soldier for his beloved. For Zhivago, too, it symbolizes his beloved, and the white branches remind him of Lara's arms. When he finally makes his escape to freedom, the tree is his landmark and guide. These images, the tree in the snow, the loved woman, the song that clarifies their relationship, and the escape to freedom which the song inspires, all merge into a symbol which is very close to the central meaning of the novel.

Although *Doctor Zhivago* abounds in scenes of death—the

opening chapter describes a funeral—there are images of resurrection as well. The very word *zhivago* means "living," and is used in the Russian Bible by the angel who greets the women at the empty tomb of Jesus: "Why seek ye the living among the dead?" (Payne, *The Three Worlds of Boris Pasternak*, p. 170). Religious imagery runs through the book as a subdued undercurrent, appearing most often in Zhivago's silent thoughts. Pasternak once protested that the critics had overstressed his religious symbolism, and asserted that he had introduced it only to add greater density of texture to his work. This sounds rather like an apology meant for the ears of the official masters of Russian literature, and probably should be discounted.

The story of Zhivago is not religious in any simple, obvious way, but the poems which conclude the novel present another picture. At least eight use explicitly Christian themes and language, and the last stanza on the last page proclaims the resurrection of Christ. Perhaps the best commentary on the novel, however, is provided by the poem "Hamlet," which heads the collection of the writings of Yurii Zhivago. In this poem the speaker, who can variously be understood as an actor, or Prince Hamlet, or Jesus Christ, or Zhivago himself, declares that he accepts his part in the tragedy he must play, but that the drama is now over and he is ready to leave the stage.

> Nothing can avert the curtain's final fall.
> I stand alone. All else is swamped in Pharisaism.
> To live life to the end is not a childish task.

These lines could be the motto for Pasternak's life as well.

The Author

One critic has remarked that the survival of Boris Pasternak into our own time is as anomalous as the survival of the coelocanth. Others have called him the last great Russian author of the nineteenth century, in the sense that he is the last major figure whose mind was formed in the intellectual atmosphere of Czarist Russia. His family was artistic: his father, Leonid Ossipovich Pasternak, was a fashionable portraitist and his mother a concert pianist. The former was a Sephardic Jew from Odessa and the latter half Jewish, but the family had converted to the Orthodox Church, and Boris inherited no special sense of Jewish identity. He was born in 1890 in Moscow, where his father had moved. The family circumstances, at first rather modest, improved as Leonid became well known. Three men especially influenced him in his youth: Tolstoi, a friend of the family whose novels Leonid Pasternak had illustrated; the poet Rainer Maria Rilke, whom Boris met through the Tolstois; and the composer Alexander Scriabin, a family friend and neighbor. Under Scriabin's influence, Boris studied music, but by the time he was nineteen he had given up any thought of becoming a composer.

Pasternak's youth was the time of Nijinsky and Pavlova, of Rasputin and the Revolution of 1905. He entered the University, studying philosophy at first and then gravitating toward literature. His life was that of any talented young student: he studied, lived simply, did tutoring, talked endlessly with his friends, and moved among the younger avant-garde writers of the day. In 1912, he spent a term at the University of Marburg studying philosophy.

In 1914, Pasternak was exempt from war service on account of a childhood leg injury. This broken leg may have saved his life. He took a clerical post in a chemical factory in the Urals and continued writing poems, translations, and a short novel. When the Revolution broke out in 1917, he returned to Moscow and served as librarian for the Soviet Ministry of Education. He married in 1923, had a son, was divorced, remarried, had more children, and continued writing.

After the first flurry of literary experimentation in the twenties, the cultural climate became increasingly unfavorable to genuine creativity. Lenin was replaced by Stalin, and a Byzantine conformity became the order of the day. Some of Pasternak's associates began to drop out of sight. Yesenin committed suicide in 1925, Mayakovsky did the same in 1930, and Gorki died under suspicious circumstances in 1936. It was the era of purges: Pasternak's principal protector and patron, the party theorist Bukharin, was executed as a traitor in 1938. Pasternak survived only because he was not a political writer and had by this time confined himself to translating into Russian classics from the Western European languages. In the political context of those days, however, merely to translate Shakespeare was to take a political stand of a sort. It indicated a wish to remain uncommitted, so that to the theorists of the class struggle Pasternak was bound to seem an ivory-tower aesthete holding himself aloof from the great issues of the age.

Doctor Zhivago was begun in 1945. After Stalin's death, there was some hope for a relaxation of doctrinal rigidity. In 1956 Pasternak submitted his manuscript to the literary periodical *Novy Mir*. The editorial board returned it with thirty pages of abusive comment, accusing him of being anti-democratic, of misrepresenting the Revolution, and of wishing to return to the days of the Czar. Not discouraged, Pasternak made plans to have the book, minus some of the more controversial passages, published by another agency. At the same time, arrangements were made for an Italian publisher, a Communist named Feltrinelli, to bring out the book in Italian. Had these plans gone through, there might have been no trouble, but unfortunately Pasternak fell ill and could not make the necessary revisions. While publication in Moscow was delayed, Feltrinelli went ahead with the translation of the original version in his possession. Now the Russian authorities began to be alarmed, and sent the Secretary of the Soviet Writers' Association, a popular author named Surkov, to stop publication. Feltrinelli hesitated a while, for the issue was becoming very complex, but he realized he had a masterpiece in his possession. When a letter arrived from Pasternak telling him to use his own judgment, he went ahead despite Surkov. The Italian version appeared in November, 1957, and the English version appeared the following year.

Pasternak's position was not awkward at first. Critics in the West recognized at once that the novel was great enough to be compared with *War and Peace*. Unfortunately, this was a tense period in the cold war, and when English and American readers started to hail *Doctor Zhivago* as an anti-Communist document, the Russians could not continue to ignore it. Then in October, 1958, the Swedish Royal Academy offered Pasternak the Nobel Prize for literature, the second time such an award had been given to a Russian author. Some felt that the prize, which had been denied to Chekhov, Tolstoi and Gorki, might at least have gone to Sholokhov, whose Communist principles were unimpeachable. A storm of protest broke out, in which the Nobel award was denounced in the press as politically motivated.

Under this pressure, Pasternak withdrew his acceptance of the prize, "in view of the interpretation placed upon this honor by the society in which I live." Meanwhile *Pravda* and *Komsomol* declared that he was a traitor and should leave the country before he was lynched. Eight hundred Soviet writers who, let it be remembered, could not possibly have read the book, urged that he be deprived of his citizenship. Sholokhov also lent his name to the attack. Pasternak was now forced to recant his errors—a painful episode which reminds one of the recantation of Galileo. He wrote a letter to Khrushchev, pleading to be allowed to remain in the country. He was deprived of his house, which he held at the pleasure of the Union of Soviet Writers, his income was cut off, and the millions of dollars of royalties accumulating abroad were of no use to him. Furthermore, he was sick. In 1960, he died of cancer of the lungs and was quietly buried without the religious funeral he had wished.

The vengeance of his enemies pursued him even after his death. Within a matter of weeks, charges were brought against his literary executor, a close friend named Mme. Olga Ivinskaya. She and her daughter were accused of illegally receiving money smuggled into the country from Pasternak's funds that were held for him beyond the Iron Curtain. Like Lara, Mme. Ivinskaya was sent to Siberia, and her daughter received a three-year sentence as well. A play on which Pasternak was working at the time of his death was also seized. In short, if there was ever any question as to whether Pasternak presented the Communist state fairly or unfairly, the Russian authorities, by their own actions, have given an answer.

Bibliography

1. Blackmur, Richard P. *Eleven Essays in the European Novel.* New York: Harcourt, 1964.
2. Bowen, Elizabeth. *Collected Impressions.* New York: Alfred A. Knopf, Inc., 1950.
3. Bree, Germaine, and Guiton, Margaret. *An Age of Fiction.* New Brunswick, New Jersey: Rutgers University Press, 1957.
4. Forster, E. M. *Aspects of the Novel.* New York: Harvest Books, Harcourt, Brace & World, 1956.
5. Gordon, Caroline, and Tate, Allen (eds.). *The House of Fiction.* New York: Scribner's, 1950.
6. James, Henry. *The Future of the Novel: Essays in the Art of Fiction,* ed. Leon Edel. New York: Vintage Books, Random House, 1956.
7. LeSage, Laurent. *The French New Novel.* University Park, Pennsylvania: Pennsylvania State University Press, 1962.
8. Lubbock, Percy. *The Craft of Fiction.* New York: Compass Books, The Viking Press, 1957.
9. Lukacs, Georg. *Realism in Our Time.* New York: Harper, 1964.
10. Mirsky, Dmitri S. *History of Russian Literature.* New York: Alfred A. Knopf, Inc., 1949.
11. Pascal, Roy. *The German Novel.* Toronto: The University of Toronto Press, 1956.
12. Peyre, Henri. *The Contemporary French Novel.* New York: Oxford, 1955.
13. Steiner, George. *Tolstoy or Dostoevsky.* New York: Alfred A. Knopf, Inc., 1959.
14. Trilling, Lionel. *The Liberal Imagination.* New York: Anchor Books, Doubleday & Co., 1953.

Index